READING
CAPITAL

READING CAPITAL

Louis Althusser and
Étienne Balibar

Translated from the French by
Ben Brewster

PANTHEON BOOKS
A Division of Random House, New York

Translator's Note on References: In the original French text of *Reading Capital*, quotations from *Capital* were taken from the Éditions Sociales version. The first three volumes of this edition, containing Volume One of *Capital*, are in the French translation of Joseph Roy, originally published by Maurice La Châtre in 1872, and discussed in the letter from Marx to La Châtre which is printed on p. 9. This translation, the proofs of which Marx read and corrected, modified the German original in many respects, both in order to simplify the text for French workers, and to incorporate Marx's later corrections and additions. This being the case, in this English translation of *Reading Capital*, I have translated the quotations from Volume One according to Roy's French text; and references are given both to the three Éditions Sociales volumes (T.I, T.II, and T.III) and to the corresponding passage in Lawrence and Wishart's edition of the English translation by Moore and Aveling (Vol. I). The French translations of Volumes Two and Three of *Capital* are more orthodox, so quotations are taken from the English translation published by Lawrence and Wishart, with minor modifications to bring them into closer accord with the German text where this is important for Althusser's or Balibar's argument. References to Volumes Two and Three are to this English edition (Vol. II and Vol. III). The occasional references to the German text are given to the edition by Dietz Verlag of the *Werke* of Marx and Engels, in which *Das Kapital* occupies the twenty-third, twenty-fourth and twenty-fifth volumes (Bd. XXIII, Bd. XXIV and Bd. XXV). Quotations and references to the *Theories of Surplus Value* are taken from the English translation of the Dietz Verlag edition of 1956–66, two volumes out of three of which have been published by Lawrence and Wishart in 1964 and 1969 (Vol. I and Vol. II). The 1857 *Introduction* to *A Contribution to the Critique of Political Economy* and the *Grundrisse der Kritik der Politischen Ökonomie* have been translated from the German text and references are given to the volume with the latter title published by Dietz Verlag in 1953, referred to as *Grundrisse*, and where applicable to *Pre-Capitalist Economic Formations*, translated from the *Grundrisse* by Jack Cohen and Eric Hobsbawm (Lawrence and Wishart, 1964) referred to as *PCEF*. Other references are explained when they occur.

Ben Brewster

Foreword to the Italian Edition

1. This edition of *Reading Capital* differs from the first edition (*Lire le Capital*, Vols. I and II, Maspero, Paris 1965) in several respects.

On the one hand, it is an abridged edition, since we have omitted a number of important contributions (the papers of Rancière, Macherey and Establet) in order to allow the book to be published in a smaller format.

On the other, it is a revised and corrected edition, and therefore in part a new edition: several pages, notably in Balibar's text, were published in French for the first time in this edition.

However, the corrections (cuts and additions) we have made to the original text concern neither the terminology nor the categories and concepts used, nor their internal relations, nor in consequence the general interpretation of Marx's work that we have given.

This edition of *Reading Capital*, although different from the first, and abridged and improved, therefore *strictly* reproduces and represents the theoretical positions of the original text.

2. This last comment was a necessary one. Indeed, out of respect to the reader and simple honesty, we have maintained an integral respect for the terminology and the philosophical positions of the first edition, although we should now find it indispensable to correct them at two particular points.

Despite the precautions we took to distinguish ourselves from the 'structuralist' ideology (we said very clearly that the 'combination' to be found in Marx 'has nothing to do with a combinatory'), despite the decisive intervention of categories foreign to 'structuralism' (determination in the last instance, domination, overdetermination, production process, etc.), the terminology we employed was too close in many respects to the 'structuralist' terminology not to give rise to an ambiguity. With a very few exceptions (some very perceptive critics have made the distinction), our interpretation of Marx has generally been recognized and judged, in homage to the current fashion, as 'structuralist'.

We believe that despite the terminological ambiguity, the profound tendency of our texts was not attached to the 'structuralist' ideology. It is our hope that the reader will be able to bear this claim in mind, to verify it and to subscribe to it.

On the other hand, we now have every reason to think that, despite all the sharpening it received, one of the theses I advanced as to the *nature of philosophy* did express a certain 'theoreticist' tendency. More precisely, the definition of philosophy as a *theory of theoretical practice* (given in *For Marx* and again in Part One of *Reading Capital*) is unilateral and therefore inaccurate. In this case, it is not merely a question of terminological ambiguity, but one of an error in the conception itself. To define philosophy in a unilateral way as the Theory of theoretical practices (and in consequence as a Theory of the differences between the practices) is a formulation that could not help but induce either 'speculative' or 'positivist' theoretical effects and echoes.

The consequences of this error in the definition of philosophy can be recognized and delimited at a few particular points in Part One of *Reading Capital*. But with the exception of a few minor details, these consequences do not affect the analysis that we have made of *Capital* ('The Object of *Capital*' and Balibar's paper).

In a forthcoming series of studies, we shall have the opportunity of rectifying the terminology and correcting the definition of philosophy.

Louis Althusser

NOTE TO THE ENGLISH EDITION

For the *conjuncture* in which this text was prepared (1965), for its character as a theoretico-ideological *intervention* in that conjuncture, and for its theoretical limits, lacunae and errors, the reader should refer to the presentation, 'To My English Readers,' in *For Marx*.

Louis Althusser, 17 May 1970

To the citizen Maurice La Châtre

Dear Citizen,

    I applaud your idea of publishing the translation of Das Kapital
*as a serial. In this form the book will be more accessible to the working-class,
a consideration which to me outweighs everything else.*

    *This is the good side of your suggestion, but here is the reverse of
the medal : the method of analysis which I have employed, and which had not
previously been applied to economic subjects, makes the reading of the first
chapters rather arduous, and it is to be feared that the French public, always
impatient to come to a conclusion, eager to know the connexion between
general principles and the immediate questions that have aroused their
passions, may be disheartened because they will be unable to move on at once.*

    *This is a disadvantage I am powerless to overcome, unless it be by
forewarning and forearming those readers who zealously seek the truth. There
is no royal road to science, and only those who do not dread the fatiguing climb
of its steep paths have a chance of gaining its luminous summits.*

Believe me,

dear citizen

Your devoted,

KARL MARX

London, 18 March 1872.

Part I

From *Capital* to Marx's Philosophy
Louis Althusser

The following papers were delivered in the course of a seminar on *Capital* held at the École Normale Supérieure early in 1965. They bear the mark of these circumstances: not only in their construction, their rhythm, their didactic or oral style, but also and above all in their discrepancies, the repetitions, hesitations and uncertain steps in their investigations. We could, of course, have gone over them at our leisure, corrected them one against the other, reduced the margin of variation between them, unified their terminology, their hypotheses and their conclusions to the best of our ability, and set out their contents in the systematic framework of a single discourse – in other words, we could have tried to make a *finished* work out of them. But rather than pretending they are what they should have been, we prefer to present them for what they are: precisely, incomplete texts, the mere beginnings of a *reading*.

I

Of course, we have all read, and all do read *Capital*. For almost a century, we have been able to read it every day, transparently, in the dramas and dreams of our history, in its disputes and conflicts, in the defeats and victories of the workers' movement which is our only hope and our destiny. Since we 'came into the world', we have read *Capital* constantly in the writings and speeches of those who have read it for us, well or ill, both the dead and the living, Engels, Kautsky, Plekhanov, Lenin, Rosa Luxemburg, Trotsky, Stalin, Gramsci, the leaders of the workers' organizations, their supporters and opponents: philosophers, economists, politicians. We have read bits of it, the 'fragments' which the conjuncture had 'selected' for us. We have even all, more or less, read Volume One, from 'commodities' to the 'expropriation of the expropriators'.

But some day it is essential to read *Capital* to the letter. To read the text itself, complete, all four volumes, line by line, to return ten times to the first chapters, or to the schemes of simple reproduction and reproduction on an enlarged scale, before coming down from the arid table-lands and plateaus

of Volume Two into the promised land of profit, interest and rent. And it is
essential to read *Capital* not only in its French translation (even Volume One
in Roy's translation, which Marx revised, or rather, rewrote), but also in the
German original, at least for the fundamental theoretical chapters and all
the passages where Marx's key concepts come to the surface.

That is how we decided to read *Capital*. The studies that emerged from
this project are no more than the various individual protocols of this reading:
each having cut the peculiar oblique path that suited him through the
immense forest of this Book. And we present them in their immediate form
without making any alterations so that all the risks and advantages of this
adventure are reproduced; so that the reader will be able to find in them
new-born the experience of a reading; and so that he in turn will be dragged
in the wake of this first reading into a second one which will take us still
further.

2

But as there is no such thing as an innocent reading, we must say what
reading we are guilty of.

We were all philosophers. We did not read *Capital* as economists, as
historians or as philologists. We did not pose *Capital* the question of
its economic or historical content, nor of its mere internal 'logic'. We read
Capital as philosophers, and therefore posed it a different question. To go
straight to the point, let us admit: we posed it the question of its *relation
to its object*, hence both the question of the specificity of its *object*, and the
question of the specificity of its *relation* to that object, i.e., the question of the
nature of the type of discourse set to work to handle this object, the question
of scientific discourse. And since there can never be a definition without a
difference, we posed *Capital* the question of the specific difference both of
its object and of its discourse – asking ourselves at each step in our reading,
what distinguishes the object of *Capital* not only from the object of classical
(and even modern) political economy, but also from the object of Marx's
Early Works, in particular from the object of the *1844 Manuscripts*; and
hence what distinguishes the discourse of *Capital* not only from the discourse
of classical economics, but also from the philosophical (ideological) discourse
of the Young Marx.

To have read *Capital* as economists would have meant reading it while
posing the question of the economic content and value of its analyses and
schemes, hence comparing its discourse with an object already defined
outside it, without questioning that object itself. To have read *Capital* as
historians would have meant reading it while posing the question of the
relation between its historical analyses and a historical object already defined
outside it, without questioning that object itself. To have read *Capital* as

logicians would have meant posing it the question of its methods of exposition and proof, but in the abstract, once again without questioning the object to which the methods of this discourse relate.

To read *Capital* as philosophers is precisely to question the specific object of a specific discourse, and the specific relationship between this discourse and its object; it is therefore to put to the *discourse-object* unity the question of the epistemological status which distinguishes this particular unity from other forms of discourse-object unity. Only this reading can determine the answer to a question that concerns the place *Capital* occupies in the history of knowledge. This question can be crystallized as follows: is *Capital* merely one ideological product among others, classical economics given a Hegelian form, the imposition of anthropological categories defined in the philosophical Early Works on the domain of economic reality; the 'realization' of the idealist aspirations of the *Jewish Question* and the *1844 Manuscripts*? Is *Capital* merely a continuation or even culmination of classical political economy, from which Marx inherited both object and concepts? And is *Capital* distinguished from classical economics not by its object, but only by its *method*, the dialectic he borrowed from Hegel? Or, on the contrary, does *Capital* constitute a real epistemological mutation of its object, theory and method? Does *Capital* represent the founding moment of a new discipline, the founding moment of a science – and hence a real event, a theoretical revolution, simultaneously rejecting the classical political economy and the Hegelian and Feuerbachian ideologies of its prehistory – the absolute beginning of the history of a science? And if this new science is the theory of *history* will it not make possible in return a knowledge of its own *prehistory* – and hence a clear view of both classical economics and the philosophical works of Marx's Youth? Such are the implications of the epistemological question posed to *Capital* by a philosophical reading of it.

Hence a philosophical reading of *Capital* is quite the opposite of an innocent reading. It is a guilty reading, but not one that absolves its crime on confessing it. On the contrary, it takes the responsibility for its crime as a 'justified crime' and defends it by proving its necessity. It is therefore a special reading which exculpates itself as a reading by posing every guilty reading the very question that unmasks its innocence, the mere question of its innocence: *what is it to read?*

3

However paradoxical it may seem, I venture to suggest that our age threatens one day to appear in the history of human culture as marked by the most dramatic and difficult trial of all, the discovery of and training in the meaning of the 'simplest' acts of existence: seeing, listening, speaking, reading – the acts which relate men to their works, and to those works thrown in their faces, their 'absences of works'. And contrary to all today's reigning appearances, we do not owe these staggering knowledges to psychology, which is built on the absence of a concept of them, but to a few men: Marx, Nietzsche and Freud. Only since Freud have we begun to suspect what listening, and hence what speaking (and keeping silent), *means* (*veut dire*); that this '*meaning*' (*vouloir dire*) of speaking and listening reveals beneath the innocence of speech and hearing the culpable depth of a second, *quite different* discourse, the discourse of the unconscious.[1] I dare maintain that only since Marx have we had to begin to suspect what, in theory at least, *reading* and hence writing *means* (*veut dire*). It is certainly no accident that we have been able to reduce all the ideological pretensions which reigned on high over the *1844 Manuscripts*, and still craftily haunt the temptations to historicist backsliding in *Capital*, to the explicit innocence of a *reading*. For the Young Marx, to know the essence of things, the essence of the historical human world, of its economic, political, aesthetic and religious productions, was simply to *read* (*lesen, herauslesen*) in black and white the presence of the 'abstract' essence in the transparency of its 'concrete' existence. This immediate reading of essence in existence expresses the religious model of Hegel's Absolute Knowledge, that End of History in which the concept at last becomes fully visible, present among us in person, tangible in its sensory existence – in which *this* bread, *this* body, *this* face and *this* man are the Spirit itself. This sets us on the road to understanding that the yearning for a reading *at sight*, for Galileo's '*Great Book of the World*' itself, is older than all science, that it is still silently pondering the religious fantasies of epiphany and parousia, and the fascinating myth of the Scriptures, in which the body of truth, dressed in its words, is the Book: the Bible. This makes us suspect that to treat nature or reality as a Book, in which, according to Galileo, is spoken the silent discourse of a language whose 'characters are triangles, circles and other geometrical figures', it was necessary to have a certain idea of *reading* which makes a written discourse the immediate transparency of the true, and the real the discourse of a voice.

The first man ever to have posed the problem of *reading*, and in consequence, of *writing*, was Spinoza, and he was also the first man in the world to have proposed both a theory of history and a philosophy of the opacity of the immediate. With him, for the first time ever, a man linked together in

[1] We owe this result, which has revolutionized our *reading* of Freud to Jacques Lacan's intransigent and lucid – and for many years isolated – theoretical effort. At a time when the radical novelty of what Jacques Lacan has given us is beginning to pass into the public domain, where everyone can make use of it and profit by it in his own way, I feel bound to acknowledge my debt to an exemplary reading lesson which, as we shall see, goes beyond its object of origin in some of its effects. I feel bound to acknowledge this *publicly*, so that 'the tailor's labour (does not) disappear . . . into the coat' (Marx), even into my coat. Just as I feel bound to acknowledge the obvious or concealed debts which bind us to our masters in reading learned works, once Gaston Bachelard and Jean Cavaillès and now Georges Canguilhem and Michel Foucault.

this way the essence of reading and the essence of history in a theory of the difference between the imaginary and the true. This explains to us why Marx could not possibly have become Marx except by founding a theory of history and a philosophy of the historical distinction between ideology and science, and why in the last analysis this foundation was consummated in the dissipation of the religious myth of *reading*. The Young Marx of the *1844 Manuscripts* read the human essence at sight, immediately, in the transparency of its alienation. *Capital*, on the contrary, exactly measures a distance and an internal dislocation (*décalage*) in the real, inscribed in its *structure*, a distance and a dislocation such as to make their own effects themselves illegible, and the illusion of an immediate reading of them the ultimate apex of their effects: *fetishism*. It was essential to turn to history to track down this myth of reading to its lair, for it was from the history in which they offered it the cult of their religions and philosophies that men had projected it onto nature, so as not to perish in the daring project of knowing it. Only from history in thought, the theory of history, was it possible to account for the historical religion of reading: by discovering that the truth of history cannot be read in its manifest discourse, because the text of history is not a text in which a voice (the Logos) speaks, but the inaudible and illegible notation of the effects of a structure of structures. A reading of some of our expositions will show that, far from making metaphorical suggestions, I take the terms I am using literally. To break with the religious myth of reading: with Marx this theoretical necessity took precisely the form of a rupture with the Hegelian conception of the whole as a 'spiritual' totality, to be precise, as an *expressive* totality. It is no accident that when we turn the thin sheet of the theory of reading, we discover beneath it a theory of *expression*, and that we discover this theory of the expressive totality (in which each part is *pars totalis*, immediately expressing the whole that it inhabits in person) to be the theory which, in Hegel, for the last time and on the terrain of history itself, assembled all the complementary religious myths of the voice (the Logos) speaking in the sequences of a discourse; of the Truth that inhabits its Scripture; – and of the ear that hears or the eye that reads this discourse, in order to discover in it (if they are pure) the speech of the Truth which inhabits each of its Words in person. Need I add that once we have broken with the religious complicity between Logos and Being; between the Great Book that was, in its very being, the World, and the discourse of the knowledge of the world; between the essence of things and its reading; – once we have broken those tacit pacts in which the men of a still fragile age secured themselves with magical alliances against the precariousness of history and the trembling of their own daring – need I add that, once we have broken these ties, a new conception of *discourse* at last becomes possible?

4

Returning to Marx, we note that not only in what he says but in what he does we can grasp the transition from an earlier idea and practice of reading to a new practice of reading, and to a theory of history capable of providing us with a new theory of *reading*.

When we read Marx, we immediately find a *reader* who *reads* to us, and out loud. The fact that Marx was a prodigious reader is much less important for us than the fact that Marx felt the need to fill out his text by reading out loud, not only for the pleasure of quotation, or through scrupulousness in his references (his accuracy in this was fanatical, as his opponents learnt to their cost), not only because of the intellectual honesty which made him always and generously recognize his debts (alas, *he* knew what a debt was), but for reasons deeply rooted in the theoretical conditions of his work of discovery. So Marx reads out loud to us, not only in the *Theories of Surplus Value*[2] (a book which remains essentially in note form), but also in *Capital*: he reads Quesnay, he reads Smith, he reads Ricardo, etc. He reads them in what seems a perfectly lucid way: in order to support himself with what is correct in what they say, and in order to criticize what is false in what they say – in sum, to *situate* himself with respect to the acknowledged masters of Political Economy. However, the reading Marx makes of Smith and Ricardo is only lucid for a certain reading of this reading: for an immediate reading that does not question what it reads, but takes the obvious in the text read for hard cash. In reality, Marx's reading of Smith-Ricardo (they will be my example here) is, on *looking* at it closely, a rather special one. It is a double reading – or rather a reading which involves two radically different reading principles.

In the *first reading*, Marx reads his predecessor's discourse (Smith's for instance) through his own discourse. The result of this reading through a grid, in which Smith's text is seen through Marx's, projected onto it as a measure of it, is merely a summary of concordances and discordances, the balance of what Smith discovered and what he missed, of his merits and failings, of his presences and absences. In fact, this reading is a retrospective theoretical reading, in which what Smith could not see or understand appears only as a radical omission. Certain of these omissions do refer to others, and the latter to a primary omission – but even this reduction restricts us to the observation of presences and absences. As for the omissions themselves, this reading does not provide reasons for them, since the observation of them destroys them: the continuity of Marx's discourse shows the lacunae in Smith's discourse which are invisible (to Smith) beneath the apparent con-

---

[2] Two volumes out of three translated into English and published by Lawrence and Wishart.

tinuity of his discourse. Marx very often explains these omissions by Smith's distractions, or in the strict sense, his *absences*: he did not *see* what was, however, staring him in the face, he did not grasp what was, however, in his hands. '*Oversights*' (*bévues*) all more or less related to the '*enormous oversight*', the confusion of constant capital and variable capital which dominates all classical economics with its 'incredible' aberration. This reduces every weakness in the system of concepts that makes up knowledge to a psychological weakness of 'vision'. And if it is absences of *vision* that explain these *oversights*, in the same way and by the same necessity, it is the presence and acuteness of 'vision' that will explain these '*sightings*' (*vues*): all the knowledges recognized.

This single logic of sighting and oversight thus reveals itself to us as what it is: the logic of a conception of knowledge in which all the work of knowledge is reduced in principle to the recognition of the mere relation of *vision*; in which the whole nature of its object is reduced to the mere condition of a *given*. What Smith did not see, through a weakness of vision, Marx sees: what Smith did not see was perfectly visible, and it was because it was visible that Smith could fail to see it while Marx could see it. We are in a circle – we have relapsed into the mirror myth of knowledge as the vision of a given object or the reading of an established text, neither of which is ever anything but transparency itself – the sin of blindness belonging by right to vision as much as the virtue of clear-sightedness – to the eye of man. But as one is always treated as one treats others, this reduces Marx to Smith minus the myopia – it reduces to nothing the whole gigantic effort by which Marx *tore* himself from Smith's supposed myopia; it reduces to a mere difference of *vision* this day in which all cats are no longer grey; it reduces to nothing the historical distance and theoretical dislocation (*décalage*) in which Marx thinks the theoretical difference that nevertheless separates him from Smith for ever. And finally, we too are condemned to the same fate of vision – condemned to see in Marx only what he *saw*.

5

But there is in Marx a *second quite different reading*, with nothing in common with the first. The latter, which is only sustained by the dual and conjoint observation of presences and absences, of sights and oversights, can itself be blamed for a remarkable oversight: it does not *see* that the combined existence of sightings and oversights in an author poses a problem, the problem of their *combination*. It does not see this problem, precisely because this problem is only visible insofar as it is invisible, because this problem concerns something quite different from given objects that can be seen so long as one's eyes are clear: a necessary invisible connexion between the field of the visible and the field of the invisible, a connexion which defines the necessity of the obscure field of the invisible, as a necessary effect of the structure of the visible field.

But in order to make what I mean by this more comprehensible, I shall leave this abrupt posing of the question in suspense for the moment, and make a detour back to it through an analysis of the *second kind of reading* we find in Marx. I only need one example: the admirable Chapter XIX of *Capital*, on wages (T.II, pp. 206ff.; Vol. I, pp. 535ff.),[3] secretly reflected backstage in Engels's extraordinary theoretical remarks in his Preface to Volume Two (pp. 14–19).

I therefore quote Marx, *reader* of the classical economists:

Classical political economy naïvely borrowed from everyday life the category 'price of labour' without any prior verification, and then asked the question, how is this price determined? It soon recognized that the relations of demand and supply explained, in regard to the price of labour, as of all other commodities, nothing but the oscillations of the market-price above or below a certain figure. If demand and supply balance, the variation in prices they produce ceases, but then the effect of demand and supply ceases, too. At the moment when demand and supply are in equilibrium, the price of labour no longer depends on their action and must be determined as if they did not exist. This price, the centre of gravity of the market prices, thus emerged as the true object of scientific analysis.

The same result was obtained by taking a period of several years and calculating the averages to which the alternative rising and falling movements could be reduced by continuous compensations. This left an average price, a relatively constant magnitude, which predominates over the oscillations in the market prices and regulates them internally. This average price, the Physiocrats' 'necessary price' – Adam Smith's 'natural price' – can, with labour, as with all other commodities, be nothing else than its *value* expressed in money. 'The commodity,' says Smith, 'is then sold for precisely *what it is worth*.'

In this way, classical political economy believed it had ascended from the accidental prices of labour to the real value of labour. It then determined this value by the value of the subsistence goods necessary for the maintenance and reproduction of the labourer. *It thus unwittingly changed terrain* by substituting for the value of labour, up to this point, *the apparent object of its investigations*, the value of labour power, a power which only exists in the personality of the labourer, and is as different from its function, labour, as a machine is from its performance. Hence the course

[3] References to *Capital* Volume One are given first to Roy's French translation in the three volumes of the Éditions Sociales version (T.I, T.II, T.III) and then to the English translation of Moore and Aveling in one volume published by Lawrence and Wishart (Vol. I). References to Volumes Two and Three are given to the English translation only (Vol. II, Vol. III).

of the analysis had led them forcibly not only from the market prices of labour to its necessary price and its value, but had led to their resolution of the so-called value of labour into the value of labour power, so that from then on the former should have been treated merely as a phenomenal form of the latter. The result the analysis led to, therefore, was *not a resolution of the problem as it emerged at the beginning, but a complete change in the terms of that problem.*

Classical economy never arrived at an awareness of this substitution, exclusively preoccupied as it was with the difference between the current prices of labour and its value, with the relation of this value to the values of commodities, to the rate of profit, etc. The deeper it went into the analysis of value in general, the more the so-called value of labour led it into inextricable contradictions . . . (T.II, pp. 208–9; Vol I, pp. 537–8).

I take this astonishing text for what it is: a protocol of Marx's *reading* of classical economics. Here again it is tempting to believe that we are destined to a conception of reading which adds up the balance of sightings and over-sights. Classical political economy certainly saw that . . . but it did not see that . . . it 'never arrived at' a sight of . . . Here again, it seems as if this balance of sights and oversights is found beneath a grid, the classical ab-sences revealed by the Marxist presences. But there is one small, one very small difference, which, I warn the reader straight away, we have no in-tention of *not seeing*! It is this: what classical political economy does not see, is not what it does not see, it is *what it sees*; it is not what it lacks, on the contrary, it is *what it does not lack*; it is not what it misses, on the contrary, it is *what it does not miss*. The oversight, then, is not to see what one sees, the oversight no longer concerns the object, but *the sight* itself. The oversight is an oversight that concerns *vision*: non-vision is therefore inside vision, it is a form of vision and hence has a necessary relationship with vision.

We have reached our real problem, the problem that exists *in* and is posed *by* the actual identity of this organic confusion of non-vision in vision. Or rather, in this observation of non-vision, or of oversight, we are no longer dealing with a reading of classical economics through the grid of Marx's theory alone, with a comparison between classical theory and Marxist theory, the latter providing the standard – for we never compare classical theory with anything *except itself*, its non-vision with its vision. We are there-fore dealing with our problem in its pure state, defined in a single domain, without any regression to infinity. To understand this necessary and paradoxi-cal identity of non-vision and vision within vision itself is very exactly to pose our problem (the problem of the necessary connexion which unites the visible and the invisible), and to pose it properly is to give ourselves a chance of solving it.

6

How, therefore, is this identity of non-vision and vision in vision possible? Let us reread our text carefully. In the course of the questions classical economics asked about the 'value of labour' something very special has happened. Classical political economy has '*produced*' (just as Engels will say, in the Preface to Volume Two, that phlogistic chemistry 'produced' oxygen and classical economics 'produced' surplus value) a correct answer: the value of 'labour' is equal to the value of the subsistence goods necessary for the reproduction of 'labour'. A correct answer is a correct answer. Any reader in the 'first manner' will give Smith and Ricardo a good mark and pass on to other observations. Not Marx. For what we shall call his eye has been attracted by a remarkable property of this answer; *it is the correct answer to a question that has just one failing: it was never posed.*

The original question as the classical economic text formulated it was: what is the value of labour? Reduced to the content that can be rigorously defended in the text where classical economics produced it, the answer should be written as follows: '*The value of* labour (   ) *is equal to the value of the subsistence goods necessary for the maintenance and reproduction of labour* (   )'. There are two *blanks*, two absences in the text of the answer. Thus Marx makes us *see* blanks in the text of classical economics' answer; but that is merely to make us see what the classical text itself says while not saying it, does not say while saying it. Hence it is not Marx who says what the classical text does not say, it is not Marx who intervenes to impose from without on the classical text a discourse which reveals its silence – *it is the classical text itself which tells us that it is silent*: its silence is *its own words*. In fact, if we suppress our 'slots', our blanks, we still have the same discourse, the same apparently 'full' sentence: '*the value of labour is equal to the value of the subsistence goods necessary for the maintenance and reproduction of labour.*' But this sentence means nothing: what is the maintenance of 'labour'? what is the reproduction of 'labour'? The substitution of one word for another at the end of the answer: 'labourer' for 'labour', might seem to settle the question. '*The value of labour is equal to the value of the subsistence goods necessary for the maintenance and reproduction of the labourer.*' But as the labourer is not the labour the term at the end of the sentence now clashes with the term at the beginning: they do not have the same content and the equation cannot be made, for it is not the labourer who is bought for the wages, but his 'labour'. And how are we to situate the first labour in the second term: 'labourer'? In even uttering this sentence, therefore, precisely at the level of the term '*labour*', at the beginning and end of the answer, there is something lacking, and this lack is strictly designated by the function of the terms themselves in the whole sentence. If we suppress our slots – our blanks – we are merely reconstituting a sentence which, if it is taken literally, itself designates in itself these *points of emptiness*, restores these slots as the marks of an omission produced by the 'fullness' of the utterances itself.

This omission, located *by the answer* in the answer itself immediately next to the word *'labour'*, is no more than the presence in the answer of the absence of its question, the omission *of its question*. For the question posed does not seem to contain anything by which to *locate* in it this omission. *'What is the value of labour?'* is a sentence identical to a concept, it is a concept-sentence which is content to *utter* the concept 'value of labour', an utterance-sentence which does not designate any omission in itself, unless it is itself as a whole, as a concept, a question *manqué*, a concept *manqué*, the omission (*manque*) of a concept. It is the answer that answers us about the question, since the question's only space is this very concept of 'labour' which is designated by the answer as *the site of the omission*. It is the answer that tells us that the question is *its own omission*, and nothing else.

If the answer, including its omissions, is correct, and if *its* question is merely the omission of its concept, it is because the answer is the answer to *a different question*, which is peculiar in one respect, it has not been uttered in the classical economic text, but is uttered as slots in its answer, precisely *in the slots in its answer*. That is why Marx can write:

> *The result the analysis led to, therefore, was not a resolution of the problem as it emerged at the beginning, but a complete change in the terms of the problem.*

That is why Marx can pose the unuttered *question*, simply by uttering the concept present in an unuttered form in the emptinesses in the *answer*, sufficiently present in this answer to produce and reveal these emptinesses as the emptinesses of a presence. Marx re-establishes the continuity of the utterance by introducing/re-establishing in the utterance the concept of *labour power*, present in the emptinesses in the utterance of classical political economy's answer – and at the same time as establishing/re-establishing the continuity of the answer, by the utterance of the concept of labour power, he produces the as yet unposed question, which the as yet un-asked-for answer answered.

The answer then becomes: *'The value of labour-power is equal to the value of the subsistence goods necessary for the maintenance and reproduction of labour power'* – and *its* question is produced as follows: *'what is the value of labour power?'*

This restoration of an utterance containing emptinesses and this production of *its* question out of the answer enable us to bring to light the reasons why classical economics was blind to what it nevertheless saw, and thus to explain the non-vision inside its vision. Moreover, it is clear that the mechanism whereby Marx is able to see what classical economics did not see while seeing it, is identical with the mechanism whereby Marx saw what classical economics did not see at all - and also, at least in principle, identical with the mechanism whereby we are at this moment reflecting this operation of the sighting of a non-sight of the seen, by *reading* a text by Marx which is itself a *reading* of a text of classical economics.

7

We have now reached the point we had to reach in order to discover from it the reason for this *oversight* where a *sighting* is concerned: we must completely reorganize the idea we have of knowledge, we must abandon the mirror myths of immediate vision and reading, and conceive knowledge as a production.

What made the mistake of political economy possible does indeed affect the *transformation of the object* of its oversight. What political economy does not see is not a pre-existing object which it could have seen but did not see – but an object which it produced itself in its operation of knowledge and which did not pre-exist it: precisely the production itself, which is identical with the object. What political economy does not see is what it *does*: its production of a new answer without a question, and simultaneously the production of a new latent question contained by default in this new answer. Through the lacunary terms of its new answer political economy produced a new question, but '*unwittingly*'. It made '*a complete change in the terms of the*' original '*problem*', and thereby produced a new problem, but without knowing it. Far from knowing it, it remained convinced that it was still on the terrain of the old problem, whereas it has '*unwittingly changed terrain*'. Its blindness and its 'oversight' lie in this misunderstanding, between what it produces and what it sees, in this '*substitution*', which Marx elsewhere calls a '*play on words*' (*Wortspiel*) that is necessarily impenetrable for its author.

Why is political economy necessarily blind to what it produces and to its work of production? Because its eyes are still fixed on *the old question*, and it continues to relate its new answer to its old question; because it is still concentrating on the old '*horizon*' (*Capital*, T.II, p. 210) within which the new problem '*is not visible*' (ibid.). Thus the metaphors in which Marx thinks this necessary 'substitution' suggest the image of a change of terrain and a corresponding change of horizon. They raise a crucial point which enables us to escape from the psychological reduction of the 'oversight' or unwittingness'. In fact, what is at stake in the production of this new problem contained *unwittingly* in the new answer is not a particular new object which has emerged among other, already identified objects, like an unexpected guest at a family reunion; on the contrary, what has happened involves a transformation of the *entire* terrain and its *entire* horizon, which are the background against which the new problem is produced. The emergence of this new critical problem is merely a particular index of a possible critical transformation and of a possible latent mutation which affect the reality of this terrain throughout its extent, including the extreme limits of its 'horizon'. Putting this fact in a language I have already used,[4] the production of a new problem endowed with this *critical* character (critical in the sense of a critical situation) is the unstable index of the possible production of a new theoretical *problematic*, of which this problem is only one symptomatic mode. Engels says this luminously in his Preface to Volume Two of *Capital*: the mere 'production' of oxygen by phlogistic chemistry, or of surplus value by classical economics, contains the wherewithal not only to modify the old theory *at one point*, but also to 'revolutionize *all* economics' or *all* chemistry (Vol. II, p. 15). Hence what is in balance in this unstable and apparently local event is the possibility of a revolution in the old theory and hence in the old problematic *as a totality*. This introduces us to a fact peculiar to the very existence of science: it can only pose problems on the terrain and within the horizon of a definite theoretical structure, its problematic, which constitutes its absolute and definite condition of possibility, and hence the absolute determination of *the forms in which all problems must be posed*, at any given moment in the science.[5]

This opens the way to an understanding of the determination of the *visible* as visible, and conjointly, of the invisible as invisible, and of the organic link binding the invisible to the visible. Any object or problem situated on the terrain and within the horizon, i.e., in the definite structured field of the theoretical problematic of a given theoretical discipline, is visible. We must take these words literally. The sighting is thus no longer the act of an individual subject, endowed with the faculty of 'vision' which he exercises either attentively or distractedly; the sighting is the act of its structural conditions, it is the relation of immanent reflection[6] between the field of the problematic and *its* objects and *its* problems. Vision then loses the religious privileges of divine reading: it is no more than a reflection of the immanent necessity that ties an object or problem to its conditions of existence, which lie in the conditions of its production. It is literally no longer the eye (the mind's eye) of a subject which *sees* what exists in the field defined by a theoretical problematic: it is this field itself which *sees itself* in the objects or problems it defines – sighting being merely the necessary reflection of the field on its objects. (This no doubt explains a 'substitution' in the classical philosophies of vision, which are very embarrassed by *having* to say *both* that the light of vision comes from the eye, *and* that it comes from the object.)

The same connexion that defines the visible also defines the invisible as its shadowy obverse. It is the field of the problematic that defines and

---

[4] *For Marx*, Allen Lane The Penguin Press, London 1969, pp. 46, 66–70, etc.
[5] Auguste Comte often came very close to this idea.
[6] 'Relation of immanent reflection': this 'reflection' itself poses a theoretical problem which I cannot deal with here, but which will be outlined at the end of this introduction (section 19).

structures the invisible as the defined excluded, *excluded* from the field of visibility and *defined* as excluded by the existence and peculiar structure of the field of the problematic; as what forbids and represses the reflection of the field on its object, i.e., the necessary and immanent inter-relationship of the problematic and one of its objects. This is the case with oxygen in the phlogistic theory of chemistry, or with surplus value and the definition of the 'value of labour' in classical economics. These new objects and problems are necessarily *invisible* in the field of the existing theory, because they are not objects of this theory, because they are *forbidden* by it – they are objects and problems necessarily without any necessary relations with the field of the visible as defined by this problematic. They are invisible because they are rejected in principle, repressed from the field of the visible: and that is why their fleeting presence in the field when it does occur (in very peculiar and symptomatic circumstances) *goes unperceived*, and becomes literally an undivulgeable absence – since the whole function of the field is not to see them, to forbid any sighting of them. Here again, the invisible is no more a function of *a subject's sighting* than is the visible: the invisible is the theoretical problematic's non-vision of its non-objects, the invisible is the darkness, the blinded eye of the theoretical problematic's self-reflection when it scans its non-objects, its non-problems without seeing them, *in order not to look at them.*

And since, to use terms adopted from some very remarkable passages in the preface to Michel Foucault's *Histoire de la Folie*,[7] we have evoked the conditions of possibility of the visible and the invisible, of the inside and the outside of the theoretical field that defines the visible – perhaps we can go one step further and show that *a certain relation of necessity* may exist between the visible and the invisible thus defined. In the development of a theory, the invisible of a visible field is not generally *anything whatever* outside and foreign to the visible defined by that field. The invisible is defined by the visible as *its* invisible, *its* forbidden vision: the invisible is not therefore simply what is outside the visible (to return to the spatial metaphor), the outer darkness of exclusion – but the *inner darkness of exclusion*, inside the visible itself because defined by its structure. In other words, the seductive metaphors of the terrain, the horizon and hence the limits of a visible field defined by a given problematic threaten to induce a false idea of the nature of this field, if we think this field literally according to the spatial metaphor[8] as a space limited by *another space outside it*. This other space is also in the

---

[7] Plon, Paris 1961; abridged translation, *Madness and Civilization*, Tavistock Press, London 1967.

[8] The recourse made in this text to spatial metaphors (field, terrain, space, site, situation, position, etc.) poses a theoretical problem: the problem of the validity of its *claim* to existence in a discourse with scientific pretensions. The problem may be formulated as follows: *why* does a certain form of scientific discourse necessarily need the use of metaphors borrowed from non-scientific disciplines?

first space which contains it as its own denegation; this other space is the first space in person, which is only defined by the denegation of what it excludes from its own limits. In other words, all its limits are *internal*, it carried its outside inside it. Hence, if we wish to preserve the spatial metaphor, the paradox of the theoretical field is that it is an *infinite* because *definite* space, i.e., it has no limits, no external frontiers separating it from nothing, precisely because it is *defined* and limited within itself, carrying in itself the finitude of its definition, which, by excluding what it is not, makes it what it is. Its *definition* (a scientific operation *par excellence*), then, is what makes it both *infinite in its kind*, and marked inside itself, in all its determinations, by what is excluded from it *in it* by its very definition. And when it happens that, in certain very special critical circumstances, the development of the questions produced by the problematic (in the present case, the development of the questions of political economy investigating the 'value of labour') leads to the *production* of the *fleeting presence of an aspect* of its invisible within the visible field of the existing problematic – this product can then only be *invisible*, since the light of the field scans it blindly without reflecting on it. This invisible thus disappears as a theoretical lapse, absence, lack of symptom. It manifests itself exactly as it is: invisible to theory – and that is why Smith made his 'oversight'.

To see this invisible, to see these 'oversights', to identify the lacunae in the fullness of this discourse, the blanks in the crowded text, we need something quite different from an acute or attentive gaze; we need an *informed* gaze, a new gaze, itself produced by a reflection of the 'change of terrain' on the exercise of vision, in which Marx pictures the transformation of the problematic. Here I take this transformation for a fact, without any claim to analyse the mechanism that unleashed it and completed it. The fact that this *'change of terrain'* which produces as its effect this metamorphosis in the gaze, was itself only produced in very specific, complex and often dramatic conditions; that it is absolutely irreducible to the idealist myth of a mental decision to change 'view-points'; that it brings into play a whole process that the subject's sighting, far from producing, merely reflects in its own place; that in this process of real transformation of the means of production of knowledge, the claims of a 'constitutive subject' are as vain as are the claims of the subject of vision in the production of the visible; that the whole process takes place in the dialectical crisis of the mutation of a theoretical structure in which the 'subject' plays, not the part it believes it is playing, but the part which is assigned to it by the mechanism of the process – all these are questions that cannot be studied here. It is enough to remember that the subject must have occupied its new place in the new terrain,[9] in other

---

[9] I retain the spatial metaphor. But the change of terrain takes place *on the spot*: in all strictness, we should speak of the mutation of the *mode* of theoretical production and of the change of function of the subject induced by this change of mode.

words that the subject must already, even partly unwittingly, have been installed in this new terrain, for it to be possible to apply to the old invisible the informed gaze that will make that invisible visible. Marx can see what escaped Smith's gaze because he has already occupied this new terrain which, in what new answers it had produced, had nevertheless been produced though unwittingly, by the old problematic.

8

Such is Marx's second reading: a reading which might well be called '*symptomatic*' (*symptomale*), insofar as it divulges the undivulged event in the text it reads, and in the same movement relates it to *a different text*, present as a necessary absence in the first. Like his first reading, Marx's second reading presupposes the existence of *two texts*, and the measurement of the first against the second. But what distinguishes this new reading from the old one is the fact that in the new one the *second text* is articulated with the lapses in the first text. Here again, at least in the way peculiar to theoretical texts (the only ones whose analysis is at issue here), we find the necessity and possibility of one reading on two bearings simultaneously.

In the papers you are about to *read*, and which do not escape the law I have pronounced – assuming that they have some claim to be treated, for the time being at least, as discourses with a theoretical meaning – we have simply tried to apply to Marx's reading the '*symptomatic*' *reading* with which Marx managed to read the illegible in Smith, by measuring the problematic initially visible in his writings against the invisible problematic contained in the paradox of *an answer which does not correspond to any question posed*. You will also find that the infinite distance which separates Marx from Smith and in consequence our relation to Marx from Marx's relation to Smith, is the following radical difference: whereas in his text Smith produces an answer which not only does not answer any of the immediately preceding questions, but does not even answer *any* other question he ever posed anywhere in his work; with Marx, on the contrary, when he does happen to formulate *an answer without a question*, with a little patience and perspicacity we can find *the question* itself *elsewhere*, twenty or one hundred pages further on, with respect to some other object, enveloped in some other matter, or, on occasion, in Engels's immediate comments on Marx, for Engels has flashes of profound inspiration.[10] And if, as I have dared suggest,

[10] If I may invoke my personal experience, I should like to give two precise examples of this presence *elsewhere* in Marx or in Engels of the question absent from its answer. At the cost of a decidedly laborious investigation, the text of which (*For Marx*, pp. 89ff) bears the mark of these difficulties, I succeeded in identifying a pertinent absence in the idea of the 'inversion' of the Hegelian dialectic by Marx: the absence of its concept, and therefore of its question. I managed to reconstruct this *question* laboriously, by showing that the 'in-

there is undoubtedly in Marx an important *answer* to a *question that is nowhere posed*, an answer which Marx only succeeds in formulating on condition of multiplying the images required to render it, the answer of the *'Darstellung'* and its avatars, it is surely because the age Marx lived in did not provide him, and he could not acquire in his lifetime, an adequate concept with which to think what he produced: *the concept of the effectivity of a structure on its elements*. It will no doubt be said that this is merely a word, and that only the word is missing, since the *object* of the word is there complete. Certainly, but this word is a *concept*, and the repercussions of the structural lack of this concept can be found in certain precise theoretical effects on certain assignable *forms* of Marx's discourse, and in certain of his identifiable *formulations* which are not without their consequences. Which may help to illuminate, but this time *from within*, i.e., not as a relic of a past, a survival, a raffish 'flirtation' (the famous *'kokettieren'*), or a trap for fools (the advantage of my dialectic is that I say things little by little – and when they think I have finished, and rush to refute me, they merely make an untimely manifestation of their asininity! – Letter to Engels, 27 June 1867), the *real presence* of certain Hegelian forms and references in the discourse of *Capital*. From within, as the exact measurement of a disconcerting but inevitable absence, the absence of the concept (and of all the sub-concepts) *of the effectivity of a structure on its elements* which is the visible/invisible, absent/present keystone of his whole work. Perhaps therefore it is not impermissible to think that if Marx does 'play' so much with Hegelian formulae in certain passages, the game is not just raffishness or sarcasm, but *the action of a real drama*, in which old concepts desperately play the part of something absent *which is nameless*, in order to call it onto the stage in person – whereas they only 'produce' its presence in their failures, in the dislocation between the characters and their roles.

If it is true that the identification and location of this omission, which is a *philosophical* omission, can also lead us to the threshold of Marx's philosophy, we can hope for other gains from it in the theory of history itself. A concep-

---

version' Marx mentions had as its effective content a revolution in the problematic. But later, reading Engels's Preface to Volume Two of *Capital*, I was stupefied to find that the question I had had such trouble in formulating was there in black and white! Engels expressly identifies the 'inversion', the 'setting right side up again' of the chemistry and political economy which had been standing on their heads, with a change in their 'theory', and therefore in their problematic. Or again: in one of my first essays, I had suggested that Marx's theoretical revolution lay not in his change of the answers, but in his change of the questions, and that therefore Marx's revolution in the theory of history consisted of a *'change of elements'* by which he moved from the terrain of ideology to the terrain of science (*For Marx*, p. 47). But recently, reading the chapter of *Capital* on wages, I was stupefied to see that Marx used the very expression *'change of terrain'* to express this change of theoretical problematic. Here again, the question (or its concept) which I had laboriously reconstituted out of its *absence* in one precise point of Marx's, Marx himself gave in black and white *somewhere else* in his work.

tual omission that has not been divulged, but on the contrary, consecrated as a non-omission, and proclaimed as a fullness, may, in certain circumstances, seriously hinder the development of a science or of certain of its branches. To be convinced of this we need only note that a science only progresses, i.e., *lives*, by the extreme attention it pays to the points where it is theoretically fragile. By these standards, it depends less for its life on what it knows than on what it *does not know*: its absolute precondition is to focus on this unknown, and to pose it in the rigour of a problem. But the unknown of a science is not what empiricist ideology thinks: its 'residue', what it leaves out, what it cannot conceive or resolve; but *par excellence* what it contains that is fragile despite its apparently unquestionable 'obviousness', certain silences in its discourse, certain conceptual omissions and lapses in its rigour, in brief, everything in it that 'sounds hollow' to an attentive ear, despite its fullness.[11] If it is true that a science progresses and lives by knowing how to hear what 'sounds hollow' in it, some part of the life of the Marxist theory of history perhaps depends on this precise point where Marx shows us in a thousand ways the presence of a concept essential to his thought, but absent from his discourse.

9

This then is the guilt of our philosophical reading of *Capital*: it reads Marx according to the rules of a reading in which he gave us a brilliant lesson in his own reading of classical political economy. Our admission of this crime is deliberate, we shall fetter ourselves to it, anchor ourselves in it, cling fiercely to it as the point which must be hung on to at all costs if we hope to establish ourselves on it one day, recognizing the infinite extent contained within its minute space: the extent of Marx's *philosophy*.

We are all seeking this philosophy. The protocols of *The German Ideology's* philosophical rupture do not give us it in person. Nor do the earlier *Theses on Feuerbach*, those few lightning flashes which break the night of philosophical anthropology with the fleeting snap of a new world glimpsed through the retinal image of the old. Nor, finally, at least insofar as their immediate form is concerned, however genial their clinical judgement, do the criticisms in *Anti-Dühring*, where Engels had to '*follow Herr Dühring into that vast territory in which he dealt with all things under the sun and some others as well*' (Moscow and London, 1959, p. 10), the territory of philosophical ideology, or of a world outlook inscribed in the form of a 'system' (p. 10). For to think that all Marx's philosophy can be found in the few quivering sentences of the *Theses on Feuerbach*, i.e., in the Works of the Break,[12] is to deceive oneself remarkably as to the conditions indispensable to the growth of a radically

[11] Pierre Macherey: 'A propos de la rupture', *La Nouvelle Critique*, Paris, May 1965, p. 139.
[12] *For Marx*, pp. 34–5.

new theory, which needs time to mature, define itself and grow. 'After its first presentation to the world in Marx's *The Poverty of Philosophy* and in *The Communist Manifesto*,' writes Engels, '*this mode of outlook of ours . . . passed through an incubation period of fully twenty years before the publication of Capital*' (p. 14). Similarly, to believe that we can get all Marx's philosophy directly from the polemical formulations of a work that joins battle on the enemy's terrain, i.e., in the terrain of philosophical *ideology*, as *Anti-Dühring* very often does (and *Materialism and Empirio-Criticism* does later), is to deceive ourselves as to the laws of ideological struggle, as to the nature of the *ideology* which is the stage on which this indispensable struggle is fought, and as to the necessary distinction between the philosophical ideology in which this ideological struggle is fought, and the Theory or Marxist philosophy which appears on this stage to give battle there. To concentrate exclusively on the Works of the Break or on the arguments of the later ideological struggle is in practice to fall into the '*oversight*' of not seeing that the place we are given in which to *read* Marx's philosophy in person is *par excellence* his masterpiece, *Capital*. But we have known this for a long time; since Engels, who told us so in black and white, particularly in the extraordinary Preface to Volume Two of *Capital*, which will be a school text some day; and since Lenin, who repeated that Marx's philosophy was entirely to be found in the '*Logic of Capital*', the Logic Marx '*did not have time*' to write.

Let no one argue against this that we are living in a different century, that much water has flowed under the bridge and that our problems are no longer the same. We are discussing living water which has not yet flowed away. We are familiar with enough historical examples, beginning with that of Spinoza, where men have worked ferociously to wall up for ever and bury deep in the earth sources which were made to quench their thirsts, but which their fear will not tolerate. For nearly a century academic philosophy has buried Marx in the earth of silence, the earth of the cemetery. In the same period, Marx's comrades and successors had to contend with the most dramatic and urgent struggles, and Marx's philosophy passed completely into their historical enterprises, their economic, political and ideological action, and into the indispensable works that guided and instructed that action. In this long period of struggles, the *idea* of Marx's *philosophy*, the *consciousness* of its specific existence and function, which are indispensable to the purity and rigour of the knowledges that underlay all the action, were safeguarded and defended against all temptations and hostility. I need no other proof of this than that cry of scientific conscience, *Materialism and Empirio-Criticism*, and all of Lenin's work, that permanent revolutionary manifesto for *knowledge*, for scientific theory – and for '*partisanship in philosophy*', the principle that dominates everything, and is nothing but the most acute consciousness of scientificity in its lucid and intransigent rigour. That is what we have been given, and what defines our task today: a number of *works*, some produced by the theoretical practice of a science (with

Capital at the top of the list), the others produced by economic and political practice (all the transformations that the history of the workers' movement has imposed on the world) or by reflection on this practice (the economic, political and ideological texts of the great Marxists). These works carry with them not only the Marxist theory of history, contained in the theory of the capitalist mode of production and in all the fruits of revolutionary action; but also Marx's *philosophical* theory, in which they are thoroughly steeped, though sometimes unwittingly, even in the inevitable approximations of its *practical* expression.

When once before[13] I claimed that it was necessary to give to this *practical* existence of Marxist philosophy, which exists in person in the practical state in that scientific practice of the analysis of the capitalist mode of production, *Capital*, and in the economic and political practice of the history of the workers' movement, the *form of theoretical existence indispensable* to its needs and our needs, I merely proposed a labour of investigation and critical elucidation, which would analyse one with another, according to the nature of their peculiar modalities, the different *degrees* of this existence, i.e., the different *works* which are the raw material of our reflection. I merely proposed a *'symptomatic' reading* of the works of Marx and of Marxism, one with another, i.e., the progressive and systematic production of a reflection of the problematic on its objects such as to make them *visible*, and the disinterment, the production of the deepest-lying problematic which will allow us to *see* what could otherwise only have existed allusively or practically. As a function of this demand, I can claim to have *read* the specific theoretical form of the Marxist dialectic in its directly political existence (and actively political: the policies of a revolutionary leader – Lenin – immersed in the revolution); as a function of this principle, I can claim to have treated Mao Tse-tung's 1937 text on contradiction as a description of the structures of the Marxist dialectic reflected in political practice. But this *reading* was not, nor could have been, a direct reading or the merely *'generalizing'* reading which Marxist philosophy is too often reduced to, but which, beneath the word *abstraction* with which it is covered, is no more than the confirmation of the religious or empiricist myth of reading, for the summation of individual readings that it resumed does not for one moment deliver us from this myth. This reading was in principle a *dual* reading, the result of a different, 'symptomatic' reading, which introduced into a *question* an answer given to its absent question.

To speak plainly, it was only possible to pose to the practical political analyses Lenin gives us of the conditions for the revolutionary explosion of 1917 the question of the *specificity* of the Marxist dialectic on the basis of an *answer* which lacked the proximity of its *question*, an answer situated *at another place* in the Marxist works at our disposal, precisely the *answer* in

[13] *For Marx*, pp. 164ff.

which Marx declared that he had '*inverted*' the Hegelian dialectic. This answer by 'inversion' was Marx's answer to the following (absent) question: what is the specific difference distinguishing the Marxist dialectic from the Hegelian dialectic? But this answer by 'inversion', like classical political economy's answer by 'the value of labour', is noteworthy in that it contains inside it an internal lack: an interrogation of the inversion metaphor shows that it cannot itself think itself, and hence that it both points to a real but absent problem, a real but absent question outside itself, and to the conceptual emptiness or ambiguity corresponding to this absence, the *absence of a concept behind a word*. Treating this absence of the concept beneath the presence of a word as a symptom put me on to the track of the formulation of the question implied and defined by its absence. However imperfect and provisional it may have been, my 'reading' of Lenin's texts was only possible on condition that it posed these texts the theoretical question whose active answer they represented, although their level of existence was far from purely theoretical (since these texts describe, for practical purposes, the structure of the conjuncture in which the Soviet Revolution exploded). This 'reading' enabled me to sharpen the question, and then to pose the question thus transformed to other, equally symptomatic texts existing at a different level, to Mao Tse-tung's text, and also to a methodological text like Marx's *1857 Introduction*. The question forged out of the first answer emerged transformed anew, and suitable for a reading of other works: today, *Capital*. But here again, to read *Capital*, we have resorted to a series of dual, i.e., 'symptomatic' readings: we have read *Capital* in order to make visible whatever invisible survivals there are in it, but in the present state of our forces, the backward step necessary for this 'reading' has taken all the space we could obtain for it from a second reading performed simultaneously of Marx's Early Works, in particular of the *1844 Manuscripts*, and therefore of the problematic which constitutes the background to his works, Feuerbach's anthropological problematic and Hegel's problematic of absolute idealism.

If the question of Marx's philosophy, i.e. of his differential specificity, emerges even only slightly altered and sharpened from this first reading of *Capital*, it should make other 'readings' possible, first other readings of *Capital*, which will give rise to new differential sharpenings, and then readings of other Marxist works: for example, an informed reading of Marxist texts which are philosophical (but trapped in the inevitable forms of ideological struggle) such as Engels's *Anti-Dühring* and *Dialectics of Nature*, and Lenin's *Materialism and Empirio-Criticism* (and the *Philosophical Notebooks*); or again a 'reading' of those other practical works of Marxism which are so abundant today and exist in the historical reality of socialism and of the newly liberated countries advancing towards socialism. I have left these classical philosophical texts so late deliberately for the simple reason that, before the definition of the essential principles of Marxist philosophy, i.e., before managing to establish the indispensable minimum for the consistent existence of Marxist philosophy in its difference from all philosophical ideology, it was not possible to *read* these classical texts, which are not scholarly but militant texts, other than to the enigmatic letter of their *ideological* expression, without being able to show why this expression had necessarily to take the *form* of ideological expression, i.e., without being able to isolate this form in its real essence. The same is true of the 'reading' of the still theoretically opaque works of the history of the workers' movement, such as the 'cult of personality' or the very serious conflict which is our present drama: perhaps this 'reading' will one day be possible on condition that we have correctly identified in the rational works of Marxism the resources for the production of the concepts indispensable to an understanding of the reasons for this unreason.[14]

May I sum up all this in one sentence? This sentence describes a circle: a philosophical reading of *Capital* is only possible as the application of that which is the very object of our investigation, Marxist philosophy. This circle is only epistemologically possible because of the existence of Marx's philosophy in the works of Marxism. It is therefore a question of producing, in the precise sense of the word, which seems to signify making manifest what is latent, but which really means transforming (in order to give a pre-existing raw material the form of an object adapted to an end), something which in a sense *already exists*. This production, in the double sense which gives the production operation the necessary form of a circle, is the *production of a knowledge*. To conceive Marx's philosophy in its specificity is therefore to conceive the essence of the very movement with which the knowledge of it is produced, or to conceive knowledge as *production*.

10

There can be no question here of making any other claim than to *take theoretical bearings* on what we obtain from our reading of *Capital*. Just as these papers are only a *first* reading, from which it must now surely be clear why we have presented them precisely in their hesitant form, so the specifications in this paper are merely the first strokes in a drawing which can as yet be no more than a sketch.

One point of principle has, I think, been established. If there are no innocent readings, that is because every reading merely reflects in its lessons and rules the real culprit: the conception of knowledge underlying the object of knowledge which makes knowledge what it is. We have glimpsed

---

[14] The same applies to the 'reading' of those new works of Marxism which, sometimes in surprising forms, contain in them something essential to the future of socialism: what Marxism is producing in the vanguard countries of the 'third world' which is struggling for its freedom, from the guerillas of Vietnam to Cuba. It is vital that we be able to 'read' these works before it is too late.

this with respect to the 'expressive' reading, the open and bare-faced reading of the essence in the existence: and behind this total presence in which all opacity is reduced to nothing we have suspected the existence of the darkness of the religious phantasm of epiphanic transparency, and its privileged model of anchorage: the Logos and its Scriptures. Our rejection of the comforting fascinations of this myth has informed us of another link, which must necessarily articulate the new reading Marx proposes to a new *conception of knowledge* on which it is based.

But I must ask the reader's indulgence for another detour, in order to approach this from the best angle. Without wishing to think within the same concept conceptions of knowledge whose historical relationship has not even been examined, let alone proved, I must nevertheless compare the conception which underlies the prescribed religious reading with another just as lively conception, and one which to all appearances is its secular transcription, *the empiricist conception of knowledge*. I use this term in its widest sense, since it can embrace a rationalist empiricism as well as a sensualist empiricism, and it is even found at work in Hegelian thought itself, which, in principle, and with Hegel's own approval, can be regarded in this respect as the reconciliation of religion and its secular 'truth'.[15]

The empiricist conception of knowledge resurrects the myth we have encountered, in a very special form. To understand this correctly, we must define the essential principles of the theoretical problematic which underlies it. The empiricist conception of knowledge presents a process that takes place between a given object and a given subject. At this level, the status of this subject (psychological, historical, or otherwise) and of this object (discontinuous or continuous, mobile or fixed) is not very important. This status only affects the precise definition of the *variants* of the basic problematic, while the basic problematic itself is all that concerns us here. The subject and object, which are given and hence pre-date the process of knowledge, already define a certain fundamental theoretical field, but one which cannot yet in this state be pronounced *empiricist*. What defines it as such is the nature of the process of knowledge, in other words a certain relationship that defines knowledge as such, as a function of the *real object* of which it is said to be the knowledge.

The whole empiricist process of knowledge lies in fact in an operation of the subject called *abstraction*. To know is to abstract from the real object its

---

[15] So long as empiricism is understood in this generic sense it is possible to accept the inclusion within the concept of empiricism of the sensualist empiricism of the eighteenth century. If the latter did not always *realize* knowledge in its real object in the way I am about to describe, if from a certain standpoint it thinks knowledge as the product of a history, it *realizes* knowledge in the *reality* of a history which is merely the development of what it originally contained. By this standard, what I am about to say about the *structure* of the real relationship between knowledge and its real object is equally valid for the relationship between knowledge and real history in eighteenth century ideology.

essence, the possession of which by the subject is then called knowledge. Whatever particular variants this concept of abstraction may adopt, it defines an invariant structure which constitutes the specific index of empiricism. Empiricist abstraction, which abstracts from the given *real* object its essence, is a *real abstraction*, leaving the subject in possession of the *real* essence. We shall see that this repetition at every moment of the process of the category *real* is characteristic of the empiricist conception. What does a *real* abstraction actually mean? It accounts for what is declared to be a real fact: the essence is abstracted from real objects in the sense of an *extraction*, as one might say that gold is *extracted* (or abstracted, i.e., separated) from the dross of earth and sand in which it is held and contained. Just as gold, before its abstraction, exists as gold unseparated from its dross in the dross itself, so the essence of the real exists as a real essence *in* the real which contains it. Knowledge is an abstraction, in the strict sense, i.e., an extraction of the essence from the real which contains it, a separation of the essence from the real which contains it and keeps it in hiding. The procedure that makes this extraction possible (e.g., the comparison of objects, their mutual tritration to wear away the dross, etc.) is of little importance; the pattern of the real, whether it is composed of discrete individuals each in its diversity containing a single essence – or of a unique individual, is of little importance. In every case, this *separation*, in the real itself, of the essence of the real from the dross that conceals the essence, imposes a very special representation both of the real and of the knowledge of it, as the very condition of this operation.

The real: it is structured as a dross of earth containing inside it a grain of pure gold, i.e., it is made of two real essences, the pure essence and the impure essence, the gold and the dross, or, if you like (Hegelian terms), the essential and the inessential. The inessential may be the form of individuality (this fruit, these particular fruits) or materiality (that which is not 'form' or essence), or 'nothingness', or anything else; it is unimportant. The fact is that the real-object contains in it, really, two distinct real parts, the essence and the inessential. Which gives us our first result: Knowledge (which is merely the essential essence) is really contained in the real as one of its parts, *in* the other part of the real, the inessential part. *Knowledge*: its sole function is to separate, in the object, the two parts which exist in it, the essential and the inessential – by special procedures whose aim is to *eliminate the inessential real* (by a whole series of sortings, sievings, scrapings and rubbings), and to leave the knowing subject only the second part of the real which is its essence, itself real. Which gives us a second result: the abstraction operation and all its scouring procedures are merely procedures to purge and eliminate *one part of the real in order to isolate the other*. As such, they leave no trace in the extracted part, every trace of their operation is eliminated along with the part of the real they were intended to eliminate.

However, something of the reality of this elimination work is represented, but not at all as one might expect, in the *result* of this operation, since this result is nothing but the pure and perfect real essence, but rather in the conditions of the operation; to be precise, in the *structure* of the *real object* from which the knowledge operation has to extract the real essence. To this end, that real object is endowed with a very special structure which we have already encountered in our analysis, but which we must now examine more closely. This structure concerns precisely the *respective positions* in the real of the two constitutive parts of the real: the inessential part and the essential part. The inessential part occupies the whole of the *outside* of the object, its *visible surface*; while the essential part occupies the *inside* part of the real object, its *invisible* kernel. The relation between the visible and the invisible is therefore identical to the relation between the outside and the inside, between the dross and the kernel. If the essence is not immediately *visible*, it is because it is concealed, in the strong sense, i.e., entirely covered and enveloped by the dross of the *inessential*. That is the only trace of the know-ledge operation – but it is a trace *realized* in the respective positions of the inessential and the essential in the real object itself; and at the same time it establishes the necessity for the operation of real extraction and for the scouring procedures indispensable to the discovery of the essence. Discovery should be taken in its most literal sense: removing the covering, as the husk is removed from the nut, the peel from the fruit, the veil from the girl, the truth, the god or the statue,[16] etc. I am not looking in these concrete examples for the origin of this structure – I cite them as a number of mirror-images in which all the philosophies of vision have reflected their complacency. Do I still need to show that this problematic of the empiricist conception of knowledge is the twin brother of the problematic of the religious vision of the essence in the transparency of existence? The empiricist conception may be thought of as a variant of the conception of vision, with the mere difference that *transparency* is not given from the beginning, but is separated from itself precisely by the *veil*, the dross of impurities, of the inessential which steal the essence from us, and which abstraction, by its techniques of separa-tion and scouring, *sets aside*, in order to give us the real presence of the pure naked essence, knowledge of which is then merely sight.

Let us now consider this *structure* of empiricist knowledge from a critical distance. We can characterize it as a conception which thinks the knowledge of that real object itself as a *real part* of the real object to be known. This part may be called essential, internal, hidden and hence invisible at first glance, but it is posed nevertheless, precisely because of these properties, as a real component part of the reality of the real object compounded with the inessential part. What represents *Knowledge*, i.e., that very special

---

[16] I am neither inventing nor joking. Michelangelo developed a whole aesthetic of artistic production based not on the production of the essential form out of the marble material, but on the *destruction* of the non-form which envelopes the form to be *disengaged* even before the first chip is cut out. A practice of aesthetic production is here buried in an empiricist realism of *extraction*.

operation performed with respect to the real object to be known, and which is not nothing, but, on the contrary, adds to the real existing object *a new existence*, precisely the existence of its knowledge (e.g., at the very least the verbal or written conceptual discourse which pronounces this knowledge in the form of a message, hence what represents that knowledge, but is performed outside the object – being the deed of an active subject), is completely *inscribed in the structure of the real object*, in the form of the difference between the inessential and the essence, between surface and depth, between outside and inside! Knowledge is therefore already *really* present in the real object it has to know, in the form of the respective dis-positions of its two real parts! Knowledge is completely and really present in it: not only its object, which is the real part called the essence, but also its operation, which is the distinction and respective positions that really exist between the two parts of the real object, of which one (the inessential) is the outer part which conceals and envelops the other (the essence or inner part).

This investment of knowledge, conceived as a real part of the real object, in the real structure of the real object, is what constitutes the specific problematic of the empiricist conception of knowledge. Once this has been firmly grasped in its concept, we can draw some important conclusions which will naturally go beyond what this conception *says*, since it will give us a confession of what it *does* while denegating it. I cannot deal with the minor conclusions here, but they are easily developed, particularly where they involve the structure of the visible and the invisible, a foretaste of whose importance can be detected here. I only want to note in passing that the categories of empiricism are at the heart of the problematic of classical philosophy; that a recognition of this problematic, even in its variants, including the mute variants and their denegrations, can give a projected history of philosophy an essential principle for the construction of its concept during this period; that this problematic *avowed* by the eighteenth century from Locke to Condillac, is profoundly present in Hegelian philosophy, however paradoxical this may seem; and that Marx, for the reasons we are analysing, *had to use it* to think the lack of a concept whose effects he had produced nevertheless, to formu-late the (absent) question, i.e., that concept, which he had answered never-theless in the analysis of *Capital*; that this problematic has survived the wear it received from its twisting and distortion by Marx who transformed it *in fact*, although he still used its terms (appearance and essence, outside and inside, inner essence of things, real and apparent movement, etc.); that we find it at work in many passages of Engels and Lenin, who found a motive for its use in the ideological battles in which the most urgent parrying was required beneath the enemy's brutal assault and on his chosen 'terrain', first of all by turning against him his own weapons and blows, i.e., his ideological arguments and concepts.

I only want to insist on one particular point: the *play on words* on which this conception is based and which involves the concept 'real'. In fact, it is possible to give a first characterization of this empiricist conception of knowledge as a *play on the word* 'real'. We have just seen that the whole of knowledge, both its peculiar object (the essence of the real object) and the distinction between the real object, to which its knowledge operation is applied, and this knowledge operation, a distinction which is *the site* itself of the operation of knowledge – we have just seen that the object as well as the operation of knowledge in its distinction from the real object, knowledge of which it proposes to produce, are posed and thought as belonging by right to the real structure of the real object. For the empiricist conception of knowledge, the whole of knowledge is thus invested *in the real*, and knowledge never arises except as *a relation inside its real object between the really distinct parts of that real object*. Once this basic structure has been firmly grasped, it provides us with a key in numerous circumstances, in particular to gauge the theoretical status of the modern forms of empiricism which present themselves to us in the innocent form of a theory *of models*,[17] which I hope I have shown is utterly foreign to Marx. More distant from us, but closer to Marx, in Feuerbach and the Works of the Break (The *Theses on Feuerbach* and *The German Ideology*), it will help us understand the perpetual *play on the words* 'real' and 'concrete' on which is based a whole series of ambiguities whose delayed effects we are suffering from today.[18] But I shall not take this

[17] Note carefully that here I only discuss and reject the theory of models as an *ideology of knowledge*. In this respect, however elaborate its forms (e.g., contemporary neo-positivism), it remains an avatar of the empiricist conception of knowledge. This rejection does not include within its ban another meaning and use of the category 'model', precisely the meaning that effectively corresponds to the technical use of 'models' as can be seen in various circumstances in the technical *practice* of planning in the socialist countries. The 'model' is then a *technical means* with which to compound the different data with a view to obtaining a certain goal. The empiricism of the 'model' is then in its place, at home, not in the theory of knowledge but in practical application, i.e., in the order of the technique for realizing certain aims as a function of certain data, on the basis of certain knowledges provided by the science of political economy. In a famous phrase which has unfortunately not had the echo it deserved in practice, Stalin condemned the confusion of political economy and economic policy, of theory with its technical application. The empiricist conception of the model as an ideology of knowledge obtains all the appearances necessary for its imposture from the confusion between the *technical instrument* that a model in fact is, and the concept of knowledge.

[18] The genial errors of Politzer's *Critique des fondements de la psychologie* largely depend on the ideological function of the uncriticized concept of the 'concrete': it is no accident that Politzer's proclamation of the arrival of '*concrete* psychology' was never followed by any works. All the virtue of the term 'concrete' was in fact exhausted in its critical use, without it ever founding the slightest amount of knowledge which only exists in the 'abstraction' of concepts. It was already possible to see this even in Feuerbach, who tried desperately to free himself from ideology by invoking the 'concrete', i.e., the ideological concept which confuses knowledge and being: obviously, ideology cannot liberate ideology. The same ambiguity and the same play on words can be found in all the interpreters of Marx who refer themselves to the Early Works, invoking 'real', 'concrete' or 'positive' humanism as the theoretical basis of his work. They do have excuses, it is true: all Marx's own expressions

extraordinarily rich critical path: I shall leave these effects to the play on words which produced them, and their refutation to the growing vigilance of our time. I am interested in the *play on words* itself.

This play on words plays on a difference it kills: at the same time it spirits away the corpse. Let us look at the name of the victim of this subtle murder. When empiricism designates the essence as the object of knowledge, it admits something important and denegates it in the same instant: it admits that the object of knowledge is not identical to the real object, since it declares that it is only a part of the real object. But it denegates what it has admitted, precisely by reducing this difference between two objects, the object of knowledge and the real object, to a mere distinction between the parts of a single object: the real object. In the admission, there are two distinct objects, the real object 'which exists outside the subject, independent of the process of knowledge' (Marx) and the object of knowledge (the essence of the real object) which is quite clearly distinct from the real object. In the denegation, there is no longer more than *one object*: the real object. Hence we are within our rights in concluding that the true play on words has deceived us as to its site, its support (*Träger*), the word which is its ambiguous seat. The true play on words is not a play on the word '*real*', which is its mask, but on the word '*object*'. It is not the word '*real*' which needs to be interrogated in connexion with the murder, but the word '*object*'; the *difference* of the *concept* of object must be produced to deliver it from the fraudulent unity of the *word* 'object'.

II

This sets us off on a path which was opened for us *almost* without our know-ledge, I think, for we have not really considered it, by two philosphers in history: Spinoza and Marx. Against what should really be called the latent dogmatic empiricism of Cartesian idealism, Spinoza warned us that the *object* of knowledge or essence was in itself absolutely distinct and different from the *real object*, for, to repeat his famous aphorism, the two objects must not be confused: the *idea* of the circle, which is the *object* of knowledge must not be confused with the circle, which is the *real object*. In the third chapter of the *1857 Introduction*, Marx took up this principle as forcefully as possible.

Marx rejected the Hegelian confusion which identifies the real object with the object of knowledge, the real process with the knowledge process: '*Hegel fell into the illusion of conceiving the real* (das Reale) *as the result of*

---

in the Works of the Break (*The Theses on Feuerbach, The German Ideology*) speak of the concrete, the real, of 'real' concrete men, etc. But the Works of the Break themselves are still trapped in the ambiguity of a *negation* which still clings to the universe of the concepts it rejects, without having succeeded in adequately formulating the new and positive concepts it brings with it (cf. *For Marx*, pp. 36–7).

thought recapitulating itself within itself, deepening itself within itself, and
moving itself from within itself, whereas the method that allows one to rise from
the abstract to the concrete is merely the mode (die Art) *of thought which*
appropriates the concrete and reproduces (reproduzieren) *it as a spiritual*
concrete (geistig Konkretes)' (*Grundrisse der Kritik der Politischen Ökonomie*,
Berlin 1953, p. 22). This confusion, which in Hegel takes the form of an
absolute idealism of history, is in principle simply a variant of the confusion
which characterizes the problematic of empiricism. Against this confusion,
Marx defends the *distinction* between the *real object* (the real-concrete the
real totality, which '*survives in its independence, after as before, outside the*
head (Kopf)' p. 22) and the *object of knowledge*, a product of the thought
which produces it in itself as a thought-concrete (*Gedankenkonkretum*), as
a thought-totality (*Gedankentotalität*), i.e., as a *thought-object*, absolutely
distinct from the real-object, the real-concrete, the real totality, knowledge
of which is obtained precisely by the thought-concrete, the thought-totality,
etc. Marx goes even further and shows that this distinction involves not
only these two objects, but also their peculiar production processes. While
the production process of a given real object, a given real-concrete totality
(e.g., a given historical nation) takes place entirely in the real and is carried
out according to the real order of *real* genesis (the order of succession of the
moments of *historical* genesis), the production process of the object of knowledge takes place entirely in knowledge and is carried out according to *a*
different order, in which the thought categories which 'reproduce' the real
categories do *not* occupy *the same* place as they do in the order of real historical genesis, but quite different places assigned them by their function in
the production process of the object of knowledge.

Let us look closely at all these themes for a moment.

When Marx tells us that the production process of knowledge, and hence
that of its object, as distinct from the real object which it is its precise aim
to appropriate in the 'mode' of knowledge takes place entirely in knowledge,
in the 'head' or in thought, he is not for one second falling into an idealism
of consciousness, mind or thought, for the '*thought*' we are discussing here
is not a faculty of a transcendental subject or absolute consciousness confronted by the real world as *matter*; nor is this thought a faculty of a psychological subject, although human individuals are its agents. This thought
is the historically constituted system of an *apparatus of thought*, founded on
and articulated to natural and social reality. It is defined by the system of
real conditions which make it, if I dare use the phrase, a determinate *mode*
of production of knowledges. As such, it is constituted by a structure which
combines ('*Verbindung*') the type of object (raw material) on which it labours,
the theoretical means of production available (its theory, its method and its
technique, experimental or otherwise) and the historical relations (both
theoretical, ideological and social) in which it produces. This definite
system of conditions of theoretical practice is what assigns any given thinking

subject (individual) its place and function in the production of knowledges. This system of theoretical production – a material as well as a 'spiritual' system, whose practice is founded on and articulated to the existing economic, political and ideological practices which directly or indirectly provide it with the essentials of its 'raw materials' – has a determinate objective reality. This determinate reality is what defines the roles and functions of the 'thought' of particular individuals, who can only 'think' the 'problems' already actually or potentially posed; hence it is also what *sets to work* their 'thought power' as the structure of an economic mode of production sets to work the labour power of its immediate producers, but according to its own peculiar mode. Far from being an essence opposed to the material world, the faculty of a 'pure' transcendental subject or 'absolute conscious- ness', i.e., the myth that idealism produces as a myth in which to recognize and establish itself, 'thought' is a peculiar real system, established on and articulated to the real world of a given historical society which maintains determinate relations with nature, a *specific* system, defined by the conditions of its existence and practice, i.e., by a *peculiar structure*, a determinate type of 'combination' (*Verbindung*) between its peculiar raw material (the object of theoretical practice), its peculiar means of production and its relations with the other structures of society.

Once it is accepted that this is how 'thought' – the very general term Marx used in the passage we are analysing – must be defined, it is perfectly legitimate to say that the production of knowledge which is peculiar to theoretical practice constitutes a process that takes place *entirely in thought*, just as we can say, *mutatis mutandis*, that the process of economic production takes place entirely in the economy, even though it implies, and precisely in the specific determinations of its structure, necessary relations with nature and the other structures (legal-political and ideological) which, taken together, constitute the global structure of a social formation belonging to a determinate mode of production. It is therefore perfectly legitimate (*richtig*) to say, as Marx does, that '*the concrete-totality as a thought-totality, as a thought-concrete, is in reality* (in der Tat) *a product of thinking and conceiving* (ein Produkt des Denkens, des Begreifens)' (p. 22); it is perfectly legitimate to imagine theoretical practice, i.e., thought's labour on its raw material (the ob- ject it works on) as the '*labour of transformation* (Verarbeitung) *of intuition* (An- schauung) *and representation* (Vorstellung) *into concepts* (in Begriffe)' (p. 22).

Elsewhere[19] I have tried to show that the *raw material* which the mode of production of knowledge works on, i.e., what Marx here calls *Anschauung* and *Vorstellung*, the material of intuition and representation, had to take very different forms according to the degree of development of knowledge in its history; for example, that there is a great difference between the raw material on which Aristotle worked and the raw material on which Galileo, Newton

---

[19] *For Marx*, pp. 190–1.

or Einstein worked – but that *formally this raw material is a part of the conditions of production of all knowledge.* I also tried to show that even though it is clear to everyone that the greater the progress of a branch of knowledge, the more elaborate becomes the raw material, though the raw material of a developed science obviously has nothing in common with 'pure' sensuous intuition or mere 'representation', nevertheless, however far back we ascend into the past of a branch of knowledge, we are never dealing with a 'pure' sensuous intuition or representation, but with an *ever-already* complex raw material, a structure of 'intuition' or 'representation' which combines together in a peculiar *'Verbindung'* sensuous, technical and ideological elements; that therefore knowledge never, as empiricism desperately demands it should, confronts a *pure object* which is then identical to the *real object* of which knowledge aimed to produce precisely . . . the knowledge. Knowledge working on its 'object', then, does not work on the *real* object but on the peculiar raw material, which constitutes, in the strict sense of the term, *its 'object'* (*of knowledge*), and which, even in the most rudimentary forms of knowledge, is distinct from the *real object.* For that raw material is ever-already, in the strong sense Marx gives it in *Capital*, a *raw material*, i.e., matter already elaborated and transformed, precisely by the imposition of the complex (sensuous-technical-ideological) structure which constitutes it as an *object of knowledge*, however crude, which constitutes it as the object it will transform, whose *forms* it will change in the course of its development process in order to produce knowledges which are constantly *transformed* but will always apply to its *object*, in the sense of *object of knowledge.*

12

It would be rash to go any further for the moment. The formal concept of the production conditions of theoretical practice alone cannot provide the specific concepts which will enable us to constitute a *history* of theoretical practice, let alone the history of the different branches of theoretical practice (mathematics, physics, chemistry, biology, history and the other 'human sciences'). To go beyond the merely *formal concept of the structure of theoretical practice,* i.e., of the production of knowledges, we must work out the *concept* of the history of knowledge, the concepts of the different *modes* of theoretical production (most important the concepts of the theoretical modes of production of ideology and science), and the peculiar concepts of the different *branches* of theoretical production and of their relations (the different sciences and their specific types of dependence, independence and articulation). This work of theoretical elaboration presupposes a very long-term investigation which will have to build on the valuable work that has already been done in the classical domains of the history of the sciences and of epistemology – i.e., an investigation which appropriates all the raw material provided by the 'facts' that have already been collected or await collection and by the first theoretical results established in these domains. But the mere collection of these 'facts', these empirical 'givens', which, with a very few remarkable exceptions,[20] are generally only presented in the form of simple sequences or chronicles, i.e., in the form of an ideological conception of history, or even in the *a priori* of a philosophy of history – the mere collection of these facts is not enough to constitute a history of knowledge, the *concept* of which must be constructed, at least in a provisional form, before it can be undertaken. In the papers you are about to read we have paid great attention to the concepts in which Marx thinks the general conditions of economic *production* and the concepts in which Marxist thought must think its theory of *history*, not only in order to grasp the Marxist theory of the *economic* region of the capitalist mode of production, but also to ascertain as far as possible the basic concepts (*production, structure* of a mode of production, *history*) whose formal elaboration is equally indispensable to the Marxist theory of the production of knowledge, and to its history.

We are now beginning to get some idea of the path these investigations are taking and will take. This path leads us to a revolution in the traditional concept of the history of the sciences, which today is still profoundly steeped in the ideology of the philosophy of the Enlightenment, i.e., in a teleological and therefore idealist rationalism. We are beginning to suspect, and even to be able to prove in a number of already studied examples, that the history of reason is neither a linear history of continuous development, nor, in its continuity, a history of the progressive manifestation or emergence into consciousness of a Reason which is completely present in germ in its origins and which its history merely reveals to the light of day. We know that this type of history and rationality is merely the effect of the retrospective illusion of a given historical result which writes its history in the 'future anterior', and which therefore thinks its origin as the anticipation of its end. The rationality of the Philosophy of the Enlightenment to which Hegel gave the systematic form of the development of the concept is merely an ideological conception both of reason and of its history. The real history of the development of knowledge appears to us today to be subject to laws quite different from this teleological hope for the religious triumph of reason. We are beginning to conceive this history as a history punctuated by radical discontinuities (e.g., when a new science detaches itself from the background of earlier ideological formations), profound re-organizations which, if they respect the continuity of the existence of regions of knowledge (and even this is not always the case), nevertheless inaugurate with their rupture the reign of a new logic, which, far from being a mere development, the 'truth' or 'inversion' of the old one, *literally takes its place.*

[20] In France, the work of Koyré, Bachelard, Cavaillès, Canguilhem and Foucault.

We are thereby obliged to renounce every teleology of reason, and to conceive the historical relation between a result and its conditions of existence as a relation of production, and not of expression, and therefore as what, in a phrase that clashes with the classical system of categories and demands the *replacement* of those categories themselves, we can call the *necessity of its contingency*. To grasp this necessity we must grasp the very special and paradoxical logic that leads to this *production*, i.e., the logic of the conditions of the production of knowledges, whether they belong to the history of a branch of still ideological knowledge, or to a branch of knowledge attempting to constitute itself as a science or already established as a science. We can expect many surprises from this series, like those we have had from Canguilhem's work on the history of the production of the reflex concept, which, despite what all the appearances (i.e. the dominant ideological conceptions) would lead us to think, was the fruit, not of a mechanistic, but of a vitalist philosophy;[21] like those we owe to Michel Foucault's studies of the disconcerting development of that complex cultural formation which in the seventeen and eighteenth centuries grouped around the over-determined word 'Madness' a whole series of medical, legal, religious, ethical and political practices and ideologies in a combination whose internal dispositions and meaning varied as a function of the changing place and role of these terms in the more general context of the economic, political, legal and ideological structures of the time;[22] like those we also owe to Michel Foucault, who has revealed to us the set of apparently heterogeneous conditions which in fact, as the outcome of a laborious 'labour of the positive' conspired in the production of what seems to us obviousness itself: the observation of the patient by the 'gaze' of clinical medicine.[23]

Even the theoretically essential and practically decisive distinction between science and ideology gets some protection from this against the dogmatist or scientistic temptations which threaten it – since in this work of investigation and conceptualization we have to learn not to make use of this distinction in a way that restores the ideology of the philosophy of the Englightenment, but on the contrary, to treat the ideology which constitutes the prehistory of a science, for example, as a real history with its own laws and as the real prehistory whose real confrontation with other technical practices and other ideological or scientific acquisitions was capable, in a specific theoretical conjuncture, of producing the arrival of a science, not as its goal, but as its surprise. The fact that this will force us to pose the problem of the conditions of the 'epistemological rupture' which inaugurates each science, i.e., returning to classical terminology, the problem

[21] Georges Canguilhem: *La formation du concept de réflexe aux XVII*e *et XVIII*e *siècles*, P.U.F., Paris 1955.
[22] Michel Foucault: *Histoire de la folie à l'âge classique*, Plon, Paris 1961, trans. *Madness and Civilization*, op. cit.
[23] Michel Feucault: *Naissance de la clinique*, P.U.F., Paris 1963.

of the conditions of scientific discovery, and the fact that we shall have to pose this problem *for Marx as well*, considerably increases our task. The fact that just as we are studying this problem we have to think (in a completely novel way) the relation between a science and the ideology which gave rise to it and which continues to accompany it silently more or less throughout its history; the fact that such an investigation confronts us with the observation that every science, in the relationship it has with the ideology it emerged from, can only be thought as a 'science of the ideology'[24], would disconcert us, were we not forewarned of the nature of the *object* of knowledge, which can only exist in the form of ideology at the moment of constitution of the science which is going to produce knowledge from it in the specific mode that defines it. If all these examples do give us a first idea of the new conception of the history of knowledge we have to produce, they also suggest the scale of the work of historical investigation and theoretical elaboration which is in store.

13

Now I come to a second of Marx's decisive comments. The text of the *1857 Introduction* which distinguishes between the real object and the object of knowledge also distinguishes between their processes, and what is crucial, brings out a difference in *order* in the genesis of these two processes. To use a different vocabulary, one that constantly recurs in *Capital*, Marx declares that the order which governs the categories of *thought* in the process of knowledge does not coincide with the order which governs the *real* categories in the process of real historical genesis. This distinction obviously has great bearing on one of the most disputed questions in *Capital*, the question as to whether there is an identity between the *so-called 'logical'* order (or order of 'deduction' of the categories in *Capital*) and the *real 'historical'* order. Most interpreters cannot really 'get out' of this question successfully because they refuse to *pose* it in adequate terms, i.e., in the field of the *problematic* this question requires. To say the same thing in a different, but now familiar way, *Capital* gives us a whole series of *answers* as to the identity or non-identity of the *'logical'* and *'historical'* orders. These answers are new answers without any explicit question: they therefore pose for us the question of their questions, i.e., they impose on us the task of formulating the unformulated question which these questions answer. It is clear that this question concerns the relation between the logical and historical orders, but in pronouncing these words we are merely adopting the terms of the answers: what governs the posing (and hence production) of a question in the last resort is a definition of the field of the problematic in which this question (problem) must be posed. But most interpreters pose this question in the field of an empiricist problematic or (its 'inversion' in the strict sense) in the field of a *Hegelian*

[24] Pierre Macherey: op. cit., pp. 136-40.

problematic, seeking to prove, in the first case that the 'logical' order, being identical in essence with the real order and existing *in* the reality of the real order as its essence itself, can only follow the real order; in the second case that the real order being identical in essence with the 'logical' order, the real order, which is then merely the existence of the logical order, must follow the logical order. In both cases the interpreters are obliged to do violence to certain of Marx's answers which manifestly contradict their hypotheses. I propose to pose this question (this problem) not in the field of an ideological problematic, but in the field of the Marxist theoretical problematic with its distinction between the real object and the object of knowledge, registering the fact that this distinction of objects implies a radical distinction between the order in which 'categories' appear in knowledge, on the one hand, and in historical reality on the other. Once the so-called problem of the *relation* between the order of real historical genesis and the order of development of the concepts in scientific discourse in the field of this problematic (the radical distinction between these two orders) has been posed we can conclude that the problem we are discussing is an *imaginary* one.

Given this hypothesis, we can respect the variety of the answers Marx gives, i.e., both the cases of correspondence and those of non-correspondence between the 'logical' order and the 'real' order – so long as we can admit no *one-to-one correspondence* between the different moments of these two distinct orders. When I say that the distinction between the real object and the object of knowledge implies the disappearance of the ideological (empiricist or absolute-idealist) myth of a one-to-one correspondence between the terms of these two orders, I include *every form, even an inverted one*, of one-to-one correspondence between the terms of the two orders: for an inverted correspondence is still a term by term correspondence according to a common order (with only a change in the sign). I evoke this last hypothesis because it has been held, by Della Volpe and his school, to be essential to understanding not only the theory of *Capital*, but also the Marxist 'theory of knowledge'.

This interpretation depends on a few sentences from Marx, the clearest of which appears in the *1857 Introduction* (*Grundrisse*, p. 28).

'Hence it would be impracticable and false to range the economic categories in the order in which they have been historically determinant. On the contrary, their order is determined by the connexion that there is between them in modern bourgeois society and which is precisely the reverse (*umgekehrte*) of what would seem their natural order or of the order corresponding to historical development.'

By appeal to this *Umkehrung*, this 'inversion' of sense, the logical order can be claimed to be a term by term inversion of the historical order. On this point, I refer the reader to Rancière's commentary.[25] But what immediately follows this passage in Marx's text leaves us in no doubt, for

---

[25] See *Lire le Capital*, first edition, 1965, Vol. I.

we learn that this dispute over the direct or inverted correspondence between the terms of the two orders has nothing to do with the problem under analysis: 'It is not a matter of the connexion which is established historically between economic relations in the succession of different social forms . . . but of their *Gliederung* (articulated combination) within modern bourgeois society' (p. 28). It is precisely this *Gliederung*, this articulated-thought-totality which has to be produced in knowledge as an object of knowledge in order to reach a knowledge of the real *Gliederung*, of the real articulated-totality which constitutes the existence of bourgeois society. The order in which the thought *Gliederung* is produced is a specific order, precisely the order of the theoretical *analysis* Marx performed in *Capital*, the order of the liaison and 'synthesis' of the concepts necessary for the production of a thought-whole, a thought-concrete, the theory of *Capital*.

The order in which these concepts are articulated in the analysis is the order of Marx's scientific proof: it has no direct, one-to-one relationship with the order in which any particular category may have appeared in history. There may be temporary encounters, fragmentary sequences apparently rhythmed by the same order, but, far from proving the existence of this correspondence or answering the question of the correspondence, they pose *a different question*. Without the theory of the distinction between the two orders it is impossible to examine whether it is legitimate to pose this question (which is by no means certain: *this question might be meaningless – we have grounds to think that it is meaningless*). Quite to the contrary, Marx spends his time showing, not without malice, that the real order contradicts the logical order, and if verbally he occasionally goes so far as to *say* that there is an *'inverted'* relationship between the two orders, we cannot take this word literally as a *concept*, i.e., as a rigorous affirmation which takes its meaning not from the fact that it has been put forward, but from the fact that it belongs by right to a definite theoretical field. Rancière's demonstration shows, on the contrary, that the term 'inversion' here as often elsewhere, is, in *Capital*, a point of *analogy*, without any theoretical rigour, i.e., without that rigour which is *imposed* on us by the theoretical problematic which underlies the whole of Marx's analysis, and which must be identified and defined before we can judge the legitimacy or weaknesses of a *term*, or even of a sentence. It would be easy to extend this demonstration successfully to all the passages which encourage the interpretation of an *inverted* one-to-one *correspondence* between the terms of the two orders.

14

I shall therefore return to the character peculiar to the order of the concepts in the exposition of Marx's analysis, i.e., in his *proof*. It is one thing to say that this order of concepts (or 'logical' order) is a *specific* order without any one-to-one relationship of its terms with those of the historical order: it is another to explain this specificity, i.e., the nature of this order as an order. To pose this question is obviously to pose the question of the *form of order* required at a given moment in the history of knowledge by the existing type of scientificity, or, if you prefer, by the norms of theoretical validity recognized by science, in its own practice, as *scientific*. This is still a problem of great scope and complexity, and one which presupposes the elucidation of a number of preliminary theoretical problems. The essential problem presupposed by the question of the existing type of *demonstrativity* is the problem of the history of the production of the *different forms* in which theoretical practice (producing knowledges, whether 'ideological' or 'scientific') recognizes the validating norms it demands. I propose to call this history the history of the *theoretical* as such, or the history of the production (and transformation) of what at a given moment in the history of knowledge constitutes the *theoretical problematic* to which are related all the existing validating criteria, and hence the *forms* required to give the order of theoretical discourse *the force and value of a proof*. This history of the *theoretical*, of the structures of theoreticity and of the forms of theoretical apodicticity, has yet to be constituted – and there, too, as Marx said when he began his work, there 'exists an enormous literature' at our disposal. But these elements at our disposal, often of considerable value (particularly in the history of philosophy treated as the history of the 'theory of knowledge'), are one thing, and their theoretical organization, which presupposes precisely the formation, the production of this theory, is another.

I have only made this detour in order to be able to say, on returning to Marx, that the apodictic character of the order of his theoretical discourse (or the 'logical' order of the categories in *Capital*) can only be thought against the background of a theory of the *history of the theoretical*, which would show what effective relationship there is between the forms of proof in the theoretical discourse of *Capital* on the one hand, and the forms of theoretical proof contemporaneous with it and close to it, on the other. In this perspective, the comparative study of Marx and Hegel is indispensable once again. But it does not exhaust our object. For we are often warned, by Marx's constant references to forms of proof other than the forms of philosophical discourse[26] – that he *also* uses forms of proof borrowed from *mathematics, physics, chemistry, astronomy*, etc. We are therefore constantly warned by Marx himself of the complex and original character of the order of proof he installs in political economy.

He says himself, in his letter to La Châtre: '*the method of analysis which I have employed, and which had not previously been applied to economic subjects,*

[26] A discourse inaugurated by Descartes, expressly conscious of the crucial importance of the 'order of reasons' in philosophy as well as in the sciences, and also conscious of the distinction between the order of knowledge and the order of being, despite his lapse into a dogmatic empiricism.

makes the reading of the first chapters rather arduous' (*Capital*, T.I, p. 44, Vol. I, p. 21). The *method of analysis* Marx mentions is the same as the *'mode of exposition'* (*Darstellungsweise*) he refers to in the Afterword to the second German edition (T.I, p. 29, Vol. I, p. 19) and carefully distinguishes from the *'mode of investigation'* (*Forschungsweise*). The 'mode of investigation' is Marx's several years long concrete investigation into the existing documents and the facts they witness to: this investigation followed paths which disappear in their result, the knowledge of its object, the capitalist mode of production. The protocols of Marx's 'investigation' are contained in part in his notebooks. But in *Capital* we find something quite different from the complex and varied procedures, the 'trials and errors' that every investigation contains and which express the peculiar logic of the process of the inventor's discovery at the level of his theoretical practice. In *Capital* we find a systematic presentation, an apodictic arrangement of the concepts in the form of that type of demonstrational discourse that Marx calls *analysis*. What is the provenance of this 'analysis', which Marx must have regarded as pre-existent since he only demanded its *application* to political economy? We pose this question as one indispensable to an understanding of Marx, and one which we are not yet in a position to give an exhaustive answer.

Our papers do bear on this *analysis*, on the forms of reasoning and proof which it sets to work, and in the first place on those almost inaudible words, those apparently neutral words which Macherey studies in the first sentences of *Capital* and to which we have all tried to lend our ears. Literally, in the actual discourse of *Capital*, these words carry the occasionally semi-silent discourse of its *proof*. If, even despite the letter of Marx's work, we have succeeded in reconstituting the sequence and the peculiar logic of this silent discourse in certain delicate points; if we have managed to identify and fill these blanks; if we have been lucky enough to replace some of these still hesitant words by other, more rigorous terms, then that is all we have done. If we have been able to establish with enough proof to state it, that Marx's discourse is in principle foreign to Hegel's, that his dialectic (the Afterword identifies it with the mode of exposition we are discussing) is quite different from the Hegelian dialectic, then that is all we have done. We have not gone on to see whence Marx took this *method of analysis* which he presents as if it were pre-existent – we have not posed the question as to whether Marx, far from borrowing it, did not himself invent this method of analysis which he thought he was merely applying, as he really did invent the dialectic which he tells us he took from Hegel, in certain well-known passages which are too often re-hashed by hurried interpreters. *And if this analysis and this dialectic are simply, as we believe, one and the same thing,* it is not a sufficient explanation of their original production to stress that it was only possible at the cost of a rupture with Hegel; we must also exhibit the positive conditions for this production, the possible positive models which, reflecting themselves in the personal theoretical conjuncture to which Marx's history had led him, produced this dialectic in his thought. We were not in a situation to do this. Of course, the differences we have brought to light will be able to serve as indices and as a theoretical guide to such a new investigation – but they cannot take its place.

And there is a more than even chance that, if as we believe this first attempt at a philosophical reading suggests, Marx really did invent a new form of *order* for axiomatic analysis, what is true of the majority of the great inventors in the history of the *theoretical* must be true of him as well: time is needed before his discovery will even be accepted, and only then will it pass into normal scientific practice. A thinker who installs a new order *in the theoretical*, a new form of apodicity or scientificity, has quite a different fate from that of a thinker who establishes a new science. He may long remain unknown and misunderstood, particularly if, as is the case with Marx, the revolutionary inventor *in* the theoretical happens to be masked in the same man by the twin who is a revolutionary inventor in a branch of science (here the science of history). The more *partial* his reflection of the concept of the revolution he has inaugurated in the theoretical, the greater the risk that he will suffer. This risk is redoubled if the cause of the limitations to his conceptual expression of a revolution which affects the theoretical through the discovery of a new science does not lie in personal circumstances or in a 'lack of time' alone: it may lie above all in the degree to which the objective theoretical conditions which govern the possibility of the *formulation* of these concepts are realized. Indispensable theoretical concepts do not magically construct themselves on command when they are needed. The whole history of the beginnings of sciences or of great philosophies shows, on the contrary, that the exact set of new concepts do not march out on parade in single file; on the contrary, some are long delayed, or march in borrowed clothes before acquiring their proper uniforms – for as long as history fails to provide the tailor and the cloth. In the meantime, the concept is certainly present in its works, but in a different form from that of a concept – in a form which is looking for itself inside a form '*borrowed*' from other custodians of formulated and disposable, or fascinating concepts. This goes to show that there is nothing incomprehensible in the paradoxical fact that Marx treated his original method of analysis as a method that already existed even in the instant when he invented it, and in the fact that he thought he was borrowing from Hegel even in the instant when he broke his Hegelian moorings. This paradox alone requires an amount of work which we have hardly more than outlined here, and which undoubtedly contains many surprises for us.

15

But we have gone far enough in this work for a return to the difference between the order of the object of knowledge and that of the real object to enable us to approach the problem whose *index* this difference is: the problem of the relation between these two objects (the object of knowledge and the real object), a relation which constitutes the very existence of *knowledge*.

I must warn the reader that we are here entering a domain which is *very difficult* to approach, for two reasons. First, because we have very few Marxist reference points with which to stake out its space and orientate ourselves within: in fact we are confronted by a problem which we not only have to solve but also to *pose*, for it has not yet *really* been posed, i.e., uttered on the basis of the required problematic and in the rigorous concepts required by this problematic. Second – and paradoxically this is the most serious difficulty, because we are literally swamped by the abundance of solutions offered to this as yet not rigorously posed problem, swamped by these solutions and blinded by their '*obviousness*'. These solutions are not, like those we have discussed with respect to Marx, answers to absent questions which can, however, be formulated in order to express the theoretical revolution contained in their answers. On the contrary, they are answers to questions and solutions to problems which have been *formulated perfectly*, since these questions and problems have been hand-picked by these answers and solutions.

I am alluding precisely to what the history of ideological philosophy classifies as the 'problem of knowledge' or 'theory of knowledge'. I say ideological *philosophy* since it is this ideological posing of the 'problem of knowledge' which defines the tradition that coincides with Western idealist philosophy (from Descartes to Husserl, via Kant and Hegel). I say that this posing of the 'problem' of knowledge is *ideological* insofar as this problem has been formulated on the basis of its 'answer', as the exact *reflection* of that answer, i.e., not as a real problem but as the problem that had to be posed if the desired *ideological* solution was to be the solution to this problem. I cannot deal here with this point which defines the essentials of ideology, in its ideological form, and which in principle reduces ideological knowledge (and *par excellence* the knowledge which ideology is discussing when it reflects knowledge in the form of the problem of knowledge or the theory of knowledge) to a phenomenon of *recognition*. In the theoretical mode of production of ideology (which is utterly different from the theoretical mode of production of science in this respect), the formulation of a *problem* is merely the theoretical expression of the conditions which allow a *solution* already produced outside the process of knowledge because imposed by extra-theoretical instances and exigencies (by religious, ethical, political or other 'interests') *to recognize itself* in an artificial problem manufactured to serve it both as a theoretical mirror and as a practical justification. All of modern Western philosophy, dominated by the 'problem of knowledge', is thus in fact dominated by the formulation of a 'problem' posed in terms and on a theoretical basis *produced* (whether consciously, as by some, or unconsciously, as with others, is not important here) in order to make possible the theoretico-practical effects expected of this *mirror recognition*. In other words, the whole history of Western philosophy is dominated not by the 'problem of knowledge', but by the ideological *solution*, i.e., the solution imposed in advance by practical, religious, ethical and political 'interests' foreign to the reality of the knowledge, which this 'problem' *had to* receive. As Marx put it so profoundly in *The German Ideology*, '*Not only in their answers but in their very questions there was a mystification*'.

Here we meet our greatest difficulty. For, practically alone in this undertaking, we have to resist the age-old 'obviousness' which *repetition*, not only the repetition of a false answer, but above all that of a false question, has produced in people's minds. We must leave the ideological space defined by this ideological question, this *necessarily closed* space (since that is one of the essential effects of the *recognition* structure which characterizes the theoretical mode of production of ideology: the inevitably closed circle of what, in another context and with other intentions, Lacan has called the '*dual mirror relation*') in order to open a new space on a different site – the space required for a *correct posing of the problem, one which does not prejudge the solution*. The whole history of the 'theory of knowledge' in Western philosophy from the famous 'Cartesian circle' to the circle of the Hegelian or Husserlian teleology of Reason *shows* us that this 'problem of knowledge' is a closed space, i.e., a vicious circle (the vicious circle of the mirror relation of ideological recognition). Its high point of consciousness and honesty was reached precisely with the philosophy (Husserl) which was prepared to take theoretical responsibility for the necessary existence of this *circle*, i.e., to think it as essential to its ideological undertaking; however, this did not *make it leave the circle*, did not deliver it from its ideological captivity – nor could the philosopher who has tried to think in an 'openness' (which seems to be only the ideological non-closure of the closure) the absolute condition of possibility of this 'closure', i.e., of the closed history of the 'repetition' of this closure in Western metaphysics – Heidegger – leave this circle. It is impossible to leave a closed space simply by taking up a position merely *outside it*, either in its exterior or its profundity: so long as this outside or profundity remain *its* outside or profundity, they still belong to *that* circle, to *that* closed space, as its 'repetition' in *its* other-than-itself. Not the repetition but the non-repetition of this space is the way out of this circle: the sole theoretically sound flight – which is precisely not a *flight*, which is always committed to what it is fleeing from, but the radical foundation of a new space, a new problematic which allows the real *problem* to be posed, the problem misrecognized in the recognition structure in which it is ideologically posed.

16

The following few reflections are devoted to a first attempt at posing this problem, though I do not intend to hide the fact that they are as precarious as they are indispensable.

In the *1857 Introduction*, Marx writes: 'the whole, as it appears (*erscheint*) in the mind as a thought-whole (*Gedankenganze*), is a product of the thinking mind, which appropriates (*aneignet*) the world (*die Welt*) in the only (*einzig*) mode (*Weise*) possible to it, a mode which is different from the artistic (*künstlerisch*), religious or practico-spiritual (*praktisch-geistig*) appropriation of this world' (*Grundrisse*, p. 22). Here the issue is not to penetrate the mystery of the concept of *appropriation* (*Aneignung*) beneath which Marx expresses the essence of a fundamental relation of which knowledge, art, religion and practico-spiritual activity (this last has still to be defined: but it probably means ethico-politico-historical activity) appear as so many distinct and specific modes (*Weise*). The text does indeed lay stress on the specificity of the mode of theoretical appropriation (knowledge) with respect to all the other modes of appropriation which are declared to be distinct from it in principle. But the expression of this distinction reveals precisely the common background of a relation-to-the-*real-world* against which this distinction is made. This clearly indicates that knowledge is concerned with the real world through its specific mode of appropriation of the real world: this poses precisely the problem of the way this function works, and therefore *of the mechanism* that ensures it: this function of the appropriation of the real world by knowledge, i.e., by the process of production of knowledges which, *despite*, or rather *because* of the fact that it takes place *entirely in thought* (in the sense we have defined), nevertheless provides that grasp (of the concept: *Begriff*) on the *real* world called its appropriation (*Aneignung*). This poses on its true terrain the question of a theory of the production of a knowledge which, as the knowledge of its object (an object of knowledge, in the sense we have defined), is the grasp or appropriation of the *real* object, the real world.

Need I comment that this question is quite unlike the ideological question of the 'problem of knowledge'? That it is not a matter of an external reflection on the *a priori* conditions of possibility which *guarantee* the possibility of knowledge? That it is not a matter of staging the characters indispensable to this scenario: a philosophical consciousness (which is very careful not to pose the question of its status, its place and its function, since in its own eyes it is Reason itself, present in its objects since the Origin, and having no dealings except with itself even in its question, i.e., posing the question to which it is itself the obligatory answer), posing scientific consciousness the question of the conditions of possibility of its knowledge relation to its *object*? Need I comment that the theoretical characters cast in this ideological scenario are the philosophical Subject (the philosophizing consciousness), the scientific Subject (the knowing consciousness) and the empirical Subject (the perceiving consciousness) on the one hand; and, on the other, the Object which confronts these three Subjects, the transcendental Object, the pure principles of science and the pure forms of perception; that the three Subjects for their part are subsumed under a single essence (e.g., this identification of the three Objects as it is seen, with significant variation, in Kant as well as Hegel and Husserl, depends on a persistent identification of the object perceived and the object known); that this parallel distribution of attributes disposes Subject and Object face to face; that this conjures away the difference in status between the object of knowledge and the real object on the Object side, and the difference in status between the philosophizing Subject and the knowing subject, on the one hand, and between the knowing subject and the empirical subject on the other, on the Subject side? That thereby the only relation which is thought is a relation of interiority and contemporaneity between a mythical Subject and Object, required to *take in charge*, if need be by falsifying them, the real conditions, i.e., the real mechanism of the history of the production of knowledges, in order to subject them to religious, ethical and political ends (the preservation of the 'faith', of 'morality' or of 'freedom', i.e., social values)?

I am not posing the question I have posed in order to produce an answer fixed in advance by instances other than knowledge itself: it is not a question closed in advance by its answer. It is not a question of *guarantees*. On the contrary, it is an open question (it is the very field that it opens), and one which if it is to be so, if it is to escape the pre-established closure of the ideological circle, must reject the services of those theoretical characters whose sole function was to ensure this ideological closure: the characters of the different Subjects and Objects, and the duties it was their mission to respect in order to play their parts, in the complicity of the ideological pact signed by the supreme instances of the Subject and the Object, with the blessing of the Western 'Freedom of Man'. It is a question which is posed and demonstrated as *open* in principle, i.e., as homogeneous in its *structure of openness* to all the actual questions posed by knowledge in its scientific existence: a question which has to express in its form this structure of openness and which must therefore be posed in the field and in the terms of the theoretical problematic which demands this structure of openness. In other words, the question of the *mode* of appropriation of the *real, specific* object of knowledge has to be posed:

(1) in terms which exclude any recourse to the ideological solution contained in the ideological characters Subject and Object, or to the mutual mirror-recognition structure, in the closed circle of which they move;

(2) in terms which form the concept of the knowledge structure, an open specific structure, and which, at the same time, are the concept of the *question* knowledge poses itself – which implies that the place and function of this question be thought even in posing the question.

This last demand is indispensable in order to establish the distinction between the theory of the history of the production of knowledge (or philosophy) and the existing content of knowledge (the sciences), without thereby making philosophy that legal instance which, in 'theories of knowledge' makes laws for the science in the name of a right it arrogates to itself. This right is no more than the *fait accompli* of mirror recognition's stage direction, which ensures philosophical ideology the *legal recognition* of the *fait accompli* of the 'higher' instances it serves.

Posed *in* these strict conditions, the problem we are concerned with can be expressed in the following form: *by what mechanism does the process of knowledge, which takes place entirely in thought, produce the cognitive appropriation of its real object, which exists outside thought in the real world?* Or again, *by what mechanism does the production of the object of knowledge produce the cognitive appropriation of the real object,* which exists outside thought in the *real world?* The mere substitution of the question of the *mechanism* of the cognitive appropriation of the real object by means of the object of knowledge, for the ideological question of *guarantees* of the possibility of knowledge, contains in it that mutation of the problematic which rescues us from the closed space of ideology and opens to us the open space of the philosophical theory we are seeking.

17

Before I go on to our question, let me run through the classic misunderstandings which lead us precisely back into the vicious circle of ideology.

Our question is often given a straight answer simply by saying, in the plain language of the pragmatism of 'obviousness': the mechanism with which the production of the object of knowledge produces the cognitive appropriation of the real object? . . . Why, it is practice! It is the role of the criterion of practice! And if this dish does not fill us, they are pleased to vary the menu or provide as many accessories as are required to satisfy us. We are told: practice is the touch-stone, the practice of scientific experiment! Economic, political, technical practice, concrete practice! Or else, to convince us of the 'Marxist' character of the answer: *social* practice! Or as a 'make-weight', the social practice of humanity repeated billions and billions of times for millenia! Or else we are served Engels's unfortunate pudding (Manchester provided him with this alimentary argument): *'the proof of the pudding is in the eating'!*

First of all, I would point out that this kind of answer does have some effectivity, and that it should therefore be used when the aim is to defeat ideology on the terrain of ideology, i.e., when the aim is ideological struggle strictly speaking: for it is an *ideological* answer, one which is situated precisely on the opponent's ideological terrain. In major historical situations it has happened and may happen again that one is obliged or forced to fight on the terrain of the ideological opponent, when it has proved impossible to draw him onto one's own terrain, if he is not ready to pitch his tents there, or if it is necessary to descend onto his terrain. But this practice, and the mode of employment of ideological arguments adapted to this struggle, must be the object of a *theory* so that ideological struggle in the domain of ideology does not become a struggle governed by the laws and wishes of the opponent, so that it does not transform us purely into subjects of the ideology it is our aim to combat. But I would add at the same time that it is not surprising that this kind of *pragmatist* answer leaves us hungry as far as our theoretical question is concerned. We can show this for one general reason and a number of special reasons, all of which depend on the same principle.

In fact, pragmatism, in its essence, drags our question into ideology, by giving it an ideological answer. Pragmatism does nothing but set out, like the ideology of the idealist 'theory of knowledge', on a hunt for *guarantees*. The only difference is that classical idealism is not content with a *de facto* guarantee but wants a *de jure* guarantee (though, as we know, this is merely the legal disguise for a *de facto* situation); that is its business – whereas pragmatism sets out in search of a *de facto* guarantee: *success* in practice, which often constitutes the sole content assignable to what is called the 'practice criterion'. At any rate, we are served with a *guarantee* which is the irrefutable index of an *ideological* question and answer, whereas we are in search of a *mechanism*! The proof of the pudding is in the eating! So what! We are interested in the *mechanism* that ensures that it really is a pudding we are eating and not a poached baby elephant, though we *think* we are eating our daily pudding! Proof by repetition for hundreds or thousands of years of the social practice of humanity (that night in which all the practices are grey)! So what! For hundreds and thousands of years this 'repetition' has produced, for example, 'truths' such as the resurrection of Christ, the Virginity of Mary, all the 'truths' of religion, all the prejudices of human 'spontaneity', i.e., all the *established* 'obviousnesses' of ideology, from the most to the least respectable! Not to speak of the trap laid jointly by idealism and pragmatism in the complicity of their action (which obeys *the same rules*). By what *right* do you tell us that practice is right? says idealism to pragmatism. Your right is no more than a disguised fact, answers pragmatism. And we are back on the wheel, the closed circle of the ideological question. In all these cases, the common rule which permits this action is in fact the question of the *guarantees* of the harmony between knowledge (or Subject) and its real object (or Object), i.e., the ideological question as such.

But let us leave this general argument for the special arguments, for they will bring us face to face with *our object*. It is enough to pronounce the word *practice*, which, understood in an ideological (empiricist or idealist) way is only the mirror image, the counter-connotation of *theory* (the pair of 'contraries' practice and theory constituting the two terms of a mirror field), to reveal the play on words that is its seat. We must recognize that there is no practice in general, but only *distinct practices* which are not related in any Manichaean way with a theory which is opposed to them in every respect. For there is not one side of theory, a pure intellectual vision without body or materiality – and another of completely material practice which 'gets its hands dirty'. This dichotomy is merely an ideological myth in which a 'theory of knowledge' reflects many 'interests' other than those of reason: those of the social division of labour, which is precisely a division between power (political, religious or ideological) and oppression (the executors who are also the executed). Even when this dichotomy is the servant of a revolutionary vision which exalts the workers' cause, their labour, their sufferings, their struggles and their experience in the undifferentiated proclamation of the primacy of practice, it still remains ideological: just as *egalitarian* communism is still an ideological conception of the aim of the workers' movement. In the strict sense, an *egalitarian conception of practice* – and I say this with the deep respect every Marxist owes to the experience and sacrifices of the men whose labour, sufferings and struggles still nourish and sustain our whole present and future, all our arguments for life and hope – *an egalitarian conception of practice* is to dialectical materialism what egalitarian communism is to scientific communism: a conception to be criticized and superseded in order to establish a scientific conception of practice exactly in its place.

But there can be no scientific conception of practice without a precise distinction between the distinct practices and a new conception of the relations between theory and practice. We can assert the *primacy of practice* theoretically by showing that all the levels of social existence are the sites of distinct practices: economic practice, political practice, ideological practice, technical practice and scientific (or theoretical) practice. We think the content of these different practices by thinking their peculiar structure, which, in all these cases, is the structure of a production; by thinking what distinguishes between these different structures, i.e., the different natures of the objects to which they apply, of their means of production and of the relations within which they produce (these different elements and their combination – *Verbindung* – obviously vary as we pass from economic practice to political practice, then to scientific practice and theoretico-philosophical practice). We think the relations establishing and articulating these different practices one with another by thinking their *degree of independence* and their type of 'relative' *autonomy*, which are themselves fixed by their *type of dependence* with respect to the practice which is 'determinant in the last instance': economic practice. But we shall go further. We are not content to suppress the egalitarian myth of practice, we acquire a completely new basis for our conception of the relation between theory and practice, which is mystified in any idealist or empiricist conception. We regard an element of 'knowledge', even in its most rudimentary forms and even though it is profoundly steeped in ideology, as always already present in the earliest stages of practice, those that can be observed even in the subsistence practices of the most 'primitive' societies. At the other extreme in the history of practices, we regard what is commonly called *theory*, in its 'purest' forms, those that seem to bring into play the powers of thought alone (e.g., mathematics of philosophy), leaving aside any direct relation to 'concrete practice', as a *practice* in the strict sense, as scientific or theoretical practice, itself divisible into several branches (the different sciences, mathematics, philosophy). This practice is *theoretical*; it is distinguished from the other, non-theoretical practices, by the *type* of object (raw material) which it transforms; by the type of means of production it sets to work, by the type of object it produces (knowledges).

To speak of the criterion of practice where theory is concerned, and every other practice as well, then receives its full sense: for *theoretical practice* is indeed its own criterion, and contains in itself definite protocols with which to *validate* the quality of its product, i.e., the criteria of the scientificity of the products of scientific practice. This is exactly what happens in the real practice of the sciences: once they are truly constituted and developed they have no need for verification from *external* practices to declare the knowledges they produce to be 'true', i.e., to be *knowledges*. No mathematician in the world waits until physics has *verified* a theorem to declare it proved, although whole areas of mathematics are applied in physics: the truth of his theorem is a hundred per cent provided by criteria purely *internal* to the practice of mathematical proof, hence by the *criterion of mathematical practice*, i.e., by the forms required by existing mathematical scientificity. We can say the same for the results of every science: at least for the most developed of them, and in the areas of knowledge which they have sufficiently mastered, they themselves provide the criterion of validity of their knowledges – this criterion coinciding perfectly with the strict forms of the exercise of the scientific practice considered. We can say this of the 'experimental' sciences: the criterion of their theory is their *experiments*, which constitute the form of their theoretical practice. We should say the same of the science which concerns us most particularly: historical materialism. It has been possible to apply Marx's theory with success because it is 'true'; it is not true because it has been applied with success. The pragmatist criterion may suit a technique which has no other horizon than the field in which it is applied – but it does not suit scientific knowledges. To be consistent we must go further and reject the more or less indirect assimilation of the Marxist theory of history to the empiricist model of a chance 'hypothesis' whose *verification* must be provided by the political practice of history *before* we can affirm its 'truth'. Later historical practice cannot give the *knowledge* that Marx produced its status as knowledge: the criterion of the 'truth' of the knowledges produced by Marx's theoretical practice is provided by his theoretical practice itself, i.e., by the proof-value, by the scientific status of the *forms* which ensured the production of those knowledges. Marx's theoretical practice is the criterion of the 'truth' of the knowledges that Marx produced: and only because it was really a matter of knowledge, and not of chance hypotheses, have these knowledges given the famous results, of which the failures as well as the successes constitute pertinent 'experiments' for the theory's reflection on itself and its internal development.

In those sciences in which it is unrestrictedly valid, this radical inwardness of the criterion of practice for scientific practice is not at all exclusive of organic relations with other practices which provide these sciences with a large proportion of their raw material, and occasionally go so far as to induce more or less profound re-organizations in their theoretical structure. I have demonstrated this sufficiently elsewhere to prevent any misunderstanding of the meaning of what has just been said. In gestatory sciences, and *a fortiori* in regions still dominated by an ideological 'knowledge', the intervention of other practices often plays a determinant critical role which may even be revolutionary. I have suggested this in unambiguous terms. But here, too, there can be no question of drowning in an egalitarian conception of practice either the specific mode of intervention of a determinate practice in the field of a theoretical practice which is still ideological or only just becoming scientific – or of drawing the precise function of this intervention, nor above all the (theoretical) *form* in which this intervention is effected. Taking Marx as an example, we know that his most personally significant practical experiences (his experience as a polemicist of 'the embarrassment of having to take part in discussions on so-called material interests' in the *Rheinische Zeitung*; his direct experience of the earliest struggle organizations of the Paris proletariat; his revolutionary experience in the 1848 period) *intervened* in his theoretical practice, and in the upheaval which led him from ideological theoretical practice to scientific theoretical practice: but they intervened in his theoretical practice *in the form of objects of experience, or even experiment*, i.e., in the form of new thought objects, 'ideas' and the concepts, whose emergence contributed, in their combination (*Verbindung*) with other conceptual results (originating in German philosophy and English political economy), to the overthrow of the still ideological theoretical base on which he had lived (i.e., thought) until then.

18

I make no apology for this long detour: it was not a detour. It was essential to clear from our way the ideological answers to our question: and to this end it was essential to reckon with an ideological conception of practice which even Marxism itself has not always avoided, and which everyone will admit reigns supreme today and surely for a long time to come, over contemporary philosophy, even over its most honest and generous representatives such as Sartre. By avoiding this market-place of egalitarian practice, or, as it has to be called in philosophy, of 'praxis', we have won through to a recognition of the fact that there is only one path before us, a narrow path certainly, but an open, or at least openable one. Let us therefore return to our question: by what *mechanism* does the production of the *object of know-ledge* produce the cognitive appropriation of the *real object* which exists outside thought in the real world? I say a mechanism, and a mechanism which must explain a specific fact: the mode of appropriation of the world by the specific practice of knowledge, whose entire space is its *object* (the object of knowledge), as distinct from the *real object* of which it is the knowledge. Here we run the greatest risks. The reader will understand that I can only claim, with the most explicit reservations, to give the first argu-ments towards a sharpening of the question we have posed, and not an answer to it.

The first step in our formulation of this sharpening must be a very im-portant distinction. When we pose the question of the *mechanism* by which the *object* of knowledge produces the cognitive appropriation of the *real object*, we are posing a quite different question from that of the conditions of the *production* of knowledge. This latter question is derived from a theory of the history of theoretical practice, which, as we have seen, is only possible given the application of the concepts which enable us to think the structure of that practice and the history of its transformations. The question we are posing is a new one, one which is precisely passed over in silence in the other. The theory of the history of knowledge or theory of the history of theoretical practice enables us to understand *how* human knowledges are produced in the history of the succession of different modes of production, first in the form of ideology, then in the form of science. It makes us spec-tators of the emergence of knowledges, their development, their diversi-fication, the theoretical ruptures and upheavals within the problematic that governs their production, and of the progressive erection, in their domain, of a division between ideological knowledges and scientific knowledges, etc. At each moment of the history of knowledges this history takes knowledges for *what they are*, whether they declare themselves knowledges or not, whether they are ideological or scientific, etc.: for *knowledges*. It considers them solely as *products*, as results. This history really does enable us to understand the mechanism of the production of knowledges, but, given a knowledge existing at a given moment in the process of the history of its production, it does not enable us to understand the *mechanism* by which the knowledge considered fulfils its function as a cognitive appropriation of the real object by means of its thought object for whoever is handling it as knowledge. But it is precisely this *mechanism* which interests us.

Need we sharpen our question even further? A theory of the history of the production of knowledges can only ever give us an observation: here is the mechanism by which these knowledges have been produced. But this observation treats the knowledge *as a fact*, whose transformations and variations it studies as so many effects of the structure of the theoretical practice which produces them, as so many products which happen to be knowledges – without ever reflecting *the fact that these products are not just any products, but precisely knowledges.* A theory of the history of the production of knowledges therefore does not account for what I propose to call the *'knowledge effect'*, which is the peculiarity of those special products which are knowledges. Our new question deals precisely with this *knowledge effect* (what Marx called the *'mode* of appropriation of the world peculiar to knowledge'). The *mechanism* I propose to elucidate is the mechanism which produces this *knowledge effect* in those very special products we call *knowledges.*

Here too (we shall never escape the destiny of having constantly to avoid false representations in order to clear the path that opens up the space of our investigation) we are confronted by illusions to be revoked and destroyed. We might indeed be tempted to refer the mechanism we are trying to discover to its origins: to say that this knowledge effect, which, as far as we are concerned, is exercised in the pure forms of some strict science, comes to us, via an infinite series of *mediations,* from reality itself. Thus, in mathematics it is tempting to think the knowledge effect of such and such an especially abstract formula as the extremely purified and formalized echo of such and such a *reality*, whether it is concrete space or the first concrete manipulations and operations of human practice. We can readily admit that at a certain moment a 'dislocation' (*décalage*) intervenes between the concrete practice of the land-surveyor and Pythagorean and Euclidean abstraction, but we can think this dislocation as a transfer (*décollage*), a retracing (*décalque*) of the concrete forms and gestures of an earlier practice in the element of 'ideality'. But all the concepts we bring into play to account for the immense space which separates the Chaldean accountant or Egyptian land-surveyor from Bourbaki will never be anything more than concepts which attempt to install, beneath the incontestable differences that have to be thought, a continuity of meaning which links in principle the *knowledge effect* of modern mathematical objects to an original meaning effect which is an integral part of an original real object, a concrete practice, original concrete gestures. Thus there would be a 'native land', an 'original ground' of the knowledge effect: either the real object itself, from which, according to empiricism, knowledge only ever extracts one part, the essence; or the Husserlian 'pre-reflexive' world of 'life', the passive ante-predicative synthesis; or, finally, the concrete of elementary behaviour and gestures, where all child psychologies, genetic or otherwise, obtain the cheap luxury of founding their own 'theories of knowledge'. In all these cases, a real, concrete, living original is made eternally and integrally responsible for the knowledge effect; the sciences throughout their history and even today are merely commenting on this heritage, i.e., subject to this heredity. Just as in good Christian theology, humanity lives only in original sin, there would be *an original knowledge effect*, emerging from the more concrete forms of the real, from life, from practice, i.e., losing itself in them, identical with them – an original knowledge effect whose indelible mark would still be borne today by the most 'abstract' scientific objects, destined as they are to its fate, condemned to knowledge. Need I set out the problematic presupposed by this 'model'? The reader will have guessed that its consistency requires support from the myth of the *origin*; from an original unity undivided between *subject* and *object*, between the real and its knowledge (that they have the same birth, that, as someone well versed in theatrical effects re-marked, knowledge is co-birth – *la connaissance soit co-naissance*); from a good *genesis*, from all the indispensable *abstractions* and, above all, *mediations*. The reader will have recognized in this passage a set of typical concepts which eighteenth-century philosophy scattered over the world and which have flourished nearly everywhere, even in the works of Marxist specialists – but concepts which we can be absolutely sure, tailor-made as they are for the ideological functions expected of them, have nothing to do with Marx.

And while we are here, let us be clear: Marxism cannot for one moment discover or rediscover itself along the path of this empiricism, whether it claims to be materialist or sublimates itself in an idealism of the ante-predica-tive, of the 'original ground' or of 'praxis' – in this idealism and in the concepts it has manufactured to play the star roles in its theatre. The concepts of origin, 'original ground', genesis and mediation should be regarded as suspect *a priori*: not only because they always more or less induce the ideology which has produced them, but because, produced solely for the use of this ideology, they are its nomads, always more or less carrying it with them. It is no accident that Sartre, and all those with none of his ability who feel a need to fill in the emptiness between '*abstract*' categories and the '*concrete*', abuse the terms *origin, genesis* and *mediations* so much. The function of the concept of origin, as in original sin, is to summarize in one word what has not to be thought in order to be able to think what one wants to think. The concept of genesis is charged with taking charge of, and masking, a production or mutation whose recognition would threaten the vital continuity of the empiricist schema of history. The concept of mediation is invested with one last role: the magical provision of post-stations in the empty space between theoretical principles and the 'concrete', as bricklayers make a chain to pass bricks. In every case, the functions are those of masks and theoretical impostures – functions which may witness both to a real embarrassment and a real good will, and to the desire not to lose theoretical control over events, but even in the best of cases, these functions are more or less dangerous theoretical fictions. Applied to our question, these concepts ensure us a cheap solution on every occasion: they make a chain between an original knowledge effect and current knowledge effects – giving us the mere posing, or rather non-posing of the problem as its solution.

19

Let us therefore try taking a few steps forward into the space we have just disengaged.

Just as we saw that recourse to a primitive real object could not save us from our responsibility to think the difference between the object of knowledge and the real object of which the first object gives us the knowledge, we have just seen that we cannot shift to an original 'knowledge effect' the responsibility for thinking for us the mechanism of this contemporary knowledge effect. And, to tell the truth, we know that these two problems are really one and the same, since only the reality of the contemporary knowledge effect, not the myth of an original effect, can give us the answer we are looking for. In this respect, we are in the same situation as Marx, who says in so many words that we must elucidate the knowledge of the '*Gliederung*' (the articulated, hierarchized, systematic combination) of *contemporary* society if we are to reach an understanding of earlier forms, and therefore of the most primitive forms. His famous remark that 'the anatomy of man is the key to the anatomy of the ape', of course, means nothing else; of course, it coincides with that other remark in the *Introduction* that it is not the historical genesis of categories nor their combination in earlier forms that enables us to understand them, but the system of their combination in contemporary society, which also opens the way to an understanding of past formations, by giving us the concept of the *variation* of this combination. Similarly, only the elucidation of the mechanism of the contemporary knowledge effect can cast light onto earlier effects. The rejection of any recourse to origins is therefore correlated with a very basic theoretical exigency which insists on the dependence of the explanation of more primitive forms on the contemporary mode of systematic combination of categories which are also found in part in earlier forms.

We must regard this exigency as constitutive of Marx's theory, *precisely in the domain of the theory of history*. Let me explain. When Marx studied modern bourgeois society, he adopted a paradoxical attitude. He first conceived that existing society as a historical *result*, i.e., as a result produced by a history. Naturally, this seems to commit us to a Hegelian conception in which the result is conceived as a result inseparable from its genesis, to the point where it is necessary to conceive it as 'the result of its becoming'. In fact, at the same time Marx takes a quite different direction! '*It is not a matter of the connexion established historically between the economic relations in the succession of different forms of society. Still less of their order of succession "in the Idea" (Proudhon) (a nebulous conception of historical movement). But of their articulated combination* (Gliederung) *within modern bourgeois society*' (*Grundrisse*, p. 28). The same idea was already rigorously expressed in *The Poverty of Philosophy*: '*How indeed, could the single logical formula of movement, of sequence, of time, explain the body of society, in which all relations coexist simultaneously* (gleichzeitig) *and support one another'* (*The Poverty of Philosophy*, New York, 1963, pp. 110–11). The object of Marx's study is therefore contemporary bourgeois society, which is thought as a historical *result*: but the understanding of this society, far from being obtained from the theory of the genesis of this result, is, on the contrary, obtained exclusively from the theory of the *'body'*, i.e., of the *contemporary structure of society*, without its genesis intervening in any way whatsoever. This attitude may be paradoxical, but Marx insists on it in categorical terms as the absolute condition of possibility of his theory of history; it reveals the existence of *two problems*, distinct in their disjoint unity. There is a theoretical problem which must be posed and resolved in order to explain the mechanism by which history has produced as its result the contemporary capitalist mode of production. But at the same time there is another absolutely distinct problem which must be posed and resolved, in order to understand that this result is indeed a *social* mode of production, that this result is precisely a form of *social* existence and not just any form of existence: this second problem is the object of the theory in *Capital* – and not for one moment is it ever confused with the first problem.

We can express this distinction, which is absolutely fundamental for an understanding of Marx, by saying that Marx regards contemporary society (and every other past form of society) both as a *result* and as a *society*. The theory of the mechanism of transformation of one mode of production into another, i.e., the theory of the forms of transition from one mode of production to the succeeding one, has to pose and solve the problem of the *result*, i.e., of the historical production of a given mode of production, of a given social formation. But contemporary society is not only a result, a product: it is *this* particular result, *this* particular *product*, which functions as a *society*, unlike other results and other products which function quite differently. This second problem is answered by the theory of the structure of a mode of production, the theory of *Capital*. In *Capital*, society is taken as a 'body', and not just as any body, but as *that body which functions as a society*. This theory completely abstracts from *society-as-a-result* – that is Marx claims that every explanation by movement, sequence, time and genesis cannot apply to this problem in principle, for it is a quite different problem. To say the same thing in more pertinent terms, I suggest the following terminology: what Marx studies in *Capital* is the mechanism which makes the result of a history's production exist *as a society*; it is therefore the mechanism which gives this product of history, that is precisely the society-product he is studying, the property of producing the *'society effect'* which makes this result exist *as a society*, and not as a heap of sand, an ant-hill, a workshop or a mere collection of men. When Marx tells us therefore that in explaining a society by its genesis we miss its *'body'*, precisely what had to be explained, he is focusing his theoretical attention on the task of explaining the mechanism by which some particular result functions precisely *as a society*, and therefore the mechanism producing the '*society effect*' peculiar to the capitalist mode of production. The mechanism of the production of this 'society effect' is only complete when all the effects of the mechanism have been expounded, down to the point where they are produced in the form of the very effects that constitute the concrete, conscious or unconscious relation of the individuals to the society as a society, i.e., down to the effects of the fetishism of ideology (or 'forms of *social* consciousness' – *Preface* to *A Contribution* . . .), in which men consciously or unconsciously live their lives, their projects, their actions, their attitudes and their functions, as *social*. In this perspective, *Capital* must be regarded as the theory of the mechanism of production of the *society effect* in the capitalist mode of production. We are beginning to suspect, even if it is only because of the works of contemporary ethnology and history, that this *society effect* differs with different modes of production. Theoretically speaking, we have every reason to believe that the *mechanism* of the production of these different society effects differs with the various modes of production. We are beginning to see that an exact consciousness of the precise problem implied by the theory in *Capital* opens new horizons in front of us by posing us new problems. But at the same time, we understand the absolutely decisive scope of those few lucid sentences from the *Poverty of Philosophy* and the *1857 Introduction*, in which Marx warns us that he is looking not for an understanding of the mechanism of the production of society as a *result* of history, but for an understanding of the mechanism of the production of the *society effect* by this result, which is effectively a real existing *society*.

By thus defining his object with this merciless distinction, Marx provides us with the wherewithal to *pose* the problem we are concerned with : the problem of the cognitive appropriation of the real object by the object of knowledge, which is a special case of the appropriation of the real world by different practices, theoretical, aesthetic, religious, ethical, technical, etc. Each of these modes of appropriation poses the problem of the mechanism of production of *its specific 'effect'*, the knowledge effect for theoretical practice, the aesthetic effect for aesthetic practice, the ethical effect for ethical practice, etc. In each of these cases we cannot merely substitute one word for another, as 'dormitive virtue' was substituted for opium. The search for each of these specific 'effects' demands the elucidation of the *mechanism* that produces it, not the reduplication of one word by the magic of another. If we want to avoid pre-judging the conclusion to which the study of these different effects may lead us, we must be content with a few indications as to the effect that concerns us here, the *knowledge effect*, produced by the existence of the theoretical object which is a knowledge. This expression *knowledge effect* constitutes a generic object which includes at least two sub-objects: the *ideological* knowledge effect and the *scientific* knowledge effect.

The ideological knowledge effect is distinguished by its properties (it is an effect of recognition-misrecognition in a mirror connexion) from the scientific knowledge effect: but insofar as the ideological effect, although it depends on other social functions which are dominant in it, really possesses its own knowledge effect, it falls in this respect within the general category with which we are concerned. I owe the reader this warning, in order to prevent any misunderstanding as to the beginnings of an analysis that follows for it is centred solely on the knowledge effect of scientific knowledge.

How can we explain the mechanism of this knowledge effect? We can now return to something we have just established: the inwardness of the 'criterion of practice' to the scientific practice under consideration – and suggest that our present question is related to this inwardness. We showed that the validity of a scientific proposition as a knowledge was ensured in a determinate scientific practice by the action of particular *forms* which ensure the *presence* of scientificity in the production of knowledge, in other words, by specific forms that confer on a knowledge its character as a ('true') knowledge. Here I am speaking of forms of scientificity – but I am also echoing this by thinking of the forms that play the same part (ensuring a different but corresponding effect) in ideological 'knowledge', and indeed in all forms of *knowing*. These *forms* are distinct from the forms in which the knowledge was produced, as a result, by the process of the history of knowledge: they deal, it will be remembered, with a knowledge already produced as a knowledge by that history. In other words, we consider the result *without its becoming*, ignoring any accusations of lese-Hegelianism or lese-geneticism, for this double crime is merely a single good deed: a liberation from the empiricist ideology of history. It is to this result that we put the question of the mechanism of production of the knowledge effect – exactly in the way Marx interrogated a given society, as a *result*, in order to pose it the question of its 'society effect', or the question of the *mechanism* which produces its existence *as a society*.

We see these specific forms in action in the discourse of scientific proof, i.e., in the phenomenon which imposes on thought categories (or concepts) *a regular order of appearance and disappearance*. We can say, then, that the mechanism of production of the knowledge effect lies in the mechanism which underlies the action of the forms of order in the scientific discourse of the proof. I say the mechanism which *underlies* and does not just *govern* the action of these forms, for the following reason: in fact these forms of order only show themselves as forms of the order of appearance of concepts in scientific discourse as a function of other forms which, without themselves being forms of order, are nevertheless the absent principle of the latter. To speak in a language which has already caught on, the forms of order (forms of proof in scientific discourse) are the *'diachrony'* of a basic *'synchrony'*. I am using these terms in a way which will be defined precisely later (Part Two), as the concepts of the two forms of existence of the object of knowledge, and hence as two forms existing purely inside knowledge. Synchrony represents the organizational structure of the concepts in the thought-totality or *system* (or, as Marx puts it, 'synthesis'), diachrony the movement of succession of the concepts in the ordered discourse of the proof. The forms of order of the discourse of the proof are simply the development of the '*Gliederung*', of the hierarchized combination of the concepts in the *system* itself. When I say that 'synchrony' thus understood is primary and governs everything, I mean two things:

(1) that the system of the hierarchy of concepts in their combination determines the definition of each concept, as a function of its place and function in the system. It is this definition of the place and function of the concept in the totality of the system which is reflected in the immanent *meaning* of this concept, when we put it in one-to-one correspondence with its real category.

(2) that the system of the hierarchy of concepts determines the 'diachronic' order of their appearance in the discourse of the proof. It is in this sense that Marx speaks of the '*development of the forms*' (of the concept) of value, surplus value, etc.: this 'development of the forms' is the manifestation, in the discourse of the scientific proof, of the systematic *dependence* which links the concepts together in the system of the thought-totality.

The knowledge effect, produced at the level of the forms of order of the discourse of the proof, and then at the level of some isolated concept, is therefore possible given the *systematicity of the system* which is the foundation of the concepts and their order of appearance in scientific discourse. The knowledge effect acts, then, in the duality or duplicity of the *existence of the system*, which is said to 'develop' in the scientific discourse, on the one hand, and on the other of the *existence of the forms of order* of the discourse, precisely in the 'play' (in the mechanical sense of the term) which constitutes the *unity of dislocation* of the system and of the discourse. The knowledge effect is produced as an effect of the scientific discourse, which exists only as a discourse *of the* system, i.e., of the object grasped in the structure of its complex constitution. If this analysis leads anywhere, it leads us to the threshold of the following new question: what is the specific difference of scientific *discourse* as a discourse? What distinguishes scientific discourse from other forms of discourse? How do other discourses produce different effects (aesthetic effect, ideological effect, unconscious effect) from the knowledge effect which is produced by scientific discourse?

20

I shall leave the question in this last form, and merely recall its terms. Unlike the 'theory of knowledge' of ideological philosophy, I am not trying to pronounce some *de jure* (or *de facto*) *guarantee* which will assure us that we really do know what we know, and that we can relate this harmony to a certain connexion between Subject and Object, Consciousness and the World. I am trying to elucidate the *mechanism* which explains to us how a *de facto* result, produced by the history of knowledge, i.e., a given determinate knowledge, functions *as a knowledge*, and not as some other result (a hammer, a symphony, a sermon, a political slogan, etc.). I am therefore trying to define its specific effect: the knowledge effect, by an understanding of its *mechanism*. If this question has been properly put, protected from all the ideologies that still weigh us down, i.e., outside the field of the ideological concepts by which the 'problem of knowledge' is usually posed, it will lead us to the question of the mechanism by which forms of order determined by the system of the existing object of knowledge, produce, by the action of their relation to that system, the knowledge effect considered. This last question confronts us definitively with the *differential* nature of *scientific discourse*, i.e., with the specific nature of a discourse which cannot be maintained as a discourse except by reference to what is present as absence in each moment of its order: the constitutive system of its object, which, in order to exist as a system, requires the absent presence of the scientific discourse that 'develops' it.

If I stop here, before a threshold we shall still have to cross, allow me to recall that it is the peculiarity of scientific discourse to be *written*; and that it therefore poses us the question of the form of its *writing*. The reader will probably remember that we began with its *reading*.

We have therefore not left the circle of one and the same question: if, without leaving it, we have avoided turning round in this circle, it is because this circle is not the closed circle of ideology, but the circle perpetually opened by its closures themselves, the circle of a well-founded knowledge.

June 1965

Part II
The Object of *Capital*
Louis Althusser

Chapter 1
Introduction

In the half-arranged, half-spontaneous division of labour which presided over the organization of this collective study of *Capital*, it fell to me to discuss *Marx's relation to his work*. Under this title, I intended to deal with the following question: what image did Marx have and give of the nature of his undertaking? With what concepts did he think his innovations, and hence the distinctions between himself and the Classical Economists? In what system of concepts did he account for the conditions which gave rise to the discoveries of Classical Economics on the one hand, and his own discoveries on the other? With these questions, I intended to interrogate Marx himself, to see where and how he had theoretically reflected the relationship between his work and the theoretico-historical conditions of its production. In this way, I meant to pose him directly the fundamental epistemological question which constitutes the object of Marxist philosophy itself – and to assess as accurately as possible the degree of explicit philosophical consciousness Marx had acquired during the elaboration of *Capital*. To make this assessment meant to compare the part Marx had illuminated in the new philosophical field that he had opened in the act of foundation of his science with the part that had remained in the shade. By assessing what Marx had done, I wanted to represent as far as possible what he himself called on us to do in order to situate this field, to estimate its extent, and to make it accessible to philosophical discovery – in short, to define as accurately as possible the theoretical space open before Marxist philosophical investigation.

Such was my project: at first sight, it might seem simple, and require only to be carried out. Indeed, Marx left us in passing in the text and notes of *Capital* a whole series of judgements of his own work, critical comparisons with his predecessors (the Physiocrats, Smith, Ricardo, etc.) and lastly very precise methodological comments comparing his *analytical* procedures with the methods of e.g., the mathematical, physical and biological sciences, and with the dialectical method defined by Hegel. Since on the other hand we possess the *1857 Introduction* to *A Contribution to the Critique of Political Economy* – an extremely profound development of the earlier theoretical and methodological comments in Chapter Two of *The Poverty of Philosophy* (1847) – it seems legitimate to believe that this set of texts really embraced the object of my reflection, and that a systematic arrangement of this already worked-out material was all that was required for the epistemological project I have mentioned to take on body and reality. Indeed, it seemed natural to think that when he spoke of his work and his discoveries, Marx was reflecting on the innovatory character, and therefore on the specific distinction of his object, in philosophically adequate terms – and that this adequate philosophical reflection was itself devoted to a definition of the *scientific object* of *Capital*, defining its specific distinction in explicit terms.

But the protocols for a reading of *Capital* which we have inherited from the history of the interpretation of Marxism, as well as the experiments in reading *Capital* we can make ourselves, confront us with real difficulties inherent in Marx's text itself. I shall assemble them under two headings, and these two headings will constitute the object of my study.

(1) Contrary to certain appearances, or at any rate, to my expectations, Marx's methodological reflections in *Capital* do not give us a developed concept, nor even an *explicit* concept of the *object of Marxist philosophy*. They always provide the means with which to recognize, identify and focus on it, and finally to think it, but often at the end of a long investigation, and only after piercing the enigma contained in certain expressions. Our question therefore demands more than a mere literal reading, even an attentive one: it demands a truly *critical* reading, one which applies to Marx's text precisely the principles of the Marxist philosophy which is, however, what we are looking for in *Capital*. This critical reading seems to constitute a circle, since we appear to be expecting to obtain Marxist philosophy from its own application. We should therefore clarify: we expect from the *theoretical work* of the philosophical principles Marx has explicitly given us or which can be disengaged from his Works of the Break, and Transitional Works – we expect from the *theoretical work* of these principles applied to *Capital* their development and enrichment as well as refinements in their rigour. This apparent circle should not surprise us: all 'production' of knowledge implies it in its process.

(2) But this philosophical investigation runs into another real difficulty, one which no longer involves the presence and distinction of the object of Marxist *philosophy* in *Capital*, but the presence and distinction of the *scientific* object of *Capital* itself. Restricting myself to a single, simple symptomatic question around which turn most of the interpretations and criticism of *Capital*, what, strictly speaking, is the *nature* of the object whose theory we get from *Capital*? Is it Economics or History? And specifying this question, if the object of *Capital* is Economics, precisely what distinguishes this object in its concept from the object of Classical Economics? If the object of *Capital* is History, what is this History, what place does Economics have in History, etc.? Here again, a merely literal reading of Marx's text, even an attentive one, will leave us unsatisfied or even make us *miss the question altogether*, dispensing us from the task of posing this question, even though it is essential to an understanding of Marx – and depriving us

of an exact consciousness of the theoretical revolution induced by Marx's discovery and of the scope of its consequences. Without doubt, in *Capital* Marx does give us, in an extremely explicit form, the means with which to identify and announce the concept of his object – what am I saying? – he announces it himself in perfectly clear terms. But if he did formulate the concept of his object without ambiguity, Marx did not always define with the same precision the concept of its *distinction*, i.e., the concept of the *specific difference* between it and the object of Classical Economics. There can be no doubt that Marx was acutely conscious of the *existence* of this distinction: his whole critique of Classical Economics proves it. But the formulae in which he gives us this distinction, this specific difference, are sometimes disconcerting, as we shall see. They do guide us onto the road to the concept of this distinction, but often only at the end of a long investigation and, once again, after piercing the enigma contained in some of his expressions. But how can we establish the differential specificity of the object of *Capital* with any precision without a critical and epistemological reading which assigns the *site* where Marx separates himself theoretically from his predecessors, and determines the meaning of this break. How can we aim to achieve this result without recourse precisely to a theory of the history of the production of knowledges, applied to the relations between Marx and his prehistory, i.e., without recourse to the principles of *Marxist philosophy*? As we shall see, a second question must be added to this one: does not the difficulty Marx seems to have felt in thinking in (*penser dans*) a rigorous concept the difference which distinguishes his object from the object of Classical Economics, lie in the *nature* of his discovery, in particular in its fantastically *innovatory character*? in the fact that this discovery happened to be theoretically *very much in advance* of the philosophical concepts then available? And in this case, does not Marx's scientific discovery imperiously demand that we pose the *new* philosophical problems required by the disconcerting nature of its *new object*? This last argument calls on philosophy to participate in any depth reading of *Capital* in order to answer the astonishing questions asked of philosophy in its pages: unprecedented questions which are decisive for the future of philosophy itself.

Such is the double object of this study, which is only possible given a constant and double reference: the identification and knowledge of the object of Marxist philosophy at work in *Capital* presupposes the identification and knowledge of the specific difference of the object of *Capital* itself – which in turn presupposes the recourse to Marxist philosophy and demands its development. It is not possible to read *Capital* properly without the help of Marxist philosophy, which must itself be read, and simultaneously, in *Capital* itself. If this double reading and constant reference from the scientific reading to the philosophical reading, and from the philosophical reading to the scientific reading, are necessary and fruitful, we shall surely be able to recognize in them the peculiarity of the philosophical revolution carried in

Marx's scientific discovery: a revolution which inaugurates an authentically new mode of philosophical thought.

We can convince ourselves that this double reading is indispensable *a contrario*, too, by the difficulties and misconstructions that simple immediate readings of *Capital* have produced in the past: difficulties and misconstructions which all revolve around a more or less serious misunderstanding of the specific difference of the object of *Capital*. We are obliged to register this remarkable fact: until relatively recently, *Capital* was hardly read, among 'specialists', except by economists and historians, of whom the former often thought that *Capital* was an economic treatise in the immediate sense of their practice, and the latter that certain parts of *Capital* were works of history, in the immediate sense of their practice. This Book, which thousands and thousands of worker militants have studied – has been read by economists and historians, but very rarely by *philosophers*,[1] i.e., 'specialists' capable of posing *Capital* the preliminary question of the differential nature of its object. With rare exceptions, all the more remarkable for that, economists and historians have not been equipped to pose it this kind of question, at least in a rigorous form, and hence they have not ultimately been equipped to identify conceptually what specifically distinguishes Marx's object from other apparently similar or related objects whether contemporaneous with him or earlier. Such an undertaking has generally only been accessible to philosophers, or to specialists with an adequate philosophical education – because it corresponds precisely to the object of philosophy.

What philosophers who are able to pose *Capital* the question of its object and of the specific difference that distinguishes Marx's object from the object of Political Economy, classical or modern, have read *Capital* and posed it this question? Knowing that *Capital* was under a radical ideologico-political interdict imposed by bourgeois economists and historians for eighty years, we can imagine the fate reserved for it by academic philosophy! The only philosophers ready to take *Capital* for an object worthy of a

---

[1] For very profound reasons, it was often in fact *political* militants and leaders who, without being professional philosophers, were best able to read and understand *Capital* as philosophers. Lenin is the most extraordinary example: his *philosophical* understanding of *Capital* gives his economic and political analysis an incomparable profundity, rigour and acuity. In our image of Lenin, the great political leader all too often masks the man who undertook the patient, detailed and profound study of Marx's great theoretical works. It is no accident that we owe to the first years of Lenin's public activity (the years preceding the 1905 Revolution) so many acute texts devoted to the most difficult questions of the theory of *Capital*. Ten years of study and meditation on *Capital* gave the man the incomparable *theoretical formation* which produced the prodigious political understanding of the leader of the Russian and international workers' movement. And this is also the reason why Lenin's political and economic works (not only the written works, but also the historical ones) are of such theoretical and philosophical value: we can study *Marxist philosophy at work* in them, in the 'practical' state, Marxist philosophy which has become politics, political action, analysis and decision. Lenin: an incomparable *theoretical and philosophical formation turned political.*

hilosopher's concern could long only be Marxist militants: only during the
st two or three decades have a few non-Marxist philosophers crossed this
orbidden frontier. But, whether Marxist or not, these philosophers could
nly pose *Capital* questions produced by their philosophy, which was not
enerally equipped to conceive a real epistemological treatment of its
object, even if it did not obstinately reject it. Among Marxists, besides the
emarkable case of Lenin, we can mention Labriola and Plekhanov, the
'Austro-Marxists', Gramsci, and more recently Rosenthal and Il'ienkov in
the USSR, the School of Della Volpe in Italy (Della Volpe, Colletti, Pietranera, Rossi, etc.) and numerous scholars in the socialist countries. The
'Austro-Marxists' were merely neo-Kantians: they produced nothing that
has survived their ideological project. The important work of Plekhanov
and particularly that of Labriola, deserve a special study – as also, and on a
quite different level, do Gramsci's great theses on Marxist philosophy. I
shall discuss Gramsci later. It is no slander on Rosenthal's work (*Problèmes
de la dialectique dans 'Le Capital'*) to reckon it partly beside the point here,
since it merely paraphrases the immediate language with which Marx
designates his object and his theoretical operations, without supposing that
Marx's very language might often be open to this question. As for the
studies of Il'ienkov, Della Volpe, Colletti, Pietranera, etc., they are indeed
the works of philosophers who have read *Capital* and pose it directly the
essential question – erudite, rigorous and profound works, conscious of the
fundamental relation linking Marxist philosophy with the understanding of
Capital. But, as we shall see, the conception they put forward of Marxist
philosophy is often debatable. However, in every case, the same exigency is
expressed everywhere in the investigations of contemporary Marxist theoreticians: a deeper understanding of the theoretical consequences of *Capital*
requires a more rigorous and richer definition of *Marxist philosophy*. In
other words, to return to classical terminology, the theoretical future of
historical materialism depends today on deepening dialectical materialism,
which itself depends on a rigorous critical study of *Capital*. History imposes
this immense task on us. Insofar as our modest means will allow, we should
like to make our contribution.

Let me return to the thesis I am going to attempt to expound and illustrate.
This thesis, it is clear, is not just an epistemological thesis which only
concerns the philosophers who take up the question of the difference between Marx and the Classical Economists: it is also a thesis which concerns
economists and historians – and, as an obvious consequence, political militants – in short, all of *Capital*'s readers. Posing the question of the object of
Capital, this thesis deals directly with the foundation of the economic and
historical analyses contained in its text: it should therefore be able to resolve
certain reading difficulties which have traditionally been opposed to Marx
by his opponents as decisive objections. The question of the object of *Capital*
is not therefore just a philosophical question. If what I have suggested about

the relation between scientific reading and philosophical reading is well-founded, the elucidation of the specific difference of the object of *Capital* may provide the means towards a better understanding of *Capital* in its economic and historical content too.

I close this foreword with the conclusion that, if I have replaced the original project for this paper, which was intended to deal with *Marx's relation to his work*, with a second project dealing with the *peculiar object* of *Capital*, this was quite necessary. In order to understand all the profundity of the comments in which Marx expresses his relation to his work, it was necessary to go beyond their letter to the essential point which is present in all these comments and in all the concepts which imply that relation – to the essential point of the *specific difference of the object of Capital*, a point which is both visible and hidden, present and absent, a point which is absent for reasons arising from the very *nature* of its presence, from the disconcerting novelty of Marx's revolutionary discovery. That these reasons may in certain cases be invisible to us at first glance surely derives in the last resort from the fact that, like all radical innovations, they are *blinding*.

Chapter 2

Marx and his Discoveries

I shall start with an immediate reading, and here I let Marx speak for himself.

In a letter to Engels on 24 August 1867, he writes:

The best points in my book are: (1) the two-fold character of labour, according to whether it is expressed in use-value or exchange value. (All understanding of the facts depends on this.) It is emphasized immediately, in the first chapter; (2) the treatment of surplus value independently of its particular forms as profit, interest, ground rent, etc. This will come out especially in the second volume. The treatment of the particular forms by classical economy, which always mixes them up with the general form, is a regular hash.

In the *Marginal Notes on Wagner's 'Lehrbuch der politischen Ökonomie'*, written in 1883, at the end of his life, Marx says of Wagner (Marx-Engels: *Werke*, Bd. XIX, pp. 370-1):

the *vir obscurus* [Wagner] has not seen:

that even in the analysis of the commodity, I do not stop at the double mode in which it is represented, but go straight on to the fact that in this double being of the commodity is represented the two-fold character of the labour whose product it is: the *useful* labour, i.e., the concrete modes of the labours which create use-values, and the abstract labour, labour as the expenditure of labour power, whatever the 'useful' mode in which it is expended (on which depends the later representation of the production process);

that in the development of the value-form of the commodity, in the last instance of its money-form, hence of money, the value of a commodity is represented in the use-value, i.e., the natural form of the other commodity;

that surplus-value itself is deduced from a 'specific' use-value of labour-power which belongs exclusively to it, etc., etc.;

and that therefore for me use-value plays a far more important part than it has in economics hitherto, but, N.B., that it only ever comes into consideration where such a consideration arises from the analysis of a given economic form, not from reasoning this way and that about the concepts or words 'use-value' and 'value'.

I quote these texts as protocols in which Marx expressly designates the basic concepts that govern his whole analysis. In these texts, therefore, Marx indicates the differences between him and his predecessors. In this way he gives us the specific difference of his object – but, note, less in the form of the *concept* of his object than in the form of concepts assisting in the analysis of that object.

These texts are far from being the only ones in which Marx announces his discoveries. We find far-reaching discoveries designated all the way through a reading of *Capital*: e.g., the genesis of money, which the whole of classical economics did not manage to think; the organic composition of capital $(c+v)$, absent from Smith and Ricardo; the general law of capitalist accumulation; the law of the tendency of the rate of profit to fall; the theory of ground rent, etc. I shall not list all these discoveries, each of which makes intelligible economic facts and practices which the Classical Economists either passed over in silence or evaded because they were incompatible with their premisses. In fact, these detailed discoveries are merely the immediate or distant consequences of the new basic concepts that Marx identified in his work as his master discoveries. Let us examine them.

The reduction of the different forms of profit, rent and interest to surplus-value is itself a discovery secondary to that of surplus-value. The basic discoveries therefore concern:

(1) the value/use-value opposition; the reference of this opposition to another opposition which the Economists were not able to identify: the opposition abstract labour/concrete labour; the particular importance which Marx, as opposed to the Classical Economists, attributes to use-value and its correlate concrete labour; the reference to the strategic points where use-value and concrete labour play a decisive part: the distinctions between constant capital and variable capital, on the one hand, and between the two departments of production on the other (Department I, production of means of production; Department II, production of means of consumption).

(2) surplus-value.

To sum up: the concepts which contain Marx's basic discoveries are: the concepts of *value* and *use-value*; of *abstract labour* and *concrete labour*; and of *surplus-value*.

That is what Marx tells us. And there is no apparent reason why we should not take him at his word. In fact, while reading *Capital* we can prove that his economic analyses do depend on these basic concepts in the last instance. We can, so long as our reading is a careful one. But this proof is not self-evident. It presupposes a great struggle for rigour – and above all it necessarily implies from the beginning something which is present in Marx's declared discoveries – but present in a strange absence – if we are to complete this proof and see clearly in the very clarity it produces.

As an index which gives a negative foretaste of this absence, one comment will do: the concepts to which Marx expressly relates his discovery and which underly all his economic analysis, the concepts of value and surplus-value, are precisely the concepts on which all the criticism addressed to Marx by modern economists has focused. It is not immaterial to know in what terms these concepts have been attacked by non-Marxist economists. Marx has been criticized on the grounds that they are concepts which, although they make allusion to economic reality, remain at heart non-economic, 'philosophical' and 'metaphysical' concepts. Even as enlightened an economist as Conrad Schmidt – who was intelligent enough to deduce the law of the tendency of the rate of profit to fall from Volume Two of *Capital* soon after its publication, even though that law was first expounded in Volume Three – even Conrad Schmidt attacked Marx's law of value as a 'theoretical fiction', a necessary one no doubt, but a fiction all the same. I do not quote these criticisms for fun, but because they are directed at the very foundation of Marx's economic analyses, the concepts of value and surplus-value, which are rejected as 'non-operational' concepts designating realities which are non-economic because they are non-measurable, non-quantifiable. Obviously, this reproach in its own way betrays the conception the economists in question have of their own object, and of the concepts it authorizes: but if this reproach does show us the point in which their opposition to Marx is at its most palpable, these economists do not give us Marx's object in their reproach, precisely because they treat that object as 'metaphysical'. However, I indicate this point as *the* point of misunderstanding, the point where the Economists misconstrue Marx's analyses. But this misunderstanding in their reading was only possible because of a misunderstanding of Marx's object itself: a misunderstanding that made the Economists read their own object into Marx, instead of reading another object in Marx which is not their own object but a quite different one. This point of misunderstanding which the Economists declare the point of Marx's theoretical weakness and error is, on the contrary, the point at which he is strongest! the point which marks him off radically from his critics, and also, on occasion, from some of his closest followers.

To demonstrate the extent of this misunderstanding, I should like to quote the letter from Engels to Conrad Schmidt (12 March 1895) from which we took the echo of Schmidt's objection above. Engels replies as follows:

There (in your objections) I find the same way of going off into details, for which I put the blame on the eclectic method of philosophizing which has made such inroads in the German universities since 1848, and which loses all general perspective and only too often winds up in rather aimless and fruitless speculation about particular points. Now of the classical philosophers it was precisely Kant with whom you had formerly chiefly occupied yourself, and Kant . . . was more or less obliged to make some apparent concessions in form to . . . Wolffian speculation. This is how I explain your tendency, which also shows in the excursus on the law of value in your letter, to become so absorbed in details . . . that you degrade the law of value to a fiction, a necessary fiction, somewhat in the manner of Kant making the existence of God a postulate of the practical reason.

The objections you raise to the law of value apply to *all* concepts, regarded from the standpoint of reality. The identity of thinking and being, to express myself in Hegelian fashion, everywhere coincides with your example of the circle and the polygon. Or the two of them, the concept of a thing and its reality, run side by side like two asymptotes, always approaching each other yet never meeting. *This difference between the two is the very difference which prevents the concept from being directly and immediately reality and reality from being immediately its own concept.* Because a concept has the essential nature of that concept and cannot therefore *prima facie* directly coincide with reality, from which it must first be abstracted, it is something more than a fiction, unless you are going to declare all the results of thought fictions because reality corresponds to them only very circuitously, and even then only with asymptotic approximation.

This reply is astounding (despite the banality of its obviousnesses) and it constitutes a kind of well-intentioned commentary on the misunderstanding, on which Marx's opponents set out to produce ill-intentioned commentaries. Engels escapes Conrad Schmidt's 'operational' objection with a theory of knowledge made to order – that looks to the approximations of abstraction to establish the inadequacy of the concept as a concept to its object! This answer is beside the point: for Marx the concept of the law of value is in fact a concept perfectly adequate to its object, since it is the concept of the limits of its variation, and therefore the adequate concept of the field of its inadequacy – and in no sense an inadequate concept by virtue of some original sin which affects all concepts brought into the world by human abstraction. Engels therefore transfers to an empiricist theory of knowledge, as a native weakness of the concept, precisely what constitutes the theoretical strength of Marx's adequate concept! This transfer is only possible with the complicity of this ideological theory of knowledge, ideological not only in its content (empiricism), but also in its use, since it is designed to answer, among other things, precisely this theoretical misunderstanding. There is a risk not only that the theory of *Capital* will be affected by it (Engels's thesis in the Preface to Volume Three: the law of value is economically valid 'from the beginning of exchange . . . until the fifteenth century A.D.' is a disturbing example), but also that Marxist philosophical theory will be marked, and with what a mark! The mark of the empiricist theory of knowledge which serves as a silent theoretical norm both in Schmidt's objection and in Engels's reply. I have dwelt on this reply in order to stress the fact that the present misunderstanding may betray not only political or ideological ill-will, but also the effects of a theoretical blindness which is a serious hazard so long as we neglect to pose Marx the question of his object.

Chapter 3

The Merits of Classical Economics

Let us therefore take things as we are told they are, and ask how Marx himself thinks himself, not only directly, when he examines in himself what distinguishes him from the Classical Economists, but also indirectly, when he thinks himself in them, i.e., registers in them the presence or presentiment of his discovery in their non-discovery, and therefore thinks his own perspicacity in the blindness of its closest pre-history.

I cannot go into every detail here, although all of them deserve a precise and exhaustive study. I propose to concentrate on a few elements only, which will act as so many pertinent indices to the problem we are concerned with.

Marx assesses his debt to his predecessors and therefore estimates what is positive in their thought (with respect to his own discovery) in two distinct forms which emerge very clearly in *Theories of Surplus Value*:

On the one hand, he pays homage to one or other of his predecessors for having isolated and analysed an important concept, even if the words that express this concept are still caught in the trap of linguistic confusion or ambiguity. In this way he registers the concept of value in Petty, the concept of surplus-value in Steuart, the Physiocrats, etc. He then makes allowances for isolated conceptual gains, usually extracting them from the confusion of a still inadequate terminology.

On the other, he stresses another merit which does not involve any particular detailed gain (any concept) but the 'scientific' mode of treatment of political economy. Two features seem to him to be discriminatory in this respect. The first, in a very classical spirit that might perhaps be called Galilean, concerns the scientific attitude itself: the method which brackets sensory appearances, i.e., in the domain of political economy, all the visible phenomena and practico-empirical concepts produced by the economic world (rent, interest, profit, etc.), in other words, all those economic categories from the 'everyday life' which, at the end of *Capital*, Marx says is the equivalent of a 'religion'. The effect of this bracketing is to unveil the hidden essence of the phenomena, their essential inwardness. For Marx, the science of political economy, like every other science, depends on this reduction of the phenomenon to the essence, or, as he puts it, in an explicit comparison with astronomy, of the *'apparent movement to the real movement'*. All the economists who have made a scientific discovery, even a minute one, have done so by way of this reduction. However, this partial reduction is not enough to constitute the science. At this point the second feature intervenes. A science is a systematic theory which embraces the totality of its object and seizes the 'internal connexion' which links together the 'reduced' essences of *all* economic phenomena. The great merit of the Physiocrats, and of Quesnay in particular, was that, even if only partially (since they restricted themselves to agricultural production), they related phenomena as diverse as wages, profit, rent, commercial gain, etc., to a *single* original essence, the surplus-value produced in the agricultural sector. It was Smith's merit that he outlined this systematic while liberating it from the agricultural presuppositions of the Physiocrats. But, at the same time, he was at fault in only half-finishing it. Smith's unforgivable weakness was that he wanted to think of as having a *single* origin objects of a different nature: both true (reduced) 'essences', and also crude phenomena not reduced to their essences: the result is that his theory is no more than the necessity – less grouping of two doctrines, the *exoteric* (which unites unreduced crude phenomena) and the *esoteric* (which unites essences), of which only the latter is scientific. This simple comment of Marx's is heavy with meaning: it implies that it is not just the form of systematicity that makes a science, but the form of systematicity of the 'essences' (of the theoretical concepts) alone, and not the systematicity of interlinked crude phenomena (elements of the *real*), or the mixed systematicity of 'essences' and crude phenomena. However, it was Ricardo's merit that he thought and went beyond this contradiction between Smith's two 'doctrines', and conceived Political Economy in the true form of scientificity, i.e., as the unified system of concepts which expresses the internal essence of its object:

> But at last Ricardo steps in . . . The basis, the starting-point for the physiology of the bourgeois system – for the understanding of its internal organic coherence and life process – is the determination of value by labour time. Ricardo starts with this and forces science to get out of the rut, to render an account of the extent to which the other categories – the relations of production and commerce – evolved and described by it, correspond to or contradict this basis, this starting-point; to elucidate how far a science, which in fact only reflects and reproduces the phenomenal forms of the process, corresponds to the basis on which rests the inner coherence, the actual physiology of bourgeois society, or to the basis which forms its starting point; and therefore how far these phenomena themselves so correspond; and in general to examine how matters stand with the contradiction between the apparent and the real movement of the system. This then is Ricardo's great historical significance for science (*Theories of Surplus Value*, Vol. II, p. 166 – modified).

The reduction of the phenomenon to the essence (of the given to its concept), the internal unity of the essence (the systematicity of the concepts unified behind their concepts): these, then, are the two positive determinations which, in Marx's eyes, constitute the conditions for the scientific character of an isolated result or a general theory. But the reader will have noted that these determinations express with respect to Political Economy the general conditions for the existing scientific rationality (the existing Theoretical): Marx merely borrowed them from the existing state of the sciences, importing them into Political Economy as the *formal* norms of scientific rationality in general. When he judges the Physiocrats, Smith or Ricardo, he applies these formal norms to them, deciding whether they have respected or ignored them – without prejudging the *content* of their objects.

However, we shall not restrict ourselves to purely formal judgements. Has the content that these forms abstract from not already been designated by Marx in the Economists themselves? Do concepts that Marx makes the foundation of his own theory, value and surplus-value, not already appear in person in the theoretical charter of the Classical Economists, together with the phenomenon-essence reduction and theoretical scientificity? But this presents us with a strange situation. It seems that, in essentials – and that is how Marx's modern critics have judged his undertaking – Marx was really no more than the heir of Classical Economics, and a decidedly well-endowed one, since he obtained from his forebears his key concepts (the content of his object) and the method of reduction, as well as the model of internal systematicity (the scientific form of his object). What, then, is peculiar to Marx, what is his historical merit? Simply the fact that he extended and completed an already almost complete work: he filled in the gaps, resolved the problems it had left open; in sum, he increased the patrimony of the classics, but on the basis of their principles, and therefore of their problematic, accepting not only their method and theory, but also together with the latter the definition of *their object* itself. The answer to the question: what is Marx's object? what is the object of *Capital*? is already inscribed, apart from a few nuances and discoveries, but in principle, in Smith, and especially in Ricardo. The great theoretical web of Political Economy was already there waiting: a few threads awry and a few holes, certainly. Marx tightened the threads, straightened the weave and added a few stitches: in other words, he finished the work, making it perfect. In this account, the possibility of a misunderstanding in reading *Capital* disappears: Marx's object is no more than Ricardo's object. The history of Political Economy from Ricardo to Marx thus becomes a beautiful unbroken continuity, which is no longer a problem. If there is a misunderstanding, it is elsewhere, in Ricardo and in Marx – no longer between Ricardo and Marx, but between the whole of the Classical Economics of labour-value, which Marx merely brilliantly touched up, and modern marginalist and neo-marginalist political economy, which rests on a quite different problematic.

And in fact, when we read certain of Gramsci's commentaries (Marxist philosophy is Ricardo generalized), Rosenthal's theoretical analyses or even the much more critical remarks of Della Volpe and his disciples, we are struck by the fact that we never forsake this *continuity of object*. These authors see no essential difference between Smith's and Ricardo's object and Marx's object. This non-difference of object has been registered in the vulgar Marxist interpretation in the following form: the only difference is in the method. The method which the classical economists applied to their object was merely *metaphysical*, but Marx's method, on the contrary, was *dialectical*. Everything therefore depends on the dialectic, which is thus conceived as a method in itself, imported from Hegel, and applied to an object in itself, already present in Ricardo. Marx simply sealed this happy union with the miracle of genius, and like all happiness, it has no history. Unfortunately, we know that there remains one 'tiny' difficulty: the history of the 'reconversion' of this dialectic, which has to be 'put back on to its feet' if it is at last to walk on the *terra firma* of materialism.

Here, too, I have not evoked the facilities of this schematic interpretation, which no doubt has its political and historical justification, simply for the fun of disagreeing with them. This hypothetical *continuity of object* from classical economics to Marx is not restricted to Marx's opponents or even to some of his supporters: it emerges silently again and again in Marx's own explicit discourse, or rather it emerges from a certain silence of Marx's which unintentionally doubles his explicit discourse. At certain moments, in certain symptomatic points, this silence emerges as such in the discourse and forces it against its will to produce real theoretical lapses, in brief blank flashes, invisible in the light of the proof: words that hang in mid-air although they seem to be inserted into the necessity of the thought, judgements which close irreversibly with a false obviousness the very space which seemed to be opening before reason. All that a simple literal reading sees in the arguments is the continuity of the text. A *'symptomatic'* reading is necessary to make these lacunae perceptible, and to identify behind the spoken words the discourse of the silence, which, emerging in the verbal discourse, induces these blanks in it, blanks which are failures in its rigour, or the outer limits of its effort: its absence, once these limits are reached, but in a space which it has *opened*.

I shall give two examples: Marx's conception of the abstractions that underly the process of theoretical practice, and the kind of criticisms he makes of the Classical Economists.

The third chapter of the *1857 Introduction* can rightly be regarded as the *Discourse on Method* of the new philosophy founded by Marx. In fact, it is the only systematic text by Marx which contains, in the form of an analysis of the categories and method of political economy, the means with which to establish a theory of scientific practice, i.e., a theory of the conditions of the process of knowledge, which is the object of Marxist philosophy.

The theoretical problematic underlying this text allows us to distinguish Marxist philosophy from every speculative or empiricist philosophy. The decisive point of Marx's thesis concerns the principle distinguishing between the *real* and *thought*. The real is one thing, along with its different aspects: the real-concrete, the process of the real, the real totality, etc. *Thought* about the real is another, along with its different aspects: the thought process, the thought-totality, the thought-concrete, etc.

This principle of distinction implies two essential theses: (1) the materialist thesis of the primacy of the real over thought about the real presupposes the existence of the real independence of that thought (the real '*survives in its independence, after as before, outside the head*' – *Grundrisse*, p. 22) (2) the materialist thesis of the specificity of thought and of the thought process, with respect to the real and the real process. This latter thesis is especially the object of Marx's reflections in the third chapter of the *Introduction*. Thought about the real, the conception of the real, and all the operations of thought by which the real is thought and conceived, belong to the order of thought, the elements of thought, which must not be confused with the order of the real, the element of the real. '*The whole, as it appears in the mind as a thought-whole, is a product of the thinking mind*' (p. 22); similarly, the thought-concrete belongs to thought and not to the real. The process of knowledge, the work of elaboration (*Verarbeitung*) by which thought transforms its initial intuitions and representations into knowledges or thought-concretes, takes place entirely in thought.

No doubt there is a relation between *thought*-about-the-real and this *real*, but it is a relation of *knowledge*,[2] a relation of adequacy or inadequacy of knowledge, not a real relation, meaning by this a relation inscribed in *that real* of which the thought is the (adequate or inadequate) knowledge. This knowledge relation between knowledge of the real and the real is not a relation *of the real* that is known in this relationship. The distinction between a relation of knowledge and a relation of the real is a fundamental one: if we did not respect it we should fall irreversibly into either speculative or empiricist idealism. Into speculative idealism if, with Hegel, we confused thought and the real by *reducing* the real to thought, by '*conceiving the real as the result of thought*' (p. 22); into empiricist idealism if we confused thought with the real by reducing thought about the real to the real itself. In either case, this double reduction consists of a projection and realization of one element in the other: of thinking the difference between the real and thought about it as either a difference within thought itself (speculative idealism) or as a difference within the real itself (empiricist idealism).

Naturally, these theses pose problems,[3] but they are problems unambiguously implied in Marx's text. Now, this is what interests us. Examining the methods of Political Economy, Marx distinguishes two such methods: a first one, that starts from '*a living whole*' ('*the population, the Nation, State, several States*'); and a second one '*that starts from simple notions such as labour,*

---

[2] Cf. Part I, sections 16 and 18.
[3] Cf. Part I, sections 16, 17 and 18.

the division of labour, money, value, etc.' There are therefore two methods, one starting from the real itself, the other from *abstractions*. Which of these two methods is correct? *'It seems to be correct to start with the real and concrete . . . but on closer inspection it is clear that this is false.'* The second method, which starts from simple abstractions in order to produce knowledge of the real in a 'thought-concrete' *'is manifestly the correct scientific method'*, and this was the method of classical Political Economy, of Smith and Ricardo. Formally, there is no need here to look beyond the obviousness of this discourse.

But in its obviousness, this discourse contains and conceals *one of Marx's symptomatic silences.* This silence is inaudible everywhere in the development of the discourse, which sticks to showing that the process of knowledge is a process of work and theoretical elaboration, and that the thought-concrete or knowledge of the real is the product of this theoretical practice. This silence is only 'heard' *at one precise point,* just where it goes unperceived: when Marx speaks of the initial *abstractions* on which the work of transformation is performed. What are these initial abstractions? By what right does Marx accept in these initial abstractions the categories from which Smith and Ricardo started, thus suggesting that he thinks in continuity with their object, and that therefore there is no break in object between them and him? These two questions are really only one single question, precisely the question that Marx does not answer, simply because *he does not pose it.* Here is the *site* of his silence, and this site, being empty, threatens to be occupied by the 'natural' discourse of ideology, in particular, of empiricism: *'The economists of the seventeenth century,'* writes Marx, *'always begin with a living whole, the population, the Nation, the State, several States, etc.; and they finish up by disengaging through analysis a number of determinant, abstract, general relations such as the division of labour, money, value, etc. Once these individual moments had been more or less abstracted and established, economic systems began to appear which ascend from simple notions such as labour, division of labour, need, exchange value'* (p. 21). Silence as to the nature of this 'analysis', this 'abstraction' and this 'establishment' – silence, or rather the inter-relationship of these 'abstractions' with the real from which they have been 'abstracted', with the 'intuition and representation' of the real, which thus seem in their purity the raw material of these abstractions without the status of this material (natural or raw?) having been expressed. An ideology may gather naturally in the hollow left by this silence, the ideology of a relation of *real* correspondence between the real and its intuition and representation, and the presence of an 'abstraction' which operates on this real in order to disengage from it these 'abstract general relations', i.e., an empiricist ideology of abstraction. The question can be posed in a different way, but its *absence* will always be noticed: how can these 'abstract general relations' be called 'determinant'? Is every abstraction as such the scientific concept of its object? Surely there are ideological abstractions and scientific

abstractions, 'good' and 'bad' abstractions? Silence.[4] The same question
can be put in another way: the famous abstract categories of the classical
economists, the abstractions that we have to start from in order to produce
knowledges, these abstractions were no problem for Marx *then*. For him,
they are the result of a process of preliminary *abstraction* about which he is
silent: the abstract categories can then 'reflect' *real* abstract categories, the
real abstract which inhabits the empirical phenomena of the economic world
as the abstraction of their individuality. The same question can be put in
yet another way: the initial abstract categories (those of the Economists) are
still there at the end, they have indeed produced 'concrete' knowledges, but
it does not look as if they have been *transformed*, it even seems that they did
not have to be transformed, for they already existed from the beginning in a
form adequate to their object, such that the 'thought-concrete' that scientific
work is to produce, can emerge as their *concretization* pure and simple, their
self-complication pure and simple, their self-comparison pure and simple
treated implicitly as their self-concretization. That is how a silence can be
extended into an explicit or implicit discourse. The whole theoretical description that Marx gives us remains a formal one since it does not question the
nature of these initial abstractions, the problem of their adequacy to their
object, in short, the object to which they relate; since, correlatively, it does
not question the transformation of these abstract categories during the
process of theoretical practice, i.e., the nature of the object implied by these
transformations. I am not attacking Marx for this: he did not have to say
everything, especially in an unpublished text, and in any case, no one can be
convicted for not saying everything at once. But his too hurried readers can
be attacked for not having *heard this silence*,[5] and for having rushed into

---

[4] The price of this silence: read Chapter VII of Rosenthal's book (*Les problèmes de la
dialectique dans 'Le Capital'*) and in particular the pages devoted to *avoiding* the problem
of the difference between 'good' and 'bad' abstraction (pp. 304–5, 325–7). Think of the
fortunes in Marxist philosophy of a term as ambiguous as '*generalization*', which is used
to think (i.e., not to think) the nature of scientific abstraction. The price of this *unheard*
silence is the empiricist temptation.

[5] There must be no misunderstanding of the meaning of this *silence*. It is part of a determinate discourse, whose object was not to set out the principles of Marxist philosophy,
the principles of the theory of the history of the production of knowledges, but to establish
the *methodological rules* indispensable to a treatment of Political Economy. Marx therefore
situated himself within an already constituted learning without posing the problem of its
production. That is why, *within the limits of this text*, he could treat Smith's and Ricardo's
'good abstractions' as corresponding to a certain real, and keep his silence as to the extraordinarily complex conditions that gave birth to classical Political Economy: he could leave
in suspense the point of knowing what process could have produced the field of the classical
problematic in which the object of classical Political Economy could be constituted as an
object, giving by its knowledge a certain grasp on the real, even though it was still dominated
by ideology. The fact that this methodological text leads us to the threshold of the requirement that we constitute that theory of the production of knowledge which is the same
thing as Marxist philosophy, is a requirement *for us*: but it is also a requirement for which
we are indebted to Marx, so long as we are attentive both to the theoretical incompleteness

empiricism. By locating accurately *the site of Marx's silence*, we can put the question which contains and coincides with this silence: precisely the question of the *differential nature of the abstractions* which scientific thought works on in order to produce new abstractions at the end of the labour process which are different from the previous ones, and, in the case of an epistemological break like the one between Marx and the classical economists, radically new.

I once tried to stress the necessity of thinking this difference by giving *different* names to the different abstractions that occur in the process of theoretical practice, carefully distinguishing between Generalities I (initial abstractions) and Generalities III (products of the knowledge process). No doubt this was to *add* something to Marx's discourse: but in a different respect, I was merely *re-establishing*, i.e., *maintaining* his discourse, without yielding to the temptation of his *silence*. I *heard* this silence as the possible weakness of a discourse under the pressure and repressive action of another discourse, which takes the place of the first discourse in favour of this repression, and speaks in its silence: the empiricist discourse. All I did was to *make this silence in the first discourse speak, dissipating the second*. The reader may think this a mere detail. Certainly, it is, but, when rigour is lacking, the more talkative and self-important discourses which deport Marx the philosopher entirely into the very ideology that he fought and rejected depend precisely on this kind of detail. We shall soon see examples of this, where the non-thought of a minute silence becomes the charter for non-thought discourses, i.e., ideological discourses.

---

of this text (its silence on this particular point) and to the *philosophical* scope of his new theory of history (in particular to what it *constrains us to think*: the articulation of ideological practice and scientific practice to the other practices, and the organic and differential history of these practices). In other words, we can treat the silence in this text in one of two ways: either by taking it for a silence *that goes without saying* because its content is the dominant theory of empiricist abstraction; or by treating it as a limit and a problem. A *limit*: the furthest point to which Marx took his thought; but then this limit, far from returning us to the old field of empiricist philosophy, opens a new field before us. A *problem*: what precisely is the nature of this new field? We now have at our disposal enough studies in the history of learning to suspect that we must look in quite different directions from the empiricist one. But in this decisive investigation, Marx himself has provided our fundamental principles (the structuration and articulation of the different practices). From which we can see the difference between the ideological treatment of a theoretical silence or emptiness, and its scientific treatment: the former confronts us with an ideological *closure*, the latter with a scientific *openness*. Here we can see immediately a precise example of the ideological threat that hangs over all scientific labour: ideology not only lies in wait for science at each point where its rigour slackens, but also at the furthest point where an investigation currently reaches its *limits*. There, precisely, philosophical ideology can intervene at the level of the life of the science: as the theoretical vigilance that protects the openness of science against the closure of ideology, on condition, of course, that it does not limit itself to speaking of openness and closure in general, but rather of *the typical, historically determined structures of this openness and closure*. In *Materialism and Empirio-Criticism*, Lenin constantly recalls this absolutely fundamental requirement which constitutes the specific function of Marxist philosophy.

Chapter 4

The Errors of Classical Economics:
Outline of a Concept of Historical Time

I now turn to my second example, in which we shall be able to size up the same problem, but in a different way: by examining the kind of criticism Marx made of the classical economists. He had many detailed criticisms of them, and one fundamental one.

I shall only discuss one of the detailed criticisms, one which concerns a point of terminology. It challenges the apparently insignificant fact that Smith and Ricardo always analyse 'surplus-value' *in the form of profit, rent and interest*, with the result that it is never called *by its name*, but always disguised beneath other names, that it is not conceived in its 'generality' as distinct from its 'forms of existence': profit, rent and interest. The style of this accusation is interesting: Marx seems to regard this confusion as a mere inadequacy of language, easy enough to rectify. And, in fact, when he reads Smith and Ricardo, he re-establishes the word absent behind the words that disguise it, he translates them, re-establishing their omission, saying precisely what they are silent about, reading their analyses of rent and profit as so many analyses of general surplus-value, although the latter is never named as the internal essence of rent and profit. But we know that the *concept* of surplus-value is, on Marx's own admission, one of the two key concepts of his theory, one of the concepts marking the peculiar difference between him and Smith and Ricardo, with respect to problematic and object. In fact, Marx treats the absence of a *concept* as if it were the mere absence of a *word*, and this is not the absence of just any concept, but, as we shall see, the absence of a concept that cannot be treated as a concept in the strict sense of the term without raising the question of the problematic which may underly it, i.e., the difference in problematic, the break that divides Marx from Classical Economics. Here again, in articulating his criticism, Marx has not thought what he is doing to the letter – since he has reduced the absence of an organic *concept*, which has 'precipitated' (in the chemical sense of the term) the revolution in his problematic, to the omission of a *word*. If this omission of Marx's is not stressed, he is reduced to the level of his predecessors, and we find ourselves back in the continuity of objects. I shall return to this point.

The fundamental criticism Marx makes of the whole of Classical Economics in texts from *The Poverty of Philosophy* to *Capital* is that it had an historical, eternal, fixed and abstract conception of the economic categories of

capitalism. Marx says in so many words that these categories must be historicized to reveal and understand their nature, their relativity and transitivity.
The Classical Economists, he says, have made the conditions of capitalist
production the eternal conditions of all production, without seeing that these
categories were historically determined, and hence historical and transitory.

> Economists express the relations of bourgeois production, the division
> of labour, credit, money, etc., as fixed, immutable, eternal categories . . .
> Economists explain how production takes place in the above-mentioned
> relations, but what they do not explain is how these relations themselves are
> produced, that is, the historical movement which gave them birth . . .
> these categories are as little eternal as the relations they express. They are
> historical and transitory products (*Poverty of Philosophy*, pp. 104, 110).

As we shall see, this critique is not the last word of Marx's *real* critique.
It remains superficial and ambiguous, whereas his real critique is infinitely
more profound. But it is surely no accident that Marx often went only half-
way with his real critique in his declared critique, by establishing the only
difference between him and the Classical Economists as the non-history of
their conception. This judgement has weighed very heavily on the interpretation not only of *Capital* and of the Marxist theory of political economy,
but also of Marxist philosophy. This is one of the strategic points in Marx's
thought – I shall go so far as to say the number one strategic point – the
point at which the theoretical incompleteness of Marx's judgement of himself has produced the most serious misunderstandings, and, as before, not
only among his opponents, who have an interest in misunderstanding him,
but also and above all among his supporters.

All these misunderstandings can be grouped round one central misunderstanding of the theoretical relationship between Marxism and history,
of the so-called radical historicism of Marxism. Let us examine the basis for
the different forms taken by this crucial misunderstanding.

In my opinion, this basis directly concerns the relation between Marx and
Hegel, and the conception of the dialectic and history. If all that divides
Marx from the Classical Economists amounts to the historical character of
economic categories, Marx need only historicize these categories, refusing
to take them as fixed, absolute or eternal, but, on the contrary, regarding them
as relative, provisional and transitory, i.e., as categories subject in the last
instance to the moment of their historical existence. In this case, Marx's
relation to Smith and Ricardo can be represented as identical with Hegel's
relation to classical philosophy. Marx would then be Ricardo set in motion,
just as it is possible to describe Hegel as Spinoza set in motion; set in motion,
i.e., historicized. In this case, Marx's whole achievement would once again
be that he Hegelianized Ricardo, made him dialectical, i.e., that he applied
the Hegelian dialectical method to thinking an already constituted content
which was only separated from the truth by the thin partition of historical

relativity. In this case, we should fall once again into schemata consecrated by a whole tradition, schemata that depend on a conception of the dialectic as method in itself, regardless of the content of which it is the law, irrespective of the specificity of the object for which it has to provide both the principles of knowledge and the objective laws. I shall not insist on this point as it has already been elucidated, at least in principle.

But I should like to point out a different confusion which has neither been denounced nor elucidated, and which dominates the interpretation of Marxism now, and probably will for a long time to come; I mean expressly *the confusion that surrounds the concept of history.*

To claim that classical economics had not a historical, but an eternalist conception of its economic categories – that, to make these categories adequate to their object, they must be thought as historical – is to propose *the concept of history,* or rather *one particular* concept of history which exists in the ordinary imagination, but without taking care to ask questions about it. In reality, it is to introduce as a solution a concept which itself poses a theoretical problem, for as it is adopted and understood it is an uncriticized concept, a concept which, like all 'obvious' concepts, threatens to have for theoretical content no more than the function that the existing or dominant ideology defines for it. It is to introduce as a theoretical solution a concept whose status has not been examined, and which, far from being a solution, is in reality a theoretical problem. It implies that it is possible to borrow this concept of history from Hegel or from the historian's empiricist practice and import it into Marx without making any difficulties of principle, i.e., without posing the preliminary critical question of the effective content of a concept which has been 'picked up' in this naïve way; as if it went without saying, when, on the contrary, and before all else, it was essential to ask what *must* be the content of the concept of history imposed by Marx's theoretical problematic.

Without anticipating the paper that follows, I should like to clarify a few points of principle. I shall take as a pertinent counter-example (why it is pertinent we shall soon see) the Hegelian concept of history, the Hegelian concept of *historical time,* which, for Hegel, reflects the essence of the historical as such.

It is well known that Hegel defined time as '*der daseiende Begriff*', i.e., as the concept in its immediate empirical existence. Since time itself directs us to the *concept* as its essence, i.e., since Hegel consciously proclaims that historical time is merely the reflection in the continuity of time of the internal essence of the historical totality incarnating a moment of the development of the concept (in this case the Idea), we have Hegel's authority for thinking that historical time merely reflects the essence of the social totality of which it is the *existence.* That is to say that the essential characteristics of historical time will lead us, as so many indices, to the peculiar structure of that social totality.

Two essential characteristics of Hegelian historical time can be isolated: its homogeneous continuity and its contemporaneity.

(1) The homogeneous continuity of time. The homogeneous continuity of time is the reflection in existence of the continuity of the dialectical development of the Idea. Time can thus be treated as a continuum *in which* the dialectical continuity of the process of the development of the Idea is manifest. On this level, then, the whole problem of the science of history would consist of the division of this continuum according to a *periodization* corresponding to the succession of one dialectical totality after another. The moments of the Idea exist in the number of historical *periods* into which the time continuum is to be accurately divided. In this Hegel was merely thinking in his own theoretical problematic the number one problem of the historian's practice, the problem Voltaire, for example, expressed when he distinguished between the age of Louis XIV and the age of Louis XV; it is still the major problem of modern historiography.

(2) The contemporaneity of time, or the category of the historical *present*. This second category is the condition of possibility of the first one, and in it we find Hegel's central thought. If historical time is the existence of the social totality we must be precise about the structure of this existence. The fact that the relation between the social totality and its historical existence is a relation with an *immediate* existence implies that this relation is itself *immediate*. In other words: the structure of historical existence is such that all the elements of the whole always co-exist in one and the same time, one and the same present, and are therefore contemporaneous with one another in one and the same present. This means that the structure of the historical existence of the Hegelian social totality allows what I propose to call an 'essential section' (*coupe d'essence*), i.e., an intellectual operation in which a *vertical break* is made at any moment in historical time, a break in the present such that all the elements of the whole revealed by this section are in an immediate relationship with one another, a relationship that immediately expresses their internal essence. When I speak of an 'essential section', I shall therefore be referring to the specific structure of the social totality that allows this section, in which all the elements of the whole are given in a co-presence, itself the immediate presence of their essences, which thus become immediately *legible in them*. It is clear that it is the specific structure of the social totality which allows this essential section: for this section is only possible because of the peculiar nature of the unity of this totality, a 'spiritual' unity, if we can express in this way the type of unity possessed by an expressive totality, i.e., a totality all of whose parts are so many '*total parts*', each expressing the others, and each expressing the social totality that contains them, because each in itself contains in the immediate form of its expression the essence of the totality itself. I am referring to the structure of the Hegelian whole which I have already discussed: the Hegelian whole has a type of unity in which each element of the whole, whether a

material or economic determination, a political institution or a religious, artistic or philosophical form, is never anything more than the presence of the concept with itself at a historically determined moment. This is the sense in which the co-presence of the elements with one another and the presence of each element with the whole are based on a *de jure* preliminary presence: the total presence of the concept in all the determinations of its existence. That is how the continuity of time is possible: as the phenomenon of the concept's continuity of presence with its positive determinations. When we speak of a *moment* of the development of the Idea in Hegel, we must be careful to observe that this term reduces *two meanings* to one: the moment as a moment of a development (which invokes the continuity of time and gives rise to the theoretical problem of periodization); and the moment as a moment of time, as the present, which is never anything but the phenomenon of the presence of the concept with itself in all its concrete determinations.

It is this absolute and homogeneous presence of the determinations of the whole with the current essence of the concept which allows the 'essential section' I have been discussing. This is what in principle explains the famous Hegelian formula, valid for all the determinations of the whole, up to and including the self-consciousness of this whole in the knowing of this whole which is the historically *present* philosophy – the famous formula according to which *nothing can run ahead of its time*. The present constitutes the *absolute horizon* of all knowing, since all knowing can never be anything but the existence in knowing of the internal principle of the whole. However far philosophy goes it can never escape the bounds of this absolute horizon: even if it takes wing *at dusk*, it still belongs to the day, to the today, it is still merely the present reflecting on itself, reflecting on the presence of the concept with itself – tomorrow is in essence forbidden it.

And that is why the ontological category of the present prevents any anticipation of historical time, any conscious anticipation of the future development of the concept, any *knowledge* of the *future*. This explains the theoretical difficulty Hegel experienced in dealing with the existence of 'great men', whose role in his reflection is therefore that of paradoxical witnesses to an impossible conscious historical forecast. Great men neither perceive nor know the future: they divine it as a presentiment. Great men are only clairvoyants who have a presentiment of but can never know the imminence of tomorrow's essence, the 'kernel in the shell', the future in invisible gestation in the present, the coming essence being born in the alienation of the current essence. The fact that there is no knowing the future prevents there being any science of politics, any knowing that deals with the future effects of present phenomena. That is why no Hegelian politics is possible strictly speaking, and in fact there has never been a Hegelian politician.

I have insisted on the nature of historical time and its theoretical conditions to this extent because this conception of history and of its relation to time is still alive amongst us, as can be seen from the currently widespread distinction between synchrony and diachrony. This distinction is based on a conception of historical time as continuous and homogeneous and contemporaneous with itself. The synchronic is contemporaneity itself, the co-presence of the essence with its determinations, the present being readable as a structure in an 'essential section' because the present is the very existence of the essential structure. The synchronic therefore presupposes the ideological conception of a continuous-homogeneous time. It follows that the diachronic is merely the development of this present in the sequence of a temporal continuity in which the 'events' to which 'history' in the strict sense can be reduced (cf. Lévi-Strauss) are merely successive contingent presents in the time continuum. Like the synchronic, which is the primary concept, the diachronic therefore presupposes both of the very two characteristics I have isolated in the Hegelian conception of time: an ideological conception of historical time.

Ideological, because it is clear that this conception of historical time is merely a reflection of the conception Hegel had of the type of unity that constitutes the link between all the economic, political, religious, aesthetic, philosophical and other elements of the social whole. Because the Hegelian whole is a 'spiritual whole' in the Leibnizian sense of a whole in which all the parts 'conspire' together, in which each part is a *pars totalis*, the unity of this double aspect of historical time (homogeneous-continuity/contemporaneity) is possible and necessary.

Now we can see the pertinence of this Hegelian counter-example. What masks from us the relationship that has just been established between the structure of the Hegelian whole and the nature of Hegelian historical time is the fact that the Hegelian idea of time is borrowed from the most vulgar empiricism, the empiricism of the false obviousness of everyday practice[6] which we find in a naïve form in most of the historians themselves, at any rate in all the historians known to Hegel, who did not pose any questions as to the specific structure of historical time. Nowadays, a few historians are beginning to pose these questions, and often in a very remarkable way (Lucien Febvre, Labrousse, Braudel, etc.); but they do not pose them explicitly as a function of the *structure of the whole* they are studying, they do not pose them in a truly conceptual form: they simply *observe that there are* different times in history, varieties of time, long times, medium times and short times, and they are content to note their interferences as so many products of their intersection; they do not therefore relate these varieties as so many *variations* to the structure of the whole although the latter directly governs the production of those variations; rather, they are tempted to relate these varieties, as so many variants measurable by their *duration*, to ordinary time itself, to the ideological time continuum we have discussed. The

[6] Hegelian philosophy has even been called a 'speculative empiricism' (Feuerbach).

Hegelian counter-example is therefore relevant because it is representative of the crude ideological illusions of everyday practice and of the practice of the historians, not only of those who do not pose any questions, but even of those who do pose some questions, because these questions are generally related not to the fundamental question of the concept of history, but to the ideological conception of time.

However, we can retain from Hegel precisely what masks from us this empiricism which he had only sublimated in his systematic conception of history. We can retain this result produced by our brief critical analysis: the fact that *the structure of the social whole* must be strictly interrogated in order to find in it the secret of the conception of history in which the 'development' of this social whole is thought; once we know the structure of the social whole we can understand the apparently 'problem-less' relationship between it and the conception of historical time in which this conception is reflected. What we have just done for Hegel is equally valid for Marx: the procedure that has enabled us to isolate the theoretical presuppositions latent in a conception of history which seemed to 'stand by itself', but which is, in fact, organically linked to a precise conception of the social whole, can be applied to Marx, with the object of constructing *the Marxist concept of historical time* on the basis of the Marxist conception of the social totality.

We know that the Marxist whole cannot possibly be confused with the Hegelian whole: it is a whole whose unity, far from being the expressive or 'spiritual' unity of Leibniz's or Hegel's whole, is constituted by a certain type of *complexity*, the unity of a *structured whole* containing what can be called levels or instances which are distinct and 'relatively autonomous', and co-exist within this complex structural unity, articulated with one another according to specific determinations, fixed in the last instance by the level or instance of the economy.[7]

Of course, we still have to define more exactly the structural nature of this whole, but this provisional definition is sufficient for us to be able to forecast that the Hegelian type of co-existence of presence (allowing an 'essential section') is incompatible with the existence of this new type of totality.

This peculiar co-existence was already fully designated by Marx in a passage from the *Poverty of Philosophy* (pp. 110–11) which deals with the relations of production alone:

> The production relations of every society form a whole. M. Proudhon considers economic relations as so many social phases, engendering one another, resulting one from the other like the antithesis from the thesis, and realizing in their logical sequence the impersonal reason of humanity. The only drawback to this method is that when he comes to examine a

---

[7] Cf. 'Contradiction and Overdetermination' and 'On the Materialist Dialectic' in *For Marx*, op. cit., pp. 87ff., and 161ff.

single one of these phases, M. Proudhon cannot explain it without having recourse to all the other relations of society, which relations, however, he has not yet made his dialectic movement engender. When, after that, M. Proudhon, by means of pure reason, proceeds to give birth to these other phases, he treats them as if they were new-born babes. *He forgets that they are of the same age* as the first. . . . In constructing the edifice of an ideological system by means of the categories of political economy, *the limbs of the social system are dislocated.* The different limbs of society are converted into so many separate societies, following one upon the other. How, indeed, could the single *logical formula of movement, of sequence, explain the body of society, in which all relations co-exist simultaneously and support one another*? (italics, L.A.).

It is all here: the *co-existence*, the articulation of the limbs 'of the social system', the mutual support of the relations between them, cannot *be thought* in the 'logical formula of movement, of sequence, of time'. If we bear in mind the fact that the 'logic' is, as Marx shows in *The Poverty of Philosophy*, merely the abstraction of 'movement' and 'time', which are here invoked directly, as the origin of Proudhon's mystification, we can see that it is essential to reverse the order of reflection and think first the specific structure of the totality in order to understand both the form in which its limbs and constitutive relations *co-exist* and the peculiar structure of history.

In the *1857 Introduction*, discussing capitalist society, Marx insists once more that the *structure of the whole* must be conceived before any discussion of temporal sequence:

It is not a matter of the connexion established historically between the economic relations in the succession of different forms of society. Still less of their order of succession 'in the Idea' (Proudhon) . . . *but of their articulated-hierarchy* (Gliederung) *within modern bourgeois society* (*Grundrisse*, p. 28).

This establishes a new point of importance: the structure of the whole is articulated as the structure of an *organic hierarchized whole.* The co-existence of limbs and their relations in the whole is governed by the order of a dominant structure which introduces a specific order into the articulation (*Gliederung*) of the limbs and their relations.

In all forms of society it is a determinate production and its relations which assign every other production and its relations their rank and influence (p. 27).

Note a crucial point here: this dominance of a structure, of which Marx gives an example here (the domination of one form of production, e.g., industrial production over simple commodity production, etc.), cannot be reduced to the primacy of a *centre*, any more than the relation between the elements and the structure can be reduced to the expressive unity of the essence within its phenomena. This hierarchy only represents the hierarchy of effectivity that exists between the different 'levels' or instances of the social whole. Because each of the levels is itself structured, this hierarchy represents the hierarchy, the degree and the index of effectivity existing between the different structured levels present in the whole: it is the hierarchy of effectivity of a structure dominant over subordinate structures and their elements. Elsewhere, I have shown that in order to conceive this 'dominance' of a structure over the other structures in the unity of a conjuncture it is necessary to refer to the principle of the determination 'in the last instance' of the non-economic structures by the economic structure; and that this 'determination in the last instance' is an absolute precondition for the necescity and intelligibility of the displacements of the structures in the hierarchy of effectivity, or of the displacement of 'dominance' between the structured levels of the whole; that only this 'determination in the last instance' makes it possible to escape the arbitrary relativism of observable displacements by giving these displacements the necessity of a function.

If the type of unity peculiar to the Marxist totality really is of this kind, several important theoretical consequences follow.

In the first place, it is impossible to think the existence of this totality in the Hegelian category of the contemporaneity of the *present*. The co-existence of the different structured levels, the economic, the political, the ideological, etc., and therefore of the economic infrastructure, of the legal and political superstructure, of ideologies and theoretical formations (philosophy, sciences) can no longer be thought in the co-existence of the Hegelian *present*, of the ideological present in which temporal presence coincides with the presence of the essence with its phenomena. And in consequence, the model of a *continuous and homogeneous time* which takes the place of immediate existence, which is the place of the immediate existence of this continuing presence, can no longer be regarded as the time of history.

Let us begin with the last point, for it will make us more sensitive to the consequences of these principles. As a first approximation, we can argue from the specific structure of the Marxist whole that it is no longer possible to think the process of the development of the different levels of the whole *in the same historical time*. Each of these different 'levels' does not have the same type of historical existence. On the contrary, we have to assign to each level a *peculiar time*, relatively autonomous and hence relatively independent, even in its dependence, of the 'times' of the other levels. We can and must say: for each mode of production there is a peculiar time and history, punctuated in a specific way by the development of the productive forces; the relations of production have their peculiar time and history, punctuated in a specific way; the political superstructure has its own history . . . ; philosophy has its own time and history . . . ; aesthetic productions have their own time and history . . . ; scientific formations have their own time and history, etc.

Each of these peculiar histories is punctuated with peculiar rhythms and can only be known on condition that we have defined the *concept* of the specificity of its historical temporality and its punctuations (continuous development, revolutions, breaks, etc.). The fact that each of these times and each of these histories is *relatively autonomous* does not make them so many domains which are *independent* of the whole: the specificity of each of these times and of each of these histories – in other words, their relative autonomy and independence – is based on a certain type of articulation in the whole, and therefore on a certain type of *dependence* with respect to the whole. The history of philosophy, for example, is not an independent history by divine right: the right of this history to exist as a specific history is determined by the articulating relations, i.e., relations of relative effectivity, which exist within the whole. The specificity of these times and histories is therefore *differential*, since it is based on the differential relations between the different levels within the whole: the mode and degree of *independence* of each time and history is therefore necessarily determined by the mode and degree of *dependence* of each level within the set of articulations of the whole. The conception of the 'relative' independence of a history and of a level can therefore never be reduced to the positive affirmation of an independence *in vacuo*, nor even to the mere negation of a dependence in itself; the conception of this 'relative' independence defines its 'relativity', i.e., the type of *dependence* that produces and establishes this mode of 'relative' independence as its necessary result; at the level of the articulation of component structures in the whole, it defines that type of dependence which produces relative independence and whose effects we can observe in the histories of the different 'levels'.

This is the principle on which is based the possibility and necessity of different *histories* corresponding respectively to each of the 'levels'. This principle justifies our speaking of an economic history, a political history, a history of religions, a history of ideologies, a history of philosophy, a history of art and a history of the sciences, without thereby evading, but on the contrary, necessarily accepting, the relative independence of each of these histories in the specific dependence which articulates each of the different levels of the social whole with the others. That is why, if we have the right to constitute these different histories, which are merely differential histories, we cannot be satisfied, as the best historians so often are today, by *observing* the existence of different times and rhythms, without relating them to the concept of their difference, i.e., to the typical dependence which establishes them in the articulation of the levels of the whole. It is not enough, therefore, to say, as modern historians do, that *there are* different periodizations for different times, that each time has its own rhythms, some short, some long; we must also think these differences in rhythm and punctuation in their foundation, in the type of articulation, displacement and torsion which harmonizes these different times with one another. To go even further, I should say that we cannot restrict ourselves to reflecting the existence of *visible* and measurable times in this way; we must, of absolute necessity, pose the question of the mode of existence of *invisible* times, of the invisible rhythms and punctuations concealed beneath the surface of each visible time. Merely reading *Capital* shows that Marx was highly sensitive to this requirement. It shows, for example, that the time of economic production is a specific time (differing according to the mode of production), but also that, as a specific time, it is a complex and non-linear time – a time of times, a complex time that cannot be *read* in the continuity of the time of life or clocks, but has to be *constructed* out of the peculiar structures of production. The time of the capitalist economic production that Marx analysed must be *constructed* in its concept. The concept of this time must be constructed out of the reality of the different rhythms which punctuate the different operations of production, circulation and distribution: out of the concepts of these different operations, e.g., the difference between production time and labour time, the difference between the different cycles of production (the turnover of fixed capital, of circulating capital, of variable capital, monetary turnover, turnover of commercial capital and of finance capital, etc.). In the capitalist mode of production, therefore, the time of economic production has absolutely nothing to do with the obviousness of everyday practice's ideological time: of course, it is rooted in certain determinate sites, in biological time (certain limits in the alternation of labour and rest for human and animal labour power; certain rhythms for agricultural production) but in essence it is not at all identified with this biological time, and in no sense is it a time that can be *read immediately* in the flow of any given process. It is an invisible time, essentially illegible, as invisible and as opaque as the reality of the total capitalist production process itself. This time, as a complex 'intersection' of the different times, rhythms, turnovers, etc, that we have just discussed, is only accessible in *its concept*, which, like every concept is never immediately 'given', never *legible* in visible reality: like every concept this concept must be *produced, constructed*.

The same could be said of political time and ideological time, of the time of the theoretical (philosophy) and of the time of the scientific, let alone the time of art. Let us take an example. The time of the history of philosophy is not immediately legible either: of course, in historical chronology we do *see* philosophers *following one another*, and it would be possible to take this sequence for the history itself. Here, too, we must renounce the ideological pre-judgement of visible succession, and undertake *to construct the concept of the time of the history of philosophy*, and, in order to understand this concept, it is absolutely essential to define the specific difference of the philosophical as one of the existing cultural formations (the ideological and scientific formations); to define the philosophical as belonging to the level of the *Theoretical* as such; and to establish the differential relation of the Theoretical as such firstly to the different existing practices, secondly to ideology and finally to the scientific. To define these differential relations is to define the peculiar type of articulation of the Theoretical (philosophical) with these other realities, and therefore to define the peculiar articulation of the history of philosophy with the histories of the different practices, with the history of ideologies and the history of the sciences. But this is not enough: in order to construct the concept of the history of philosophy it is essential to define in philosophy itself the specific reality which constitutes philosophical formations as such, and to which one must refer in order to think the mere possibility of *philosophical events*. This is one of the essential tasks of any theoretical attempt to produce the concept of history: to give a rigorous definition of the *historical fact* as such. Without anticipating this investigation, I should like to point out that, in its generality, the *historical* fact, as opposed to all the other phenomena that occur in historical existence, can be defined as *a fact which causes a mutation in the existing structural relations*. In the history of philosophy it is also essential, if we are to be able to discuss it as a history, to admit that *philosophical facts, philosophical events of historical scope*, occur in it, i.e., precisely *philosophical facts* which cause real mutations in the *existing philosophical structural relations*, in this case the *existing theoretical problematic*. Obviously, these facts are not always *visible*, rather, they are sometimes the object of a real repression, a real and more or less lasting historical denegation. For·example, the mutation of the dogmatic classical problematic by Locke's empiricism is a philosophical event with historical scope, one which still dominates idealist critical philosophy today, just as it dominated the whole of the eighteenth century, Kant, Fichte and even Hegel. This historical fact and above all the length of its range (and in particular its importance for the understanding of German idealism from Kant to Hegel) is often suspected; its real profundity is rarely appreciated. Its role in the interpretation of Marxist philosophy has been absolutely decisive, and we are still largely held prisoner by it. For another example, Spinoza's philosophy introduced an unprecedented theoretical revolution in the history of philosophy, probably the greatest philosophical revolution of all time, insofar as we can regard Spinoza as Marx's only direct ancestor, from the philosophical standpoint. However, this radical revolution was the object of a massive historical repression, and Spinozist philosophy suffered much the same fate as Marxist philosophy used to and still does suffer in some countries: it served as damning evidence for a charge of 'atheism'. The insistence of the seventeenth and eighteenth century establishment's hounding of Spinoza's memory, and the distance every writer had ineluctably to take with respect to Spinoza in order to obtain the right to speak (cf. Montesquieu) are evidence both of the repulsion and the extraordinary attraction of his thought. The history of philosophy's repressed Spinozism thus unfolded as a subterranean history acting at *other sites* (*autres lieux*), in political and religious ideology (deism) and in the sciences, but not on the illuminated stage of visible philosophy. And when Spinoza re-appeared on this stage in German idealism's '*Atheismusstreit*', and then in academic interpretations, it was more or less under the aegis of a *misunderstanding*. I think I have said enough to suggest what direction the construction of the concept of history in its different domains must take; and to show that the construction of this concept incontestably produces a reality which has nothing to do with the visible sequence of events recorded by the chronicler.

We have known, since Freud, that the time of the unconscious cannot be confused with the time of biography. On the contrary, *the concept of the time of the unconscious must be constructed* in order to obtain an understanding of certain biographical traits. In exactly the same way, it is essential to construct the concepts of the different historical times which are never given in the ideological obviousness of the continuity of time (which need only be suitably divided into a good periodization to obtain the time of history), but must be constructed out of the differential nature and differential articulation of their objects in the structure of the whole. Are more examples necessary to convince us of this? Read Michel Foucault's remarkable studies in the 'history of madness', or the 'birth of clinical medicine', and you will see the distance between the elegant sequences of the official chronicle, in which a discipline or a society merely reflect its good conscience, i.e., the mask of its bad conscience – and the absolutely unexpected temporality that constitutes the essence of the process of constitution and development of those cultural formations: there is nothing in true history which allows it to be read in the ideological continuum of a linear time that need only be punctuated and divided; on the contrary, it has its extremely complex and peculiar temporality which is, of course, utterly paradoxical in comparison with the disarming simplicity of ideological pre-judgement. An understanding of the history of cultural formations such as those of 'madness' and of the origins of the 'clinical gaze' (*regard clinique*) in medicine, presupposes a vast effort not of abstraction but *in* abstraction, in order to construct and identify the object itself, and in order to construct from this *the concept of its history*. This is antipodal to the empirically visible history in which the time of all histories is the simple time of continuity and in which the 'content' is the vacuity of events that occur in it which one later tries to determine with dividing procedures in order to 'periodize' that continuity. Instead of these categories, continuity and discontinuity, which summarize the banal mystery of all history, we are dealing with infinitely more complex categories specific to each type of history, categories in which new logics come into play, in which, naturally, the Hegelian schemata, which are merely the sublimation of the categories of the 'logic of movement and time', no longer have more than a highly approximate value, and even this *only on condition that they are used approximately (indicatively) in accordance with their approximate nature* – for if we had to take these Hegelian categories for adequate categories, their use would become theoretically absurd, and practically either vain or disastrous.

This specific reality of the complex historical time of the levels of the whole can, paradoxically, be tested experimentally by trying to take an 'essential section' through this specific and complex time, the crucial experiment of the *contemporaneity* structure. A historical break of this kind, even if it is applied to a break in a periodization sanctioned by the phenomena of a major mutation either in the economic or the political order, never produces a 'present' with a structure of so-called 'contemporaneity', a presence that corresponds to the expressive or spiritual type of unity of the whole. The co-existence which can be observed in the 'essential section' does not reveal any omnipresent essence which is also the present of each of these 'levels'. The break 'valid' for a determinate level, political or economic, the break that would correspond to an 'essential section' in politics, for example, does not correspond to anything of the kind in the other levels, the economic, the ideological, the aesthetic, the philosophical or the scientific – which live in different times and know other breaks, other rhythms and other punctuations. The present of one level is, so to speak, the absence of another, and this co-existence of a 'presence' and absences is simply the effect of the structure of the whole in its articulated decentricity. What is thus grasped as absences in a localized presence is precisely the non-localization of the structure of the whole, or more accurately, the type of effectivity peculiar to the structure of the whole on its 'levels' (which are themselves structured) and on the 'elements' of those levels. What the impossibility of this essential section reveals, even in the absences it shows up negatively, is the form of historical existence peculiar to a social formation arising from a determinate mode of production, the peculiar type of what Marx calls the development process of the determinate mode of production. And this process, too, is what Marx, discussing the capitalist mode of production in *Capital*, calls the type of *intertwining of the different times* (and here he only mentions the economic level), i.e., the type of 'dislocation' (*décalage*) and torsion of the different temporalities produced by the different levels of the structure, the complex combination of which constitutes the peculiar time of the process's development.

To avoid any misunderstanding of what I have just said, I think it is necessary to add the following comments.

The theory of historical time which I have just outlined allows us to establish the possibility of a history of the different levels considered in their 'relative' autonomy. But we should not deduce from this that history is made up of the juxtaposition of different 'relatively' autonomous histories, different historical temporalities, living the same historical time, some in a short-term mode, others in a long-term mode. In other words, once we have rejected the ideological model of a continuous time subject to essential sections into presents, we must avoid substituting for this idea another which, although different in style, in fact surreptitiously restores the same ideology of time. There can therefore be no question of relating the diversity of the different temporalities to a single ideological base time, or of measuring their *dislocation* against the line of a single continuous reference time, remaining content, therefore, to think these dislocations as backwardnesses or forwardnesses *in time*, i.e., in the ideological reference time. If we try to make an 'essential section' in our new conception, we find that it is impossible. But this does not mean that we are dealing with an *uneven section*, a stepped or multiply toothed section in which the forwardness or backwardness of one time with respect to another is illustrated in temporal space in the way that the lateness or earliness of trains are illustrated in the SNCF's notice-boards by a spatial forwardness or backwardness. If we were to accept this, we should relapse, as even the best of our historians usually do, into the trap of the ideology of history in which forwardness and backwardness are merely variants of the reference continuity and not the effects of the structure of the whole. We must break with all the forms of this ideology if we are to be able to relate the phenomena *observed* by the historians themselves correctly *to their concepts*, to the concept of the history of the mode of production considered – and not to any homogeneous and continuous ideological time.

This conclusion is absolutely crucial if we are to establish the status of a whole series of notions which have a major strategic role in the language of this century's economic and political thought, e.g., the notions of *unevenness of development*, of *survivals*, of *backwardness* (in consciousness) in Marxism itself, or the notion of '*under-development*' in contemporary economic and political practice. Where these notions are concerned, therefore, we must be thoroughly precise as to the meaning we can give this concept of differential temporality, for they have far-reaching consequences in practice.

*

In order to respond to this point we must once again purify our concept of the theory of history, and purify it radically, of any contamination by the obviousness of empirical history, since we know that this 'empirical history' is merely the bare face of the empiricist ideology of history. This empiricist temptation is enormous, but it is as lightly borne by the ordinary man and even the historian as the inhabitants of this planet bear the weight of the enormous layer of air that crushes them. In view of this, we must clearly and unequivocally see and understand that the *concept of history* can no longer be empirical, i.e., *historical* in the ordinary sense, that, as Spinoza has already put it, *the concept dog cannot bark*. We must grasp in all its rigour the absolute necessity of liberating the theory of history from any compromise with 'empirical' temporality, with the ideological concept of time which underlies and overlies it, or with the ideological idea that the theory of history, *as history*, could be subject to the 'concrete' determinations of 'historical time' on the pretext that this 'historical time' might constitute its object.

We must have no illusions as to the incredible power of this prejudice, which still dominates us all, which is the basis for contemporary historicism and which would have us confuse the object of knowledge with the real object by attributing to the object of knowledge the same 'qualities' as the real object of which it is the knowledge. The knowledge of history is no more historical than the knowledge of sugar is sweet. But before this simple principle can 'finally assert itself' in our consciousnesses, we shall no doubt need a whole 'history'. We must therefore be content for the moment to clarify a few points. We should indeed be relapsing into the ideology of a homogeneous-continuous/self-contemporaneous time if we related the different temporalities I have just discussed to this single, identical time, as so many discontinuities in its continuity; these temporalities would then be thought as the backwardnesses, forwardnesses, survivals or unevennesses of development that can be assigned to this time. In fact, despite any dene-gations, this would be to institute a reference time in the continuity of which we should measure these unevennesses. On the contrary, we must regard these differences in temporal structure as *and only as*, so many objective indices of the mode of articulation of the different elements or structures in the general structure of the whole. This amounts to saying that if we cannot make an 'essential section' in history, it is only in the specific unity of the complex structure of the whole that we can think the concept of these so-called backwardnesses, forwardnesses, survivals and unevennesses of development which *co-exist* in the structure of the real historical present: the present of the *conjuncture*. To speak of differential types of historicity therefore has no meaning in reference to a base time in which these back-wardnesses and forwardnesses might be measured.

This amounts to saying that, on the contrary, the ultimate meaning of the metaphorical language of backwardness, forwardness, etc., must be sought in the structure of the whole, in the site peculiar to such and such an element of such and such a structural level in the complexity of the whole. To speak of differential historical temporality therefore absolutely obliges us to situate *this site* and to think, in its peculiar articulation, the *function* of such an element or such a level in the current configuration of the whole; it is to determine the relation of articulation of this element as a function of other elements, of this structure as a function of other structures, it obliges us to define what has been called its *overdetermination* or *underdetermination* as a function of the structure of the determination of the whole, it obliges us to define what might be called, in another language, the *index of determination*, the *index of effectivity* currently attributable to the element or structure in question in the general structure of the whole. By *index of effectivity* we may understand the character of more or less dominant or subordinate and therefore more or less 'paradoxical' determination of a given element or structure in the current mechanism of the whole. And this is nothing but the theory of the conjuncture indispensable to the theory of history.

I do not want to go any further with this analysis, although it has still hardly been elaborated at all. I shall restrict myself to drawing two conclusions from these principles, one of which concerns the concepts of synchrony and diachrony, the other the concept of history.

(1) If what I have just said has any objective meaning, it is clear that the synchrony/diachrony opposition is the site of a misconception, since to take it for a knowledge would be to remain in an epistemological vacuum, i.e. – ideology abhorring a vacuum – in an ideological fullness, precisely in the fullness of the ideological conception of a history whose time is continuous-homogeneous/self-contemporaneous. If this ideological conception of history falls, this opposition falls with it. However, something of it remains: the aim of the epistemological operation of which this opposition is an unconscious reflection, precisely this epistemological operation itself, once it has been stripped of its ideological reference. What the synchrony aims at has nothing to do with the *temporal* presence of the object as a *real object*, but on the contrary, concerns a different type of presence, and the presence of a *different object*: not the temporal presence of the concrete object, not the historical time of the historical presence of the historical object, but the presence (or the 'time') *of the object of knowledge of the theoretical analysis itself*, the presence of *knowledge*. The synchronic is then nothing but *the conception* of the specific relations that exist between the different elements and the different structures of the structure of the whole, it is *the knowledge* of the relations of dependence and articulation which make it an organic whole, a system. *The synchronic is eternity in Spinoza's sense*, or the adequate knowledge of a complex object by the adequate knowledge of its complexity. This is exactly what Marx is distinguishing from the concrete-real historical sequence in the words:

> How, indeed, could the single logical formula of movement, of sequence, of time, explain the body of society, in which all economic relations co-exist simultaneously and support one another? (*Poverty of Philosophy*, pp. 110–11).

If this is really what synchrony is, it has nothing to do with simple concrete temporal presence, it concerns the knowledge of the complex articulation that makes the whole a whole. It is not that concrete co-presence, but the knowledge of the complexity of the object of knowledge, which gives the knowledge of the real object.

If this is the case for synchrony, similar conclusions must be drawn where diachrony is concerned, since it is on the ideological conception of synchrony (of the contemporaneity of the essence with itself) that the ideological conception of diachrony is built. There is hardly any need to show how diachrony admits its destitution in those thinkers who assign to it the role of history.

Diachrony is reduced to the sequence of events (*à l'événementiel*), and to the effects of this sequence of events on the structure of the synchronic: the historical then becomes the unexpected, the accidental, the factually unique, arising or falling in the empty continuum of time, for purely contingent reasons. In this context, therefore, the project of a 'structural history' poses serious problems, and a laborious reflection of this can be found in the passages devoted to it by Lévi-Strauss in *Structural Anthropology*. Indeed, by what miracle could an empty time and momentary events induce de- and re-structurations of the synchronic? Once synchrony has been correctly located, diachrony loses its 'concrete' sense and nothing is left of it either but its epistemological use, on condition that it undergoes a theoretical conversion and is considered in its true sense as a category not of the concrete but of knowing. Diachrony is then merely the false name for the *process*, or for what Marx called the *development of forms*.[8] But here too we are *within knowledge*, in the process of knowledge, not in the development of the real-concrete.[9]

(2) I now come to the concept of historical time. To define it strictly, one must accept the following condition. As this concept can only be based on the complex and differentially articulated structure in dominance of the social totality that constitutes the social formation arising from a determinate mode of production, it can only be assigned a content as a function of the structure of that totality, considered either as a whole, or in its different 'levels'. In particular, it is only possible to give a content to the concept of historical time by defining historical time as the specific form of existence of the social totality under consideration, an existence in which different structural levels of temporality interfere, because of the peculiar relations of correspondence, non-correspondence, articulation, dislocation and torsion which obtain, between the different 'levels' of the whole in accordance with its general structure. It needs to be said that, just as there is no production in general, there is no history in general, but only specific structures of historicity, based in the last resort on the specific structures of the different modes of production, specific structures of historicity which, since they are merely the existence of determinate social formations (arising from

---

[8] Cf. Part I, section 13.

[9] To avoid any misunderstanding, I should add that this critique of the latent empiricism which haunts the common use of the *bastard* concept of 'diachrony' today obviously does not apply to the *reality* of historical transformations, e.g., the transition from one mode of production to another. If the aim is to *designate* this reality (the fact of the real transformation of structures) as 'the diachrony', this is merely to apply the term to the historical itself (which is never purely static) or, by making a distinction within the historical, to what is *visibly* transformed. But once the aim is to think the concept of these transformations, we are no longer in the real (the 'diachronic') but in knowledge, in which – insofar as the *real* 'diachronic' itself is concerned – the epistemological dialectic that has just been set out comes into play: the concept and the 'development of its forms'. On this point cf. Balibar's essay below.

specific modes of production), articulated as social wholes, have no meaning except as a function of the essence of those totalities, i.e., of the essence of their peculiar complexity.

This definition of historical time by its *theoretical* concept is aimed directly at historians and their practice. For it should draw their attention to the empiricist ideology which, with a few exceptions, overwhelmingly dominates every variety of history (whether it be history in the wide sense or specialized economic, social or political history, the history of art, literature, philosophy, the sciences, etc.). To put it crudely, history lives in the illusion that it can do without *theory* in the strong sense, without a theory of its object and therefore without a definition of its theoretical object. What acts as its theory, what it sees as taking the place of this theory is its *methodology*, i.e., the rules that govern its effective practices, practices centred around the scrutiny of documents and the establishment of facts. What it sees as taking the place of its theoretical object is its 'concrete' object. History therefore takes its methodology for the theory it lacks, and it takes the 'concrete' of the concrete obviousnesses of ideological time for its theoretical object. This dual confusion is typical of an empiricist ideology. What history lacks is a conscious and courageous confrontation of one of the essential problems of any science whatsoever: the problem of the nature and constitution of its *theory*, by which I mean the theory within the science itself, the system of theoretical concepts on which is based every method, and every practice, even the experimental method and practice, and which simultaneously defines its theoretical object. But with a few exceptions historians have not posed history's vital and urgent problem, the problem of its *theory*. And, as inevitably happens, the place left empty by scientific theory has been occupied by an ideological theory whose harmful influence can be shown in detail precisely at the level of the historian's methodology.

The object of history as a science therefore has the same kind of theoretical existence and occupies the same theoretical level as the object of Marx's political economy. The only difference that can be established between the theory of political economy, of which *Capital* is an example, and the theory of history as a science, lies in the fact that the theory of political economy only considers one relatively autonomous component of the social totality, whereas the theory of history in principle takes the complex totality as such for its object. Other than this difference, there can be no distinction between the science of political economy and the science of history, from a theoretical view-point.

The opposition often suggested between the 'abstract' character of *Capital* and the supposedly 'concrete' character of history as a science is purely and simply a misunderstanding, but one which is worth discussing, for it has a special place in the realm of the prejudices which govern us. It is true that the theory of political economy is worked out and developed by the investigation of a raw material provided in the last resort by the practices of real concrete history; it is true that it can and must be realized in what are called 'concrete' economic analyses, relating to some given conjuncture or given period of a given social formation; and these truths are exactly mirrored in the fact that the theory of history, too, is worked out and developed by the investigation of a raw material provided by real concrete history, and that it, too, is realized in the 'concrete analysis' of 'concrete situations'. The misunderstanding lies entirely in the fact that history hardly exists other than in this second form, as the 'application' of a theory . . . which does not exist in any real sense, and that therefore the 'applications' of the theory of history somehow occur behind this absent theory's back and are naturally mistaken for it . . . if they do not depend (for they do need a minimum of theory to exist) on more or less ideological outlines of theories. We must take seriously *the fact that the theory of history, in the strong sense, does not exist*, or hardly exists as far as historians are concerned, that the concepts of existing history are therefore nearly always 'empirical' concepts, more or less in search of their theoretical basis – 'empirical', i.e., cross-bred with a powerful strain of an ideology concealed behind its 'obviousnesses'. This is the case with the best historians, who can be distinguished from the rest precisely by their concern for theory, but who seek this theory at a level on which it cannot be found, at the level of historical *methodology*, which cannot be defined without the *theory* on which it is based.

On the day that history also exists as theory in the sense defined, its dual existence as theoretical science and empirical science will pose no more problems than does the dual existence of the Marxist theory of political economy as theoretical science and empirical science. On that day, the theoretical imbalance between the banal opposition of the abstract science of political economy and the supposedly 'concrete' science of history will disappear, and along with it all the religious dreams and rituals of the resurrection of the dead and the communion of saints which, one hundred years after Michelet, some historians still spend their time celebrating, not in the catacombs but in today's public places.

I have one more word to say on this subject. The present confusion between history as theory of history and history as supposed 'science of the concrete', history trapped in the empiricism of its object – and the confrontation of this 'concrete' empirical history with the 'abstract' theory of political economy, give rise to a significant number of conceptual confusions and false problems. It could even be said that this misunderstanding itself *produces* ideological concepts, whose function it is to *fill in the gap*, i.e., the vacuum, between the theoretical part of existing history on the one hand and empirical history on the other (which is existing history only too often). I do not want to discuss each of these concepts one by one, another book would be necessary to do so. I shall point out three of them as examples: the classical oppositions: essence/phenomena, necessity/contingency, and the 'problem' of the action of the individual in history.

According to the economistic or mechanistic hypothesis, the role of the essence/phenomena opposition is to explain the non-economic as a phenomenon of the economic, which is its essence. In this operation, the theoretical (and the 'abstract') is surreptitiously substituted for the economy (since we have its theory in *Capital*) and the empirical or 'concrete' for the non-economic, i.e., for politics, ideology, etc. The essence/phenomena opposition performs this role well enough so long as we regard the 'phenomena' as the empirical and concrete, and the essence as the non-empirical, as the abstract, as the truth of the phenomenon. The result is to set up an absurd relationship between the theoretical (the economic) and the empirical (the non-economic) by a change in partners which compares the knowledge of one object with the existence of another – which is to commit us to a fallacy.

The necessity/contingency or necessity/accident oppositions are of the same kind and have the same function: to fill in the gap between the theoretical part of one object (e.g., the economy) and the non-theoretical part, the empirical part of another (the non-economic, in which the economy 'asserts itself': the 'circumstances', 'individuality', etc.). To say, for example, that necessity 'asserts itself' amid the contingent givens and diverse circumstances, etc., is to set up an astonishing mechanism in which two realities with no direct relationship are compared. 'Necessity', in this case, designates a *knowledge* (e.g., the law of determination in the last instance by the economy), and the 'circumstances' *what is not known*. But instead of comparing a knowledge with a non-knowledge, the non-knowledge is put into parenthesis and the *empirical existence* of the unknown object (called the 'circumstances' or contingent givens, etc.) is substituted for it – which allows the *terms to be crossed*, achieving a fallacious short-circuit in which the *knowledge* of a determinate object (economic necessity) is compared with the empirical existence of a different object (the 'circumstances', political or otherwise, amid which this 'necessity' is said to 'assert itself').

The most famous form of this fallacy is found in the 'problem' of the 'role of the individual in history' . . . a tragic argument which consists of a comparison between the theoretical part or knowledge of a determinate object (e.g., the economy) which represents the essence of which the other objects (the political, the ideological, etc.) are regarded as the phenomena – and that fiendishly important (politically!) empirical reality, individual action. Here again we are dealing with a short-circuit between crossed terms which it is illegitimate to compare: for to do so is to compare the knowledge of one definite object with the empirical existence of another! I do not want to insist on the difficulties which these concepts put in the way of their users, who cannot escape them in practice except by questioning critically the Hegelian (and more generally classical) philosophical concepts which are fish in the water of this fallacy. But I should like to signal that this false problem of the 'role of the individual in history' is nevertheless an index to a true problem, one which arises by right in the theory of history: the problem of the concept of *the historical forms of existence of individuality. Capital* gives us the principles necessary for the posing of this problem. It defines for the capitalist mode of production the different forms of individuality required and produced by that mode according to functions, of which the individuals are 'supports' (*Träger*), in the division of labour, in the different 'levels' of the structure. Of course, even here, the mode of historical existence of individuality in a given mode of production is not legible to the naked eye in 'history'; its concept, too, must therefore be *constructed*, and like every concept it contains a number of surprises, the most striking of which is the fact that it is nothing like the false obviousnesses of the 'given' – which is merely the mask of the current ideology. The concept of the variations in the mode of historical existence of individuality opens the way to what is really left of the '*problem*' of '*the role of the individual in history*', which, posed in its familiar form, is a false problem, false because unbalanced, theoretically 'hybrid', since it compares the theory of one object with the empirical existence of another. So long as the real theoretical problem has not been posed (the problem of the forms of historical existence of individuality), we shall be beating about in the dark – like Plekhanov, who ransacked Louis XV's bed to prove that the secrets of the fall of the *Ancien Régime* were not hidden there. As a general rule, concepts are not hidden in beds.

Once we have, at least in principle, elucidated the specificity of the Marxist concept of historical time – once we have criticized as ideologies the commonsense notions that encumber the *word* '*history*', we can better understand the different effects that this misunderstanding about history has had on the interpretation of Marx. An understanding of the main confusions *ipso facto* reveals to us the pertinence of certain essential distinctions which have often been misconceived, despite the fact that they appear in so many words in *Capital*.

In the first place, it is clear why the mere project of 'historicizing' classical political economy leads to the theoretical impasse of a fallacy in which the classical economic categories, far from being thought within the theoretical concept of history, are merely projected onto the ideological concept of history. This procedure restores to us the classical schema, once again linked with the misconception of Marx's specificity: all that Marx did was to seal the union of classical political economy on the one hand, and the Hegelian dialectical method (a theoretical concentrate of the Hegelian concept of history) on the other. But this leads directly to the foisting of a pre-existing and exoteric method onto a pre-determined object, i.e., to the theoretically dubious union of a method defined independently of its object, whose agreement with its object can only be sealed against the common ideological background of a misunderstanding which marks Hegelian historicism as much as economic eternalism. And it follows that the two terms of the eternity/history opposition derive from a common problematic, Hegelian 'historicism' being only the historicized counter-connotation of economistic 'eternalism'.

But, *in the second place*, we also see the meaning of the still unclosed debates about the relation between economic theory and history in *Capital* itself. These debates have lasted until today largely under the influence of a confusion between the status of economic *theory* itself and that of history. When, in *Anti-Dühring* (London 1959, p. 204), Engels writes that 'Political economy is . . . essentially a *historical* science,' because 'it deals with material which is *historical, that is, constantly changing*,' he touches the exact spot of the ambiguity: the word '*historical*' may either fall towards the Marxist concept or towards the ideological concept of history, according to whether this word designates the *object of knowledge* of a theory of history, or, on the contrary, the real object of which this theory gives the knowledge. We have every right to say that the theory of Marxist political economy derives from the Marxist theory of history, as one of its regions; but we might also think that the theory of political economy is affected even in its concepts by the peculiar *quality* of real history (its 'material' which is '*changing*'). Engels rushes us into this latter interpretation in a number of astonishing texts which introduce history (in the empiricist-ideological sense) even into Marx's theoretical categories. I am referring particularly to his insistence that Marx could not produce real *scientific definitions* in his theory because of the properties of his real object, because of the *moving, changing nature* of a *historical reality which in essence rebels against any treatment by* definitions, *whose fixed and 'eternal' forms can only betray the perpetual mobility of historical development.*

In his Preface to Volume Three of *Capital*, Engels, quoting Fireman's criticisms, writes:

They rest upon the *misunderstanding* that Marx wishes to *define* where he only *develops*, and that in general one might expect fixed, cut-to-measure once and for all applicable definitions in Marx's works. It is self-evident that where things and their inter-relations are conceived, not as fixed, but as changing, their mental reflections, *the concepts, are likewise subject to change and transformation*; and they are not encapsulated in rigid definitions, but are *developed* in their *historical* or *logical* process of formation. This makes clear, of course, why in the beginning of Volume One Marx proceeds from simple commodity production as the *historical* premise, ultimately arriving from this basis at *capital* . . . (*Capital*, Vol. III, pp. 13–14 – modified).

The same theme recurs in the preparatory notes for *Anti-Dühring* (p. 470):

To science definitions are worthless because always inadequate. The only *real* definition is the *development* of the *thing* itself, but *this is no longer a definition*. To know and show what life is we must examine all forms of life and present them in their inter-connexion. On the other hand, *for ordinary purposes*, a brief exposition of the commonest and at the same time most significant features of a so-called definition is often useful and even necessary, and can do no harm if no more is expected of it than it can convey (italics, L.A.).

Unfortunately, these texts leave no room for ambiguity, since they go so far as to designate quite precisely the site of the '*misunderstanding*' and to formulate its terms. All the characters in this misunderstanding are on stage here, each playing the part ascribed to it by the effect expected of this theatre. We only have to change their places for them to admit the role that has been assigned to them, abandon it and begin to speak to a quite different text. The whole misunderstanding in this reasoning lies in fact in the fallacy which confuses the theoretical development of concepts with the genesis of real history. But Marx carefully distinguished between these two *orders*, when, in the *1857 Introduction*, he showed that it was impossible to institute any one-to-one correlation between the terms which feature in the order of succession of concepts in the discourse of scientific proof on the one hand, and those which feature in the genetic order of real history on the other. Here Engels postulates precisely such an impossible correlation, unhesitatingly identifying 'logical' development and 'historical' development. And with extraordinary honesty he points out the theoretical precondition for this identification: the affirmation that these two developments are identical in order depends on the fact that the necessary concepts of any theory of history are affected in their conceptual substance, by the *properties* of the *real* object. 'Where things . . . are conceived . . . as changing, their mental reflections, *the concepts, are likewise subject to change and transformation*.' In order to be able to identify the development of the concepts and the development of real history, he therefore had to identify the object of knowledge with the real object, and to subject the concepts to the real determination of real history. In this way, Engels applies to the concepts of the theory of history a *coefficient of mobility* borrowed directly from the concrete empirical sequence (from the ideology of history), transposing the 'real-concrete' into the 'thought-concrete' and the historical as real change into the concept itself. Given these premisses, the argument is bound to conclude that every definition is unscientific: '*to science, definitions are worthless*', since '*the only real definition is the development of the thing itself, but this is no longer a definition*'. Once again the *real* thing has been substituted for the concept and the development of the real thing (i.e., the real history of concrete genesis) has been substituted for the '*development of forms*', which was explicitly described, in the *Introduction* as well as in *Capital*, as occurring exclusively in knowledge and concerning exclusively the necessary order of appearance and disappearance of concepts in the discourse of the scientific proof. Need I demonstrate that Engels's interpretation contains a theme we have already encountered in his answer to Conrad Schmidt: the theme of the original weakness of the concept? If 'to science, definitions are worthless', it is because they are '*always inadequate*'; in other words, the concept is in essence at fault, and this fault is inscribed in its very conceptual nature: his awareness of this original sin forces him to relinquish any claim to *define* the real, which 'defines' itself in the historical production of the forms of its genesis. If the question of the status of the *definition*, i.e., of the concept, is posed from this starting point, there is no alternative but to confer on it a role which is quite different from the role it claims theoretically: a 'practical' role, good enough for 'ordinary purposes', a role of general designation without any theoretical function. Paradoxically, it is not without interest to note that Engels, after beginning by crossing the terms implied in his question, is led to conclude with a definition whose meaning is crossed, too, i.e., dislocated (*décalé*) with respect to the object it is aimed at, since in this purely practical (ordinary) definition of the role of the scientific concept he also gives us the starting-point for a theory of one of the functions of the *ideological* concept: its function as a practical allusion and index.

This is where we are led by ignoring the basic distinction Marx was careful to draw between the object of knowledge and the real object, between the 'development of forms' of the concept in knowledge and the development of the real categories in concrete history: to an empiricist ideology of knowledge, and to the identification of the *logical* and the *historical* in *Capital* itself. It should hardly surprise us that so many interpreters go round in circles in the question that hangs on this definition, if it is true that all problems concerned with the relation between the logical and the historical in *Capital* presuppose a *non-existent relation*. Whether this relation is imagined as one which brings the terms featured in the two orders of development (the development of the concept; the development of real history) into *direct* one-to-one correspondence; or whether the same relation is imagined as one which brings the terms of the two orders of development into *inverse* correspondence (the basis for the theses of Della Volpe and Pietranera analysed by Rancière),[10] there remains the hypothesis of a relation *where no relation exists*. Two conclusions can be drawn from this error. The first is simply practical: the difficulties encountered in the solution of this problem are serious ones, indeed insurmountable ones: if it is not always possible to solve a problem that does exist, we can rest assured that it is never possible to solve *a problem that does not exist*.[11] The second is

[10] See *Lire le Capital*, first edition, Paris 1965, Vol. I, pp. 170ff.

[11] We are indebted to Kant for the suspicion that *problems which do not exist* may give rise to massive theoretical efforts, and the more or less rigorous production of solutions as fantastic as their object, for his philosophy may be broadly conceived as a theory of the possibility of the existence of '*sciences*' *without objects* (rational metaphysics, cosmology and psychology). If it so happens that the reader does not have the heart to tackle Kant, he can consult directly the producers of 'sciences' without objects: e.g., theologians, most social psychologists, some 'psychologists', etc. I should also add that in certain circumstances, the theoretical and ideological conjuncture may make these 'sciences without objects' produce or contain, during the elaboration of the theory of their supposed 'objects', the theoretical

theoretical: an imaginary solution is required for an imaginary problem, and not just any imaginary solution but *the* imaginary solution required by the (imaginary) posing of this imaginary problem. Every imaginary (ideological) posing of a problem (which may be imaginary, too) in fact carries it in a determinate problematic, which defines both the possibility and the form of the posing of this problem. This problematic *recurs* as its mirror-image in the solution given to this problem by virtue of the mirror action peculiar to the ideological imagination (cf. Part One); if it is not in fact found directly as such in the aforesaid solution, it will emerge elsewhere, openly, when it is explicitly in question, in the latent 'theory of knowledge' which underlies the identification of the historical and the logical: an *empiricist* ideology of knowledge. It is no accident therefore that we see Engels literally precipitated by his *question* into this empiricist temptation, nor that, in a different way, Della Volpe and his pupils support their thesis of the *inverse* identification of the historical and logical orders in *Capital* by arguing a theory of 'historical abstraction', which is a higher form of historicist empiricism.

To return to *Capital*, the effect of the mistake I have just pointed out, which postulates the imaginary existence of a non-existent relation, is to make a *different relation* invisible, a relation which is legitimate because it exists and is established by right between the theory of the economy and the theory of history. If the first relation (theory of the economy and concrete history) was imaginary, the second relation (theory of the economy and theory of history) is a true *theoretical* relation. Why has it remained until now, if not invisible, at least opaque to us? Because the first relation had the advantage of 'obviousness', i.e., of the empiricist temptations of the historians who, reading pages of 'concrete' history in *Capital* (the struggle for the reduction of the working day, the transition from manufacture to modern industry, primitive accumulation, etc.), felt in some sense 'at home' in it and therefore posed the problem of economic theory as a function of the existence of this 'concrete' *history*, without feeling any need to pose the question of its status. They gave an empiricist interpretation of analyses of Marx's which, far from being historical analyses in the strict sense, i.e., analyses sustained by the development of the concept of history, are more the half-finished materials *for a history* (cf. Balibar's paper) than a real *historical* treatment of those *materials*. They used the presence of these half-elaborated materials as an argument for an ideological concept of history, and therefore posed the question of this ideology of 'concrete' history for the 'abstract' theory of political economy: hence both the fascination of *Capital* for them, and their unease before a discourse which seemed to them to be 'speculative' in many places. The economists had much the same reaction, torn between (concrete) economic history and (abstract) economic

---

forms of existing rationality: e.g., in the Middle Ages, theology *undoubtedly* contained and elaborated the *forms* of the theoretical then in existence.

theory. Both hoped to find in *Capital* what they sought, but they also found something else which they had not 'sought' and which they therefore tried to *reduce*, by posing the imaginary problem of the relation, one-to-one or otherwise, between the abstract order of concepts and the concrete order of history. They did not see that what they had *found* did not answer their question but a quite different question, which, of course, should have given the lie to the ideological illusion of the concept of history which they had brought with them and projected into their reading of *Capital*. They did not see that the 'abstract' theory of political economy is the theory of a region which, as a region (level or instance) is an organic component of the object of the theory of history itself. They did not see that history features in *Capital* as an object of theory, not as a real object, as an 'abstract' (conceptual) object and not as a real-concrete object; and that the chapters in which Marx applies the first stages of a historical treatment either to the struggles to shorten the working day, or to primitive capitalist accumulation refer to the theory of history as their principle, to the construction of the *concept* of history and of its 'developed forms', of which the economic theory of the capitalist mode of production constitutes one determinate 'region'.

One word more on one of the current effects of this misunderstanding. In it we have one of the origins of the interpretation of *Capital* as a 'theoretical model', a formula whose use can, *a priori*, always be seen as a symptom, in the precise clinical sense of the word, of the empiricist misunderstanding about the object of a given knowledge. This conception of theory as a 'model' is in fact only possible on peculiarly ideological conditions; firstly that the distance separating theory from the empirical concrete is included *within* theory itself; and secondly, equally ideologically, that this distance is itself conceived as an *empirical* distance, and hence as belonging to the concrete itself, which one then has the privilege (i.e., the banality) of defining as what is 'always-richer-and-more-living-than-theory'. No doubt this proclamation of the exalted status of the superabundance of 'life' and 'concreteness', of the superiority of the world's imagination and the green leaves of action over the poverty of grey theory, contains a serious lesson in intellectual modesty, healthy for the right (presumptuous and dogmatic) ears. But we are also aware of the fact that the concrete and life may be the pretext for facile chatter which serves to mask either apologetic ends (a god, whatever his plumage, is always lining his nest with the feathers of the superabundance, i.e. 'transcendence' of the 'concrete' and 'life') or mere intellectual laziness. What matters is precisely the *use* made of this kind of endlessly repeated commonplace about the concrete's surplus of transcendence. But in the conception of knowledge as a 'model', we find the real and the concrete intervening to enable us to think the relation, i.e., the distance, between the 'concrete' and theory as both *within* theory itself and *within* the real itself, not as in a real outside this real object, knowledge of which is produced precisely by theory, but as *within this real object itself*, as a relation of the *part* to the *whole*, of a 'partial' part to a superabundant whole (cf. Part One, section 10). The inevitable result of this operation is to make theory seem one empirical instrument among others, in other words, to reduce any theory of knowledge as a model directly to what it is: a form of theoretical pragmatism.

We have therefore obtained, with the last effect of this mistake, a precise principle of understanding and criticism: it is this establishment of a relation of one-to-one correspondence in the real of the object between a theoretical ensemble (the theory of political economy) and the *real* empirical ensemble (concrete history) of which the first ensemble is the knowledge, which has given rise to misconstructions where the question of the 'relations' between 'Logic' and 'history' in *Capital* is concerned. The most serious of these misconstructions is the blinding effect of the question: it has sometimes prevented any perception that *Capital* really does *contain* a theory of history which is indispensable for any understanding of the theory of the economy.

Chapter 5
Marxism is not a Historicism

But this brings us to one last misunderstanding, of the same breed but perhaps even more serious, for it does not only involve our reading of *Capital*, or Marxist philosophy, but also the relationship between *Capital* and Marxist philosophy, hence the relationship between historical materialism and dialectical materialism – i.e., the meaning of Marx's work as a whole – and, lastly, the relationship between real history and Marxist theory. This misunderstanding stems from the *oversight* which *sees* in Marxism a historicism, and the most radical historicism of all, an *'absolute historicism'*. This claim presents the relationship Marxist theory has with *real history* in the form of the relationship between the science of history and Marxist philosophy.

I should like to suggest that, from the theoretical stand-point, Marxism is no more a historicism than it is a humanism (cf. *For Marx*, pp. 219ff); that in many respects both historicism and humanism depend on the same ideological problematic; and that, *theoretically speaking*, Marxism is, in a single movement and by virtue of the unique epistemological rupture which established it, an anti-humanism and an anti-historicism. Strictly speaking, I ought to say an a-humanism and an a-historicism. But in order to give these terms all the weight of a declaration of rupture which far from going without saying is, on the contrary, very hard to accept, I have deliberately used this doubly *negative* formula (anti-humanism, anti-historicism) instead of a simple privative form, for the latter is not sufficiently imperative to repel the humanist and historist assault which, in some circles, has threatened Marxism continuously for the past forty years.

We know precisely what were the circumstances in which this humanist and historicist interpretation of Marx was born, and what recent circumstances have reinvigorated it. It was born out of a vital reaction against the mechanism and economicism of the Second International, in the period just preceding and, above all, in the years just following the 1917 Revolution. In this respect it has real historical merits; just as the recent renaissance of this interpretation after the Twentieth Congress's denunciation of the dogmatic errors and crimes of the 'Cult of Personality' has real historical sanction, though in a somewhat different way. This recent reinvigoration is merely a repetition and usually a generous or skilful but 'rightist' misappropriation of a historical reaction which then had the force of a protest that was revolutionary in spirit, although 'leftist'. It cannot therefore provide the norm with which we judge the historical significance of its former state. The themes of a revolutionary humanism and historicism emerged from the German Left, initially from Rosa Luxemburg and Mehring, and then, after the 1917 Revolution, from a whole series of theoreticians, some of whom, like Korsch, were lost later, while others, like Lukács, played an important part, or even, like Gramsci, a very important part. We know the terms in which Lenin judged this movement of 'leftist' reaction against the mechanistic conventionality of the Second International: he condemned its theoretical fables and its political tactics (cf. *Left-Wing Communism, an Infantile Disorder*), while recognizing that it did then contain authentically revolutionary elements, for example in Rosa Luxemburg and in Gramsci. One day we shall have to illuminate this whole past. Such a historical and theoretical study is indispensable if we are to distinguish rightly in our present itself between the real and ghostly characters, and if we are to establish on indisputable bases the results of a critique which was then conducted amidst the confusions of a battle in which the reaction against the mechanicism and fatalism of the Second International necessarily took the form of an appeal to the consciousness and wills of men, to *make* the revolution at last which history had given them to make. When this has been done, we may perhaps be a little clearer about the paradoxical title of a famous article in which Gramsci celebrated 'The Revolution against *Capital*', proclaiming brutally that the anti-capitalist revolution of 1917 had had to be made *against* Karl Marx's *Capital* by the voluntary and conscious action of men, of the masses and the Bolsheviks, and not by virtue of a Book in which the Second International *read* the fatality of the advent of socialism as if in a Bible.[12]

Even without this scientific study of the conditions which produced the first, 'leftist' form of this humanism and historicism, we are equipped to identify in Marx what was used to authorize this interpretation, and obviously cannot but justify its recent form in the eyes of contemporary readers of Marx. We shall not be astonished to discover that the same ambiguities in formulation which fostered a mechanistic and evolutionist reading have also authorized a historicist reading: Lenin has given us enough examples of the common theoretical bases of opportunism and leftism for us not to be disconcerted by such a paradoxical coincidence.

I have referred to ambiguous formulations. Here too we have stumbled on a reality the extent of whose effects we have already registered: Marx did *produce* in his work the distinction between himself and his predecessors, but – as is the fate of all inventors – he did not think the *concept* of this dis-

[12] Gramsci: 'No, the mechanical forces never predominate in history; it is the men, the consciousnesses and the spirit which mould the external appearance and always triumph in the end. . . . The pseudo-scientists' natural law and fatal course of events has been replaced by man's tenacious will' (from a text published in *Rinascità*, 1957, pp. 149–58, quoted by Mario Tronti in *Studi Gramsciani*, Editori Riuniti, Rome, 1959, p. 306).

tinction with all the sharpness that could be desired; he did not think theoretically, or in an adequate and advanced form, either the concept or the
theoretical implications of the theoretically revolutionary step he had taken.
Sometimes, for want of anything better, he thought it partly in borrowed
concepts, particularly Hegelian ones, introducing an effect of dislocation
between the semantic field of origin from which he borrowed his concepts,
and the field of conceptual objects to which they were applied. At others he
did think this difference for itself, but only partially or as an indicative
outline, as an obstinate search for equivalents,[13] without succeeding in
directly formulating the original and strict sense of what he was producing
in the adequacy of a concept. This dislocation, which can only be revealed
and reduced by a critical reading, *is objectively part of the text of Marx's
discourse.*[14]

This, rather than any tendentiousness on their part, is the reason why so
many of Marx's inheritors and supporters have produced inaccurate estimates
of his thought, while claiming, text in hand, that they remain true *to the
letter* of what he wrote.

Here I should like to go into some detail in order to show on which
particular texts it is possible to base a *historicist* reading of Marx. I shall not
discuss Marx's Early Works or the texts of the Break (*For Marx*, p. 34), for
it is easy to prove it with them. There is no need to do violence to texts
such as the *Theses on Feuerbach* or *The German Ideology* which still rever-
berate profoundly with humanist and historicist echoes, to make them
pronounce the words demanded of them: they pronounce them of their
own accord. I shall discuss only *Capital* and the *1857 Introduction*.

The texts of Marx's which can be used to support a historicist reading
of Marx can be grouped under two heads. The first of these concerns the
definition of the conditions in which the object of any historical science is
given.

In the *1857 Introduction*, Marx writes:

> As in general in every historical social science, it must always be borne
> in mind in the march of economic categories, that *the subject, here modern
> bourgeois society, is given in the mind as well as in reality*, and that therefore
> the categories express forms of existence, conditions of existence and often
> only single aspects of this determinate society, of this subject (op. cit.,
> p. 26–7).

[13] Here we need a full study of his typical metaphors and their proliferation around a centre
which it is their mission to *focus* as they cannot call it by its right name, the name of its
concept.

[14] The fact and necessity of this dislocation are not peculiar to Marx but common to every
scientific founding moment and to all scientific production generally: a study of them is
part of a theory of the history of the production of knowledges and a history of the theoretical
the necessity for which we feel here also.

This can be compared with a passage in *Capital* (T.I., p. 87; Vol. I, p. 75):

> Man's reflection on the forms of social life, and consequently, also, his scientific analysis of those forms, takes a course directly opposite to the real movement. It begins, *post festum*, with already established givens, *with the results of the development.*

Not only do these texts suggest that the object of all of the social and historical sciences is an evolved object, a result, but also that the activity of knowledge which is applied to this object, too, is defined by *the present* of this given, by the current moment of this given. This is what some Italian Marxist interpreters, reverting to a term of Croce's, have called the category of the *'contemporaneity'* of the 'historical present', a category that defines historically and defines as historical the conditions for all knowledge concerning a historical object. As we know, this term contemporaneity can contain an ambiguity.

Marx himself seems to recognize this absolute condition in the *Introduction* a few lines earlier than the text referred to above:

> Historical development so-called generally depends on the fact that the latest form treats the past forms as stages leading up to itself, and, as it is itself only rarely and *under very specific circumstances able to criticize itself* . . . it always conceives them unilaterally. The Christian religion was only able to help in the objective understanding of earlier mythologies once it had, so to speak, *dynamei*, developed its own self-criticism to a certain level. And bourgeois economics first arrived at an understanding of the feudal, ancient and oriental economies insofar as *bourgeois society had begun its self-criticism* (p. 26).

To sum up: every science of a historical object (and political economy in particular) applies to a given, present, historical object, an object that has evolved as a result of past history. Hence every operation of knowledge, starting from the present and applied to an evolved object, is merely the projection of the present onto the past of that object. Marx is here describing the retrospection which Hegel had criticized in 'reflective' history (*Introduction to the Philosophy of History*). This inevitable retrospection is only scientific if the present attains the science of itself, criticism of itself, its self-criticism, i.e., if the present is an *'essential section'* which makes the essence *visible*.

But here the second group of texts come in, and this is the decisive point at which we might speak of a historicism in Marx. This point concerns precisely what Marx calls in the text above, *'the very specific circumstances'* of a present's self-criticism. In other words, in order that the retrospection of the self-consciousness of a present should cease to be subjective, this present must be capable of self-criticism, in order to attain the *science of itself*. But what do we find if we examine the history of political economy?

We find thinkers who have merely thought *within the limits of their present*, unable to run ahead of their times. Aristotle: with all his genius he could only write the equation: 'x objects A = y objects B' as an equation, and declare that the common substance in this equation was unthinkable since it was absurd. What prevented him from going further?

> *Aristotle could not* READ (herauslesen) out of the value form of commodities the fact that all labour is here expressed as indistinct human labour, and consequently as labour of equal quality, *because* Greek society was founded upon slave-labour, and had, therefore, for its natural basis the inequality of men and of their labour-powers (*Capital*, T.I., p. 73; Vol. I, pp. 59–60).

The present that enabled Aristotle to make this genial intuitive reading, simultaneously presented him from solving the problem he had posed.[15] The same goes for all the other great inventors of classical political economy. The Mercantilists merely reflected their own present, making their monetary theory out of the monetary policy of their time. The Physiocrats merely reflected their own present, outlining a general theory of surplus-value, but of natural surplus-value, the surplus-value of agricultural labour where the corn could be *seen* growing, and the surplus unconsumed by a corn-producing agricultural labourer could be *seen* passing into the farmer's granary: in doing this they were merely formulating the *essence of their present*, the development of agrarian capitalism in the rich plains of the Paris Basin which Engels lists: Normandy, Picardy and the Ile-de-France (*Anti-Dühring*, Part II, Ch. X, p. 336). Even they could not run ahead of their times; they only acquired knowledges insofar as their times offered these knowledges to them in a *visible* form, had produced them for their consciousnesses: in sum, they described what they *saw*. Did Smith and Ricardo go any further, did they describe what they *did not see*? Did they run ahead of their times? No. If they attained a science which was more than the mere *consciousness* of their present, it was because this consciousness contained a real *self-criticism* of this present. Why was this self-criticism possible at this point? The logic of this essentially Hegelian interpretation tempts one to answer: they attained science itself in the consciousness of their present because this consciousness was, as a consciousness, *its own self-criticism*, i.e., *a science of itself*.

In other words, what distinguished their living and lived present from all the other *presents* (of the past) was that, for the first time, this present produced in itself *its own critique of itself*, and that it therefore possessed the historical privilege of producing the science of itself precisely in the form of a self-consciousness. But this present has a name: it is the present of *absolute knowledge*, in which consciousness and science are one and the

---

[15] This is not untrue, of course, but when this limitation is directly related to 'history' there is once again a risk of merely invoking the *ideological* concept of history.

same, in which science exists in the immediate form of consciousness, and truth can be *read* openly in the phenomena, if not directly, at least with little difficulty, since the abstractions on which the whole historico-social science under consideration depends are really present in the real empirical existence of the phenomena.

Immediately after his discussion of Aristotle, Marx says:

> The secret of the expression of value, namely, that all kinds of labour are equal and equivalent because and insofar as they are human labour in general, cannot be deciphered until the notion of human equality has already acquired the fixity of a popular prejudice. This, however, is possible *only in a society in which the commodity form has become the general form of the produce of labour*, in which, consequently, the dominant social relation has become the relation between men as producers and exchangers of commodities (*Capital*, T.I, p. 75; Vol. I, p. 60).

> It requires a fully developed production of commodities before, *from experience* alone, the *scientific truth* springs up, that all the different kinds of private labour, which are carried on independently of each other, and yet intertwine as branches of the spontaneous social system of the division of labour, are continually being reduced to the quantitative proportions in which society requires them (*Capital*, T.I, p. 87; Vol. I, p. 75).

> The recent scientific discovery, that the products of labour, insofar as they are values, are but material expressions of the human labour spent in their production, makes, indeed, an epoch in the history of the development of the human race. (*Capital*, I, 86; I, 75).

This historical epoch of the foundation of the science of Political Economy does seem here to be brought into relationship with experience itself (*Erfahrung*), i.e., with the straightforward reading of the essence in the phenomenon. Or, if you prefer, the sectional reading of the essence in the slice of the present seems to be brought into relationship with the essence of a particular epoch of human history in which the generalization of commodity production and hence of the category commodity appears simultaneously as the absolute condition of possibility and the immediate given of this direct reading from experience. In fact, in the *Introduction* as well as in *Capital*, Marx says that the reality of labour in general, of abstract labour, is produced as a phenomenal reality by capitalist production. In some sense, history has reached the point and produced the exceptional, specific present in which *scientific abstractions exist in the state of empirical realities*, in which science and scientific concepts exist in the form of the *visible* part of experience as so many directly accessible *truths*.

See how this is expressed in the *Introduction*:

This abstraction of labour in general is not only the result in thought (*geistige*) *of a concrete totality of labours.* The indifference towards determinate labour is the expression of a form of society in which individuals move easily from one kind of labour to another and the determinate kinds of labour they perform are accidental, and hence indifferent to them. Here labour has become a means towards the creation of wealth in general not only as *a category* but in *reality* (*in der Wirklichkeit*) and, as a determination, *it no longer coincides with the individuals only in one particular aspect.* Such a situation is most developed in the most modern form of existence of bourgeois society – the United States of America. *There the abstraction of the categories 'labour', 'labour in general', labour* sans phrase, *modern economics' starting-point, is for the first time true in practice* (wird praktisch wahr). *Hence the simplest abstraction, which modern economics puts before all else and which expresses an ancient relation and one valid for all forms of society, nevertheless only appears in this abstraction as true in practice* (praktisch wahr) *as a category of the most modern society* (op. cit., p. 25 – italics, L.A.).

If the present of capitalist production has produced scientific truth itself in its visible reality (*Wirklichkeit, Erscheinung, Erfahrung*), in its self-consciousness, and if therefore its self-consciousness, its own phenomenon, is therefore its own self-criticism in act (*en acte*) – then it is perfectly clear why the present's retrospection of the past is no longer ideology but true knowledge, and we can appreciate the *legitimate epistemological primacy of the present over the past*:

Bourgeois society is *the most developed and the most varied* organization of production. Hence the categories which express its relations, our understanding of its articulation, at the same time *guarantee insight into the articulation and production relations of all past forms of society, with debris and elements of which bourgeois society is built, certain unsubdued remnants of which still survive inside it, and certain mere hints of which it develops to their full significance, etc. The anatomy of man is the key to the anatomy of the ape.* The *pointers* to higher species of animals in the lower species can only be understood if the higher species itself is already known. Thus the bourgeois economy provides the key to the economy of antiquity, etc. (op. cit., pp. 25-6).

We need take only one more step in the logic of absolute knowledge, think the development of a history which culminates and is fulfilled in the present of a science identical with consciousness, and reflect this result in a justified retrospection, to be able to conceive all economic (or any other) history as the development, in the Hegelian sense, of a simple, primitive, original form, e.g., value, immediately present in commodities, and to read *Capital* as a logico-historical deduction of all the economic categories from one original category, the category of value, or even the category of *labour*. Given this, the method of exposition in *Capital* would coincide with the speculative genesis of the concept. And this speculative genesis of the concept is identical with the genesis of the real concrete itself, i.e., with the process of empirical history. We should thus be dealing with an essentially Hegelian work. That is why the question of the starting-point becomes of such critical value, for everything may depend on an incorrect reading of the first chapter of Volume One. That is also why any critical reading must, as the exposition above has shown, elucidate the status of the concepts and mode of analysis of the first chapter of Volume One, if it is not to fall into this misunderstanding.

This form of historicism may be regarded as a *limit-form*, insofar as it culminates and destroys itself in the negation of absolute knowledge. As such, it may be regarded as the common matrix of the other, less peremptory and often less visible, though occasionally more 'radical', forms of historicism, because it provided us with a way to understand them.

As proof of this I shall take some contemporary forms of historicism, forms in which the work of certain interpreters of Marxism, particularly in Italy and France, is steeped, sometimes consciously, sometimes unconsciously. It is in the Italian Marxist tradition that the interpretation of Marxism as an 'absolute historicism' has the most pronounced features and the most rigorous forms: allow me to dwell on this for a few moments.

This tradition goes back to Gramsci, who inherited it largely from Labriola and Croce. I shall have to discuss Gramsci, therefore. I do not do so without profound misgivings, fearing not only that my necessarily schematic remarks may disfigure the spirit of this enormously delicate and subtle work of genius, but also that the reader may be drawn against my will to extend to Gramsci's fruitful discoveries in the field of *historical materialism*, the theoretical reservations I want to formulate with respect only to his interpretation of *dialectical materialism*. I ask therefore that this distinction be kept carefully in mind, for without it this attempt at a critical reflection will trespass beyond its limits.

First of all, I should like to draw attention to one elementary precaution: I shall refuse to take Gramsci immediately at his word on every occasion and on any pretext or text; I shall only consider his *words* when I have confirmed that they have the function of *'organic' concepts*, concepts which really belong to his most profound philosophical problematic, and not when they simply play the part of a language entrusted either with a polemical role or with a function of 'practical' designation (designation either of an *existing* problem or object, or of a *direction* to take, in order best to pose and solve a problem). For example, it would be completely unfair to Gramsci to dub him a 'humanist' and 'absolute' 'historicist' on a first reading of a polemical text such as this famous note on Bukharin (*Il materialismo storico e la filosofia di Benedetto Croce*, Einaudi, Milan, 1948, p. 159):

There is no doubt that Hegelianism is (relatively speaking) the most important of the philosophical motivations of our author [Marx], also, and in particular, for the reason that it attempted to go beyond the traditional conceptions of idealism and materialism in a new synthesis which undoubtedly had a quite exceptional importance and which represents a world-historical moment of philosophical enquiry. So when the *Manual* [of Bukharin] says that the term 'immanence' in the philosophy of praxis is used in a metaphorical sense, it is saying nothing. In reality the term immanence has here acquired a special meaning which is not that of the 'pantheists' nor any other metaphysical meaning, but one which is new and needs to be made precise. It has been forgotten that in the case of a certain very common expression [*historical materialism*] one should put the accent on the first term – 'historical' – and not on the second, which is of metaphysical origin. *The philosophy of praxis is absolute 'historicism', the absolute secularization and earthliness of thought, an absolute humanism of history.* It is along this line that one must trace the thread of the new conception of the world.

It is only too clear that these 'absolute' 'humanist' and 'absolute' 'historicist' statements of Gramsci's are primarily critical and polemical in meaning; their functions are, first and foremost: (1) to reject any metaphysical interpretation of Marxist philosophy, and (2) to *indicate*, as 'practical' concepts,[16] the site on which the Marxist conception should be established and the direction it should take in order to break all ties with the previous metaphysics: the site of 'immanence', of the 'down here' which Marx himself opposed as *'diesseits'* (down-here) to transcendence, the beyond (*jenseits*) of classical philosophies. This distinction is featured in so many words in one of the *Theses on Feuerbach* (the second). However, we can already draw one first conclusion from the 'indicative-practical' nature of these two concepts which Gramsci combines in one and the same function (humanism, historicism); a restricted conclusion, it is true, but a theoretically important one: if these concepts are polemical-indicative, they indicate the direction in which an investigation must be begun, the kind of domain in which the problem of the interpretation of Marxism must be posed, but they do not provide the *positive concept* of this interpretation. In order to be able to judge Gramsci's interpretation we must first of all bring to light the positive concepts in which it is expressed. What does Gramsci mean by 'absolute historicism'?

If we go beyond the purely critical aims of his formulations, we immediately find a first *positive sense*. By presenting Marxism as a historicism, Gramsci is stressing an essential determination of Marxist theory: its practical role in *real history*. One of Gramsci's constant concerns is the practico-historical role of what, adopting Croce's conception of religion,

[16] In the sense defined in *For Marx*, pp. 242ff.

he calls the great 'conceptions of the world', or 'ideologies': theoretical formations which are capable of penetrating deep into men's practical lives, and hence of inspiring and animating a whole historical epoch, by providing not only the 'intellectuals' but also and above all the 'ordinary' men, with both a general view of the course of events and *at the same time* rules of practical conduct.[17] In this respect, the historicism of Marxism is no more than the consciousness of a task and a necessity: Marxism cannot claim to be the theory of history unless, *even in its theory*, it can think the conditions of this penetration into history, into all strata of society, even into men's everyday lives. This perspective enables us to understand a number of Gramsci's expressions; where, for instance, he says that philosophy must be concrete, real, must be history, that the real philosopher is simply the politician, that philosophy, politics and history are absolutely one and the same.[18] This perspective enables us to understand his theory of intellectuals and ideology, his distinction between individual intellectuals, who can produce more or less subjective and arbitrary ideologies, and 'organic' intellectuals or the 'collective intellectual' (the Party), who ensure the 'hegemony' of a ruling class by carrying its 'conception of the world' (or organic ideology) into the everyday life of all men; and to understand his interpretation of Machiavelli's *Prince*, whose heritage has, in new conditions, fallen to the

---

[17] 'Assuming Benedetto Croce's definition of religion as a conception of the world which has become a norm of life, since norm of life is not understood in a bookish sense but as a norm realized in practical life, the majority of men are philosophers insofar as they work practically; a conception of the world, a philosophy is implicit in their working practice' (Gramsci: *Il materialismo storico e la filosofia di Benedetto Croce*, Milan 1948, p. 21).

'But at this point we reach the fundamental problem facing any conception of the world, any philosophy which has become a cultural movement, a "religion", a "faith", any that has produced a form of practical activity or will in which the philosophy is contained as an implicit theoretical "premiss". One might say "ideology" here, but on condition that the word is used in its highest sense of a conception of the world that is implicitly manifest in art, in law, in economic activity and in all manifestations of individual and collective life. This problem is that of preserving the ideological unity of the entire social *bloc* which that ideology serves to cement and unify' (ibid., p. 7).

The reader will have noted that the conception of an ideology which is 'implicitly' manifest in art, law, economic activity and 'all the manifestions of individual and collective life' is very close to the Hegelian conception.

[18] 'All men are philosophers' (ibid., p. 3).

'Since all action is *political*, can one not say that the real philosophy of each man is contained in its entirety in his political action?.... Hence the reason why philosophy cannot be divorced from politics. And one can show furthermore that the choice and the criticism of a conception of the world is also a political matter' (ibid., p. 6).

'If it is true that every philosophy is the *expression* of a society, it must react on that society and determine certain positive and negative effects; the precise extent to which it reacts is the measure of its historical scope, of the extent to which it is not an individual "elucubration" but a "historical fact" ' (ibid., pp. 23–4).

'The identity of history and philosophy is immanent in historical materialism. . . . The proposition that the German proletariat is the heir of classical German philosophy contains precisely the identity between history and philosophy . . .' (ibid., p. 217). Cf. pp. 232–4.

modern Communist Party, etc. In all these cases Gramsci is merely expressing a necessity which is inherent in Marxism, not only practically, but *consciously* and *theoretically*. Hence the historicism of Marxism is no more than one of the *aspects* and *effects* of its own theory, correctly conceived, no more than its own internally consistent theory. A theory of real history, too, must, as other 'conceptions of the world' have already done, pass into real history. What was true of the great religions must *a fortiori* be true of Marxism itself, not despite but because of the difference between it and those ideologies, because of what is philosophically new in it, since this *novelty* is that it includes in its theory itself the practical meaning of that theory.[19]

However, as the reader will have realized, this last sense of 'historicism', which refers us to a theme within Marxist theory, is still very largely a *critical indication*, designed to condem all 'bookish' Marxists, all those who hope to reduce it to one of the 'individual philosophies', destined never to achieve any hold on history – and even all those ideologists who, like Croce, return to the unfortunate tradition of the intellectuals of the Renaissance, wishing to educate the human race 'from above', without engaging in political action and real history. The historicism Gramsci affirms means a vigorous protest against this aristocratism of theory and of its 'thinkers'.[20] The old protest against the bookish phariseeism of the Second International ('The Revolution against *Capital*') is still echoing here; this is a direct appeal to 'practice', to political action, to 'changing the world', without which Marxism would be no more than the prey of bookworms and passive political functionaries.

Does this protest *necessarily* contain a new theoretical interpretation of Marxist theory? Not *necessarily*; it may simply develop one of the essential themes of Marx's theory in the practical form of an absolute reminder: the theme of the new relationship between 'theory' and 'practice' which Marx installed *within his theory itself*. We find this theme in Marx *in two places*: in historical materialism (in the theory of the role of ideologies and the role of scientific theory in the transformation of existing ideologies) on the one hand, and, on the other, in dialectical materialism with respect to the Marxist theory of theory and practice and their relationship, in what is commonly called 'the materialist theory of knowledge'. In both these cases what Marx vigorously affirms and what is at stake in our problem is Marxist *materialism*. Hence the stress Gramsci lays on the 'historicism' of Marxism, in the very precise sense we have just defined, is *in reality* an allusion to the resolutely *materialist* character of Marx's conception (both in historical and dialectical materialism). But this *reality* leads on to a disconcerting comment

[19] What *corresponds* here to the concept of 'historicism', in this interpretation, has a precise name in Marxism: it is the problem of the union of theory and practice, more particularly, the problem of the union of Marxist theory and the workers' movement.

[20] Gramsci, op. cit., pp. 8–9.

which contains three aspects, each of which is as disturbing as the next. (1) Whereas it is precisely *materialism* which is at stake, Gramsci declares that in the expression 'historical materialism' 'one should put the accent on *the first term – "historical" – and not the second which,*' he says, '*is of metaphysical origin*'. (2) Whereas the materialist stress involves not only historical materialism but also dialectical materialism, Gramsci hardly ever speaks of anything but historical materialism – indeed, he suggests that the term 'materialism' inevitably sounds 'metaphysical', or perhaps more than sounds. (3) It is clear that Gramsci makes the expression 'historical materialism', which designates only the scientific theory of history, bear a double sense: it means *simultaneously* both historical materialism and Marxist philosophy; hence Gramsci tends to make the theory of history and dialectical materialism coincide within *historical materialism alone*, although they form two distinct disciplines. Obviously I am not basing these remarks or drawing this last conclusion on the authority of the single sentence I am analysing, but on that of a very large number of Gramsci's other arguments,[21] which confirm it unambiguously and so give it a conceptual meaning. I believe that here we have a new sense of Gramsci's 'historicism', one that can no longer be reduced to the legitimate use of a polemical or critical indicative concept – but one which must be regarded as a *theoretical interpretation* affecting the very content of Marx's thought, and one to which our criticisms and reservations must therefore apply.

Finally, as well as his polemical and practical use of the concept, Gramsci also has a truly 'historicist' conception of Marx: a 'historicist' conception of the theory of the *relationship between Marx's theory and real history*. It is not completely accidental that Gramsci is constantly haunted by Croce's theory of religion; that he accepts its terms, and extends it from actual religions to the new 'conception of the world', Marxism; that he ranges these religions and Marxism under the same concept as 'conceptions of the world' and 'ideologies'; that he so easily identifies religion, ideology, philosophy

---

[21] Cf. e.g.: 'The philosophy of praxis derives certainly from the immanentist conception of reality, but it derives from it insofar as it is purified of any speculative aroma and reduced to pure history or historicity or to pure humanism. . . . Not only is the philosophy of praxis connected to immanentism. It is also connected to the subjective conception of reality, to the extent precisely that it turns it on its head, explaining it as a historical fact, as the "historical subjectivity of a social group [class]", as a real fact, which presents itself as a phenomenon of philosophical "speculation" and is simply a practical act, the form of a concrete social content and the means of leading the ensemble of society to shape for itself a moral unity' (ibid., p. 191).

Or again: 'If it is necessary, in the perennial flux of events, to fix concepts without which reality cannot be understood, one must also, and it is indeed quite indispensable, fix and recall that reality in movement and concept of reality, though *logically* they may be distinct, *historically* must be conceived as an inseparable unity' (ibid., p. 216).

Echoes of Bogdanov's empiricism are obvious in the first text; the second features the empiricist-speculative thesis of all historicism: the identity of the concept and the *real* (historical) object.

and Marxist theory, without calling attention to the fact that what distinguishes Marxism from these ideological 'conceptions of the world' is less the (important) formal difference that Marxism puts an end to any supra-terrestrial 'beyond', than the distinctive *form* of this absolute immanence (its 'earthliness'): *the form of scientificity*. This 'break' between the old religions or ideologies, even the 'organic' ones, and Marxism, *which is a science*, and which must become the 'organic' ideology of human history by producing a *new* form of ideology in the masses (an ideology which will depend on a science this time – *which has never been the case before*) – this break was not really reflected by Gramsci, and, absorbed as he was by the necessity and the practical conditions for the penetration of the 'philosophy of praxis' into real history, he neglected the theoretical significance of this break and its theoretical and practical consequences. Hence he often tends to *unite under the same head* the scientific theory of history (historical materialism) and Marxist philosophy (dialectical materialism), and to think this unity as a 'conception of the world' or as an 'ideology' basically comparable with the old religions. Similarly, he tends to think the relationship between Marxist *science* and real history according to the model of the relationship between an 'organic' (historically dominant and active) *ideology* and real history; and ultimately to think this relationship between Marxist scientific theory and real history according to the model of a relationship of *direct expression*, which does give a fair account of the relationship between an organic ideology and its age. It is here, it seems to me, that the disputable principles of Gramsci's historicism lie. It is here that he spontaneously rediscovers the language and theoretical problematic indispensable to every 'historicism'.

Given these premises it is possible to give a theoretically historicist sense to the formulae I referred to at the beginning – for, given the whole underlying context I have just indicated, they also take on this sense in Gramsci – and if I now go on and try to draw out their implications as rigorously as I can in a short space, I do not do so as an attack on Gramsci (who had too fine a historical and theoretical sensitivity not to keep every distance when necessary) so much as to make *visible* a latent logic, knowledge of which can help us to understand certain of their theoretical effects, whose occurrence would otherwise remain a riddle, whether in Gramsci's own work, or in the works of certain of those inspired by him or comparable with him. So I shall be expounding a *limit-situation* here, too, just as I did with respect to the 'historicist' reading of certain passages from *Capital*, and I shall be defining not so much any particular interpretation (Gramsci, Della Volpe, Colletti, Sarte) as the *field* of the theoretical problematic which haunts their reflections and which emerges from time to time in certain of their concepts, problems or solutions.

To this end, and with these reservations, which are not merely stylistic, I shall now take the statement that Marxism must be conceived as an '*absolute historicism'*, as a symptomatic thesis which will enable us to bring a whole latent problematic to light. How are we to understand this statement in our present perspective? If Marxism is an absolute historicism, it is because it historicizes even what was peculiarly the theoretical and practical negation of history for Hegelian historicism: the end of history, the unsurpassable present of Absolute Knowledge. In absolute historicism there is no longer any Absolute Knowledge, and hence no end for history.

There is no longer any privileged present in which the totality becomes visible and legible in an 'essential section', in which consciousness and science coincide. The fact that there is no Absolute Knowledge – which is what makes the historicism *absolute* – means that Absolute Knowledge itself is historicized. If there is no longer any privileged present, all presents are privileged to the same degree. It follows that historical time possesses in each of its presents a structure which allows each present the 'essential section' of contemporaneity. Nevertheless, the Marxist does not have the same structure as the Hegelian totality, and in particular it contains different levels or instances which do not directly express one another. Therefore in order to make it susceptible to the 'essential section' these levels must be linked together in such a way that the present of each of them coincides with the presents of all the others: i.e., they must all be 'contemporaneous'. Thus re-organized, their relationship will exclude the effects of distortion and dislocation, which, in the authentic Marxist conception, contradict this ideological reading of a contemporaneity. Hence the project of thinking Marxism as an (absolute) historicism automatically unleashes a logically necessary chain reaction which tends to reduce and flatten out the Marxist totality into a variation of the Hegelian totality, and which, even allowing for more or less rhetorical distinctions, ultimately tones down, reduces, or omits the real differences separating the levels.

The symptomatic point at which this reduction of the levels shows its face – i.e., hides behind the cover provided by an 'obviousness' which betrays it (in both senses of the word) – can be defined precisely: in the status of scientific and philosophical *knowledge*. We have seen that Gramsci was so insistent on the practical unity of the conception of the world and history that he neglected to retain what distinguishes Marxist theory from every previous organic ideology: its character as *scientific* knowledge. Marxist philosophy, which he does not clearly distinguish from the theory of history, suffers the same fate: Gramsci relates it to present history as its direct expression; philosophy is then, as Hegel intended (in a conception readopted by Croce) 'the history of philosophy', and, in short, *history*. As all science and all philosophy are at bottom real history, real history itself can be called philosophy and science.

But how can one think this double radical affirmation in Marxist theory and create the theoretical conditions which will permit its formulation? By a whole series of conceptual slides (*glissements*), whose effect is precisely to *reduce* the distance between the levels which Marx had distinguished. Each of these slides is the less perceptible the less attention has been paid to the theoretical distinctions registered in the precision of Marx's concepts.

In this way, Gramsci constantly declares that a scientific theory, or such and such a category of a science, is a 'superstructure'[22] or a 'historical category' which he assimilates to a 'human relation'.[23] In fact, this is to attribute to the concept 'superstructure' a breadth Marx never allowed, for he only ranged within it: (1) the politico-legal superstructure, and (2) the ideological superstructure (the corresponding 'forms of social consciousness'): except in his Early Works (especially the *1844 Manuscripts*), Marx *never included scientific knowledge in it*. Science can no more be ranged within the category 'superstructure' than can language, which as Stalin showed escapes it. To make science a superstructure is to think of it as one of those 'organic' ideologies which form such a close 'bloc' with the structure that they have the same 'history' as it does! But even in Marxist theory we read that ideologies may survive the structure that gave them birth (this is true for the majority of them: e.g., religion, ethics, or ideological philosophy), as may certain elements of the politico-legal superstructure in the same way (Roman law!). As for science, it may well arise from an ideology, detach itself from its field in order to constitute itself as a science, but precisely this detachment, this 'break', inaugurates a new form of historical existence and temporality which together save science (at least in certain historical conditions that ensure the real continuity of its own history – conditions that have not always existed) from the common fate of a single history: that of the 'historical bloc' unifying structure and superstructure. Idealism is an ideological reflection of the temporality peculiar to science, the rhythm of its development, the kind of continuity and punctuation which seem to save it from the vicissitudes of political and economic history in the form of a historicity and atemporality; in this way it hypostasizes a real phenomenon which needs quite different categories if it is to be thought, but which *must be thought* by distinguishing between the relatively autonomous and peculiar history of scientific knowledge and the other modalities of historical existence (those of the ideological and politico-legal superstructures, and that of the economic structure).

The *reduction* and *identification* of the peculiar history of science to the history of organic ideology and politico-economic history ultimately reduces science to history as its 'essence'. The collapse of science into history here is no more than the index of a theoretical collapse: a collapse that precipitates the theory of history into *real* history; reduces the (theoretical) object of the science of history to real history; and therefore confuses the object of knowledge with the real object. This collapse is nothing but a collapse into

[22] Cf. Gramsci's astonishing pages on science in *Il materialismo storico*, pp. 54-7.
[23] ibid., p. 160.

empiricist ideology , with the roles in this presentation played by philosophy and real history. Despite his enormous historical and political genius, Gramsci did not avoid this empiricist temptation in his attempt to think the status of science and above all that of philosophy (for he is little concerned with science). He is constantly tempted to think the relation between real history and philosophy as a relation of expressive unity, whatever mediations may be responsible for the maintenance of this relation.[24] As we have seen, for him, a philosopher is, in the last instance, a 'politician'; for him, philosophy is the direct product (assuming all the 'necessary mediations') of the activity and experience of the masses, of politico-economic praxis: professional philosophers merely lend their voices and the forms of their discourse to this 'common-sense' philosophy, which is already complete without them and speaks in historical praxis – they cannot change it substantially. Gramsci spontaneously rediscovers, as an opposition indispensable to the expression of his thought, the very formulations which Feuerbach used in a famous text of 1839 which opposed the philosophy produced by real history to the philosophy produced by philosophers – the formulations opposing praxis to speculation. And Gramsci's intention to retain what was valuable in Croce's historicism is expressed in the very terms of Feuerbach's 'inversion' of speculation into 'concrete' philosophy: he proposes to 'invert' Croce's speculative historicism, to set it back on to its feet, in order to make it into Marx's historicism – in order to rediscover real history and 'concrete' philosophy. If it is true that the 'inversion' of a problematic retains the same structure as that problematic, it is not surprising that the relationship of direct expression (given all the necessary 'mediations') between real history and philosophy conceived by Hegel and Croce recurs in the inverted theory: precisely the relationship of direct expression Gramsci is tempted to set up between politics (real history) and philosophy.

But it is not enough to reduce to a minimum the distance within the social structure between the specific site of theoretical, philosophical and scientific formations on the one hand and political practice on the other; that is, the site of theoretical practice and the site of political practice – it is also essential to provide a conception of *theoretical practice* which illustrates and consecrates the proclaimed identity of philosophy and politics. This latent requirement explains some new conceptual slides, whose effect is once again to *reduce* the distinction between the levels.

In this interpretation, theoretical practice tends to lose all specificity and to be reduced to *historical practice* in general, a category which is made to include forms of production as different as economic practice, political practice, ideological practice and scientific practice. Nevertheless, this assimilation poses critical problems: Gramsci himself recognized that absolute historicism threatens to run aground on the rock of the theory of

[24] On the concept of 'mediation' see Part I, section 18.

ideologies. But he himself provided the arguments for a solution when he compared the *Theses on Feuerbach* with a phrase of Engels's (history as '*industry and experiment*'), by proposing as his model a practice which is capable of uniting all these different practices within its concept. The problematic of absolute historicism *required* that this problem be solved: it is no accident that it has usually given this empiricist problem a solution which is empiricist in spirit. The model may, for example, be that of *experimental practice*, borrowed not so much from the reality of modern science as from a certain ideology of modern science. Colletti has taken up this hint of Gramsci's and maintains that history, and even reality itself, have an '*experimental structure*', and therefore that in essence they are structured like an experiment. If real history on the one hand is declared to be 'industry and experiment' in this way – and if all scientific practice on the other is defined as experimental practice, it follows that historical practice and theoretical practice have one and the same structure. Colletti pushes this comparison to its extremes, and suggests that history includes in its being, just like science, the moment of *hypothesis* which is indispensable to a presentation of the experimental structure, in Claude Bernard's schemata. As history is constantly anticipating itself in living political action (in the predictions of the future indispensable to any action) it is thus hypothesis and verification in action, just like the practice of experimental science. This identity of essential structures makes it possible to assimilate theoretical practice *directly, immediately* and adequately to historical practice – and the reduction of the site of theoretical practice to that of political or social practice can then be based on the reduction of these practices to a single structure.

I have taken Gramsci and Colletti as my examples. This is not because they are the only possible examples of theoretical *variations* on a single theoretical invariant: the problematic of historicism. In no sense does a problematic impose absolutely identical variations on the thoughts that cross its field: a field can be crossed by quite different paths, since it can be approached from many different directions. But to come upon it means to submit to its law, which produces as many different effects as there are different thoughts which come upon it: however, all these effects have certain identical features in common: the features of the problematic they have come upon. To give a paradoxical example, we all know that Sartre's thought in no sense derives from Gramsci's interpretation of Marxism: it has quite different origins. However, when he came upon Marxism, for his own peculiar reasons Sartre immediately gave a historicist interpretation of it (although he would undoubtedly refuse to call it that), declaring that the great philosophies (he cites Marx's philosophy after those of Locke and Kant-Hegel) are '*insurpassable until the historical moment whose expression they are has been surpassed*' (*Critique de la raison dialectique*, Paris 1960, p. 17; English translation: *The Problem of Method*, London 1965, p. 7). Here once again we find, in a form peculiar to Sartre, the structures of contemporaneity, expression and the insurpassable (Hegel's 'no one can run ahead of his time'), which *for him* represent specifications of his major concept: *totalization* – but which nevertheless realize the necessary conceptual effects of his encounter with the structure of the historicist problematic, in the form of specifications of this concept which is peculiar to him. These are not the only effects: we are not surprised to see Sartre using his own means to rediscover a theory of 'ideologists' (ibid., pp. 17–18; trans. pp. 7–8) (who cash and comment on a great philosophy, transferring it into men's practical lives) in many respects very close to Gramsci's theory of organic intellectuals;[25] nor are we surprised to see Sartre make the same *necessary reduction* of the different practices (the different levels distinguished by Marx) to a single practice: for him, for reasons related precisely to his peculiar philosophical origins, it is not the concept of experimental practice, but the concept of 'praxis' as such, which is responsible for the unity of practices as different as scientific practice and economic or political practice, at the price of innumerable mediations (Sartre is the philosopher of mediations *par excellence*: their function is precisely to ensure unity in the negation of differences).

I cannot develop these very schematic comments. But they will serve to give some idea of the implications necessarily contained in any historicist interpretation of Marxism, and of the particular concepts this interpretation *has to* produce in order to solve the problems it poses for itself – at least when it aims, as is the case with Gramsci, Colletti or Sartre, to be theoretically demanding and rigorous. This interpretation can itself only be thought on condition of a whole series of reductions which are the effect of the empiricist character of its project on the order of the production of concepts. For example, only on condition that it reduces all practice to experimental practice, or to 'praxis' in general, and then assimilates this mother-practice to political practice, can all practices be thought as arising from 'real' historical practice, can philosophy, even science, and hence Marxism, too, be thought as the 'expression' of real history. The result is to flatten even scientific knowledge or philosophy, and at any rate Marxist theory, down to the unity of politico-economic practice, to the heart of 'historical' practice, *to 'real' history*. In this way one reaches the result required by all historicist interpretations of Marxism as their theoretical precondition: the transformation of the Marxist totality into a variant of the Hegelian totality.

The historicist interpretation of Marxism may lead to one last effect: the practical negation of the distinction between the science of history (historical materialism) and Marxist philosophy (dialectical materialism). In this final reduction, Marxist philosophy loses in practice its *raison d'être*, to the

---

[25] Gramsci even gives Sartre's distinction between philosophy and history in so many words (*Il materialismo storico*, op. cit., p. 197).

advantage of the theory of history: dialectical materialism disappears into historical materialism.[26] This is clearly visible in Gramsci, and in most of his followers: not only do they have serious reservations about the *word* dialectical materialism, but also about the *concept* of a Marxist philosophy defined by a peculiar object. They think that the mere idea of a theoretically autonomous philosophy (autonomous in its object, theory and method), i.e., one which is distinct from the science of history, tips Marxism back into metaphysics, into the restoration of the Philosophy of Nature, for which Engels made himself responsible.[27] Since all philosophy is history, the 'philosophy of praxis' can, as a philosophy, only be the philosophy of the philosophy-history identity, or of the science-history identity. Deprived of any object of its own, Marxist philosophy loses the status of an autonomous discipline and is reduced, according to Gramsci, quoting Croce, to a mere 'historical methodology', i.e., to the mere self-consciousness of the historicity of history, to a reflection on the presence of real history in all its manifestations:

> Separated from the theory of history and politics, philosophy cannot be other than metaphysics, whereas the great conquest in the history of modern thought, represented by the philosophy of praxis, is precisely the *concrete historicization* of philosophy and its identification with history (Gramsci: *Il materialismo storico*, p. 133).

This historicization of philosophy reduces it then to the status of a historical methodology:

> To think of a philosophical affirmation as true in a particular historical period (that is, as the necessary and inseparable expression of a particular historical action, of a particular praxis) but as superseded and rendered 'vain' in a succeeding period, without however falling into scepticism and moral and ideological relativism, in other words *to see philosophy as historicity*, is quite an arduous and difficult mental operation . . . [Bukharin] does not succeed in elaborating the concept of the philosophy of praxis as '*historical methodology*' and of that in turn as 'philosophy', as the only *concrete philosophy*. That is to say he does not succeed in posing and resolving, from the point of view of the *real dialectic, the problem which Croce has posed and has attempted to resolve from the speculative point of view.*

These last words bring us full circle: we have returned to Hegelian historicism 'radicalized' by Croce, which only needs to be 'inverted' to change from speculative philosophy into 'concrete' philosophy, from the speculative dialectic into the real dialectic, etc. The theoretical undertaking

---

[26] The same structural causes can give rise to the *opposite* effect: with Sartre, we can say just as easily that the Marxist science of history *becomes philosophy*.

[27] Cf. Gramsci's critique of Bukharin, and Colletti's introduction to Lenin's *Philosophical Notebooks*, now in *Il Marxismo e Hegel*, Bari 1969.

which interprets Marxism as a historicism does not escape the *absolute limits* within which this 'inversion' of speculation into praxis and of abstraction into the concrete has been performed since Feuerbach: these limits are defined by the empiricist problematic, sublimated in Hegelian speculation, and no 'inversion' can deliver us from them.[28]

In the different theoretical reductions indispensable to the historicist interpretation, and in their effects, we can therefore clearly see the basic structure of all historicism: the contemporaneity which makes possible a reading in essential section. And of theoretical necessity we can also see this structure imposed willy-nilly on the structure of the Marxist totality, transforming it and reducing the real distance between its different levels. Marxist history 'relapses' into the ideological concept of history, the category of temporal presence and continuity; into the politico-economic practice of real history, by flattening the sciences, philosophy and ideologies into the unity of the relations and forces of production, i.e., in fact, into the *infrastructure*. Paradoxical as this conclusion may seem – and I shall doubtless be attacked for expressing it – it must be drawn: from the standpoint of its *theoretical problematic*, and not of its political style and aims, this humanist and historicist materialism has rediscovered the basic theoretical principles of the Second International's economistic and mechanistic interpretation. If this single theoretical problematic can underly policies of different inspiration, one fatalist, the other voluntarist, one passive, the other conscious and active – it is because of the scope for theoretical *'play'* contained in this ideological theoretical problematic as in every ideology. In this case, this kind of historicism can be opposed politically to the theses of the Second International by conferring on the infrastructure the most active qualities of the political and ideological superstructure, in a compensating crossed connexion. This transfer of qualities can be conceived in different ways: e.g., by endowing political practice with the qualities of philosophy and theory (spontaneism); by attributing to economic practice all the active and even explosive virtues of politics (anarcho-syndicalism); or by entrusting to political consciousness and determination the determinism of the economic (voluntarism). In other words, if there really are two distinct ways of identifying the superstructure with the infrastructure, or consciousness with the economy – one which sees in consciousness and politics only

[28] A moment ago I spoke of the peculiar origins of Sartre's philosophy. Sartre thinks with Descartes, Kant, Husserl and Hegel: but his most profound thought undoubtedly comes from *Politzer* and (paradoxical as this juxtaposition might appear) secondarily from Bergson. But Politzer is the Feuerbach of our time: his *Critique des fondements de la psychologie* is a critique of *speculative* Psychology in the name of a *concrete* Psychology. Sartre may have treated Politzer's themes as 'philosophemes': he has not abandoned his inspiration; when Sartre's historicism inverts the 'totality', the *abstractions* of dogmatic Marxism, he is also 'repeating' in a different place and with respect to different objects an 'inversion' which, from Feuerbach to the Young Marx and Politzer, has merely *conserved* the same problematic behind an apparent critique.

the economy, while the other imbues the economy with politics and consciousness, there is never more than one *structure* of identification at work –
the structure of the problematic which, by reducing one to the other,
theoretically identifies the levels present. It is this common structure of the
problematic which is made visible when, rather than analysing the theoretical or political *intentions* of mechanicism-economism on the one hand
and humanism-historicism on the other, we examine the internal logic of
their conceptual mechanisms.

Allow me one more comment on the relation between humanism and
historicism. It is only too clear that a non-historicist humanism is perfectly
conceivable, as is a non-humanist historicism. Of course, here I always mean
a *theoretical* humanism and historicism, considered in their function as
theoretical foundations for Marxist science and philosophy. To live by ethics
or religion, or by that politico-ethical ideology known as social-democracy
is enough to erect a *humanist but non-historicist* interpretation of Marx:
all that is required is to read Marx in the 'light' of a theory of 'human
nature', be it religious, ethical or anthropological (cf. Fathers Calvez and
Bigo, and Monsieur Rubel, as well as the Social Democrats Landshut and
Mayer, the first editors of Marx's Early Works). It is child's play to reduce
Capital to an ethical inspiration, whether or no one relies on the radical
anthropology of the *1844 Manuscripts*. But, inversely, it is just as easy to
imagine a *historicist but non-humanist* reading of Marx: if I understand him
correctly, Colletti's best efforts tend in this direction. To justify this historicist non-humanist reading of Marx it is necessary to refuse, as Colletti does,
to reduce the Forces of Production/Relations of Production unity, which
constitutes the essence of history, to the mere phenomenon of a human
nature, even a historicized one. But let us leave these two possibilities at this
point.

It must be said that the union of humanism and historicism represents
the gravest temptation, for it procures the greatest theoretical advantages,
at least in appearance. In the reduction of all knowledge to the historical
social relations a second underhand reduction can be introduced, by treating
the *relations of production* as mere *human relations*.[29] This second reduction
depends on something 'obvious': is not history a 'human' phenomenon
through and through, and did not Marx, quoting Vico, declare that men can
know it since they have '*made*' all of it? But this 'obviousness' depends on a
remarkable presupposition: that the 'actors' of history are the authors of its
text, the subjects of its production. But this presupposition too has all the
force of the 'obvious', since, as opposed to what the theatre suggests, concrete
men are, in history, the actors of roles of which they are the authors, too.
Once the stage-director has been spirited away, the actor-author becomes the
twin-brother of Aristotle's old dream: the doctor-who-cures-himself; and

[29] This surreptitious practice is common to all the humanist interpretations of Marxism.

the *relations of production*, although they are the real stage-directors of history, are reduced to mere *human relations*. Is not *The German Ideology* stuffed with formulations about the 'real men', the 'concrete individuals', who, 'with their feet firmly on the ground', are the real subjects of history? Do not the *Theses on Feuerbach* declare that objectivity itself is the completely human result of the 'practico-sensuous' activity of these subjects? Once this human nature has been endowed with the qualities of 'concrete' historicity, it becomes possible to avoid the abstraction and fixity of theological or ethical anthropologies and to join Marx in the very heart of his lair: historical materialism. This human nature will therefore be conceived as something produced by history, and changing with it, while man changes, as even the Philosophers of the Enlightenment intended, with the revolutions of his own history, and is affected by the social products of his objective history even in his most intimate faculties (seeing, hearing, memory, reason, etc. Even Helvetius claimed this, and Rousseau too, in opposition to Diderot; Feuerbach made it one of the main articles of his philosophy – and in our own day, a horde of cultural anthropologists have adopted it). History then becomes the transformation of a human nature, which remains the real subject of the history which transforms it. As a result, history has been introduced into human nature, making men the contemporaries of the historical effects whose subjects they are, but – and this is absolutely decisive – the relations of production, political and ideological social relations, have been reduced to historicized *'human relations'*, i.e., to inter-human, inter-subjective relations. This is the favourite terrain of historicist humanism. And what is its great advantage? The fact that Marx is restored to the stream of an ideology much older than himself, an ideology born in the eighteenth century; credit for the originality of a revolutionary theoretical rupture is taken from him, he is often even made acceptable to modern forms of 'cultural' anthropology, and so on. Is there anyone today who does not invoke this historicist humanism, in the genuine belief that he is appealing to Marx, whereas such an ideology takes us away from Marx?

But this has not always been the case, at least not *politically speaking*. I have said why and how the historicist-humanist interpretation of Marxism came to birth in the portents and in the wake of the 1917 Revolution. Its significance then was that of a violent protest against the mechanicism and opportunism of the Second International. It appealed directly to the consciousness and will of *men* to reject the War, overthrow capitalism and make the revolution. It rejected absolutely anything, *even in theory*, which might defer or stifle this urgent appeal to the historical responsibility of the real men hurled into the revolution. In the same movement, it demanded the *theory of its will*. That is why it proclaimed a radical return to Hegel (the young Lukács and Korsch) and worked out a theory which put Marx's doctrine into a directly *expressive* relationship with the working class. From this period, too, dates the famous opposition between 'bourgeois science' and 'proletarian science', in which triumphed an idealist and voluntarist interpretation of Marxism as the exclusive product and expression of proletarian practice. This 'left-wing' humanism designated the proletariat as the site and missionary of the human essence. The historical role of freeing man from his 'alienation' was its destiny, through the negation of the human essence whose absolute victim it was. The alliance between the proletariat and philosophy announced in Marx's early texts was no longer seen as an alliance between two mutually exclusive components, The proletariat, the human essence in revolt against its radical negation, because the revolutionary affirmation of the human essence: the proletariat was thus *philosophy in deed* and its political practice philosophy itself. Marx's role was then reduced to having conferred on this philosophy which was acted and lived in its birthplace, the mere form of *self-consciousness*. That is why Marxism was proclaimed 'proletarian' 'science' or 'philosophy', the direct expression, the direct production of the human essence by its sole historical author: the proletariat. Kautsky's and Lenin's thesis that Marxist theory is produced by a specific theoretical practice, *outside* the proletariat, and that Marxist theory must be *'imported'* into the proletariat, was absolutely rejected – and all the themes of spontaneism rushed into Marxism through this open breach: the humanist universalism of the proletariat. *Theoretically*, this revolutionary 'humanism' and 'historicism' together laid claim to Hegel and to those of Marx's early texts then available. As for its *political* effects, some of Rosa Luxemburg's theses on imperialism and the disappearance of the laws of 'political economy' in the socialist regime; the Proletkult; the conceptions of the 'Workers' Opposition', etc.; and in a general way the 'voluntarism' which deeply marked the period of the dictatorship of the proletariat in the USSR, even in the paradoxical forms of Stalinist dogmatism. Even today, this 'humanism' and 'historicism' find genuinely revolutionary echoes in the political struggles waged by the people of the Third World to conquer and defend their political independence and set out on the socialist road. But these ideological and political advantages themselves, as Lenin admirably discerned, are offset by certain effects of the *logic* that they set in motion, which eventually and inevitably produce idealist and empiricist temptations in economic and political conceptions and practice – if they do not, given a favourable conjuncture, induce, by a paradoxical but still necessary inversion, conceptions which are tainted with reformism and opportunism, or quite simply revisionist.

Indeed, it is a peculiarity of every *ideological* conception, especially if it had conquered a scientific conception by diverting it from its true meaning, that it is governed by 'interests' beyond the necessity of knowledge alone. In this sense, i.e., on condition that it is given the object of which it speaks without knowing it, historicism is not without theoretical value, since it gives an adequate description of an essential aspect of all *ideology*, which takes its meaning from the *current* interests in whose service it is subjected. If the *ideology* does not express the total objective essence of its time (the essence of the historical present), it can at least express the current changes in the historical situation reasonably well by the effect of slight internal displacements of accent: unlike a science, an ideology is both theoretically closed and politically supple and adaptable. It bends to the interests of the times, but without any apparent movement, being content to *reflect* the historical changes which it is its mission to assimilate and master by some imperceptible modification of its peculiar internal relations. The ambiguous example of the Vatican II *'aggiornamento'* is a sufficiently striking proof: the effect and sign of an indisputable evolution, but at the same time a skilful adjustment to history, thanks to an intelligently handled conjuncture. Ideology changes therefore, but imperceptibly, conserving its ideological form; it moves, but with an immobile motion which maintains it *where it is*, in its place and its ideological role. It is the immobile motion which, as Hegel said of philosophy itself, reflects and expresses what happens in history without ever running ahead of its own time, since it is merely that time *caught* in the trap of a mirror reflection, precisely so that men will be *caught* in it too. That is the essential reason why the revolutionary humanism of the echoes of the 1917 Revolution can serve today as an ideological *reflection* for various political or theoretical preoccupations, some still related to this origin, others more or less foreign to it.

This historicist humanism may, for example, serve as a theoretical warning to intellectuals of bourgeois or petty-bourgeois origin, who ask themselves, sometimes in genuinely tragic terms, whether they really have a right to be members of a history which is made, as they know or fear, outside them. Perhaps this is Sartre's profoundest problem. It is fully present in his double thesis that Marxism is the 'unsurpassable philosophy of our time', and yet that no literary or philosophical work is worth an hour's effort in comparison with the sufferings of a poor wretch reduced by imperialist exploitation to hunger and agony. Caught in this double declaration of faith, on the one hand in an idea of Marxism, on the other in the cause of all the exploited, Sartre reassures himself of the fact that he really does have a role to play, beyond the 'Words' he produces and regards with derision, in the inhuman history of our times, with a theory of 'dialectical reason' which assigns to all (theoretical) rationality, and to every (revolutionary) dialectic, the unique transcendental origin of the human 'project'. Thus in Sartre historicist humanism takes the form of an exaltation of human freedom, in which by freely committing himself to their fight, he can commune with the freedom of all the oppressed, who have always been struggling for a little human light since the long and forgotten night of the slave revolts.

The same humanism, with some shift in accent, can serve other causes, according to conjuncture and needs: e.g., the protest against the errors and crimes of the period of the 'cult of personality', the impatience to see them dealt with, the hope for a real socialist democracy, etc. When these political sentiments want a theoretical basis, they always look for it in the same texts and concepts: in one of the theoreticians who emerged in the great post-1917 period (that is the reason for all these editions of the young Lukács and Korsch, and the passion for certain ambiguous formulations of Gramsci), or in Marx's humanist texts: his Early Works; in 'real humanism', in 'alien-ation', in the 'concrete', in 'concrete' history, philosophy and psychology.[30]

Only a critical reading of Marx's *Early Works* and a thorough study of *Capital* can enlighten us as to the significance and risks involved in a *theoretical* humanism and historicism, for they are foreign to Marx's problematic.

*

The reader will probably remember the point from which we set out on this analysis of a misunderstanding of history. I pointed out that the way Marx thought of himself might emerge from the judgements in which he weighs the merits and faults of his predecessors. At the same time, I suggested that we had to submit Marx's text not to an immediate reading, but to a *'symptomatic' reading*, in order to discern in the apparent continuity of the discourse the lacunae, blanks and failures of rigour, the places where Marx's discourse is merely the unsaid of his silence, arising in his discourse itself. I uncovered one of these theoretical symptoms in the judgement Marx himself gave of the absence of a concept in his predecessors, the absence of the *concept* of surplus-value, which (as Engels puts it) Marx 'disdained' to treat as more than a matter of the absence of a word. We have just seen what happens when another *word*, the word *'history'*, arises in the critical discourse Marx addressed to his predecessors. This apparently full word is in fact theoretically an empty word, in the immediacy of its obviousness – or rather, it is the ideology-fulfilment (*plein-de-l'idéologie*)[31] which surfaces in this lapse of rigour. Anyone who reads *Capital* without posing the critical question of its object sees no malice in this word that 'speaks' to him: he happily continues the discourse whose first word this word may be, the ideological discourse of history, and then the historicist discourse. As we have seen and as we understand, the theoretical and practical consequences are not so innocent. In an epistemological and critical reading, on the contrary, we cannot but hear behind the proferred word the silence it con-ceals, see the blank of suspended rigour, scarcely the time of a lightning-flash in the darkness of the text: correlatively, we cannot but hear behind this discourse which seems continuous but is really interrupted and gov-erned by the threatened irruption of a repressive discourse, the silent voice

---

[30] Cf. *La Nouvelle Critique*, nos. 164, 165, etc.

[31] This example can, by analogy, be compared with that of the symptom, the slip of the tongue and the dream – which is, for Freud, a 'wish-fulfilment' (*plein du désir*). [Cf. Louis Althusser: 'Freud and Lacan', *New Left Review* No. 55, May-June 1969, p. 61, n. 6].

of the real discourse, we cannot but restore its text, in order to re-establish its profound continuity. It is here that the identification of the precise points of weakness in Marx's rigour is the same thing as the recognition of that rigour: it is his rigour that shows us its weaknesses; and in the brief moment of his temporary silence we are simply returning to him the speech that is his own.

Chapter 6

The Epistemological Propositions

of *Capital*

(Marx, Engels)

After this long digression, let us take stock of our analysis. We are looking for Marx's peculiar object.

In a first moment, we examined the texts in which Marx tells us what *his real discovery* is, and we isolated the concepts of value and surplus-value as the bearers of this discovery. But we were forced to note that these concepts were precisely the site of the misunderstanding not only of the economists, but also of a number of Marxists about the peculiar object of the Marxist theory of political economy.

Then, *in a second moment*, we examined Marx through his own judgement of his predecessors, the founders of classical Political Economy, in the hope of grasping Marx himself in the judgement he pronounced on his own scientific prehistory. Here too we stumbled on disconcerting or inadequate definitions. We found that Marx did not really succeed in thinking the concept of the difference between himself and Classical Economics, and that by thinking this difference in terms of a continuity of content, he either projected us into a merely formal distinction, the dialectic, or into the foundation of this Hegelian dialectic, a certain ideological conception of history. We have assessed the theoretical and practical consequences of these ambiguities; we have seen that the ambiguity in the texts did not affect only the definition of the specific object of *Capital*, but also and at the same time the definition of Marx's theoretical practice, the relationship between his theory and earlier theories – in short, the theory of science and the theory of the history of science. In this we were no longer dealing only with the theory of political economy and history, or historical materialism, but also with the theory of science and of the history of science, or dialectical materialism. And we can *see*, if only in relief, that there is an essential relationship between what Marx produced in the theory of history and what he produced in philosophy. We can *see it* in at least the following sign: the mere existence of an emptiness in the system of concepts of historical materialism is enough to establish in it immediately the fullness of a philosophical ideology, the empiricist ideology. We can only recognize this emptiness by emptying it of the obviousnesses of the ideological philosophy of which it is full. We can only rigorously define Marx's few and as yet inadequate scientific concepts on the absolute condition that we recognize the ideological nature of the philosophical concepts which have usurped their places: in short, on the absolute condition that at the same time we begin to define the concepts of Marxist philosophy adapted to knowing and recognizing as ideological the philosophical concepts which mask the weaknesses of the scientific concepts from us. In this we are absolutely committed to a theoretical destiny: we cannot *read* Marx's scientific discourse without at the same time writing at his dictation the text of another discourse, inseparable from the first one but distinct from it: the discourse of Marx's *philosophy*.

Let us now begin the *third moment* of this examination. *Capital*, Engels's prefaces, certain letters and the Notes on Wagner in fact contain what we need to start us off in a productive direction. What until now we have had to recognize negatively in Marx we shall from here on discover positively.

First we shall look at a few comments on *terminology*. We know that Marx criticized Smith and Ricardo for constantly *confusing* surplus-value with its forms of existence: profit, rent and interest. The great Economists' analyses are therefore lacking a word. When Marx reads them he re-establishes this missing word in their texts: surplus-value. This act of re-establishing an absent *word* may seem insignificant, but it has considerable theoretical consequences: in fact, this word is not a word, but a *concept*, and a theoretical concept, which is here the *representative* of a new conceptual system, the correlative of the appearance of a new object. Every word is of course a concept, but every concept is not a theoretical concept, and every theoretical concept is not the representative of a new object. If the word surplus-value has such importance it is because it directly affects the structure of the object whose future is at stake in the simple act of naming. It does not matter that all these consequences were nowhere near Marx's mind or pen when he criticized Smith and Ricardo for having skipped a *word*. Marx should not be expected to say everything at once any more than anybody else: what is important is that *elsewhere* he should say what he does not say when he says it *here*. Now Marx undoubtedly regarded as a theoretical requirement of the first order the need to constitute an adequate scientific terminology, i.e., a consistent system of defined terms in which not only would the words already used be concepts but in which the new words would also be concepts and moreover ones which define a new object. Criticizing Wagner's confusion of use-value and value, Marx wrote:

> The only stable thing in this German imbecility is that the *words* value or worth (*Wert, Würde*) are applied *literally* directly to the useful things themselves, which existed for a long time, even as 'products of labour' before they became commodities. But this has as much to do with the *scientific definition* of commodity 'value' as the fact that the

word salt was first applied to cooking salt by the ancient world, and that therefore since Pliny *sugar*, etc., have figured as *kinds of salt*, etc. (*Werke*, Bd. XIX, p. 372)

– and slightly earlier:

This is reminiscent of the old chemists before chemistry was a science: because edible butter, which in ordinary life was just called butter (according to nordic custom), has a soft consistency, they called chlorides butter of zinc, butter of antimony, etc., or butyrous humours (ibid., p. 371).

This text is especially clear, for it distinguishes between the '*literal*' meaning of a word and its scientific and conceptual meaning, on the basis of a theoretical revolution in the object of a science (chemistry). If Marx proposes a *new object*, he must necessarily provide a corresponding new conceptual terminology.[32]

Engels put this particularly well in a passage from his Preface to the English edition of *Capital* (1886 – T.I, pp. 35-6; Vol. I, pp. 4-6):

There is, however, one difficulty we could not spare the reader: the use of certain terms in a sense different from what they have, not only in common life, but *in ordinary Political Economy*. But *this was unavoidable*. Every new aspect of a science involves a revolution in the technical terms (*Fachausdrücken*) of that science. This is best shown by chemistry, where the whole of the terminology (*Terminologie*) is radically changed about once in twenty years, and where you will hardly find a single organic compound that has not gone through a whole series of different names. Political Economy has generally been content to take, just as they were, the terms of commercial and industrial life, and to operate with them, entirely failing to see that *by so doing, it confined itself within the narrow circle of ideas expressed by those terms*. Thus, *though perfectly aware that* both profits and rent are but sub-divisions, fragments of that unpaid part of the product which the labourer has to supply to his employer (its first appropriator, though not its ultimate exclusive owner), yet even classical Political Economy *never went beyond the received notions* (übliche Begriffe) *of profits and rents, never examined this unpaid part of the product* (called by Marx surplus-product) *in its integrity as a whole,* and therefore never arrived at a *clear comprehension,* either of its origin and nature, or of the laws that regulate the subsequent distribution of its value. Similarly all industry, not agricultural or handicraft, is indiscriminately comprised in the term of manufacture, and thereby the distinction is obliterated

---

[32] Cf. *Capital*, T.I, p. 17; Vol. I, p. 8n, where Marx speaks of the 'new terminology created' by him.

between two great and essentially different periods of economic history: the period of manufacture proper, based on the division of manual labour, and the period of modern industry based on machinery. It is, however, self-evident that a *theory which views modern capitalist production as a mere passing stage in the economic history of mankind, must make use of terms different from those habitual to writers who look upon that form of production as imperishable and final.*[33]

We should retain the following basic theses from this text:

(1) every revolution (new aspect of a science) in its object necessarily leads to a revolution in its terminology;

(2) every terminology is linked to a definite circle of ideas, and we can translate this by saying: every terminology is a function of the theoretical system that provides its bases, every terminology brings with it a determinate and limited theoretical system;

(3) classical political economy was confined within a circle defined by the identity of its system of ideas and its terminology;

(4) in revolutionizing classical economic theory, Marx necessarily had to revolutionize its terminology;

(5) the sensitive point in this revolution concerns precisely *surplus-value*. Their failure to think it in a word which was the concept of its object kept the classical economists in the dark, imprisoning them in words which were merely the ideological or empirical concepts of economic practice;

(6) in the last resort, Engels reveals the difference between the terminology of classical political economy and Marx's terminology as a difference in their conceptions of the object: the classics regarding it as imperishable, Marx as passing. We know what to think of this idea.

Despite this last weakness, this text is quite remarkable, since it reveals an intimate relationship between the *object* of a determinate scientific discipline on the one hand, and the system of its terminology and that of its ideas, on the other. It therefore reveals an intimate relationship between the object, the terminology and the corresponding conceptual system – a relationship which, once the object has been modified (once its 'new aspects' have been grasped), must necessarily induce a correlative modification in the system of ideas and conceptual terminology.

Or else, to put the same thing in a different language, Engels asserts the existence of a necessary functional connexion between *the nature of the object, the nature of the theoretical problematic* and *the nature of the conceptual terminology*.

---

[33] This is a very remarkable, even exemplary text. It gives us a quite different idea of Engels's exceptional epistemological sensitivity from that which we have gathered from him in other circumstances. There will be other occasions on which we shall be able to signal Engels's theoretical genius, for he is far from being the second-rate commentator usually contrasted unfavourably with Marx.

This connexion is even clearer in another astonishing text of Engels's, the Preface to Volume Two of *Capital*, a text which can be related directly to the analysis Marx gives of the blindness of the classical economists with regard to the wages problem (T.II, pp. 206ff; Vol. I, pp. 535ff).

In this text, Engels poses the question sharply:

Capitalistic man has been producing surplus-value for several hundred years and has gradually arrived at the point of pondering over its origin. The view first propounded grew directly out of commercial practice: surplus-value arises out of an addition to the value of the product. This idea was current among the mercantilists. But James Steuart already realized that in that case one would necessarily lose what the other would gain. Nevertheless, this view persisted for a long time afterwards, especially among the Socialists. But it was thrust out of classical science by Adam Smith (Vol. II, p. 8).

Engels then shows that Smith and Ricardo knew the origin of capitalist surplus-value. If they *'did not separate surplus-value as such, considered as a special category, from the special forms which it assumes in profit and ground rent'* (ibid., p. 10), they did *'produce'* the basic principle of the Marxist theory in *Capital*: surplus-value.

Whence the epistemologically pertinent question:

But what is there new in Marx's utterances on surplus-value? How is it that Marx's theory of surplus-value struck home like a thunderbolt out of a clear sky, and that in all civilized countries, while the theories of all his socialist predecessors, Rodbertus included, vanished without having produced any effect? (ibid., p. 14).

Engels's recognition of the enormous effect of the emergence of a new theory – the 'thunderbolt out of a clear sky' – is of interest to us as a brutal index of Marx's *novelty*. This is no longer a matter of the ambiguous differences (fixist eternalism, history in movement) in which Marx tries to express his relationship with the economists. Engels does not hesitate: he *directly* poses the true problem of Marx's epistemological *rupture* with classical economics; he poses it at the most pertinent, and also the most paradoxical point: *surplus-value*. Surplus-value is precisely not *new*, since it has already been 'produced' by classical economics! Engels therefore poses the question of Marx's *novelty* with respect to a reality which *is not new* in Marx! The extraordinary intelligence of this question reveals Engels's genius: he braves the question in its last hiding-place, without retreating an inch; he confronts it just where it was presented in the crushing form of its *answer*; where rather the answer's crushing claims to obviousness enabled it to prevent the slightest question being posed! He is so bold as to pose the question of the novelty of the non-novelty of a reality which appears in *two different discourses*, i.e., the question of the *theoretical modality* of this 'reality' inscribed in two theoretical discourses. A simple reading of his answer reveals that he has not posed it out of malice or at random, but within the field of a theory of science based on a theory of the history of the sciences. In fact, it is a comparison with the history of chemistry which enables him to formulate his question and define its answers.

What is there new in Marx's utterances on surplus value? . . .

The history of chemistry offers an illustration which explains this.

We know that late in the past century the phlogistic theory still prevailed. It assumed that combustion consisted essentially in this: that a certain hypothetical substance, an absolute combustible named phlogiston, separated from the burning body. This theory sufficed to explain most of the chemical phenomena then known, although it had to be considerably strained in some cases. But in 1774 Priestley produced a certain kind of air 'which he found to be so pure, or so free from phlogiston, that common air seemed adulterated in comparison with it,' He called it 'dephlogisticated air'. Shortly after him Scheele obtained the same kind of air in Sweden and demonstrated its existence in the atmosphere. He also found that this kind of air disappeared whenever some body was burned in it or in ordinary air and therefore he called it 'fire-air'.

Priestley and Scheele had *produced* oxygen *without knowing* what they had laid their hands on. They '*remained prisoners of the*' phlogistic '*categories as they came down to them*'. The element which was destined to *upset all* phlogistic views (*die ganze phlogistische Anschauung umstossen*) and *to revolutionize chemistry* remained barren in their hands. But Priestley had immediately communicated his discovery to Lavoisier in Paris, and Lavoisier, by means of this *new* fact (*Tatsache*), analysed *the entire phlogistic chemistry* and came to the conclusion that this new kind of air was a new chemical element, and that combustion was not a case of the mysterious phlogiston *departing* from the burning body, but of this new element *combining with that body*, Thus he was the first *to place all chemistry, which in its phlogistic form had stood on its head, squarely on its feet* (*stellte so die ganze Chemie, die in ihrer phlogistischen Form auf dem Kopf gestanden, erst auf die Füsse*). And although he did not produce oxygen simultaneously and independently of the other two, as he claimed later on, he nevertheless is the real *discoverer* (*der eigentliche Entdecker*) of oxygen *vis-à-vis* the others who had only produced it (*dargestellt*) without knowing what (*was*) they had produced.

Marx stands in the same relation to his predecessors in the theory of surplus-value as Lavoisier stood to Priestley and Scheele. The *existence* (*die Existenz*) of that part of the value of products which we now call (*nennen*) surplus-value had been ascertained long before Marx. It had also been stated with more or less precision what it consisted of, namely, of the product of the labour for which its appropriator had not given any equivalent. But one did not get any further (*Weiter aber kam man nicht*). Some – the classical bourgeois economists – investigated at most the proportion in which the product of labour was divided between the labourer and the owner of the means of production. Others – the Socialists – found that the division was unjust and looked for utopian means for abolishing this injustice. They all remained prisoners (*befangen*) of the economic categories as they had come down to them (*wie sie sie vorgefunden hatten*).

Now Marx appeared upon the scene. *And he took a view directly opposite to that of all his predecessors* (*in direktem Gegensatz zu allen seinen Vorgänger*). What they had regarded as a *solution* (*Lösung*), he considered but a *problem* (*Problem*). He saw that he had to deal neither with dephlogisticated air nor with fire-air, but with oxygen – that here it was not simply a matter of stating an economic fact (*Tatsache*) or of pointing out the conflict between this fact and eternal justice and true morality, but of explaining a fact (*Tatsache*) which was destined to revolutionize (*umwälzen*) all economics, and which offered to him who knew how to use it the key to an understanding of all (*gesamten*) capitalist production. With this fact as his starting-point he examined (*untersuchte*) all the economic categories which he found at hand, just as Lavoisier proceeding from oxygen had examined the categories of phlogistic chemistry which he found at hand. In order to understand what surplus-value was, Marx had to find out what value was. He had to criticize above all the Ricardian theory of value. Hence he analysed labour's value-producing property and was the first to ascertain *what* labour it was that produced value, and why and how it did so. He found that value was nothing but congealed labour of *this* kind, and this is a point which Rodbertus never grasped to his dying day. Marx then investigated the relation of commodities to money and demonstrated how and why, thanks to the property of value immanent in commodities, commodities and commodity-exchange must engender the opposition of commodity and money. His theory of money, founded on this basis, is the first exhaustive (*erschöpfende*) one and has been tacitly accepted everywhere. He analysed the transformation of money into capital and demonstrated that this transformation is based on the purchase and sale of labour-power. By *substituting* (*an die Stelle . . . setzen*) labour-power, the value-producing property, for labour, he solved with one stroke (*löste er mit einem Schlag*) one of the difficulties which brought about the downfall of the Ricardian school, viz., the impossibility of harmonizing the mutual exchange of capital and labour with the Ricardian law that value is determined by labour. By establishing the distinction of capital into constant and variable he was enabled to represent (*darzustellen*) the real course of the process of the formation of surplus-value in its minutest details and thus to explain (*erklären*) it, a feat which none of his predecessors had accomplished. Consequently he established a distinction inside of capital itself with which neither Rodbertus nor the bourgeois economists knew in the least what to do, but which furnishes the key for the solution of the most complicated economic problems, as is strikingly proved again by Book II and will be proved still more by Book III. He analysed surplus-value further and found its two forms, absolute and relative surplus-value. And he showed that they had played a different, and each time a decisive role, in the historical development of capitalist production. On the basis of this surplus-value he developed the first rational theory of wages we have, and for the first time drew up an outline of the history of capitalist accumulation and an exposition of its historical tendency.

And Rodbertus? After he has read all that, he . . . finds that he himself has said much more briefly and clearly what surplus-value evolves from, and finally declares that all this does indeed apply to 'the present form of capital', that is to say to capital as it exists historically, but not to the 'concept of capital', namely the utopian idea which Herr Rodbertus has of capital. Just like old Priestley, who swore by phlogiston to the end of his days and refused to have anything to do with oxygen. The only thing is that Priestley had actually produced oxygen first, while Rodbertus had merely rediscovered a commonplace in his surplus-value, or rather his 'rent', and that Marx, unlike Lavoisier, disdained to claim that he was the first to discover the fact (*Tatsache*) of the existence of surplus-value' (Vol. II, pp. 14–16).

Let us summarize the theses of this remarkable text.

(1) Priestley and Scheele, in the period dominated by phlogistic theory, 'produced' (*stellt dar*) a strange gas, which the former called dephlogisticated air – and the latter: fire-air. In fact, it was the gas that would later be called oxygen. But, notes Engels, they '*had produced it without having the least idea of what they had produced*', i.e., without its *concept*. That is why '*the element which was determined to upset all phlogistic views and to revolutionize chemistry remained barren in their hands*'. Why this barrenness and blindness? Because they '*remained prisoners of the "phlogistic" categories as they came down to them*'. Because, instead of seeing in oxygen a problem, they merely saw '*a solution*'.

(2) Lavoisier did just the opposite: '*Lavoisier, by means of this new fact, analysed the entire phlogistic chemistry*'; '*thus he was the first to place all chemistry, which in its phlogistic form had stood on its head, squarely on its feet*'. Where the others saw a solution he saw a problem. That is why, if it can be said that the first two '*produced*' oxygen, it was Lavoisier alone who *discovered* it, by giving it its concept.

Exactly the same is true of Marx, in his relation with Smith and Ricardo, as of Lavoisier, in his relation with Priestley and Scheele: he truly *discovered* the surplus-value his predecessors had merely *produced*.

This mere comparison and the terms in which it is expressed, open up vistas deep into Marx's work and into Engels's epistemological insight. In order to understand Marx we must treat him as one scientist among others and apply to his scientific work the same epistemological and historical concepts we would apply to others: in this case to Lavoisier. Marx thus appears as the founder of a science, comparable with Galileo or Lavoisier. What is more, in order to understand the relation between Marx's work and that of his predecessors, in order to understand the nature of the *break* or *mutation* which distinguishes him from them, we must examine the work of other founders who also had to break with their predecessors. An understanding of Marx, of the mechanism of his discovery and of the nature of the epistemological break which inaugurated his scientific foundation, leads us therefore to the concepts of a general theory of the history of the sciences, a theory capable of thinking the essence of these *theoretical events*. It is one thing whether this general theory as yet only exists as a project or whether it has already partially materialized; it is another that it is *absolutely indispensable to a study of Marx*. The path Engels designates for us in what he has done is a path we must take at all costs: it is none other than the path of the philosophy founded by Marx in the act of founding the science of history.

Engels's text goes further. He gives us in so many words the first theoretical outline of the concept of the *break*: the mutation by which a new science is established in a new problematic, separated from the old ideological problematic. But the most astonishing point is this: Engels thinks this theory of the mutation of the problematic, i.e., of the *break*, in the terms of the *'inversion'* which *'places squarely on its feet'* a discipline which *'had stood on its head'*. Here we have a familiar idea! *the very terms in which Marx*, in the Afterword to the Second Edition of *Capital, defined the treatment he applied to the Hegelian dialectic in order to change it from the idealist state to the materialist state*. Here we find the very terms in which Marx defined the relationship between himself and Hegel in a phrase that still weighs very heavily on Marxism. But what a difference! Instead of Marx's enigmatic phrase, Engels gives us a luminous one – and in Engels's phrase, at last, for the first and perhaps *the only time* in all the classical texts, we find a *clear* explanation of Marx's phrase. *'To put chemistry which had stood on its head squarely on its feet'*, means, without any possible ambiguity, in Engels's text: to *change* the theoretical base, to *change* the theoretical problematic of chemistry, replacing the old problematic with a new one. This is the meaning of the famous 'inversion': in this image, which is no more than an image and has neither the meaning nor the rigour of a concept, Marx was simply trying to indicate for his part the *existence* of the mutation of the problematic which inaugurates every scientific foundation.

(3) In fact, Engels describes to us one of the formal conditions for an event in theoretical history: precisely a *theoretical revolution*. We have seen

that it is essential to construct the concepts of theoretical *fact* and theoretical *event*, of the theoretical revolution which intervenes in the history of knowledge, in order to be able to constitute the history of knowledge – just as it is essential to construct and articulate the concepts of historical fact and historical event, of revolution, etc., in order to be able to think political or economic history. With Marx we are at the site of a historical break of the first importance, not only in the history of the science of history, but also in the history of philosophy, to be precise, in the history of the *Theoretical*; this break (which enables us to resolve a periodization problem in the history of science) coincides with a *theoretical event*, the revolution in the science of history and in philosophy constituted by the problematic introduced by Marx. It does not matter that this event went wholly or partly unperceived, that *time* is needed before this theoretical revolution can make all its effects felt, that it has suffered an incredible repression in the visible history of ideas; the event took place, the break took place, and the history which was born with it is grubbing its subterranean way beneath official history: 'well grubbed, old mole!' One day the official history of ideas will fall behind it, and when it realizes this it will be too late for it unless it is prepared to recognize this event and draw the consequences.

Indeed Engels shows us the other side of this revolution: the insistence with which those who have lived through it *deny it*: 'the old Priestley . . . swore by phlogiston to the end of his days and refused to have anything to do with oxygen'. Like Smith and Ricardo, he held to the *system of existing ideas*, refusing to question the theoretical problematic from which the new discovery had just broken.[34] I am justified in putting forward this term 'theoretical *problematic*' because in doing so I am giving a name (which is a concept) to what Engels *says* to us: Engels in fact sums up the critical interrogation of the old theory and the constitution of the new one, in the act of *posing as a problem* what had hitherto been given as a *solution*. This is no more than Marx's own conception, in the famous chapter on wages (T.II, pp. 206ff.; Vol. I, pp. 535ff.). Examining what it was that allowed classical political economy to define wages by the value of the necessary subsistence goods, Marx wrote: 'It *thus unwittingly changed terrain* by substituting for the value of labour, up to this point the apparent object of its investigations, the value of labour-power . . . The result the analysis led to therefore was *not a resolution of the problem as it emerged at the beginning, but a complete change in the terms of that problem.*' Here, too, we can see the content of the 'inversion': this 'change of terrain' identical with the 'change of terms', and therefore the change in the theoretical basis from which the *questions* are formulated and the *problems* posed. Here, too, we

---

[34] The history of science is no different from social history here: there are those in both 'who have learnt nothing and forgotten nothing', especially when they have seen the show from the front row.

can see that there is no difference between 'inverting', 'placing what had stood on its head squarely on its feet', 'changing terrain' and 'changing the terms of the problem': each of these transformations is the same, affecting the peculiar structure of the basic theory in respect to which every problem is posed in the terms and in the field of the new theory. To change theoretical base is therefore to *change theoretical problematic*, if it is true that the theory of a science at a given moment in its history is no more than the *theoretical matrix of the type of questions* the science poses its object – if it is true that with a new basic theory a new organic way of putting questions to the object comes into the world, a new way of posing questions and in consequence of producing new answers. Speaking of the *question* that Smith and Ricardo put to wages, Engels writes: '*The question* (die Frage) *is indeed insoluble* (unlöslich), *if put in this form. It has been correctly* (richtig) *formulated by Marx and thereby been answered*' (Vol. II, p. 17). This *correct formulation* of the problem is not a chance effect: on the contrary, it is *the effect of a new theory*, which is the system for posing problems in a correct form – the effect of a new problematic. Hence every theory is in its essence a problematic, i.e., the theoretico-systematic matrix for posing every problem concerning the object of the theory.

(4) But Engels's text contains something further. It contains the idea that the reality, the new fact (*Tatsache*), in this case the existence of surplus-value, cannot be reduced to '*simply a matter of stating an economic fact*': that, on the contrary, it is a fact destined to revolutionize all economics, and provide an understanding of '*all capitalist production*'. Marx's discovery is not therefore a subjective problem (merely a way of interrogating a given reality, or a changed 'view-point', both purely subjective): in correlation with the transformation of the theoretical matrix for posing every problem concerning the object, it concerns the *reality of the object: its objective definition*. To cast doubt on the definition of the object is to pose the question of a differential definition of the *novelty of the object* aimed at by the new theoretical problematic. In the history of the revolutions of a science, every upheaval in the theoretical practice is correlated with a transformation in the definition of the object, and therefore with a difference which can be assigned to the *object* of the theory itself.

In drawing this conclusion, have I gone beyond Engels? Yes and no. *No*, for Engels does not only take into account the existence of a system of phlogistic ideas, which, before Lavoisier, determined the way every problem was posed, and therefore the meaning of every corresponding solution; as he takes into account the existence of a system of ideas in Ricardo when he notes the ultimate necessity which forced Marx to '*criticize above all the Ricardian theory of value*' (Vol. II, p. 15). Perhaps *yes*, if it is true that however acute he may have been in his analysis of this theoretical event and scientific revolution, Engels was not so bold when it came to thinking this revolution's effects *on the object* of the theory. We have already noted the ambiguities of his conception on this point of which he was very much aware: they can all be reduced to the empiricist confusion between the object of knowledge and the real object. Engels clearly fears that by risking himself beyond the (imaginary) security of the empiricist thesis he may lose the guarantees he obtains by proclaiming a *real* identity between the object of knowledge and the real object. He has difficulty in imagining what he is saying, although he does say it and the history of science reveals it to him at every step: the fact that the process of production of a knowledge necessarily proceeds by the constant transformation of its (conceptual) object; that it is precisely the effect of this transformation, which is the same thing as the history of knowledge, that it produces a *new* knowledge (a new object of knowledge) which still concerns the *real object*, knowledge of which is deepened precisely by this reorganization of the object of knowledge. As Marx says profoundly, the *real* object, of which knowledge is to be acquired or deepened, *remains what it is*, after as before the process of knowledge which involves it (cf. the *1857 Introduction*); if, therefore, it is the absolute reference point for the process of knowledge which is concerned with it – the deepening of the knowledge of this real object is achieved by *a labour of theoretical transformation* which necessarily affects the *object of knowledge*, since it is only applied to the latter. Lenin understood this essential condition of scientific practice perfectly – it is one of the major themes of *Materialism and Empirico-Criticism: the theme of the incessant deepening of the knowledge of a real object by incessantly reorganizing the object of knowledge*. This transformation of the object of knowledge may take various forms: it may be continuous and impalpable – or, on the contrary, discontinuous and spectacular. When a well-established science is developing smoothly, the transformation of the object (of knowledge) takes on a continuous, progressive form: the transformation of the object makes 'new aspects' visible in the object, aspects which were *not at all visible* before; the object is then like a geographical map of a region which is still little known but in process of exploration: the blanks in the interior are being filled in with new details and corrections, but without modifying the already recognized and accepted general outlines of the region. For example, this is how we have been able since Marx to pursue the systematic investigation of the object Marx defined: we shall certainly add new details, 'see' what we could not see before – but inside an object whose structure will be confirmed rather than revolutionized by our results. The reverse is the case in the *critical* periods in the development of a science when real *mutations* take place in the theoretical problematic: the *object* of the theory then suffers a corresponding mutation, which now does not only affect 'aspects' of the object, details of its structure, but this structure itself. What is then made visible is a new structure of the object, often so different from the old that it is legitimate to speak of a *new object*: the history of mathematics from the beginning of the nineteenth century until today, or the history of modern physics, are rich in mutations of this kind. *A fortiori*, the same is true when a new science is born – when it detaches itself from the field of the ideology from which it breaks at its birth: this theoretical 'uncoupling' always and inevitably induces a revolutionary change in the theoretical problematic, and just as radical a modification of the *object* of theory. In this case, it is strictly correct to speak of a *revolution*, of a qualitative leap, of a modification affecting the *very structure of the object*.[35] The new object may well still retain some link with the old ideological object, *elements* may be found in it which belong to the old object, too: but the meaning of these elements changes with the new *structure*, which precisely confers on them their meaning. These apparent similarities in isolated elements may mislead a superficial glance unaware of the function of the structure in the constitution of the meaning of the elements of an object, just as certain technical similarities in isolated elements may deceive those interpreters who rank structures as different as contemporary capitalism and socialism within the same category ('industrial societies'). In fact, this theoretical revolution which is visible in the break which separates a new science from the ideology which gave it birth, reverberates profoundly in the object of the theory, which is at the same moment itself the site of a revolution – and becomes peculiarly a *new object*. This mutation in the *object*, like the mutation in the corresponding problematic, may become the object of a rigorous epistemological study. And as a single movement constitutes both the new problematic and the new object, the study of this double mutation is in fact only a single study, belonging to the discipline which reflects on the history of the forms of knowledge and on the mechanism of their production: philosophy.

With this we reach the threshold of our question: what is the *peculiar object* of the economic theory founded by Marx in *Capital*, what is the object of *Capital*? What is the specific difference between Marx's object and that of his predecessors?

---

[35] A good example: Freud's 'object' is a radically new object with respect to the 'object' of the psychological or philosophical ideologies of his predecessors. Freud's object is the *unconscious*, which has nothing to do with the objects of all the varieties of modern psychology, although the latter can be multiplied at will! It is even possible to see the number one task of every new discipline as that of *thinking* the specific difference of the new object which it *discovers*, distinguishing it rigorously from the old object and constructing the peculiar concepts required to think it. It is in this basic theoretical work that a science wins its effective right to autonomy in open combat.

Chapter 7
The Object of Political Economy

To answer this question, I shall take literally the sub-title of *Capital* – 'A Critique of Political Economy'. If the view I have put forward is correct, 'to criticize' Political Economy cannot mean to criticize or correct certain inaccuracies or points of detail in an existing discipline – nor even to fill in its gaps, its blanks, pursuing further an already largely initiated movement of exploration. 'To criticize Political Economy' means to *confront* it with a new problematic and a new object: i.e., to question the very *object* of Political Economy. But since Political Economy is defined as Political Economy by its object, the critique directed at it from the new object with which it is confronted could strike Political Economy's vital spot. This is indeed the case: Marx's critique of Political Economy cannot challenge the latter's object without disputing Political Economy itself, in its theoretical pretensions to autonomy and in the 'divisions' it creates in social reality in order to make itself the theory of the latter. Marx's critique of Political Economy is therefore a very radical one: it queries not only the object of Political Economy, but also *Political Economy itself as an object*. In order to give this thesis the benefit of its radicalism, let us say that Political Economy, as it is defined by its *pretensions*, has no right to exist as far as Marx is concerned: if Political Economy thus conceived cannot exist, it is for *de jure*, not *de facto* reasons.

If this really is the case, we can understand what misunderstanding separates Marx not only from his predecessors, critics and certain of his supporters – but also from the 'economists' who have come after him. This misunderstanding is a simple one, but at the same time it is paradoxical. Simple because the economists make their living from Political Economy's pretensions to existence – and these pretensions revoke all its rights to exist. Paradoxical, because the consequence Marx has drawn from the *de jure* non-existence of Political Economy is a vast book called *Capital* which seems to speak of *nothing but* political economy from beginning to end.

We must therefore go into detail, uncovering the indispensable corrections, little by little, in the rigorous relationship that unites them. In order to anticipate them, which is necessary if we are to understand them, let us give one first reference point. Political Economy's pretensions to existence are a function of the nature and hence of *the definition of its object*. Political Economy gives itself as an object the domain of 'economic facts' which it regards as having the obviousness of *facts*: absolute givens which it takes as they 'give' themselves, without asking them for any explanations. Marx's revocation of the pretensions of Political Economy is identical with his revocation of the obviousness of this 'given', which in fact it *'gives itself'* arbitrarily as an object, pretending that this object *was given it*. Marx's whole attack is directed at this object, at its pretensions to the modality of a 'given' object: Political Economy's pretensions being no more than the mirror reflection of its object's pretensions to have been *given* it. By posing the question of the 'givenness' of the object, Marx poses the question of the object itself, of its nature and limits, and therefore of the domain of its existence, since the *modality* according to which a theory thinks its object affects not only the nature of that object but also the situation and extent of its domain of existence. As an indication, let us adopt a famous thesis of Spinoza's: as a first approximation, we can suggest that Political Economy's existence is no more possible than the existence of any science of 'conclusions' as such: a science of 'conclusions' is not a science, since it would be the actual ignorance (*'ignorance en acte'*) of its 'premises' – it is only the Imaginary in action (the 'first kind'). The science of conclusions is merely an effect, a product of the science of premises: but if we suppose that this science of premises exists, the *pretended* science of conclusions (the 'first kind') is known as imaginary and as the imaginary in action: once known it disappears with the disappearance of its pretensions and its object. The same is true *grosso modo* of Marx. If Political Economy cannot exist for itself, it is because its object does not exist for itself, because it is not the object of its concept, or because its concept is the concept of an inadequate object. Political Economy cannot exist unless the science of its premises, or if you prefer, the theory of its concepts, already exists – but once this theory exists, then Political Economy's pretensions disappear into what they are: imaginary pretensions. From these very schematic indications, we can draw two provisional conclusions. If the 'Critique of Political Economy' does have the meaning we have proposed, it must at the same time be a construction of *the true concept of the object*, at which classical Political Economy is aiming in the Imaginary of its pretensions – a construction which will produce the concept of the new object with which Marx confronts Political Economy. If any understanding of *Capital* depends on the construction of the concept of this new object, those who can read *Capital* without looking for this concept in it and without relating everything to this concept, are in serious danger of being tripped up by misunderstandings or riddles: living merely in the 'effects' of invisible causes, in the Imaginary of an economy as close to them as the sun's distance of two hundred paces in the 'first kind of knowledge' – as close, precisely because it is an infinite number of leagues away from them.

This reference point is sufficient as an introduction to our analysis. We shall proceed as follows: in order to reach a differential definition of Marx's object we shall make an initial detour: an analysis of the object of Political Economy, which will show us by its structural features the type of object Marx rejected in order to constitute his own object (A). A critique of the categories of this object will indicate to us the positive concepts in Marx's theoretical practice which are constitutive of his object (B). We can then define this object, and draw a number of conclusions from its definition.

A. THE STRUCTURE OF THE OBJECT OF POLITICAL ECONOMY

I cannot here provide a detailed examination of the classical theories, nor *a fortiori* of the modern theories, of political economy, in order to draw from it a definition of the *object* to which they are related in their theoretical practice, even if they do not reflect this object for itself.[36] I propose only to locate the most general concepts that constitute the *theoretical structure* of the object of Political Economy: in essentials, this analysis concerns the object of classical Political Economy (Smith, Ricardo), but it is not restricted to the classical forms of Political Economy, since the same basic *theoretical* categories still underly the work of many economists today. With this in mind, I think I can take as my elementary theoretical guide the definitions proposed in A. Lalande's *Dictionnaire Philosophique*. Their inconsistencies and inaccuracies, even their 'banality', are not without advantages: they can be taken as so many indices not only of a common theoretical background, but also of the possible resonances and inflexions of sense this background provides.

Lalande's Dictionary defines Political Economy as follows: '*a science whose goal is knowledge of the phenomena, and (if the nature of those phenomena allows) the determination of the laws, which concern the distribution of wealth, and its production and consumption, insofar as the latter phenomena are linked to those of distribution. Wealth means, technically, everything which is capable of utilization*' (I, p. 187). The various definitions Lalande proposes, quoting Gide, Simiand, Karmin, etc., put the concept of *distribution* in the forefront. The definition of the extension of Political Economy to the three fields of production, distribution and consumption is taken from the classics – particularly from Say. Discussing production and consumption, Lalande notes that they are '*only economic from one point of view. Taken in their totality they imply a great many notions foreign to political economy, notions borrowed, as far as production is concerned, from technology, ethnography and the science of social mores. Political economy deals with production and consumption; but only insofar as they are related to distribution, either as cause or as effect.*'

---

[36] On the modern theories, Maurice Godelier's remarkable article 'Objets et méthodes de l'anthropologie économique' (*L'Homme*, October 1965 and in *Rationalité et irrationalité en économie*, Paris 1966) can be read with profit.

Let us take this schematic definition as the most general basis of Political Economy, and see what it implies, from a *theoretical* point of view, where the *structure* of its object is concerned.

(a) First of all, it implies the existence of 'economic' facts and phenomena distributed within a definite field which has the property of being a *homogeneous field*. The field and the phenomena that constitute it and fill it are *given*, i.e., accessible to direct observation and attention: their apprehension does not depend on the prior theoretical construction of their concepts. This homogeneous field is a defined space in which the different economic determinations, facts or phenomena are, by virtue of the homogeneity of the field in which they exist, comparable, and, to be precise, *measurable*, i.e., *quantifiable*. Every economic fact is therefore in essence measurable. This was already the great principle of classical economics: precisely the first point at which Marx directed his critique. Smith's great error was, in Marx's eyes, the fact that he sacrificed the analysis of the value-form to a consideration of the *quantity* of value only: *'their attention is entirely absorbed in the analysis of the magnitude of value'* (T.I, p. 83 n1; Vol. I, p. 80 n2). On this point modern economists, despite the differences in their conception are on the side of the classics in attacking Marx for producing in his theory concepts which are 'non-operational', i.e., which exclude the measurement of their object: e.g., surplus-value. But this attack back-fires on its authors, since Marx accepts and uses measurement – for the 'developed forms' of surplus-value (profit, rent and interest). If surplus-value is not measurable, that is precisely because it is the *concept* of its forms, which are measurable. Of course, this simple distinction changes everything: the homogeneous planar space of the phenomena of political economy is no longer a mere *given*, since it requires the posing of its *concept*, i.e., the definition of the conditions and limits which allow phenomena to be treated as homogeneous, i.e., measurable. Let us merely note this difference – but without forgetting that modern political economy remains faithful to the empiricist, 'quantitative' tradition of the classics, if it is true that, to use a phrase of André Marchal's, it knows only 'measurable' facts.

(b) But this empiricist-positivist conception of economic facts is not as 'plain' (*'plat'*) as it might seem. Here I am talking about the 'plainness' of the *planar* (*'plan'*) space of its phenomena. If this homogeneous space does not refer to the depth of its concept, it does do so to a certain world outside its own plane which has the theoretical role of underlying it in existence and founding it. The homogeneous space of economic phenomena implies a determinate relationship with the world of the *men* who produce, distribute, receive and consume. This is the second theoretical implication of the object of Political Economy. This implication is not always as visible as it is in Smith and Ricardo, it may remain latent and not be so directly thematized in Economics: but it is no less essential to the structure of its object for that. Political Economy relates economic facts to their origin in the *needs* (or 'utility') of human *subjects*. It therefore tends to reduce exchange-values to use-values, and the latter ('wealth', to use the expression of Classical Economics) to human needs. This is also the position of F. Simiand (quoted by Lalande): *'What makes a phenomenon economic? Instead of defining that phenomenon with respect to wealth* (richesses – *a classical term in the French tradition, but one that could be imposed on*) *I believe it would be better to follow more recent economists who take as their central notion the satisfaction of material needs'* (Lalande, I, p. 188). Simiand is wrong to put forward his request as a novelty: his definition merely repeats the classical one, for behind men and their needs it presents their *theoretical function* as the *subjects* of the economic phenomena.

That is to say that Classical Economics can only think economic facts as belonging to the homogeneous space of their positivity and measurability on condition that it accepts a *'naïve' anthropology* which founds all the acts involved in the production, distribution, reception and consumption of economic objects on the economic subjects and their needs. Hegel provided the philosophical concept of the *unity* of this 'naïve' anthropology with the economic phenomena in his famous expression *'the sphere of needs'*, or 'civil society',[37] as distinct from political society. In the concept of the sphere of needs, economic facts are thought as based in their economic essence on human subjects who are a prey to 'need': on the *homo oeconomicus*, who is a (visible, observable) given, too. The homogeneous positivist field of measurable economic facts depends on a world of subjects whose activity as productive subjects in the division of labour has as its aim and effect the production of objects of consumption, destined to satisfy these same subjects of needs. The subjects, as subjects of needs, support the activity of the subjects as producers of use-values, exchangers of commodities and consumers of use-values. The field of economic phenomena is thus, in origin as in aim, founded on the ensemble of human subjects whose needs define them as economic subjects. *The peculiar theoretical structure of Political Economy depends on immediately and directly relating together a homogeneous space of given phenomena and an ideological anthropology which bases the economic character of the phenomena and its space on man as the subject of needs (the givenness of the homo oeconomicus).*

Let us examine this more closely. We have been speaking of a homogeneous space of *given, economic* facts or phenomena. And now, behind this given, we have discovered a world of given human subjects indispensably underlying its existence: The first given is therefore a false given: or rather it is really a given, given *by* this anthropology, which is itself given. This and this alone,

[37] The concept of 'civil society', as found in Marx's mature writings and constantly repeated by Gramsci to designate the sphere of *economic* existence, is ambiguous and should be struck from Marxist theoretical vocabulary – unless it is made to designate not the economic as opposed to the political, but the 'private' as opposed to the public, i.e., a combined *effect* of law and legal-political ideology on the economic.

indeed, allows us to declare that the phenomena which are grouped within the space of Political Economy are *economic*: they are economic as (more or less immediate or 'mediated') effects of the *needs* of human subjects, in short, of what it is that makes man, besides his rational (*animal rationale*), loquacious (*animal loquax*), laughing (*ridens*), political (*politicus*), moral and religious natures, a subject of *needs* (*homo oeconomicus*). It is the need (of the human subject) that defines the *economic* in economics. The *given* in the homogeneous field of economic phenomena is therefore given us as *economic* by this silent anthropology. But if we look closer we see that this 'giving' anthropology is, in the strongest sense, the absolute given! unless someone refers us to God as its founder, i.e., to the Given who himself gives himself, *causa sui*, God-Given. Let us leave this point in which we can see well enough that there can never be a given on the fore-stage of obviousnesses, except by means of a giving ideology which stays behind, with which we keep no accounts and which gives us what it wants. If we do not go and look behind the curtain we shall not see its act of 'giving': it disappears into the given as all workmanship does into its works. We are its spectators, i.e., its beggars.

This is not all: the same anthropology that underlies the space of economic phenomena in this way, allowing them to be called economic, re-emerges in them later in other forms, some of which we know: if classical political economy was able to present itself as a happy providential order, as economic harmony (from the Physiocrats to Say via Smith), it was by the direct projection of the moral or religious attributes of its latent anthropology onto the space of economic phenomena. The same type of intervention was at work in liberal bourgeois optimism or in the moral protests of Ricardo's socialist commentators, with whom Marx constantly crossed swords: the content of the anthropology changes but the anthropology survived, along with its role and the site of its intervention. This latent anthropology also re-emerges in certain myths of modern political economists, e.g., in concepts as ambiguous as economic 'rationality', 'optimum', 'full employment' or welfare economics, 'humane' economics, etc. The same anthropology which serves as the original foundation for economic phenomena comes to the fore as soon as there is a question of defining the meaning of these phenomena, i.e., their *end*. The homogeneous given space of economic phenomena is thus doubly given by the anthropology which grips it in the vice of origins and ends.

And if this anthropology seems *absent* from the immediate reality of the phenomena themselves, it is in the interval between origins and ends, and also by virtue of its universality which is merely repetition. As all the subjects are equally subjects of needs their effects can be dealt with by bracketing the ensemble of these subjects: their universality is then reflected in the universality of the laws of the effects of their needs – which naturally leads Political Economy towards its pretensions to deal with economic phenomena in the absolute, in all forms of society, past, present and future. The taste for false eternity Marx found in the Classics may have come to them *politically* from their wish to make the bourgeois mode of production everlasting: this is obvious enough for some of them: Smith, Say, etc. But it may have come to them from a different cause, one older than the bourgeoisie, living in the time of a different history, not from a political cause but from a *theoretical* cause: from theoretical effects produced by this silent anthropology, which ratifies the structure of the object of Political Economy. This is surely the case with Ricardo, who knew perfectly well that one day the bourgeoisie would have had its day, who already read this destiny into the mechanism of its economy and yet continued to speak the discourse of eternity at the top of his voice.

Need we go further in our analysis of the structure of the object of Political Economy than this functional unity between the homogeneous field of given economic phenomena – and a latent anthropology, and reveal the presuppositions, the theoretical (philosophical) concepts which in their specific connexions underly this unity? We should then be faced by philosophical concepts as fundamental as: given, subject, origin, end, order – and connexions such as that of linear and teleological causality. All these concepts deserve a detailed analysis showing the role they are forced to play in Political Economy's stage direction. But this would lead us much too far afield – and, in any case, we shall come across them again from the other side when we see Marx either rejecting them or giving them quite different roles.

Chapter 8

Marx's Critique

Marx rejected both the positive conception of a homogeneous field of given economic phenomena – and the ideological anthropology of the *homo oeconomicus* (etc.) which underlies it. Along with this unity he therefore rejected the very structure of the object of Political Economy.

First let us see what was the fate of *classical anthropology* in Marx's work. For this purpose I shall make a rapid survey of the major regions of the economic 'space': consumption, distribution and production – in order to see what *theoretical* place is occupied in it by anthropological concepts.

A. CONSUMPTION

We can begin with *consumption*, which seems a direct concern of anthropology since it involves the concept of human *'needs'*. In the *1857 Introduction*, Marx showed that economic needs cannot be defined unambiguously by relating them to the 'human nature' of the economic subjects. In fact, consumption is *double*. It does include the *individual consumption* of the men in a given society, but also *productive consumption*, which would have to be defined as the consumption which satisfies the needs of production to consecrate the universal use of the concept of need. This kind of consumption includes: the 'objects' of production (natural materials or raw materials, the result of labour transforming natural materials) and the instruments of production (tools, machines, etc.) necessary for production. A full part of consumption is therefore directly and exclusively the concern of production itself. A full part of consumption is therefore devoted not to the satisfaction of the needs of individuals, but to allowing either simple or extended reproduction of the conditions of production. From this statement Marx drew two absolutely essential distinctions, both of which are absent from classical Political Economy: the distinction between *constant capital* and *variable capital*, and the distinction between two departments of production, Department I, devoted to the reproduction of the conditions of production on a simple or extended basis, and Department II, devoted to the production of the objects of individual consumption. The proportion between these two departments is governed by the *structure* of production which intervenes directly to determine the nature and the quantity of a full part

of the use-values which never enter consumption for need but only production itself. This discovery plays an essential part in the theory of the
realization of value, in the process of capitalist accumulation, and in all the
laws that flow from it. This point is the object of an interminable polemic of
Marx's against Smith, which he returns to several times in Volumes Two and
Three and which is echoed in Lenin's critique of the populists and their
teacher, the 'romantic' economist Sismondi.[38]

However, this distinction does not settle all the questions. It may be
true that the 'needs' of production avoid any anthropological determination,
but it remains true also that part of the product is consumed by individuals,
who satisfy their 'needs' with it. But here, too, we find that anthropology's
theoretical pretensions have been shattered by Marx's analysis. Not only
does Marx define these 'needs' as 'historical' and not as absolute givens
(*The Poverty of Philosophy*, pp. 41–2; *Capital*, T.I, pp. 174, 228; Vol. I,
pp. 171, 232; Vol. III, p. 837, etc.), but also and above all he recognizes
them as 'needs' in their economic function, on condition that they are
'effective' (Vol. III, pp. 178, 189). The only needs that play an economic
part are those that can be satisfied economically: those needs are not defined
by human nature in general but by their effectivity, i.e., by the level of the
income at the disposal of the individuals concerned – and by the *nature* of
the products available, which are, at a given moment, the result of the
technical capacities of production. The determination of the needs of
individuals by the forms of production goes even further, since production
produces not only definite means of consumption (use-values), but also their
mode of consumption, including even the wish for these products (*1857 Introduction*, op. cit., p. 13). In other words, individual consumption itself, which
interconnects use-values and needs in an apparently immediate fashion (and
therefore seems to derive directly from an anthropology, but a historicized
one), refers us to the technical capacities of production (the level of the
forces of production) on the one hand, and on the other to the *social relations
of production*, which fix the distribution of income (the forms of the division

---

[38] Although there is no time to do it here, I should like to note that it would be of great
interest to study these long critiques of Marx's in order to find out on the one hand what
distinguishes Marx from Smith in this crucial matter and on the other *how and where he
locates the essential difference* – in order to find out how he explains Smith's incredible
'*oversight*', '*blindness*', '*misconstruction*' and '*forgetfulness*' which are at the root of the
'absurd dogma' that dominates all modern economics, and finally, in order to find out why
Marx felt the need to begin this critique four or five times over, as if he had not got to the
bottom of it. And we should then discover, among other epistemologically relevant conclusions, that Smith's 'enormous oversight' was directly related to his *exclusive consideration
of the individual capitalist*, i.e., of the economic subjects considered outside *the whole* as the
ultimate subjects of the global process. In other words, we should discover once again the
determinant presence of the anthropological ideology in its directly effective form (essential
references: *Capital*, Vol. II, pp. 189–227 and 359–436; Vol. III, pp. 811–30; *Theories of
Surplus Value*, Vol. I, pp. 90–100.)

into surplus-value and wages). This last point leads on to the distribution of men into *social classes*, which then become the 'real' 'subjects' (insofar as that term is applicable) of the production process. The direct relationship between 'needs' thus defined and an anthropological basis becomes therefore purely mythical: or rather, we must invert the order of things and say that the idea of an anthropology, if it is possible at all, must first take into consideration the economic (non-anthropological) definition of those 'needs'. Those needs are subject to a double *structural*, i.e., no longer anthropological, determination: the determination which divides the products between Departments I and II, and assigns to needs their content and meaning (the structure of the relation between the productive forces and the relations of production). This conception therefore rejects classical anthropology's founding role in economics.

B. DISTRIBUTION

Since distribution has been revealed as an essential factor in the determination of needs – alongside production – let us examine this new category. Distribution, too, has two aspects. It is not only the distribution of income (which refers to the relations of production), but also the distribution of the use-values produced by the production process. But we know that these use-values include the products of Department I, or means of production – and the products of Department II, or means of consumption. The products of Department II are exchanged for individual's incomes, hence as a function of their incomes, hence as a function of the distribution of incomes, hence as a function of the first distribution. As for the products of Department I, the means of production, intended for the reproduction of the conditions of production, they are not exchanged for income, but directly between the owners of the means of production (this results from the realization diagrams in Volume Two): between the members of the capitalist class, who have a monopoly of the means of production. Behind the distribution of use-values, therefore, we can trace the outline of a different distribution: the distribution of men into social classes exercising functions in the production process.

In its most banal conception, distribution appears as the distribution of products, and thus as further away from and quasi-independent of production. But before distribution is distribution of the product, it is: (1) the distribution of the instruments of production, and (2) *what is a further definition of the same relationship*, the distribution of the members of the society into the different kinds of production (subsumption of the individuals under determinate relations of production). The distribution of the product is obviously only the result of this distribution which is included within the production process itself and determines the articulation of production (Marx: *1857 Introduction*, op. cit., p. 17).

In both cases, whether by the distribution of income or by the distribution of means of consumption and means of production, the index of the distribution of the members of society into distinct classes, we are therefore referred to the *relations* of production and *production* itself.

Our examination of categories which at first sight seemed to demand the theoretical intervention of an anthropology of the *homo oeconomicus* and, for this reason, might have seemed to make it well-founded, has therefore produced two results: (1) the disappearance of anthropology, which has ceased to play its founding role (determination of the economic as such, determination of the 'subjects' of the economy). The 'planar space' of economic phenomena is no longer doubled by the anthropological space of the existence of human subjects; (2) A necessary reference, implied by the analysis of consumption and distribution, to the site of the true determination of the economic: *production*. Correlatively, we see this theoretical deepening as a transformation of the field of economic phenomena: their former 'planar space' has been replaced by a new pattern in which the economic 'phenomena' are thought within the domination of the *'relations of production'* which define them.

The reader will have recognized one of Marx's basic theses in this second result: *it is production* that governs consumption and distribution, not the reverse. Marx's whole discovery is often reduced to this basic theory and its consequences.

But this 'reduction' runs into one small difficulty; this discovery is as old as the Physiocrats, and Ricardo, the economist 'of production *par excellence*' (Marx), gave it its systematic form. In fact, Ricardo proclaimed the primacy of production over distribution and consumption. We must go even further and admit, as Marx does in the *1857 Introduction*, that Ricardo claimed that distribution constituted the peculiar object of Political Economy because he was alluding to the aspect of distribution which concerns the division of the agents of production into social classes (*1857 Introduction*, op. cit., p. 17). But here too we must apply to Ricardo what Marx said of him with respect to surplus-value. Ricardo gave every outward token of recognizing the reality of surplus-value – but he always spoke of it in the forms of profit, rent and interest, i.e., within other concepts than its own. Similarly, Ricardo gives every outward token of recognizing the existence of the relations of production – but he always speaks of them in the form of the distribution of income and products alone – i.e., without producing their *concept*. When it is only a question of identifying the *existence* of a reality behind its disguise, it does not matter if the word or words which designate it are inadequate concepts. This is what enabled Marx to translate the *language* of his predecessor in an immediate substitutional reading, and to pronounce the words *surplus-value* where Ricardo had pronounced the word profit – or the words *relations of production* where Ricardo had pronounced the words distribution of income. This is all right so long as there is no need to do more than designate an existence: it is enough to correct a word in order to call the thing by its name. But when it is a matter of the theoretical consequences arising from this disguise, the affair becomes much more grave: since this word then plays the part of a concept whose inadequacy or absence has serious theoretical effects, whether the author in question recognizes them (as Ricardo did the contradictions he ran into) or not. Then one learns that what one had taken for a reality disguised in an inaccurate word is a disguised second disguise: the theoretical function of a concept disguised in a word. On this condition, variations in terminology may be the real index of a variation in the problematic and the object. However, it is just as if Marx had made his own division of labour. On the one hand, he was content to carry out a substitutional reading of his predecessors: this was a sign of the 'generosity' (Engels) which always made him calculate his debts unselfishly, and in practice treat 'producers' as 'discoverers'. But on the other hand, though in different places, Marx revealed that he was as pitiless towards the theoretical consequences drawn by his predecessors in this blindness as he was to the conceptual meaning of the facts which they had produced. When Marx criticized Smith or Ricardo with the utmost severity because they were unable to distinguish between surplus-value and its forms of existence, he was in fact attacking them because they did not give a *concept* to the fact that they had managed to 'produce'. We can clearly see that the mere 'omission' of a word is really the absence of a *concept*, since the presence or absence of a concept is decisive for a whole chain of theoretical consequences. And in return, this illuminates the effects of the absence of a word on the theory which 'contains' this absence: the absence of a 'word' from it is the presence in it of a *different* concept. In other words, anyone who thinks he only has to re-establish a 'word' which is absent from Ricardo's discourse is in danger of deceiving himself as to the *conceptual* effect of that absence, he is reducing Ricardo's very concepts to mere 'words'. In this cross-over of false identifications (the belief that the construction of a concept is no more than the re-establishment of a word; the belief that Ricardo's concepts are mere words) we must look for the reason why Marx could both exalt his predecessors' discoveries when they had often only 'produced' them without 'discovering' them, and criticize them just as sharply for the theoretical consequences, although these consequences have merely been drawn from the 'discoveries'. I had to go into this amount of detail in order to situate the meaning of the following judgement of Marx's:

Ricardo, who was concerned to conceive modern production in its determinate social articulation, and who is the economist of production *par excellence, precisely for this reason* explains not production but distribution as the basic theme of modern economics (*1857 Introduction*, op. cit., p. 18).

'*Precisely for this reason*' means:

> ... [he] *instinctively* conceived the forms of distribution as the most definite expression of the *fixed relations between the agents of production in a given society* (ibid., p. 17).

The 'fixed relation between the agents of production in a given society' are precisely the *relations of production*, and when Marx took them into consideration, not in the form of an '*instinctive*' feeling, i.e., in the form of the '*unknown*' – but in the form of a *concept* and its consequences, it revolutionized the object of classical economics, and with the object, the science of Political Economy as such.

Marx's peculiarity, indeed, does not lie in his having claimed or even demonstrated the primacy of production (Ricardo had already done this in his own way), but in his having transformed the *concept of production* by assigning to it an object radically different from the object designated by the old concept.

C. PRODUCTION

According to Marx, all production is characterized by two indissociable elements: the *labour process*, which deals with the transformations man inflicts on natural materials in order to make use-values out of them, and the *social relations of production* beneath whose determination this labour process is executed. We shall examine these two points in succession: the labour process (a) and the relations of production (b).

(a) *The labour process*
The analysis of the labour process involves the *material and technical conditions* of production.

> The labour process, . . . the activity whose aim is the production of use-values, the appropriation of external substances for needs, is the general condition for exchanges of matter between man and nature, a physical necessity of human life, and is therefore independent of all its social forms, or rather common to all of them (*Capital*, T.I, p. 186; Vol. I, pp. 183–4).

This process can be reduced to the combination of simple elements, of which there are three: ' . . . (1) the personal activity of man, or labour strictly speaking; (2) the object on which that labour acts; (3) the means with which it acts' (T.I, p. 181; Vol. I, p. 178). The labour process therefore implies an expenditure of the labour-power of men who, using defined instruments of labour according to adequate (technical) rules, transform the *object* of labour (either a natural material or an already worked material or raw material) into a useful product.

This analysis brings out *two essential features* which we shall examine in succession: the *material* nature of the conditions of the labour process, and the dominant role of the *means of production* in the labour process.

First feature. Every productive expenditure of labour power presupposes *material* conditions for its performance, which can all be reduced to the existence of nature, either directly, or as modified by human activity. When Marx writes that 'labour is, in the first place, a process which takes place between man and nature, and in which man starts, regulates, and controls by his own activity the material exchanges between himself and nature. He opposes himself to nature as a natural force', he is stating that the trans-formation of material nature into products, and therefore the labour process as a material mechanism, is dominated by the physical laws of nature and technology. Labour-power, too, is included in this mechanism. This deter-mination of the labour-*process* by these material conditions is at its own level a denial of every 'humanist' conception of human labour as pure creativity. As we know, this idealism has not remained in the state of a myth, but has reigned in political economy itself, and from there, in the economic utopias of vulgar socialism: e.g. in Proudhon (the people's bank project), Gray ('labour bonds'), and finally in the Gotha Programme, whose opening line proclaimed:

Labour is the source of all wealth and culture,

to which Marx replied:

Labour is not the source of all wealth. Nature is just as much the source of use-values (and it is surely of such that material wealth consists!) as labour, which itself is only the manifestation of a force of nature, human labour-power. The above phrase is to be found in all children's primers and is correct insofar as it is implied that labour is performed with the appurtenant objects and instruments. But a socialist programme cannot allow such bourgeois phrases to pass over in silence the *conditions* that alone give them meaning .... The bourgeois have very good grounds for falsely ascribing *supernatural creative power* to labour. ('Critique of the Gotha Programme,' *Selected Works in One Volume*, London 1968, p. 319).

It was this same utopianism that led Smith and all the utopians who have followed him on this point, to leave out of their economic concepts *any formal representation of the necessity for the reproduction of the material conditions of the labour process*, as essential to the existence of that process – and therefore to abstract from the *current* materiality of the productive forces (the object and the material instruments of labour) implied in every pro-duction process (in this respect, Smith's Political Economy lacks a theory of *reproduction*, an indispensable element of any theory of production). The same idealism of labour made it possible for Marx, in the *1844 Manuscripts*, to call Smith the 'Luther of Political Economy' because he reduced all wealth (all use-value) to human *labour* alone; and to seal the theoretical union of Smith and Hegel: the first because he reduced the whole of political economy to the subjectivity of labour, the second because he conceived 'labour as the essence of man'. In *Capital*, Marx breaks with this idealism of labour by thinking the concept of the material conditions of every labour process and by providing the concept of the *economic forms of existence* of these material conditions: in the capitalist mode of production, the decisive distinctions between constant capital and variable capital on the one hand, and between Department I and Department II on the other.

This simple example enables us to assess the theoretical and practical effects induced in the field of economic analysis itself by merely thinking the *concept of its object*. Once Marx thought the reality of the material conditions of production as belonging to the concept of production, economically 'operational' concepts emerged in the field of economic analysis (constant capital, variable capital, Department I, Department II) which revolution-ized its arrangement and nature. The concept of its object is not a para-economic concept, it is the concept of the construction of the economic concepts necessary for an understanding of the nature of the economic object itself: the economic concepts of constant capital and variable capital, of Department I and Department II, are merely the economic determinations, in the field of economic analysis itself, of the concept of the *material con-ditions of the labour process*. The concept of the object exists immediately then in the form of directly 'operational' economic concepts. But without the concept of the object, these concepts would not have been produced, and we should have remained in Smith's economic idealism, exposed to all the temptations of ideology.

This is a crucial point, for it shows us that to call ourselves Marxists it is not enough for us to believe that the economy, and in the economy, pro-duction, govern all the other spheres of social existence. It is possible to proclaim these positions and yet, at the same time, develop an idealist conception of the economy and of production, by declaring that labour constitutes both the 'essence of man' and the essence of political economy, in short by developing an anthropological ideology of labour, of the 'civiliza-tion of labour', etc. Marx's materialism, on the contrary, presupposes a materialist conception of economic production, i.e., among other conditions, a demonstration of the irreducible material conditions of the labour process. This is one of the points where a sentence from one of Marx's letters to Engels which I have referred to above is directly applicable: the sentence in which Marx points out that he 'attributed much more importance *to the category use-value*' than did any of his predecessors. This is a stumbling-block for all the interpretations of Marxism as a 'philosophy of labour', whether ethical, personalist or existentialist: especially Sartre's theory of the practico-inert, since it lacks any concept of the modality of the material conditions of the labour process. Smith had already related the current material con-ditions of the labour process to past labour: he thus dissolved the *currency* of the material conditions required at a given moment for the existence of the labour process in an infinite regression, in the *non-currency* of earlier labours, in their memory, Hegel was to resurrect this idea in his theory of '*Erinnerung*'). Similarly, Sartre dissolves the *current* material conditions whose structural combination governs all effective labour and every current transformation of a raw material into a useful product in the philosophical memory of an earlier praxis, itself second to another or several other earlier praxes, and so on down to the praxis of the original subject. In Smith, who was writing an economic work, this ideal dissipation had important theoretical consequences in the realm of the economy itself. In Sartre, it is immediately elevated into its explicit philosophical 'truth': the anthropology of the subject, latent in Smith, takes the open form of a philosophy of freedom in Sartre.

Second feature. The same analysis of the labour process reveals the dominant role of the '*means of labour*'.

The use and fabrication of means of labour . . . is characteristic of the *specifically human* labour-process, and Franklin therefore defines man as a tool-making animal. Relics of by-gone means of labour possess the same importance for the investigation of extinct economic forms of society, as does the structure of fossil bones for a knowledge of the organization of extinct species of animals. It is less what is produced (*macht*) than how (*wie*) it is produced, and by what means of labour, that enables us to distinguish different economic epochs. Means of labour supply a standard of the degree of development of the labourer and they are also indicators (*Anzeiger*) of the social relations in which he labours (*Capital*, T.I, pp. 182–3; Vol. I, pp. 179–80).

One of the three constitutive elements of the labour process (object of labour, means of labour, labour-power) is therefore dominant: the *means of labour*. It is this last element which enables us to identify within the labour process common to every economic epoch the specific difference which will distinguish between its essential forms. The 'means of labour' determine the typical form of the labour process considered: by establishing the 'mode of attack' on the external nature subject to transformation in economic production, they determine the *mode of production*, the basic category of Marxist analysis (in economics and history); at the same time, they establish the level of *productivity* of productive labour. The concept of the pertinent differences observable in a variety of labour processes, the concept which makes possible not only the 'periodization' of history, but above all the construction of the concept of history: the concept of the *mode of production* is thus established, with respect to our present considerations, in the qualitative differences between different means of labour, i.e., in their productivities. Need I point out that there is a direct relationship between the concept of the dominant role of the means of labour and the economically 'operational' concept of productivity? Need I note the fact that classical

economics was never able to isolate and identify this concept of productivity –
a fact Marx attacked it for – and that its misconception of history was linked
to the absence in it of the concept of *mode of production*?[39]

By producing his key concept of the mode of production, Marx was indeed
able to express the differential degree of material attack on nature by production, the differential mode of unity existing between 'man and nature',
and the degree of variation in that unity. But as well as revealing to us the
theoretical significance of taking into consideration the *material conditions*
of production, the concept of the mode of production simultaneously
reveals to us another determinant reality, corresponding to the degree of
variation in the 'man–nature' unity: *the relations of production*:

> Means of labour not only supply a standard of the degree of develop-
> ment to which human labour power has attained, but they are also indices
> (*Anzeiger*) of the social relations under which production is carried on . . .

Here we discover that the man–nature unity expressed in the degree of
variation in that unity is at the same time both the unity of the man–nature
relationship and the unity of the *social relations* in which production takes
place. The concept of the mode of production therefore contains the concept
of the unity of this double unity.

(b) *The relations of production*

We have thus arrived at a *new condition* of the production process. After
studying the *material* conditions of the production process, which express
the specific nature of the relations between men and nature, we must now
turn to a study of the *social* conditions of the production process: *the social
relations of production*. These new conditions involve the specific type of
relations *between the agents of production* which exist as a function of the
relations between these agents on the one hand and the *material means* of
production on the other. This adjustment is crucial: *the social relations of
production are on no account reducible to mere relations between men, to relations which only involve men, and therefore to variations in a universal
matrix, to inter-subjectivity* (recognition, prestige, struggle, master–slave
relationship, etc.). For Marx, the social relations of production do not bring
men alone onto the stage, but the *agents* of the production process and the
material conditions of the production process, in specific 'combinations'. I
insist on this point, for reasons which are related to Rancière's analysis of
certain of Marx's expressions,[40] where, in a terminology still inspired by
his early anthropological philosophy, it is tempting to oppose, literally,
relations between men and relations between things. But the *relations of
production* necessarily imply relations between men and things, such that the

---

[39] For all these questions, barely outlined in this chapter, see Étienne Balibar's essay –
especially his important analysis of the concept of *productive forces*.
[40] See Lire *le Capital*, first edition, 1965, Vol. I, pp. 93ff.

relations between men and men are defined by the precise relations existing between men and the material elements of the production process.

How did Marx think these relations? He thought them as a 'distribution' or 'combination' (*Verbindung*). Discussing distribution in the *1857 Introduction*, Marx wrote (op. cit., pp. 17–18):

> In its most banal conception, distribution appears as the distribution of products, and thus as further away from and quasi-independent of production. But before distribution is distribution of the product, it is: (1) the distribution of the instruments of production, and (2) what is a further definition of the same relationship, the distribution of the members of the society into the different kinds of production (subsumption of the individuals under determinate relations of production). The distribution of the product is obviously only the result of this distribution which is included within the production process itself and determines the *articulation of production* (*Gliederung*). It is obviously an empty abstraction to consider production while ignoring this distribution which is included in it, while, on the contrary, the distribution of products is implied by this distribution, which originally forms a moment (*Moment*) of production . . . Production must start from a certain *distribution* of the instruments of production . . .

This distribution thus consists of a certain *attribution* of the means of production to the agents of production, in a certain regular proportion fixed between, on the one hand, the means of production, and on the other, the agents of production. This distribution-attribution can be formally conceived as the *combination* (*Verbindung*) of a certain number of elements which belong either to the means of production or to the agents of production, a combination which occurs according to definite modalities.

This is Marx's own expression:

> Whatever the social form of production, labourers and means of production always remain factors of it. But in a state of separation from each other either of these factors can be such only potentially. For production to go on at all they must combine. The *specific manner* (*die besondere Art und Weise*) in which thus combination is accomplished distinguishes the different economic epochs of the structure of society (*Gesellschaftsstruktur*) from one another (*Capital*, Vol II, p. 34 modified).

In another and probably more important text (*Capital*, Vol. III, pp. 770–04), on the feudal mode of production, Marx writes:

> The specific economic form, in which unpaid surplus-labour is pumped out of direct producers, determines the relationship of rulers and ruled, as it grows directly out of production itself and, in turn reacts upon it as a determining element. Upon this, however, is founded the entire formation

(*Gestaltung*) of the economic community which grows out of the production relations themselves, thereby simultaneously its specific political form (*Gestalt*). It is always the direct relationship of the owners of the conditions of production to the direct producers – a relation always naturally corresponding to a definite stage in the development of the methods (*Art und Weise*) of labour and thereby its social productivity – which reveals the innermost secret (*innerste Geheimnis*), the hidden basis (*Grundlage*) of the entire social structure (*Konstruktion*), and with it the political form of the relation of sovereignty and dependence, in short, the corresponding specific form of the State.

This text's developments reveal behind the two elements hitherto considered (agents of production, means of production) distinctions of quite crucial importance. On the side of the means of production we find the already familiar distinction between the object of production, e.g., the land (which played a determinant part *directly* in all the modes of production before capitalism), and the instruments of production. On the side of the *agents* of production we find, besides the distinction between labourer and labour power, an essential distinction between the *direct agents* (Marx's own expression) whose labour power is set to work in production, and other men whose role in the general process of production is that of owners of the means of production, but who do not feature in it as labourers or direct agents, since their labour power is not used in the production process. By combining or *inter-relating* these different elements – labour power, direct labourers, masters who are not direct labourers, object of production, instruments of production, etc. – we shall reach a definition of the different *modes of production* which have existed and can exist in human history. This operation inter-relating determinate pre-existing elements might make us think of a *combinatory*, if the very special specific nature of the relations brought into play in these different combinations did not strictly define and limit its field. To obtain the different modes of production these different elements do have to be combined, but by using *specific modes of combination* or '*Verbindungen*' which are only meaningful in the peculiar nature of the *result* of the combinatory (this result being real production) – and which are: *property, possession, disposition, enjoyment, community*, etc. The application of specific relations to the different distributions of the elements present produces a limited number of formations which constitute the relations of production of the defined modes of production. These relations of production determine the connexions between the different groups of agents of production and the objects and instruments of production, and thereby they simultaneously divide the agents of production into functional groups, each occupying a definite place in the production process. The relations between the agents of production are then the result of the typical relations they maintain with the means of production (object, instruments) and of their distribution into groups defined and localized functionally in their relations with the means of production by the structure of production.

I cannot give a theoretical analysis of this concept of 'combination' and of its different forms here: on this point I refer the reader to Balibar's paper. But it is clear that the theoretical nature of this concept of 'combination' may provide a foundation for the thesis I have already suggested in a critical form, the thesis that Marxism *is not a historicism*: since the Marxist concept of history depends on the principle of the variation of the forms of this 'combination'. I should just like to insist on the special nature of these relations of production, which are remarkable *in two respects*.

In the text I have just quoted we have seen Marx prove that a certain form of combination of the elements present necessarily implied a certain form of domination and servitude indispensable to the survival of this combination, i.e., a certain *political* configuration (*Gestaltung*) of society. We can see precisely where the necessity and form of the political 'formation' is founded: at the level of the *Verbindungen* which constitute the modes of liaison between the agents of production and the means of production, at the level of the relations of property, possession, disposition, etc.[41] These types of connexion, according to the diversification or non-diversification of the agents of production into direct labourers and masters, make the existence of a political organization intended to impose and maintain the defined types of connexions by means of material force (that of the State) and of moral power (that of ideologies) either *necessary* (class societies) or *super-fluous* (classless societies). This shows that certain relations of production presuppose the existence of a legal-political and ideological *superstructure* as a condition of their peculiar existence, and why this superstructure is necessarily *specific* (since it is a function of the specific relations of production that call for it). It also shows that certain other relations of production do not call for a political superstructure, but only for an ideological superstructure (classless societies). Finally, it shows that the nature of the relations of production considered not only calls or does not call for a certain form of superstructure, but also establishes the *degree of effectivity* delegated to a certain level of the social totality. Irrespective of all these consequences, we can draw one conclusion at any rate where the relations of production are concerned: they relate to the superstructural forms they call for as so many conditions of their own existence. The relations of production cannot therefore be thought in their concept while abstracting from their specific superstructural conditions of existence. To take only one example, it is quite clear that the analysis of the buying and selling of labour power in which capitalist relations of production *exist* (the separation between the

---

[41] One important specification. The term 'property' used by Marx can lead to the belief that the relations of production are *identical* with legal relations. But law is not the relations of production. The latter belong to the infrastructure, the former to the superstructure.

owners of the means of production on the one hand and the wage-workers on the other), directly presupposes, for an understanding of its object, a consideration of the *formal legal relations* which establish the buyer (the capitalist) as much as the seller (the wage-labourer) as legal subjects – as well as a whole political and ideological superstructure which maintains and contains the economic agents in the distribution of roles, which makes a minority of exploiters the owners of the means of production, and the majority of the population producers of surplus-value. The whole super-structure of the society considered is thus implicit and present in a specific way in the relations of production, i.e., in the fixed structure of the distri-bution of means of production and economic functions between determinate categories of production agents. Or in other words, if the structure of the relations of production defines the economic as such, a definition of the concept of the relations of production in a determinate mode of production is necessarily reached via the definition of the concept of the totality of the distinct levels of society and their peculiar type of articulation (i.e. effectivity).

In no sense is this a formal demand; it is the absolute theoretical condition governing the definition of the *economic* itself. It is enough to refer to the innumerable problems raised by this definition where modes of production other than the capitalist one are concerned to realize the decisive importance of this recourse: Marx often says that what is hidden in capitalist society is clearly visible in feudal society or in the primitive community, but precisely in the latter societies we can clearly see that *the economic is not directly and clearly visible*! – just as in these same societies we *can also clearly see* that the degree of effectivity of the different levels of the social structure *is not clearly visible*! Anthropologists and ethnologists 'know' what to confine themselves to when, seeking the economic, they come upon kinship relations, religious institutions, etc.; specialists in mediaeval history 'know' what to confine themselves to when, seeking for the dominant determination of history in the 'economy', they find it in politics or religion.[42] In all these cases, there is no *immediate* grasp of the economic, there is no raw economic 'given', any more than there is any immediately 'given' effectivity in any of the levels. In all these cases, the identification of the economic is achieved by *the construction of its concept*, which presupposes a definition of the specific existence and articulation of the different levels of the structure of the whole, as they are necessarily implied by the structure of the mode of production considered. To construct the concept of the economic is to define it rigorously as a level, instance or region of the structure of a mode of production: it is therefore to define its peculiar *site*, its *extension*, and its *limits* within that structure; if we like to return to the old Platonic image, it is to 'divide up' the region of the economic correctly in the whole, according

[42] Cf. Godelier's article 'Objet et méthode de l'anthropologie économique' (*L'Homme*, October 1965 and in *Rationalité et irrationalité en économie*, Paris 1966).

to its peculiar 'articulation', *without mistaking this articulation*. The 'division' of the 'given', or empiricist division, always mistakes the articulation, precisely because it projects on to the 'real' the arbitrary articulations and divisions of its underlying ideology. There is no correct division and therefore no correct articulation, except on condition of possessing and therefore constructing its concept. In other words, in primitive societies it is not possible to regard any *fact*, any *practice* apparently unrelated to the 'economy') (such as the practices which are produced by kinship rites or religious rites, or by the relations between groups in 'potlatch' competition), *as rigorously economic*, without first having constructed the concept of the differentiation of the structure of the social whole into these different practices or levels, without having *discovered* their peculiar meaning in the structure of the whole, without having identified in the disconcerting diversity of these practices the *region* of economic practice, its configuration and its modalities. It is probable that the majority of the difficulties of contemporary ethnology and anthropology arise from their approaching the 'facts', the 'givens' of (descriptive) ethnography, without taking the theoretical precaution of constructing the concept of their object: this omission commits them to projecting on to reality the categories which define the economic for them in practice, i.e., the categories of the economics of contemporary society, which to make matters worse, are often themselves empiricist. This is enough to multiply aporia. If we follow Marx here, too, this detour via primitive societies, etc., will only have been necessary in order to see clearly in them what our own society hides from us: i.e., in order to *see clearly* in them that the economic is *never clearly visible*, does not coincide with the 'given' in them any more than in any other reality (political, ideological, etc.). This is all the more 'obvious' for the capitalist mode of production in that we know that the latter is the mode of production in which *fetishism* affects the economic region *par excellence*. Despite the massive 'obviousness' of the economic 'given' in the capitalist mode of production, and precisely because of the 'massive' character of this fetishised 'obviousness', the only way to the essence of the economic is to construct its concept, i.e., to reveal the *site* occupied in the structure of the whole by the region of the economic, therefore to reveal the articulation of this region with other regions (legal-political and ideological superstructure), and the degree of *presence* (or effectivity) of the other regions in the economic region itself. Here, too, this requirement can be faced directly as a positive theoretical requirement: it can also be omitted, and it then reveals itself in peculiar effects, either theoretical (contradictions and thresholds in the explanation) or practical (e.g., difficulties in planning techniques, whether socialist or capitalist). That, very schematically, is the first conclusion we can draw from Marx's determination of the economic by the *relations of production*.

The second conclusion is not less important. If the relations of production now appear to us as a regional *structure*, itself *inscribed* in the structure of the social totality, we are interested in this because of its *structural* nature. Here both the mirage of a theoretical anthropology and the mirage of a homogeneous space of *given* economic phenomena dissolve simultaneously. Not only is the economic a structured region occupying its peculiar place in the global structure of the social whole, but even in its own site, in its (relative) regional autonomy, it functions as a regional *structure* and as such determines its elements. Here once again we find the results of the other papers in this book: i.e., the fact that the structure of the relations of production determines the *places* and *functions* occupied and adopted by the agents of production, who are never anything more than the occupants of these places, insofar as they are the 'supports' (*Träger*) of these functions. The true 'subjects' (in the sense of constitutive subjects of the process) are therefore not these occupants or functionaries, are not, despite all appearances, the 'obviousnesses' of the 'given' of naïve anthropology, 'concrete individuals', 'real men' – but *the definition and distribution of these places and functions. The true 'subjects' are these definers and distributors: the relations of production* (and political and ideological social relations). But since these are 'relations', they cannot be thought within the category *subject*. And if by chance anyone proposes to reduce these relations of production to relations between men, i.e., *'human relations'*, he is violating Marx's thought, for so long as we apply a truly critical reading to some of his rare ambiguous formulations, Marx shows in the greatest depth that the *relations* of production (and political and ideological social relations) are irreducible to any anthropological inter-subjectivity – since they only combine agents and objects in a specific structure of the distribution of relations, places and functions, occupied and 'supported' by objects and agents of production.

It is clear once again, then, how the *concept* of his object distinguishes Marx radically from his predecessors and why criticisms of him have run wide of the mark. To think the concept of production is to think the concept of the unity of its conditions: the mode of production. To think the mode of production is to think not only the material conditions but also the social conditions of production. In each case, it is to produce the concept which governs the definition of the economically 'operational' concepts (I use the word 'operational' deliberately, since it is often used by economists) out of the concept of their object. We know which concept in the capitalist mode of production expressed the fact of capitalist relations of production in economic reality itself: *the concept of surplus-value*. The unity of the material and social conditions of capitalist production is expressed by the direct relationship between variable capital and the production of surplus-value. The fact that surplus-value is not a measurable reality arises from the fact that it is not a thing, but the concept of a relationship, the concept of an existing social structure of production, of an existence visible and measurable *only in its 'effects'*, in the sense we shall soon define. The fact that it only exists in its effects does not mean that it can be grasped completely in any one of its determinate effects: for that it would have to be *completely present* in that effect, whereas it is only present there, as a structure, in its *determinate* absence. It is only present in the totality, in the total movement of its effects, in what Marx calls the 'developed totality of its form of existence', for reasons bound up with its very nature. It is a relation of production between the agents of the production process and the means of production, i.e., the very structure that dominates the process in the totality of its development and of its existence. The *object* of production, the land, minerals, coal, cotton, the *instruments of production*, tools, machines, etc., are *'things'* or visible, assignable, measurable realities: they are not *structures*. The relations of production are structures – and the ordinary economist may scrutinize economic 'facts': prices, exchanges, wages, profits, rents, etc., all those 'measurable' facts, as much as he likes; he will no more 'see' any *structure* at that level than the pre-Newtonian 'physicist' could 'see' the law of attraction in falling bodies, or the pre-Lavoisierian chemist could 'see' oxygen in 'dephlogisticated' air. Naturally, just as bodies were 'seen' to fall before Newton, the 'exploitation' of the majority of men by a minority was 'seen' before Marx. But the concept of the economic 'forms' of that exploitation, the concept of the economic existence of the relations of production, of the domination and determination of the whole sphere of political economy by that *structure* did not then have any theoretical existence. Even if Smith and Ricardo did 'produce', in the 'fact' of rent and profit, the 'fact' of surplus-value, they remained in the dark, not realizing what they had 'produced', since they could not think it in its concept, nor draw from it its theoretical consequences. They were a hundred miles away from being able to *think* it, since neither they nor the culture of their time had ever imagined that a 'fact' might be the existence of a *relation* of 'combination', a relation of complexity, consubstantial with the entire mode of production, dominating its present, its crisis, its future, determining as the law of its structure the entire economic reality, down to the visible detail of the empirical phenomena – while remaining *invisible* even in their blinding obviousness.

Chapter 9

Marx's Immense

Theoretical Revolution

We can now go back to the past and assess the distance between Marx and his predecessors – and between his *object* and theirs.

From now on we can abandon the issue of anthropology, whose function in Political Economy was to establish both the *economic* nature of economic phenomena (by the theory of the *homo oeconomicus*) and their existence in *the homogeneous space of a given*. Once this anthropological 'given' has been removed, the space remains, which is precisely what interests us. What happens to it, in its being, once it can no longer be based on an anthropology, what effects does this omission have on it?

Political Economy thought the economic phenomena as deriving from a planar space governed by a transitive mechanical causality, such that a determinate effect could be related to an object-cause, a different pheno-menon; such that the necessity of its immanence could be grasped completely in the sequence of a given. The homogeneity of this space, its planar charac-ter, its property of givenness, its type of linear causality: these are so many theoretical determinations which, as a system, constitute the structure of a theoretical problematic, i.e., of a certain way of conceiving its object, and at the same time of posing it definite questions (defined by the problematic itself) as to its being, while anticipating the form of its answers (the quanti-tative schema): in short, an empiricist problematic. Marx's theory is radically opposed to this conception. Not that it is an 'inversion' of it: it is different, theoretically unrelated to it, and therefore in rupture with it. Because he defined the economic *by its concept*, Marx does not present economic pheno-mena – to illustrate his thought temporarily with a spatial metaphor – in the infinity of a homogeneous planar space, but rather in *a region* determined by a regional structure and itself inscribed in a site defined by a global structure: therefore as a complex and deep space, itself inscribed in another complex and deep space. But let us abandon this spatial metaphor, since this first opposition exhausts its virtues: everything depends, in fact, on the nature of this depth, or, more strictly speaking, of this *complexity*. To define economic phenomena by their concept is to define them by the concept of this complexity, i.e., by the concept of the (global) *structure* of the mode of production, insofar as it determines the (regional) *structure* which constitutes as economic objects and determines the phenomena of this defined region, located in a defined site in the structure of the whole. At the economic level, strictly speaking, the *structure* constituting and determining economic objects is the *following*: the unity of the productive forces and the relations of production. The concept of this last *structure* cannot be defined without the concept of the global structure of the mode of production.

Once we have simply put Marx's fundamental theoretical concepts in their places and posed them in the unity of a theoretical discourse, a number of important consequences follow.

First: the economic cannot have the qualities of a *given* (of the immediately visible and observable, etc.), because its identification requires the concept of the structure of the economic, which in turn requires the concepts of the structure of the mode of production (its different levels and their specific articulations – because its identification therefore presupposes the construction of its *concept*. The concept of the economic must be constructed *for each mode of production*, as must the concept of each of the other 'levels' that belong to the mode of production: the political, the ideological, etc. Like every other science, therefore, all economic science depends on the construction of the concept of its object. On this condition, there is no contradiction between the theory of Economics and the theory of History: on the contrary, the theory of economics is a subordinate region of the theory of history, understood of course in the non-historicist, non-empiricist sense in which we have outlined the theory of history.[43] And just as any 'history' which does not work out the concept of its object, but claims to 'read' it immediately in what is visible in the 'field' of historical phenomena, is still bound willy-nilly to be tainted with empiricism, any 'political economy' which goes to the 'things themselves', i.e., to the 'concrete', the 'given', without constructing the concept of its object, is still willy-nilly caught in the toils of an empiricist ideology and constantly threatened by the re-emergence of its true 'objects', i.e., its objectives (whether these are the ideals of classical liberalism or those of a 'humanism' of labour, even a socialist one).

Second: if the 'field' of economic phenomena no longer has the *homogeneity* of an infinite plane, its objects are no longer *de jure* homogeneous at all points with one another: they are therefore no longer uniformly susceptible to comparison and *measurement*. This by no means excludes from economics the possibility of measurement or of the intervention of the instruments of mathematics and its peculiar modalities, etc., but it does make it from now on subject to a prior conceptual definition of the sites and limits of the measurable, and of the sites and limits to which the other resources of mathematical science (e.g., the instruments of econometrics and other formalization procedures) can be applied. Mathematical formalization must be subordinate to conceptual formalization. Here, too, the limits between political economy and empiricism, even formalistic empiricism,

[44] Cf. Chapter 3.

coincide with the boundary between the concept of the (theoretical) object and the 'concrete' object, along with even the 'mathematical' protocols of its manipulation.

The practical consequences of this principle are obvious: e.g., in the solution of the 'technical' problems of planning, in which 'problems' which arise quite simply from the absence of the concept of the object, i.e., from economic empiricism, are frequently treated as real 'technical' problems. The intellectual 'technocracy' lives by this kind of confusion, securing its full-time employment with it; for nothing takes so long to resolve as a problem which does not exist or has been badly posed.

Third: if the field of economic phenomena is no longer this planar space but a deep and complex one, if economic phenomena are determined by their *complexity* (i.e., their structure), the concept of linear causality can no longer be applied to them as it has been hitherto. A different concept is required in order to account for the new form of causality required by the new definition of the object of Political Economy, by its 'complexity', i.e., by its peculiar determination: *the determination by a structure.*

This third consequence deserves our whole attention, for it introduces us to an absolutely new theoretical domain. An object cannot be defined by its immediately visible or sensous appearance, it is necessary to make a detour via its concept in order to grasp it (*begreifen* grasp, *Begriff* concept): these theses have a familiar ring to them – at least they are the lesson of the whole history of modern science, more or less reflected in classical philosophy, even if this reflection took place in the element of an empiricism, whether transcendent (as in Descartes), transcendental (Kant and Husserl) or 'objective'-idealist (Hegel). It is true that much theoretical work is needed to deal with all the forms of this empiricism sublimated in the 'theory of knowledge' which dominates Western philosophy, to break with its problematic of subject (*cogito*) and object – and all their variations. But at least all these philosophical ideologies do 'allude' to a real necessity, imposed against this tenacious empiricism by the theoretical practice of the real sciences: i.e., that the knowledge of a real object is not reached by immediate contact with the 'concrete' but by the production of the *concept* of that object (in the sense of object of knowledge) as the absolute condition of its *theoretical* possibility. If, *formally*, the task which Marx has allotted to us in forcing us to produce the concept of the economic in order to be able to constitute a theory of political economy, in obliging us to define *by its concept* the domain, limits and conditions of validity of a mathematization of that object, if it does break with all the empiricist-idealist traditions of Western critical philosophy, then it is in no sense in rupture with effective scientific practice. On the contrary, Marx's requirements restate in a new domain the requirements which have long been imposed on the practices of those sciences which have achieved autonomy. These requirements often conflict with the practices that have reigned and still do reign in economic science, practices which are deeply steeped in empiricist ideology, but this is undoubtedly because of the youth of this 'science', and also because 'economic science' is especially exposed to the pressures of ideology: the sciences of society do not have the serenity of the mathematical sciences. As Hobbes put it, geometry unites men, social science divides them. 'Economic science' is the arena and the prize of history's great political battles.

But our third conclusion is quite different, and so is the requirement it imposes on us to think the economic phenomena as *determined by a (regional) structure* of the mode of production, itself determined by *the (global) structure* of the mode of production. This requirement poses Marx a problem which is not only a *scientific* problem, i.e., one that arises from the theoretical practice of a definite science (Political Economy or History), but a theoretical, or philosophical problem, since it concerns precisely the production of a concept or set of concepts which necessarily affect the forms of existing scientificity or (theoretical) rationality themselves, the forms which, at a given moment, define the *Theoretical* as such, i.e., the object of philosophy.[44] This problem certainly does involve the production of a theoretical (philosophical) concept which is absolutely indispensable to the constitution of a rigorous discourse in the theory of history and the theory of political economy: the production of an indispensable philosophical concept *which does not exist in the form of a concept.*

Perhaps it is too soon to suggest that the birth of every new science inevitably poses theoretical (philosophical) problems of this kind: Engels thought so – and we have every reason to believe him, if we examine what happened at the time of the birth of mathematics in Greece, at the time of the constitution of Galilean physics, of infinitesimal calculus, at the time of the foundation of chemistry and biology, etc. In several of these conjunctures we find the following remarkable phenomenon: the 'reprise' of a basic scientific discovery in philosophical reflection, and the production by philosophy of *a new form of rationality* (Plato after the discoveries of the mathematicians of the fifth and fourth centuries before Christ, Descartes after Galileo, Leibniz with infinitesimal calculus, etc.). This philosophical 'reprise', this production by philosophy of new theoretical concepts which solve the *theoretical problems* contained 'in the practical state', if not explicitly posed, in the great scientific discoveries in question, mark the great breaks in the history of the Theoretical, i.e., in the history of philosophy. However, it seems that certain scientific disciplines have established themselves or thought themselves established by the mere extension of an existing form of rationality (psycho-physiology, psychology, etc.) which would tend to suggest that not *any* scientific foundation *ipso facto* induces a revolution in the Theoretical, but presumably only a scientific foundation which is obliged to

[44] Cf. Part I, section 14.

reorganize *practically* the existing problematic in the Theoretical in order to think its object; the philosophy capable of reflecting the upheaval produced by the emergence of such a science by bringing to light a new form of rationality (scientificity, apodicticity, etc.) would then mark by its existence a decisive punctuation, a revolution in the history of the Theoretical.

Bearing in mind what has been said elsewhere of the delay required for the philosophical production of this new rationality and even of the historical repressions to which certain theoretical revolutions may be subjected, it seems that Marx offers us precisely an example of this importance. The epistemological problem posed by Marx's radical modification of Political Economy can be expressed as follows: *by means of what concept is it possible to think the new type of determination which has just been identified as the determination of the phenomena of a given region by the structure of that region?* More generally, *by means of what concept, or what set of concepts, is it possible to think the determination of the elements of a structure, and the structural relations between those elements, and all the effects of those relations, by the effectivity of that structure? And* a fortiori, *by means of what concept or what set of concepts is it possible to think the determination of a subordinate structure by a dominant structure; In other words, how is it possible to define the concept of a structural causality?*

This simple theoretical question sums up Marx's extraordinary scientific discovery: the discovery of the theory of history and political economy, the discovery of *Capital*. But it sums it up as an extraordinary theoretical question *contained* 'in the practical state' in Marx's scientific discovery, the question Marx 'practiced' in his work, in answer to which he gave his scientific work, without producing *the concept* of it in a philosophical *opus* of the same rigour.

This simple question was so new and unforseen that it contained enough to smash all the classical theories of causality – or enough to ensure that it would be unrecognized, that it would pass unperceived and be buried even before it was born.

Very schematically, we can say that classical philosophy (the existing Theoretical) had two and only two systems of concepts with which to think effectivity. The mechanistic system, Cartesian in origin, which reduced causality to a *transitive* and analytical effectivity: it could not be made to think the effectivity of a whole on its elements, except at the cost of extraordinary distortions (such as those in Descartes' 'psychology' and biology). But a second system was available, one conceived precisely in order to deal with the effectivity of a whole on its elements: the Leibnizian concept of *expression*. This is the model that dominates all Hegel's thought. But it presupposes in principle that the whole in question be reducible to an *inner essence*, of which the elements of the whole are then no more than the phenomenal forms of expression, the inner principle of the essence being present at each point in the whole, such that at each moment it is possible to write the immediately adequate equation: *such and such an element* (economic, political, legal, literary, religious, etc., in Hegel) = *the inner essence of the whole*. Here was a model which made it possible to think the effectivity of the whole on each of its elements, but if this category – inner essence/outer phenomenon – was to be applicable everywhere and at every moment to each of the phenomena arising in the totality in question, *it presupposed that the whole had a certain nature, precisely the nature of a 'spiritual' whole in which each element was expressive of the entire totality as a* 'pars totalis'. In other words, Leibniz and Hegel did have a category for the effectivity of the whole on its elements or parts, but on the absolute condition that the whole was not a structure.

If the whole is posed as *structured*, i.e., as possessing a type of unity quite different from the type of unity of the spiritual whole, this is no longer the case: not only does it become impossible to think the determination of the elements by the structure in the categories of analytical and transitive causality, *it also becomes impossible to think it in the category of the global expressive causality of a universal inner essence immanent in its phenomenon*. The proposal to think the determination of the elements of a whole by the structure of the whole posed an absolutely new problem in the most theoretically embarrassing circumstances, for there were no philosophical concepts available for its resolution. The only theoretician who had had the unprecedented daring to pose this problem and outline a first solution to it was Spinoza. But, as we know, history had buried him in impenetrable darkness. Only through Marx, who, however, had little knowledge of him, do we even begin to guess at the features of that trampled face.

This is merely to return to the most general form of a fundamental and dramatic theoretical problem of which the preceding studies have given us a precise idea. I call it a fundamental problem because it is clear that by other paths contemporary theory in psycho-analysis, linguistics, other disciplines such as biology, and perhaps even physics, has had to confront it, without suspecting that Marx had 'produced' it in the true sense, long ago. I call it a *dramatic* theoretical problem because although Marx *'produced' this problem he did not pose it as a problem*, but set out to solve it practically in the absence of its concept, with extraordinary ingenuity, but without completely avoiding a relapse into earlier schemata which were necessarily inadequate to pose and solve this problem. It is on this problem that Marx is attempting to focus in the tentative sentences we can read in the *Introduction*:

> In all forms of society it is a determinate production and its relations which assign every other production and its relations their rank and influence. It is a general illumination (*Beleuchtung*) in which all the other colours are plunged and which modifies their special tonalities. It is a special ether which defines the specific weight of every existence arising in it (op. cit., p. 27).

This text is discussing the determination of certain structures of production which are subordinate to a dominant structure of production, i.e., the determination of one structure by another and of the elements of a subordinate structure by the dominant, and therefore determinant structure. I have previously attempted to account for this phenomenon with the concept of *overdetermination*, which I borrowed from psycho-analysis; as one might suppose, this transfer of an analytical concept to Marxist theory was not an arbitrary borrowing but a necessary one, *for the same theoretical problem is at stake in both cases: with what concept are we to think the determination of either an element or a structure by a structure?* It is this same problem that Marx has in view and which he is trying to focus by introducing the metaphor of a variation in the *general illumination*, of the *ether* in which bodies are immersed, and of the subsequent alterations produced by the domination of one particular structure in the localization, function and relations (in his own words: the relations, their rank and influence), in the original colour and the specific weight of the objects. The constant and real presence of this problem in Marx has been demonstrated by the rigorous analysis of his expressions and forms of reasoning in the preceding papers. It can be entirely summed up in the concept of '*Darstellung*', the key epistemological concept of the whole Marxist theory of value, the concept whose object is precisely to designate the mode of *presence* of the structure in its *effects*, and therefore to designate structural causality itself.

The fact that we have isolated the concept of '*Darstellung*' does not mean that it is the only one which Marx uses in order to think the effectivity of the structure: a reading of the first thirty pages of *Capital* shows that he uses at least a dozen different expressions of a metaphorical kind in order to deal with this specific reality, *unthought before him*. We have retained this term because it is both the least metaphorical and, at the same time, the closest to the concept Marx is aiming at when he wants to designate at once both absence and presence, i.e., *the existence of the structure in its effects*.

This is an extremely important point if we are to avoid even the slightest, in a sense inadvertent relapse into the diversions of *the classical conception of the economic object*, if we are to avoid saying that the Marxist conception of the economic object is, for Marx, determined *from the outside by a non-economic structure*. The structure is not an essence *outside* the economic phenomena which comes and alters their aspect, forms and relations and which is effective on them as an absent cause, *absent because it is outside them. The absence of the cause in the structure's 'metonymic causality'*[45] *on its effects is not the fault of the exteriority of the structure with respect to the economic phenomena; on the contrary, it is the very form of the interiority of the structure, as a structure, in its effects.* This implies therefore that the effects are not outside the structure, are not a pre-existing object, element or space in which

[45] An expression Jacques-Alain Miller has introduced to characterize a form of structural causality registered in Freud by Jacques Lacan.

the structure arrives to *imprint its mark*: on the contrary, it implies that the structure is immanent in its effects, a cause immanent in its effects in the Spinozist sense of the term, that *the whole existence of the structure consists of its effects*, in short that the structure, which is merely a specific combination of its peculiar elements, is nothing outside its effects.

This specification is very important when we have to deal with the occasionally strange form which the discovery of this reality and the search for expressions for it take, even in Marx. To understand these strange forms it is essential to note that the exteriority of the structure with respect to its effects can be conceived either as a pure exteriority or as an *interiority* on the sole condition that this exteriority or interiority are posed as *distinct from their effects*. In Marx, this distinction often takes the classical form of the distinction between the inside and the outside, between the 'intimate essence' of things and their phenomenal 'surface', between the 'intimate relations', the 'intimate links' of things and the external relations and links of the same things. And it is well known that this opposition, which derives in principle from the classical distinction between essence and phenomenon, i.e., from a distinction which situates *in being itself, in reality itself, the inner site of its concept*, and therefore opposes it to the 'surface' of concrete appearances; which therefore transposes as a difference of level or of components *in the real object itself*, a distinction which does not belong to that real object since it is a matter of the distinction which separates the concept or knowledge of the real from that real as an existing object; – it is well known that this opposition sometimes leads Marx to the following disarming pleonasm: *if the essence were not different from the phenomena, if the essential interior were not different from the inessential or phenomenal exterior, there would be no need for science.*[46] It is also well known that this singular formula may gain strength from all those arguments of Marx's which present the development of the concepts as the transition from the *abstract* to the *concrete*, a transition understood *as the transition from the essential, in principle abstract interiority to the concrete, visible and palpable outer determinations*, a transition summed up in the transition from Volume One to Volume Three. All these ambiguous arguments depend once again on the confusion between the thought-concrete, which Marx completely isolated from the real-concrete in the *Introduction*, and this same real-concrete – whereas in reality, the concrete of Volume Three, i.e., the *knowledge* of ground rent, profit and interest, is, like all knowledge, *not the empirical concrete but the concept*, and therefore still always an abstraction: what I have been able to and have had to call a 'Generality III', in order to stress that it was still a product of thinking, the *knowledge* of an empirical existence and not that empirical *existence* itself.

---

[46] *Capital*, Vol. III, p. 797: 'All science would be superfluous if the outward appearance and the essence of things directly coincided.' This re-echoes the old dream which haunted all classical political reflection: all politics would be superfluous if men's passions and reasons coincided.

It is therefore essential to be rigorous and draw the conclusion that *the transition from Volume One to Volume Three of* Capital *has nothing to do with the transition from the abstract-in-thought to the real-concrete, with the transition from the abstractions of thought necessary in order to know it to the empirical concrete*. We never leave abstraction on the way from Volume One to Volume Three, i.e., we never leave knowledge, the 'product of thinking and conceiving': *we never leave the concept*. We simply pass within the abstraction of knowledge from the concept of the structure and of its most general effects, to the concepts of the structure's particular effects – never for an instant do we set foot beyond the absolutely impassable frontier which separates the 'development' or specification of the concept from the development and particularity of things – and for a very good reason: *this frontier is impassable in principle because it cannot be a frontier, because there is no common homogeneous space (spirit or real) between the abstract of the concept of a thing and the empirical concrete of this thing which could justify the use of the concept of a frontier.*

I am very insistent on this ambiguity because I want to show clearly the difficulty Marx found when he had to think in a really reflected concept the epistemological problem which he had nevertheless produced: *how was he to account theoretically for the effectivity of a structure on its elements?* This difficulty was not without its consequences. I have pointed out that theoretical reflection before Marx had provided two and only two models for an effectivity in thought: the model of a transitive causality, Galilean and Cartesian in origin, and the model of an expressive causality, Leibnizian in origin and adopted by Hegel. But by playing on the ambiguity of the two concepts, these two models could quite easily find common ground in the classical opposition between *phenomenon and essence*. The ambiguity of these concepts is indeed obvious: the essence does refer to the phenomenon, but at the same time secretly to the *inessential*. The phenomenon does refer to the essence of which it can be the manifestation and expression, but at the same time, and secretly, it refers to what appears to be an empirical subject, to perception, and therefore to the empirical state of mind of a possible empirical subject. It then becomes quite simple to accumulate these ambiguous determinations in reality itself, and *to locate in the real itself* a distinction which is only meaningful as a function of a distinction *outside the real*, since it brings into play a distinction between the real and the knowledge of the real. In his search for a concept with which to think the remarkable reality of the effectivity of a structure on its elements, Marx often slipped into the really almost inevitable use of the *classical* opposition between *essence and phenomenon*, adopting its ambiguities by force rather than merit, and *transposing the epistemological difference between the knowledge of a reality and that reality itself* into reality in the form of the '*inside and the outside*', of the real, of the '*real movement and the apparent movement*' of the '*intimate essence*' and its concrete, phenomenal determinations, perceived and manipulated by subjects. There are surely consequences in this for his conception of science, as we could have seen when Marx had to provide the concept of what his predecessors had either found or missed – or the concept of the difference between himself and them.

But there were also consequences in this ambiguity for the interpretation of the phenomenon he baptized *'fetishism'*. We have proved that fetishism is not a subjective phenomenon related either to the illusions or to the perceptions of the agents of the economic process, that it cannot be reduced therefore to the *subjective effects* produced in the economic subjects by their place in the process, their site in the structure. But how many of Marx's texts present *fetishism as an 'appearance'*, an 'illusion' arising purely in 'consciousness', show us the real, inner movement of the process *'appearing'* in a fetishized form to the 'consciousness' of the same subjects in the form of the apparent movement! And yet how many other texts of Marx's assure us that this appearance is not subjective at all, but, on the contrary, objective through and through, the 'illusion' of the 'consciousness' and perceptions being itself secondary, and dislocated by the structure of this primary, purely objective 'illusion'! At this point we see Marx most clearly struggling with reference concepts which are inadequate to their objects, now accepting, now rejecting them in a necessarily contradictory movement.

However, and by virtue of these same contradictory hesitations, Marx often takes the side of what he was actually saying: and he then produces concepts adequate to their object, but it is just as if, producing them in a lightning gesture, he had not marshalled and confronted this production theoretically, had not reflected it in order to impose it on the total field of his analysis. For example, when dealing with the rate of profit, Marx wrote:

> In fact, the formula $\frac{s}{C}$ [the rate of profit] expresses the degree of self-expression of the total capital advanced ... taken in conformity with its inner conceptual connexions (*seinem begrifflichen, innern Zusammenhang entsprechend gefasst*) and the nature of surplus-value (*Capital*, Vol. III, p. 45).

In this passage, and in several others, Marx is unambiguously 'practising' the truth that *interiority* is nothing but the *'concept'*, that it is not the *real* 'interior' of the phenomenon, but knowledge of it. If this is true, the reality that Marx studies can no longer be presented as a *two-level reality*, inside and outside, the inside being identified with the pure essence and the outside with a phenomenon, sometimes purely subjective, the state of mind of a 'consciousness', sometimes impure, because it is foreign to the essence, or inessential. *If the 'inside' is the concept*, the 'outside' can only be the specification of the concept, exactly as the effects of the structure of the whole can only be the existence of the structure itself. Here, for example is what Marx says of ground rent:

> As important as it may be for a scientific analysis of ground rent – that is, the independent and specific economic form of landed property on the

basis of the capitalist mode of production – to study it in *its pure form* free of all distorting and obfuscating irrelevancies, it is just as important for an understanding of the practical effects of landed property – even for *a theoretical comprehension of a multitude of facts* which contradict the *concept* and *nature* of ground-rent and yet appear as *modes of existence of ground-rent* – to learn the sources which give rise to such muddling in theory (Vol. III, p. 610).

Here we have in black and white the double status Marx attributes to his analysis. He is analysing a pure form which is none other than the concept of capitalist ground-rent. He thinks this purity both as the modality and the definition of the concept, and at the same time he thinks it as what he distinguishes from *empirical impurity*. Still, he does at once think this same empirical impurity in a second correcting movement as the *'modes of existence'*, i.e., as theoretical determinations of the concept of ground-rent itself. In this latter conception we leave the empiricist distinction between pure essence and impure phenomenon, we abandon the empiricist idea of a purity which is thus only the result of an empirical *purge* (since it is a purge of the empirical) – we really think the purity as *the purity of the concept*, the purity of a knowledge adequate to its object, and the determinations of this concept as the effective knowledge of the modes of existence of ground-rent. It is clear that this language itself revokes the distinction between inside and outside, and substitutes for it the distinction between the concept and the real, or between the object (of knowledge) and the real object. But if we take this indispensable substitution seriously, it directs us towards a conception of scientific practice and of its object which no longer has anything in common with empiricism.

Marx states unambiguously the principles of this quite different conception of scientific practice in the *1857 Introduction*. But it is one thing to develop this concept and quite another to set it to work in order to solve the unprecedented theoretical problem of the production of the concept of the effectivity of a structure on its elements. We have seen Marx *practising* this concept in the use he makes of the *'Darstellung'*, and trying to pinpoint it in the images of changes in the illumination or in the specific weight of objects by the ether in which they are immersed, and it is sometimes directly exposed in Marx's analyses, in passages where it is expressed in a novel but extremely precise language: a language of metaphors which are nevertheless already *almost perfect concepts*, and which are perhaps only incomplete insofar as they have not yet been *grasped*, i.e., retained and elaborated as concepts. This is the case each time Marx presents the capitalist system as a mechanism, a machinery, a machine, a construction (*Triebwerk, Mechanismus, Getriebe* . . . Cf. *Capital*, Vol. III, p. 858 – Marx-Engels *Werke*, Bd. XXV, p. 887 – *Capital*, Vol. III, p. 859; Vol. II, p. 216; Vol. II, p. 421; Vol. II, p. 509); or as the complexity of a 'social metabolism' (*Capital*, Vol. III, p.

793 – modified). In every case, the ordinary distinctions between outside and inside disappear, along with the 'intimate' links within the phenomena as opposed to their visible disorder: we find a different image, a new quasi-concept, definitely freed from the empiricist antinomies of phenomenal subjectivity and essential interiority; we find an objective system governed in its most concrete determinations by the laws of its *erection* (*montage*) and *machinery*, by the specifications of its concept. Now we can recall that highly symptomatic term *'Darstellung'*, compare it with this 'machinery' and take it literally, as the very existence of this machinery in its effects: the mode of existence of the stage direction (*mise en scène*) of the theatre which is simultaneously its own stage, its own script, its own actors, the theatre whose spectators can, on occasion, be spectators only because they are first of all forced to be its actors, caught by the constraints of a script and parts whose authors they cannot be, since it is in essence *an authorless theatre*.

Need I add anything more? Marx's repeated efforts to break down the objective limits of the existing Theoretical, in order to forge a way of thinking the question that his scientific discovery has posed philosophy, his failures and even his relapses are a part of the theoretical drama he lived, in absolute solitude, long ago, and we are only just beginning to suspect from the signs in our heavens that *his question is our question*, and will be for a long time, that it commands our whole future. Alone, Marx looked around him for allies and supporters: who can reproach him for allowing himself to lean on Hegel? As for us, we can thank Marx for the fact that we are not alone: our solitude only lies in our ignorance of what he said. We should accuse this ignorance in us and in all those who think they have forstalled him, and I only include the best of them – when they were only on the threshold of the land he discovered and opened for us. We even owe it to him that we can see his weaknesses, his lacunae, his omissions: they concur with his greatness, for, in returning to them we are only returning to the beginnings of a discourse interrupted by death. The reader will know how Volume Three ends. A title: *Classes*. Forty lines, then silence.

Appendix

On the 'Ideal Average' and
the Forms of Transition

Just a few words on two important theoretical problems which are directly related to Marx's discovery and to the forms in which he expressed it: the problem of the definition of the object of *Capital* as 'the ideal average' of real capitalism – and the problem of the forms of transition from one mode of production to another.

> In a general analysis of this kind [writes Marx], it is usually always assumed that the *real* relations correspond to their *concept*, or, what is the same, that the real relations are represented only to the extent that they express their peculiar *general type* (*allgemeinem Typus*) (*Capital*, Vol. III, p. 141 – modified).

Marx defines this general type several times as the 'ideal average' (*idealer Durchschnitt*) of capitalist production. This name, in which average and ideality are combined on the concept's side while being referred to a certain existing real, poses anew the question of the philosophical problematic which underlies this terminology: is it not tainted with empiricism? This is certainly the impression given by a passage from the Preface to the first German edition of *Capital*:

> The physicist, when accounting for the processes of nature, either observes the phenomena where they occur in their most marked form, and most free from disturbing influences, or he makes experiments under conditions that assure as far as possible the regularity of their occurrence. In this work I have to examine the capitalist mode of production, and the relations of production and exchange corresponding to that mode. Their classical ground is England. That is the reason why I have taken the chief facts and examples which illustrate the development of my theories from England (T.I, p. 18; Vol. I, p. 8).

Marx therefore chooses the English example. However, he subjects even this example to a remarkable 'purification', since, on his own admission, he analyses it on the assumption that there are only ever two classes present in his object (a situation which has never existed anywhere), and that the world market is entirely subject to the capitalist mode of production, which is just as far from reality. Marx therefore does *not even study the English example*, however classical and pure it may be, but a non-existent example, precisely what he calls the 'ideal average' of the capitalist mode of production. Lenin restated this apparent difficulty in 1899 in his 'Once more on the theory of realization', *Collected Works*, Moscow 1960, Vol. IV, pp. 86–7).

Let us dwell for a while on the problem that has 'long interested' Struve: what is the real scientific value of the theory of realization?

It has exactly the same value as have all the other postulates of *Marx's abstract theory*. If Struve is bothered by the circumstances that 'perfect realization is the ideal of capitalist production, but by no means its reality', we must remind him that all the other laws of capitalism, revealed by Marx, also depict only *the ideal of capitalism and not its reality*. 'We need present,' wrote Marx, 'only the inner organization of the capitalist mode of production, in its ideal average (*in ihrem idealen Durchschnitt*), as it were' (*Capital*, Vol. III, p. 810). The theory of capital assumes that the worker receives the full value of his labour-power. This is the ideal of capitalism, but by no means its reality. The theory of rent presupposes that the entire agrarian population has been completely divided into landowners, capitalists and hired labourers. This is the ideal of capitalism, but by no means its reality. The theory of realization presupposes the proportional distribution of production. This is the ideal of capitalism, but by no means its reality.

Lenin is merely repeating Marx's own words, opposing the ideality of Marx's object to actual historical reality on the basis of the term '*ideal*' in the expression 'ideal average'. It would not be necessary to take this opposition very far to fall back into the traps of empiricism, particularly if we remember that Lenin described Marx's theory as an '*abstract*' theory, a theory which seems to be naturally opposed to the concrete-historical character of the reality of the actual forms of capitalism. But here again we can grasp Marx's true intention if we conceive this '*ideality*' as an '*idea-ness*', i.e., as the mere conceptuality of his object, and the 'average' as the content of the concept of his object – and not as the result of an empirical abstraction. Marx's object is not an *ideal* object opposed to a real object and distinct from it through this opposition, as 'ought' is from 'is', the norm from the fact – the object of his theory is an *idea*, i.e., it is defined in terms of knowledge, in the abstraction of the concept. Marx says so himself, when he writes that, '*its [the capitalist system's] specific difference ... is revealed (sich darstellt) in all its core form (in ihrer ganzen Kerngestalt)*' (*Capital*, Vol. III, p. 239 – modified). It is this '*Kerngestalt*' and its determinations that constitute the object of Marx's analysis, insofar as this specific difference defines the capitalist *mode* of production as the *capitalist* mode of production. What to vulgar economists like Struve seems to contradict reality for Marx constitutes reality itself, *the reality of his theoretical object*. In order to understand this we need only remember what I have said about the object of the theory of history and therefore of the theory of political economy: they study the basic forms of unity of historical existence, the *modes of production*. Besides, Marx tells us this himself if we are prepared to take his expressions seriously, in the Preface to the first German edition, where he is discussing England:

> In this work I have to examine the capitalist mode of production, and the relations of production and exchange corresponding to that mode (T.I, p. 18; Vol. I, p. 8).

As for England, a close reading of Marx's text shows that it only appears as *a source of illustrations and examples*, not as the theoretical object studied:

> Their classical ground in England. That is the reason why I have taken the chief facts and examples which *illustrate* the development of my theories from England (ibid.).

This unambiguous statement puts into correct perspective the earlier sentence in which the example of physics was evoked in a way that might suggest that Marx was investigating a 'pure' object *'free from disturbing influences'*. In this respect, England, too, is an impure disturbed object, but these 'impurities' and 'disturbances' cause no theoretical trouble *since Marx's theoretical object is not England but the capitalist mode of production in its* 'Kerngestalt' *and the determinations of that* 'Kerngestalt'. When Marx tells us that he is studying an 'ideal average', we must therefore understand that this ideality connotes not the unreal or the ideal norm, but the *concept* of the real; and that this 'average' is not an empiricist average, i.e., it does not connote the non-unique, but on the contrary, it connotes the concept of the specific difference of the mode of production concerned.

Let us go further. For, if we return to the English example, if we compare it with Marx's apparently purified and simplified object, the two-class capitalist mode of production, we have to admit that we must confront a *real residue*: precisely, restricting ourselves to this one pertinent point, the real existence of *other classes* (landowners, artisans, small-scale agriculturalists). We cannot in honesty suppress this real residue merely by invoking the fact that Marx proposed as his whole object only the concept of the specific difference of the capitalist mode of production, and by invoking the difference between the real and the knowledge of it!

But it is in this apparently urgent difficulty, which is also the major argument of the empiricist interpretation of the theory of *Capital*, that what has been said of the theory of history acquires all its meaning. For Marx could only study the specific difference of the capitalist mode of production on condition that at the same time he studied *the other modes of production*, not only the other modes of production as types of specific *Verbindung* unity between the factors of production, but also the *relations between different modes of production* in the process of the constitution of modes of production. The impurity of English capitalism is a real, definite object which Marx did not propose to study in *Capital*, but which is relevant to Marxist theory nevertheless: this impurity is, in its immediate form, what we can for the time being call the '*survivals*' of forms within the dominant capitalist mode of production in Britain from modes of production subordinate to but not yet eliminated by the capitalist mode of production. This supposed 'impurity' constitutes an object relevant to the theory of modes of production: in particular to *the theory of the transition from one mode of production to another*, which is the same thing as *the theory of the process of constitution of a determinate mode of production*, since every mode of production is constituted solely out of the existing forms of an earlier mode of production. This object is in principle part of Marxist theory, and the fact that we can recognize the status of this object in principle does not mean that we can criticize Marx for not providing us with the theory of it. All Marx's texts on the primitive accumulation of capital constitute the material if not already the outline of this theory, where the constitution process of the capitalist mode of production is concerned – i.e., the transition from the feudal mode of production to the capitalist mode of production. We must recognize what Marx actually gave us and what he enabled us to obtain for ourselves, although he could not give it to us. Just as we can say that we possess only the outline of a Marxist theory of the modes of production before the capitalist mode of production – we can say, and even, since the existence of this problem and above all the necessity of posing it in its peculiar theoretical form are not generally recognized, we must say that *Marx did not give us any theory of the transition from one mode of production to another, i.e., of the constitution of a mode of production.* We know that this theory is indispensable: without it we shall be unable to complete what is called the construction of socialism, in which the transition from the capitalist mode of production to the socialist mode of production is at stake, or even to solve the problems posed by the so-called '*under-developed*' countries of the Third World. I cannot go into any detail concerning the theoretical problems posed by this new object, but we can regard it as certain that posing and solving these burning contemporary problems is a first priority of Marxist investigation. Not only the problem of the period of the 'cult of personality', but also the current problems expressed in the form of 'national roads to socialism', 'peaceful roads', etc., relate directly to these theoretical investigations.

Here, too – even if certain of his formulations take us to the brink of ambiguity – Marx did not leave us without suggestions or resources. If we can pose the question of the transition from one mode of production to another as a theoretical problem, and therefore account not only for past transitions, but also anticipate the future and 'run ahead of our time' (which Hegelian historicism could not do), it is not because of any claim to the 'experimental structure' of history, but because of the Marxist theory of history as a theory of modes of production, of the definition of the constitutive elements of the different modes of production, and of the fact that the theoretical problems posed by the process of the constitution of a mode of production (in other words, the problems of the transformation of one mode of production into another) are directly a function of the theory of the modes of production concerned.[47] That is why we can say that Marx did give us enough to think this theoretically and practically decisive problem: knowledge of the modes of production considered provides the basis for posing and solving the problems of transition. That is why we can anticipate the future and theorize not only that future, but also and above all the roads and means that will secure us its reality.

The Marxist theory of history understood as I have just defined it secures us this right, given that we are able to define its conditions and limits very accurately. But at the same time, it gives us a measure of what remains to be done – and it is immense – in order to define with all desirable rigour these roads and means. If it is true that mankind always sets itself only such tasks as it can solve, given that this formula is not understood in any historicist way, it remains essential that mankind has an exact consciousness of the relationship between these tasks and its capacities, that it is prepared to proceed via a knowledge of these terms and their relationships, and therefore via an examination of these tasks and capacities, in order to define the right means to produce and dominate its future. If not, even in the 'transparency' of its new economic relations it will risk, as it has already discovered in the silences of the terror – and may do so again in the velleities of humanism – it will risk entering a future still charged with dangers and shades, with a virgin conscience.

[47] Cf. Balibar's paper.

Part III
On the Basic Concepts
of Historical Materialism
Étienne Balibar

The preceding papers have already formulated the idea that Marx's work contains a general scientific theory of history. In particular, they have shown that, in the formulation of this theory, Marx's construction of the central concept of the 'mode of production' has the function of an epistemological break with respect to the whole tradition of the philosophy of history. For in its generality it is absolutely incompatible with the principles of idealism, whether dogmatic or empiricist, and it progressively revolutionizes the whole problematic of society and history.

If this is the case, we know that it is because Marx's 'historical materialism' gives us not only *elements* of scientific historical knowledge (e.g., elements restricted to the history of 'bourgeois' society, in its economic and political aspects), but, in principle, a true theoretical science, and therefore an abstract science. The concept of the 'mode of production' and the concepts immediately related to it thus appear as the first abstract concepts whose validity is not as such limited to a given period or type of society, but on which, on the contrary, the concrete knowledge of this period and type depends. Hence the importance of defining them at the level of generality that they demand, i.e., in fact, the importance of posing a number of problems which the science of history has been waiting for since Marx.

Althusser however, in his paper, has shown us that the explicit formulation (and therefore recognition) of an abstract theory of history is surrounded by difficulties and ambiguities. He has shown the historical and philosophical reasons for this. Marx's theory was able to realize the paradox of having as its constant object the very history whose scientific knowledge it inaugurated, and yet of offering nowhere the adequate concept of this history, reflected for itself. I should like first to add a few specifications of this point, which will serve as a direct introduction to my particular problem.

It is not quite accurate to say that this theoretical formulation is missing: several texts give a remarkable outline of it, e.g., the first section of *The German Ideology* (which already contained a whole new definition of 'production'), the various preparatory drafts for *Capital* collected into the *Grundrisse der Kritik der politishen Ökonomie*,[1] and above all the Preface to

---

[1] *Grundrisse der Kritik der politischen Ökonomie* (Rohentwurf 1857–8), Dietz Verlag, Berlin 1953. Notable among these manuscripts is the one called *Formen, die der kapitalistischen*

A Contribution to the Critique of Political Economy, the terms of which have been constantly discussed in the Marxist tradition. These are very general, prospective or summary texts; texts in which the sharpness of the distinctions and the peremptoriness of the claims are only equalled by the brevity of the justifications, the elliptical nature of the definitions. By an unfortunate accident, which is really a true historical necessity, the only expositions of the principles of the theory of history and the main expositions of its method (the *1857 Introduction*) are of this type, and most of them were also intentionally left as incomplete and unpublished manuscripts. So despite the malicious critical intentions that inspire those readers of Marx who have asked '*Where* precisely did Marx set out his conception of history?', they have not been completely unfair.

The reader will be familiar with the young Lenin's answer in *What the Friends of the People Really Are*:[2] this theory is everywhere, but in two forms; the Preface to *A Contribution* presents 'the hypothesis of historical materialism'; *Capital* sets this hypothesis to work and *verifies* it against the example of the capitalist social formation. These concepts enable Lenin to formulate what is for us a decisive commentary: in the expression 'historical materialism', 'materialism' means no more than *science*, and the expression is strictly synonymous with that of 'science of history'. But at the same time, these concepts belong organically to the empiricist, even pragmatist theory of science, and this text of Lenin's is throughout an application of such a theory (hypothesis/verification). However, let us reconsider its movement in other terms.

In reality, this Preface to *A Contribution*, if it is read attentively, does not present us with the form of a hypothesis, but explicitly that of an answer, an answer to a question we must try to reconstitute.

As an example, let us take a familiar text, one of those programme-texts whose interest I have just discussed, in which Marx states *what was new in what he had proved*: his letter to Weydemeyer on 5 March 1852:

> No credit is due to me for discovering the existence of classes in modern society, nor yet the struggle between them. Long before me bourgeois historians had described the historical development of this struggle of the classes, and bourgeois economists the economic anatomy of the classes. What I did that was new was to prove: (1) that the existence of classes is only bound up with particular historical phases in the development of production. . . .

Produktion vorhergehen, pp. 375–413. References below are to this text and to the English translation by Jack Cohen, edited and introduced by E. J. Hobsbawm, *Pre-Capitalist Economic Formations*, Lawrence and Wishart, London 1964.
[2] Lenin: 'What the Friends of the People Really Are and How they Fight the Social-Democrats', *Collected Works*, Vol. I.

Here we find a procedure characteristic of Marx when he wants to think his own 'novelty', i.e., his rupture, his scientificity: the delimitation of a *classicism*. Just as there is an economic classicism (in England), there is a historical classicism, represented by the French and German historians of the early nineteenth century (Thierry, Guizot and Niebuhr). *This, therefore, is Marx's point of departure: their point of arrival.* Historical knowledge in its most advanced form shows the succession of 'civilizations', 'political regimes', 'events', 'cultures', organized and rationalized by a series of *class struggles*, a general form whose patterns can be listed: slaves and free citizens, patricians and plebeians, serfs and feudal lords, masters and journeymen, land-owners and bourgeois, bourgeois and proletarians, etc. This heritage, this *fact*, proposed by history, but itself already the result of a labour of knowledge, is reflected in the famous opening of the *Manifesto*: 'The history of all hitherto existing society is the history of class struggles.' This sentence is not the first statement of Marx's theory, *it predates it*, it summarizes the raw material of its work of transformation.

This is a very important point, for it enables us to formulate Marx's *question* more precisely, the question contained in the Preface to *A Contribution: on what conditions can the claim that history is the history of class struggles be a scientific utterance?* In other words what classes are these? what are classes? what is their struggle?

If we turn to the text of the Preface itself, we do indeed find an exposition of a relationship between the 'social formation' (*Gesellschaftsformation*) and its 'economic base' or 'economic structure' (*Struktur*), the anatomy of which is constituted by the study of the *mode of production*. The social formation is the site of a first 'contradiction' between the classes which Marx describes in terms of struggle, war, and opposition, a 'contradiction' which can be 'now hidden, now open', and whose terms are 'in a word, oppressor and oppressed' (*The Communist Manifesto*). Here it is related just as to its essence to a second form of 'contradiction' which Marx is always very careful not to confuse with the first, even terminologically: he calls it an 'antagonism', 'not in the sense of individual antagonism' (*nicht im individuellen Sinn*), i.e., not a struggle between men but an antagonistic structure; it is *inside the economic base*, typical of a determinate mode of production, and its terms are called 'the level of the productive forces' and 'the relations of production'. The antagonism between the productive forces and the relations of production has the effect of a revolutionary rupture, and it is this effect which determines the transition from one mode of production to another ('progressive epochs in the economic formation of society'), and thereby the transformation of the whole social formation. Marx himself chose to restrict his study to the level of the relatively autonomous sphere or stage of this 'antagonism' inside the economic structure.

But it remains strictly impossible for us to locate this sphere, since the terms that define it do not yet have any meaning. Indeed, it would be absolutely wrong to take the descriptive style of some of these terms or the direct simplicity with which Marx presents them as a pretext for believing them to be *given* in immediate experience and of obvious significance. On the contrary, they have been *produced* by Marx (who is careful to remind us – notably in his use of the term 'civil society' – that a considerable part of the raw material of this production had been constituted by economic and philosophical tradition), and they are so little obvious that it is extremely difficult to make use of them in actual sociological analyses without first mastering the definitions that Marx gave of them elsewhere. That is why they are often described from the standpoint of bourgeois empiricist sociology as paradoxical, heteroclite or inconsistent, or else assimilated without further ado to other terms: technology, economics, institutions, human relations, etc.

Taking this textual reading further, we can draw from it the two principles on which is based the transformation of history into a science: the principle of *periodization* and the principle of the *articulation of the different practices* in the social structure. One diachronic principle, it seems, and one synchronic principle. The principle of the articulation of the practices refers to the construction (*Bau*) or mechanism of 'correspondence' in which the social formation is presented as constituted out of different levels (we shall also speak of them as instances and practices). Marx lists *three*: the economic base, the legal and political superstructures, and the forms of social consciousness. As for periodization, it distributes history according to the *epochs* of its economic structure. These two principles introduce a double *reduction* of temporal continuity. Leaving aside the problem of primitive societies (i.e., the way Marx conceived the origin of society: there is no allusion to this here, any more than there is in the *Manifesto*), there is, first, a reduction to an absolute invariance in the elements which are found in *every social structure* (an economic base, legal and political forms, and ideological forms); second, there is a division into periods which replaces historical continuity with a discontinuity, a succession of temporarily invariant *states of the structure* which change by rapid mutation ('revolution'): the antagonism that induces the mutation can only be defined by this invariance itself, i.e., by the permanence of the terms which it opposes.

These states of the structure are the *modes of production*, and the history of society can be reduced to a discontinuous succession of modes of production.

Now it is essential to pose the question of the theoretical status of these concepts. Are they all *positive* concepts? Does the text as a whole have a homogeneous content of theoretical knowledge, at the level of scientific abstraction which I have just discussed, as Gramsci thinks, for example, regarding it as he does as the most exact exposition of the 'philosophy of praxis'?

I think, on the contrary, that within theoretical practice itself, this text has the status of what is called a set of *practical* concepts.[3] In other words, this text offers

---

[3] Louis Althusser: 'A Complementary Note on Real Humanism', *For Marx*, pp. 242–7.

us concepts which still depend in their *formulation* precisely on the problematic which has to be displaced; at the same time, without being able to think it in its concept they indicate *where we must go* in order to pose otherwise (and at the same stroke solve) a new problem which has arisen within the old problematic.

To demonstrate this characteristic, I shall take as my main example the concept of *periodization*. This concept belongs completely to the traditional conception of history which Marx is questioning here. It is the concept of discontinuity in continuity, the concept which fragments the line of time, thereby finding the possibility of understanding historical phenomena in the framework of an autonomous totality (in this general form, the problem does not change whether we look for 'civilizations' or for 'structures' as opposed to 'conjunctures'). Thus the concept of periodization gives theoretical form to a problem which historians have never been able to evade in their practice, but without itself providing them with a theoretical solution, a precise theoretical *methodology*, for fundamental reasons which the rest of this paper will reveal. A problem which manifestly haunts these texts of Marx's, too: the problem of the 'right break'. If the right break or breaks are found, history, without ceasing to unfold in the linear flux of time, becomes intelligible as the relationship between an essential permanence and a subordinate movement. The questions necessarily contained in this problematic do not differ in their essence whether it is economic structures or *ages* (the 'age of Louis XIV') that have to be distinguished. The latter formulation even has the advantage that it constantly reminds us that these problems are constrained to respect the conditions imposed on them by the linearity of time: or in other words to transpose all discontinuities onto the plane of temporal discontinuities. It is in this way that it has been possible for the main instrument of historical conceptualization which emerged in modern economic history to have been a distinction between *the long term* and *the short term*, i.e., a distinction entirely 'rotated' into the linearity of time. The historian seeks to distinguish the long-term phenomena from the short-term phenomena, and to show how the latter are *inserted* into the movement of the former and into their determinism. At the same time, he perpetuates two kinds of difficulties: those relating to the notion of the historical *event*, which is assessed according to the single criteria of *brevity* (suddenness) and is therefore almost of necessity confined to the sphere of political events; and those relating to the impossibility of making *clean* breaks.

Marx therefore seems to treat matters in exactly the same way; simply proposing a new criterion of periodization, a means of making the right break, the one which gives the best periods, the periods which must not be described as *artificial* but not *arbitrary*, but which correspond to the very nature of historical social reality.[4] In fact, if we are to take the idea of an

---

[4] 'Artificial but not arbitrary.' Here I have adopted Auguste Comte's very words in the *Cours de philosophie positive* (First Lecture, Vol. I, p. 24) about the division of science

epistemological rupture seriously, we should have to say that the very nature of the critierion chosen (epochs in the economic structure) implies a complete transformation of the way the problem has to be posed. Marx would say: in order to periodize the history of mankind, we must approach it from the side of economic science *rather than* from that of art, politics, science or law. But it is then clear that what is theoretically essential in this concept, what is new in its contribution, *what defines it differentially*, cannot lie in the general form that it has in common with all the other periodizations, but in its particular answer to the question.

We must now think in all its epistemological singularity the form in which Marx proposes his own theory to us here: the theoretical specificity of Marx's own concept of periodization lies *solely* in the fact that it is a *particular answer* to a question which, for its part, belongs to an old problematic, a question which is not decisive in the constitution of the science. Such a situation necessarily implies and envelops Marx's own inability to *justify* his particular answer at this level – in fact it is impossible to justify it at this level – and that is perhaps why the text we are discussing is so dogmatically brief; and also Marx's inability to formulate the true theoretical concept of this periodization, since it would be the concept of the only way to periodize which abolishes the earlier problematic of periodization based on the linear conception of time and at grips with it.

What is true of the concept of periodization is also necessarily true of the concepts in the Preface which designate the different instances of the social structure other than the *economic base* (which, as we have seen, is designated by new concepts which are specific if not yet defined: productive forces, relations of production, mode of production). These concepts and all the terms which designate the peculiar articulation of their objects ('*corresponds*', 'on which rises', etc.) are remarkably vague and yet they have sustained all Marxist reflection on the problem of ideologies and superstructures. They have no other function than to *indicate* where, provisionally, Marx *is not going to go* on this occasion; they do not therefore constitute a knowledge of these levels and their mutual relations, but merely a practical *registration* (practical in the sense of theoretical practice, of course) which disengages the level of the economic structure which Marx is now undertaking to study, in its relative autonomy. Nevertheless, if this registration is to be possible,

---

into several branches. The problem of the 'break' between the different states of a single science is of the same nature: 'It is impossible to assign a precise origin to this revolution . . . It is constantly more and more complete. . . . However, . . . it is convenient to fix an epoch in order to prevent our ideas from straying' (ibid., p. 10). Bacon, Descartes and Galileo thus determine the transition of physics to positivity, and at the same time the beginning of the general preponderance of the positive state. With his double articulation of the sciences and the law of the three states, Comte is the most rigorous thinker so far of this general theoretical problem: how the distinct practices which constitute a 'division of labour' are articulated together, and how this articulation varies with the mutations in these practices ('breaks').

certain theoretical conditions must be met which constitute its real meaning: on condition that its concept is redefined, the economic structure must really possess the relative autonomy which allows us to delimit it as an independent field of research. A *plurality* of instances must be an essential property of every social structure (but we shall regard their number, names and the terms which designate their articulation as subject to revision); the problem of the science of society must be precisely the problem of *the forms of variation of their articulation*.[5]

Finally, these same comments are valid for the concept *'men'*: the 'men' who support the whole process. Let me say without prevarication that all the rest of this paper is governed by a principle of *critical* reading, which I hope will be granted me: I shall refrain from pre-judging the meaning of such a term ('men') until I have elucidated its conceptual function in the theoretical structure which contains it – since its theoretical meaning depends entirely on this function. The 'obviousness', the 'transparency' of the word 'men' (here charged with every carnal opacity) and its anodyne appearance are the most dangerous of the traps I am trying to avoid. I shall not be satisfied until I have either situated it and *founded* it in the necessity of the theoretical system to which it belongs, or *eliminated* it as a foreign body, and in this latter case, replaced it by something else. The formulations in this Preface ('In the social production of their life, *men enter into* definite relations . . . *their* material productive *forces* . . . It is not the consciousness *of men* that determines *their being* . . . ideological forms in which *men* become conscious

[5] Here we should note a serious difficulty for our reading, not only where the *Contribution* is concerned, but also *Capital*: the term 'social formation' which Marx uses, may be either an empirical concept designating the object of a concrete analysis, i.e., an *existence*: England in 1860, France in 1870, Russia in 1917, etc., or else an abstract concept replacing the ideological notion of 'society' and designating the object of the science of history insofar as it is a totality of instances articulated on the basis of a determinate mode of production. This ambiguity includes, first, *philosophical* problems of a theory of science and of the concept, which are not explicitly solved, and the empiricist tendency to think the theoretical object of an abstract science as a mere 'model' of existing realities (see Althusser's paper on this point). But, secondly, it also includes an objective *omission* from historical materialism itself, which can only be imputed to the inevitably gradual character of its development: *Capital*, which expounds the abstract theory of the capitalist mode of production, does not undertake to analyse concrete social formations which generally contain *several* different modes of production, whose laws of coexistence and hierarchy must therefore be studied. The problem is only implicitly and partially contained in the analysis of *ground rent* (Volume Three); it is only present practically in Marx's historical and political works (*The Eighteenth Brumaire*, etc.); Lenin alone, in *The Development of Capitalism in Russia* and the works of the period of the transition to socialism, begins to treat this problem theoretically.

And we should also note that the insufficient elaboration, in this first draft, of the concepts which designate the *articulation* of the instances of the social formation, is in itself the (negative) cause of a constant confusion in Marxist literature between the *social formation* and its economic infra-structure (which is itself often related to *one* mode of production). Many of the contemporary discussions of non-capitalist or pre-capitalist modes of production bear witness to this.

of this conflict . . .') must be compared with many others in *The German Ideology*, in *The Poverty of Philosophy*, in the correspondence (notably in Engels's letter to Bloch: 'We (=men) make our history ourselves, but, in the first place, under very definite assumptions and conditions . . .'). All these formulations are the matrices of the idea that *it is men who make history on the basis of previous conditions*. But who are these 'men'? A first, 'naïve' reading of our Preface suggests that they are *firstly* the agents of the process of the historical transformation of the social structure via the mediation of the activity of economic production. We are to understand that men *produce* their material means of survival, and at the same time, the social relations in which they produce, which are either maintained or transformed. In consequence, they are *secondly* the real (concrete) supports of the different practices articulated into the social structure: this articulation is precisely given only *by the men* who at one and the same time take part in the production process, are legal subjects and are consciousnesses. The importance of this concept can thus be measured by the function of structural cohesion it fulfils in theory. But its ambiguity is revealed in the fact that it belongs simultaneously to several incompatible systems of concepts: theoretical and non-theoretical, scientific and ideological. The concept of 'men' thus constitutes a real point where the utterance *slips away* towards the regions of philosophical or commonplace ideology. The task of epistemology here is to stop the utterance slipping away by fixing the meaning of the concept.

If this really is the ambiguous status of these concepts, if they really are practical concepts, signal concepts within a still unbalanced problematic (periodization, correspondence – articulation of the practices, men), then this task becomes necessary. I propose to begin this work here, an explicit labour which *transforms* these '*practical*' concepts into *theoretical* concepts of the Marxist theory of history, a labour which strips them of their present theoretical form in order to make them theoretically adequate to their practical content. At the same time, those concepts, which are no more than expressions of the exigencies of the old ideological problematic, will disappear completely. And at the same time, too, weak and open points will appear which will demand the production of new theoretical concepts even in the region explored by Marx, and make this production possible. For, at the *most abstract* level, the fruitful incompleteness of Marx's work is the necessary effect of its scientific character.

Since the theoretical concepts of the Preface to *A Contribution* have this compound status as the anticipations and summaries (or 'results') of an analysis, the text of *Capital* cannot therefore constitute a mere 'verification' or application of them. The text of *Capital*, in its necessary order of exposition, is the process of the production, construction and definition of these theoretical concepts, or at least of some of them. If we take the 'mode of production' as the main object of our analysis, it is because *in* that very exposition Marx himself designates the theoretical object of *Capital* as *the concept of the capitalist mode of production*.

Chapter 1

From Periodization to the
Modes of Production

In my reconstitution of the concept of a mode of production, I shall start with what seem the most external and formal determinations, and attempt to enrich them progressively. I shall therefore return to the first question of the theory of history, the question of the breaks, of the right break. Scattered throughout Marx's writings is a series of comments with a common form: they all begin as follows: 'What defines a historical epoch of production is . . .' or again, 'what defines a historical mode of production is the specific way in which it . . .'; then follow several phrases whose comparison is only too likely to be quite instructive, for they are all *equivalent* in principle, without this equivalence being at all tautological. In other words, we can try to extract from these equivalent answers to a single question which depends in principle on a method of comparison, the determination of the *criteria* for the identification of a 'mode of production' (for the moment this term is still no more than a name, as far as we are concerned, the name of the unit of periodization peculiar to Marx), the determination of the *pertinent differences* which make it possible to define the concept of each mode of production. If we do reveal such pertinent differences, we shall face a second task, that of characterizing the *ensembles* within which these differences act.[6]

(1) MODE OF PRODUCTION: MANNER OF PRODUCING

Even more than its French or English equivalent, the German term *Produktionsweise* retains some echo of the simple and original meaning of the word *Weise*, mode, i.e., *manner*, way to do something (there is a standard German expression for this, the doublet *Art und Weise*). This warns us immediately what kind of analysis we are dealing with: a *descriptive* analysis which isolates forms or qualities. Thus the mode 'of production' first

---

[6] Periodization, thought of as the periodization of the modes of production themselves, in their purity, first gives form to the theory of history. Thus the majority of the indications in which Marx assembles the elements of his definition are *comparative* indications. But behind this descriptive terminology (men do not produce in the same way in the different historical modes of production, capitalism does not contain the universal nature of economic relations), there is the indication of *what makes the comparisons possible at the level of the structures*, the search for the *invariant determinations* (for the 'common features') of 'production in general', which does *not exist* historically, but whose *variants* are represented by all the historical modes of production (cf. the *1857 Introduction* to *A Contribution*).

exists on the same plane as the many other *modes* we find in the course of an analysis of *Capital*. For example:

> *Modes of exchange*: 'It is not the economy, i.e., the process of production itself that is emphasized as the distinguishing mark of the two categories, money-economy and credit-economy, but rather the mode of exchange ... between the various agents of production or producers' (*Verkehrsweise*) (*Capital*, Vol. II, p. 116). *Modes of circulation*: 'What determines that a portion of the capital-value invested in means of production is endowed with the character of fixed capital is exclusively the peculiar manner in which this value circulates. This specific manner of circulation (*diese eigene Weise der Zirkulation*) arises from the specific manner in which the instrument of labour transmits its value to the product, or in which it behaves (*sich . . .verhält*) as a creator of value during the process of production. This manner again arises from the special way in which the instruments of labour function in the labour-process (*aus der besonderen Art der Funktion der Arbeitsmittel*)' (*Capital*, Vol. II, p. 160). *Modes of consumption*: 'Even the number of so-called natural needs, as also the modes of satisfying them (*die Art ihrer Befriedigung*), are themselves a historical product' (*Capital*, T.I, p. 174; Vol. I, p. 171).

I could give other examples, too, taken from the 'economic' sphere and elsewhere.

This descriptive and comparative character indicates that the expression 'mode of production' does not initially contain any reference to the breadth of its application other than in the form of a tendency towards generality: we find the capitalist mode of production, in the narrow sense of the industrial mode of production, the utilization of machinery, steadily extended to the various branches of industry:

> But when surplus-value has to be produced by the conversion of necessary labour into surplus-labour, it no longer suffices for capital, while leaving intact the traditional labour process, simply to prolong the duration of that process. The technical and social conditions of the process, and consequently the very mode of production must be transformed. Only then can the productivity of labour be increased, thus decreasing the value of labour-power, and thereby shortening the time necessary for the reproduction of that value (*Capital*, T.II, p. 9; Vol. I, p. 315).

This text is preceded by the following definition:

> a revolution in the conditions of production, i.e., an alteration in his *tools* or his *mode of working*, or in both.

Here we have descriptions of processes, manners, methods, forms – all expressions which have meaning only by *what they exclude*. Firstly, *quantitative* measurements. Thus the *productivity* of labour, which determines the relative quantities necessary for the satisfaction of the producer's needs and for surplus-value, only intervenes here insofar as it depends in each historical epoch, on a certain *form* of the labour process, i.e., on the relationship between certain instruments (means of labour) and certain forms of labour organization (which include non-organizations, such as when the individual producer alone sets to work the tools which enable him to obtain an actual useful product). Then they exclude any consideration of the material *nature* of the objects which produce or undergo a transformation, insofar as such a consideration refers to the special features of branches of the *social division of production* which produce special *use*-values with peculiar technological characteristics. In this sense, Marx had already written in the *1857 Introduction* that 'political economy is not technology' in the sense that the latter term had acquired at the beginning of the nineteenth century, and whose historical origins he reveals in the chapter in Volume One on Modern Industry. These two negative determinations are to be found in the text of the chapter on the *labour process*:

> Relics of by-gone means of labour possess the same importance for the investigation of extinct economic forms of society, as does the structure of fossil bones for a knowledge of the organization of extinct species of animals. It is less what is produced than how it is produced (*Nicht was . . . sondern wie*), and by what means of labour, that enables us to distinguish different economic epochs. Means of labour supply a standard of the degree of development of the labourer and they are indicators of the social relations in which he labours (*Nicht nur Gradmesser der Entwicklung der menschlichen Arbeitskraft, sondern auch Anzeiger der gesellschaftlichen Verhältnissen, worin gearbeitet wird*) (*Capital*, T.I, p. 182; Vol. I, pp. 179–80).

If means of labour are to be 'indicators' of social relations, they must obviously be justifiable by a type of analysis different from the measurement of their effectivity or the technological description of their elements. Otherwise we should fall back into Proudhon's error and take machines for social relations (cf. *The Poverty of Philosophy*, op. cit., p. 133).

We can define this analysis as *a differential determination of forms*, and define a 'mode' as a system of forms which represents *one state of the variation* of the set of elements which necessarily enter into the *process considered*. This definition, which I am about to put to the test, is true for all modes, and on each occasion it requires two things: a listing of the *places* (or functions) which feature in the process concerned, and a determination of *the pertinent criteria* which enable us to distinguish between the forms occupying these places. Thus, if we return to the above-mentioned example of the mode of circulation (*Capital*, Vol. II, p. 160), we find that this criterion consists of the fact that it transmits its value to the product either *in toto* or only in parts spread over several periods of production. At the same time, we can derive from it the concepts by which Marx designates existence as an element of the process: function, factor. But in order to list these places we must refer to another 'mode', the 'mode of production' itself; we are not dealing with a relatively autonomous process with its own consistency. It is different with the mode of production itself, and there we find that consistency.

(2) THE ELEMENTS OF THE SYSTEM OF FORMS

In the case, therefore, of the *mode of production* (in the strict sense), we still have to identify these elements. Here we shall find it necessary to compare several of Marx's texts which complement one another, and even to suggest interpretations of them whose well-foundedness will, I hope, emerge later in the paper.

We find a first extremely clear text in *Capital* Volume Two:

Whatever the social form of production, labourers and means of production always remain *factors* (*Faktoren*) of it. But in a state of separation from each other either of these factors can be such only potentially (*der Möglichkeit nach*). For production to go on at all they must *combine* (*Verbindung*). The specific manner in which this combination is accomplished distinguishes the different epochs of the structure of society one from another (*Capital*, Vol. II, p. 34 – modified).

Two of the elements we are seeking are indicated here:

(1) *The labourer* (labour power);
(2) *The means of production.*

The text goes on:

In the present case, the separation of the free worker from his means of production is the starting-point given, and we have seen how and under what conditions these two elements are united in the hands of the capitalist, namely, as the productive mode of existence of his capital.

Here we find straightaway a third element which, like the other two, also deserves to be called a 'factor':

(3) *The non-worker, appropriating surplus-labour.* Elsewhere, Marx describes him as the representative of the 'class of large proprietors' (*Grossbesitzerklasse – Capital*, T.II, p. 185; Vol. I, p. 511). This is the capitalist. Besides this, we find here an element of a different kind which we could call a *connexion* (*relation*) between the preceding elements: it can take two exclusive values: separation (*Trennung*)/property.

If we compare the results of our analysis of this text with a series of other texts, particularly those contained in Marx's unpublished draft *Pre-Capitalist Economic Formations* (op. cit.), and in the Chapter in Volume Three of *Capital* on the 'Genesis of Capitalist Ground Rent', we find the same elements and long descriptions of their combinations. The *labourer* is specified as the *direct producer*; the property relation is itself specified according to several complex forms, notable the duality of 'possession' (use, enjoyment) and 'property' (property strictly speaking).

But the essential interest of these texts is that they oblige us to introduce into the structure *a second connexion distinct from the first*, a second relation between the 'factors' of the combination. This is a very important point, for it governs our whole understanding of the structure. We must therefore try to define the nature of this connexion very clearly, starting from Marx's texts themselves. This connexion corresponds to what Marx designates by various terms such as *the real material appropriation of the means of production by the producer in the labour process* (*Aneignung, Appropriation, wirkliche Aneignung*), or simply as the appropriation of nature by man. Two points must be clearly established:

(1) this connexion is distinct from the preceding one;

(2) this, too, really is a connexion, a relation between the previously listed elements.

The relative looseness of Marx's vocabulary on this point in the texts I have mentioned (particularly *Pre-Capitalist Economic Formations*) makes it difficult to prove the first point. Marx uses a whole series of practically equivalent terms (*Aneignung, Appropriation; Besitz, Benutzung*, etc.) to describe all the connexions between the producer and his means of production. This looseness depends in reality on the difficulty Marx felt in clearly thinking the distinction between the two connexions, a difficulty I shall explain. Nevertheless, let us take the text of Volume One of *Capital* on *absolute surplus-value and relative surplus-value* (T.II, pp. 183ff.; Vol. I, pp. 508ff.): there we find two uses of the word *Aneignung* (appropriation) less than two pages apart but with obviously different meanings corresponding to the two connexions I have been discussing:

> *in der individuellen Aneignung von Naturgegenständen zu seinem Lebenszwecken kontrolliert er sich selbst. Später wird er kontrolliert* (In the individual appropriation of natural objects the labourer controls himself. Afterwards his labour is controlled by others);
>
> '*die Aneignung dieser Mehrarbeit durch das Kapital*' (the appropriation of that surplus-labour by capital).

The second '*Aneignung*' describes a property relation, the one we first met. It describes one of the presuppositions of capitalist production: capital is the owner of all the means of production *and* of labour, and therefore it is the owner of the entire product.

But the first does not designate a property relation: it belongs to the analysis of what Marx called the 'labour process', or rather it situates the analysis of that labour process as part of the analysis of the mode of production. Nowhere in it does the capitalist intervene *as an owner*, but only the labourer, the means of labour and the object of labour.

In the light of this distinction, we can now re-read for example the chapter on the labour process (T.I, pp. 186–7; Vol. I, pp. 184–5). Marx writes:

The labour process, turned into the process by which the capitalist consumes labour-power, exhibits two characteristic phenomena. First, the labourer works under the control of the capitalist . . . Secondly, the product is the property of the capitalist and not that of the labourer, its immediate producer . . . (T.I, p. 187; Vol. I, p. 185).

In these 'two phenomena' characteristic of the capitalist mode of production, we find precisely the two connexions in the specific form they take in the capitalist mode of production.

From the point of view of property, the labour process is an operation between things which the capitalist has purchased. 'The product of this process belongs, therefore, to him, just as much as does the wine which is the product of a process of fermentation completed in his cellar.'

In the capitalist mode of production, the labour process is such that individual labour does not set to work the society's means of production, which are the only means of production able to function as such. Without the capitalist's 'control', which is a technically indispensable moment of the labour process, labour does not possess the *fitness (Zweckmässigkeit)* it requires if it is to be social labour, i.e., labour used by society and recognized by it. The fitness peculiar to the capitalist mode of production implies the cooperation and division of the functions of control and execution. It is a form of the second connexion I have discussed, which can now be defined as *the direct producer's ability to set to work the means of social production*. In the pages of *Capital*, Marx defines several forms of this connexion: the *autonomy (Selbständigkeit)* of the direct producer, and the forms of mutual *dependence* of the producers (co-operation, etc.).

We can already see that recognition of this *second* connexion in its conceptual independence, in its difference from the 'property' connexion (A), is the key to several very important theses of *Capital*. Notably the *double function* of the capitalist as the exploiter of labour-power ('property') and as the organizer of production ('real appropriation'); a double function expounded by Marx in the chapters on co-operation, manufacture and modern industry (Volume One). This double function is an index of what I shall call the double nature of the *division of labour* in production (the 'technical' division of labour and the 'social' division of labour); at the same time, it is an index of the *interdependence* or intersection of these two divisions, which itself reflects the fact that the two connexions which I have distinguished both belong to *a single 'Verbindung'*, to a single combination, i.e., to the structure of a single mode of production.

That is why the distinction between these two connexions finally enables us to understand what constitutes the *complexity* of the combination, the complexity which characterizes the Marxist totality as opposed to the Hegelian totality. When the concept of structural complexity was introduced,[7] it was a question of the complexity of the social structure as a whole, insofar as several relatively autonomous levels were articulated in it. Now we find that *production* itself is a complex totality, i.e., that nowhere is there a simple totality, and we can give a precise meaning to this complexity: it consists of the fact that the elements of the totality are not linked together once, but twice, by two distinct connexions. What Marx called a *combination* is not therefore *a simple relationship between the 'factors' of any production, but the relationship between these two connexions and their interdependence.*

Finally, therefore, we can draw up a table of the elements of any mode of production, a table of the invariants in the analysis of forms:

(1) labourer;
(2) means of production;
    (i) object of labour;
    (ii) means of labour;
(3) non-labourer;
(A) property connexion;
(B) real or material appropriation connexion.

Marx's difficulty in clearly distinguishing between the two connexions in certain historically retrospective texts can be explained by the particular form these connexions take in the capitalist mode of production. In the capitalist mode of production, both connexions can indeed be characterized by a *'separation'*: the labourer is 'separated' from all the means of production, he is stripped of all property (save that of his labour-power); but at the same time, as a human individual, the labourer is 'separated' from any ability to set in motion the instruments of social labour by himself; he has lost his craft skill, which no longer corresponds to the means of labour; as Marx says, the labour is no longer 'his property'. In the capitalist mode of production, strictly speaking, these two 'separations', these two distinctions overlap and coincide in the image of the opposition between the 'free' labourer and the means of production instituted as capital, to the extent that the labourer himself becomes an element of capital: that is why Marx constantly confounds them in a single concept, the concept of *the separation of the labourer from his condition of labour.* Now in all the historical inquiries which trace the history of the constitution of the elements of the capitalist mode of production back to earlier modes of production, Marx takes this concept as his guiding thread. This explains his difficulty, a difficulty which is patent in the semantic hesitations of *Pre-Capitalist Economic Formations*, in isolating the two connexions; for the homology between the two connexions, the overlap between their forms, which characterizes the capitalist structure,

---

[7] Louis Althusser: 'On the Materialist Dialectic', *For Marx*, op. cit., Chapter 6.

does not so characterize those earlier modes of production. Marx only finds it again in the hypothetical 'natural community' which inaugurates history: then the form of each of the two connexions was, on the contrary, the *union*, the *belonging together* of the labourer and the means of production: on the one hand the almost biological collective property of the land, on the other the biological naturalness of the labour (the earth as 'man's laboratory', indistinctly object and means of labour).

But the entire difficulty, and any looseness in Marx's terminology, disappear once our analysis deals with the *effects* of this double articulation of the mode of production, i.e., with the *double nature* of the 'immediate production process' as a labour process and (in its capitalist form) as a process of self-expansion (*Verwertung*) of value (the distinction between these two constitutes the object of Volume One, Chapter VII).

By varying the combination of these elements according to the two connexions which are part of the structure of every mode of production, we can therefore reconstitute the various modes of production, i.e., we can set out the 'presuppositions' for the theoretical knowledge of them, which are quite simply the concepts of the conditions of their historical existence. In this way, we can even to a certain extent generate modes of production which have never existed in an *independent* form, and which do not therefore strictly speaking form part of our 'periodization' – modes of production such as Marx called the 'mode of commodity production' (the reunion of individual small producers owning their own means of production and setting them to work without co-operation); or modes of production for which it is only possible to *foresee* the general conditions, such as the socialist mode of production. The final result would be *a comparative table of the forms* of different modes of production which all combine the same 'factors'.

However, this is by no means a *combinatory* in the strict sense, i.e., a form of combination in which only the places of the factors and their relations change, but not their nature. Before we go on to prove this in a second section, we can nevertheless draw from what has already been established a number of conclusions as to the nature of the 'determination in the last instance' of the social structure by the form of the production process; which amounts to a justification of what I announced when I referred to the Preface to *A Contribution*: that the new principle of periodization proposed by Marx contained a complete transformation of the historian's problematic.

(3) DETERMINATION IN THE LAST INSTANCE

By a double necessity, the capitalist mode of production is both the mode of production in which the economy is most easily recognized as the 'motor' of history, and the mode of production in which the essence of this 'economy' is unrecognized in principle (in what Marx calls 'fetishism'). That is why the first explanations of the problem of the 'determination in the last instance by the economy' that we find in Marx are directly linked to the problem of fetishism. They occur in the texts in *Capital* on the 'fetishism of commodities' (T.I, pp. 88–90; Vol. I, pp. 76–8), on the 'genesis of capitalist ground rent' (Vol. III, pp. 763–93) and on the 'trinity formula' (Vol. III, pp. 794–811), where Marx replaces the false conception of this 'economy' as a relation between things by its true definition as a system of social relations. At the same time, he presents the idea that the capitalist mode of production is the only one in which exploitation (the extortion of surplus-value), i.e., the specific form of the social relation that binds classes together in production, is 'mystified', 'fetishized' into the form of a relation between the things themselves. This thesis follows directly from his proof where the *commodity* is concerned: the social relation which constitutes its reality, knowledge of which enables us to assess its fetishism, is precisely the commodity relation as a relation of production, i.e., the commodity relation as generalized by the capitalist mode of production. A social ('human') relation cannot therefore be found behind 'things' in general, but only behind the thing of this capitalist relation.[8]

At this point there is a refutation of an objection raised against the general thesis of the Preface to *A Contribution*, which introduces the general idea of determination in the last instance. We shall only find this refutation intelligible if we constantly think the 'economy' as the structure of *relations* that I have defined:

> According to these objections: 'my view . . . that the mode of production of material life dominates the development of social, political and intellectual life generally . . . is very true for our own times, in which material interests preponderate, but not for the middle ages, in which Catholicism, nor for Athens and Rome, where politics, reigned supreme. In the first place it strikes one as an odd thing for anyone to suppose that those well-worn phrases about the middle ages and the ancient world are unknown to anyone else. This much, however, is clear, that the middle ages could not live on Catholicism, nor the ancient world on politics. *On the contrary, it is the economic conditions of the time that explain why here politics and there Catholicism played the chief part.* It requires but a slight acquaintance with the history of the Roman Republic, for example, to be aware that its secret history is the history of its landed property. On the other hand, Don Quixote long ago paid the penalty for wrongly imagining that knight errantry was compatible with all economic forms of society' (*Capital*, T.I, p. 93n; Vol. I, p. 81n).

---

[8] It is not my aim to give a theory of 'fetishism', i.e., of the ideological effects directly implied by the economic structure, nor even to examine in detail what Marx himself tells us about it, but merely to retain and use the *index* he provides by explicitly linking the problem of fetishism with that of the *place* of the economy in the structure of various social formations.

We can therefore first make a specification that can be added to those that the preceding papers have proposed with respect to fetishism: Marx's thesis does not mean that in modes of production other than capitalism the structure of the social relations is *transparent to the agents*. 'Fetishism' is not absent from them, but *displaced* (onto Catholicism, politics, etc.). In reality certain of Marx's formulations leave no doubt on this point. For example, at the beginning of the text on *Pre-Capitalist Economic Formations*, Marx writes about the so-called 'primitive' community:

> The earth is the great laboratory, the arsenal which provides both the means and the materials of labour, and also the seat, the basis of the community. Men relate to it *naïvely* as the property of the community, and of the community producing and reproducing itself in living labour. Only insofar as the individual is a limb or member of such a community, does he regard himself as an owner or possessor. Real appropriation by means of the process of labour takes place under these pre-conditions, which are not the product of labour but appear as its *natural or divine* pre-conditions (*Grundrisse*, p. 376; *PCEF*, p. 64).

In other words, the transparency which characterizes the relation between the direct producer and his product in non-commodity modes of production has as its counterpart this specific form of 'naïvety' in which the existence of a *community*, i.e., certain kinship relations and forms of political organization, can appear as 'natural or divine' and not as implied by the structure of a particular mode of production.

But this point, which Marx touches on only too briefly (for lack of historical material), is in principle quite clearly linked to the problem of determination in the last instance. Indeed, it emerges that the 'mystification' applies not to the economy (the mode of material production) as such, but precisely to that instance of the social structure which, according to the nature of the mode of production, is determined as occupying the place of determination, the place of the last instance.

We can now understand why *analogous* causes produce analogous effects here: in the event, it is possible to give this formulation a precise sense; that is to say, whenever the place of determination is occupied by a single instance, the relationship of the agents will reveal phenomena analogous to 'fetishism'. Perhaps it is not an exaggeration to say that this is the sense of the following passage from *Pre-Capitalist Economic Formations* on the 'Asiatic' mode of production:

> In most Asiatic fundamental forms . . . the all-embracing *unity* (*Einheit*) which stands above all these small communities may appear as the higher or sole proprietor, the real communities only as heredity possessors. Since the *unity* is the real owner, and the real pre-condition of common ownership, it is perfectly possible for it to appear as a particular being

above the numerous real, particular communities. The individual is then in fact propertyless, or property . . . appears to be mediated by means of a grant from the total unity – which is realized in the despot as the father of the many communities – to the individual through the mediation of the particular community. It therefore follows that the *surplus-product* (which, incidentally, is legally determined as a consequence of the real appropriation through labour) *belongs of itself* (von sich selbst) *to this higher unity* . . . (*Grundrisse*, pp. 376–7; *PCEF*, pp. 69–70).

This '*of itself*' must be taken in the strongest sense, noting that in other modes of production, e.g., the feudal mode of production, the surplus-product does not 'of itself' belong to the representatives of the ruling class. As we shall see, something further is explicitly required for the feudal mode of production: a political relationship, either in the 'pure' form of violence, or in the adapted and improved forms of law. In the 'Asiatic' mode of production and the capitalist mode of production, on the contrary, to modes of production as far apart chronologically, geographically, etc., as possible, and despite the fact that the agents who enter into the relationship are different in other respects (here capitalist and wage-labourer, there State and communities), the same *direct* determination by the functions of the process of production produces the same effects of fetishism: the product belongs 'of itself' to this higher 'unity' because it appears to be the *work* of that unity. This is what Marx writes a little further on in the same text:

> The communal conditions of real appropriation through labour, such as irrigation systems (very important among the Asian peoples), means of communication, etc., *will then appear as the work of the higher unity* – the despotic government which is poised above the lesser communities.

This reasoning recurs in the chapter in *Capital* on *co-operation*, where Marx systematically compares the Asiatic forms of despotism with capitalist forms of 'despotism', i.e., the joining of the function of control or direction, indispensable to the performance of the labour process (the real appropriation of the object of labour), with the function of ownership of the means of production.

> Because social labour power costs capital nothing, and because, on the other hand, the wage-labourer himself does not develop it before his labour belongs to capital, it appears as a power with which capital is endowed *by nature* – a productive force that is immanent in capital. The colossal effects of simple co-operation are to be seen in the gigantic structures of the ancient Asiatics, Egyptians, Etruscans, etc. . . . This power of Asiatic and Egyptian kings, Etruscan theocrats, etc., has in modern society been transferred to the capitalist, whether he be an isolated or a collective capitalist (*Capital*, T.II, p. 26; Vol. I, pp. 333–4).

It would therefore be possible and legitimate to look in Asiatic despotism for an analogy to the forms of appearance which mean that in the capitalist mode of production, 'all faculties of labour are projected as faculties of capital, just as all forms of value commodity are projected as forms of money' (*Capital*). We should then in fact be basing ourselves on the analogy of the relations between the two connexions with the 'combination' in these two modes of production, i.e., *on the analogy of the articulation of the double division of labour* (see above).

But above all, these texts imply that all the levels of the social structure have the structure of a 'mode' in the sense in which I have analysed the mode of production strictly speaking. In other words, they are themselves presented in the form of specific complex *combinations* (*Verbindungen*). They therefore imply specific *social relations*, which are no more patterns of the inter-subjectivity of the agents than are the social relations of production, but depend on functions of the process concerned: in this sense, I shall be rigorous in speaking of political social relations or *ideological social relations*. In the analysis of each of these modes of combination, I shall appeal to criteria of pertinence specific to each occasion.

The problem which I wish to approach is therefore the following: how is the determinant instance in the social structure in a given epoch itself determined, i.e., how does a specific mode of *combination* of the elements constituting the structure of the mode of production determine the place of determination in the last instance in the social structure, i.e., how does a specific mode of production determine the relations between the various instances of the structure, i.e., ultimately, the *articulation* of that structure? (What Althusser has called the *matrix* role of the mode of production.)

In order to answer this question, at least in principle, I shall consider, not an ideal, but a *reduced* case: that of a social structure reduced to the articulation of *two* different instances, an 'economic' instance and a 'political' instance, which will enable me to follow closely certain passages where Marx compares, *vis-à-vis ground rent*, the feudal mode of production with the capitalist mode of production.

On the simplest form of feudal ground rent, labour rent (*corvée*), Marx writes:

It is . . . evident that in all forms in which the direct labourer remains the 'possessor' of the means of production and labour conditions necessary for the production of his own means of subsistence, the property relationship must simultaneously appear *as a direct relation of lordship and servitude* (*als unmittelbares Herrschafts- und Knechtschaftsverhältnis*), so that the direct producer is not free; a lack of freedom (*Unfreiheit*) which may be reduced from serfdom with enforced labour to a mere tributary relationship. The direct producer, according to our assumption, is to be found here in possession of his own means of production, the necessary material labour conditions required for the realization of his labour and the production of his own means of subsistence. He conducts his agricultural activity and the rural home industries connected with it independently . . .

Under such conditions the surplus-labour for the nominal owner of the land can only be extorted from them *by other than economic pressure*, whatever the form assumed may be . . . Thus, personal conditions of personal dependence are requisite, a lack of personal freedom, no matter to what extent, and being tied to the soil as its accessory (*Zubehör*), bondage in the true sense of the word. . . .

The specific economic form, in which unpaid surplus-labour is pumped out of direct producers, determines the relationship of rulers and ruled, as it grows directly out of production itself and in turn, reacts upon it as a determining element. Upon this, however, is founded the entire formation of the economic community which grows up out of the production relations themselves, *thereby simultaneously its specific political form. It is always the direct relationship of the owners of the conditions of production to the direct producers . . . which reveals the innermost secret, the hidden basis of the entire social structure, and with it the political form of the re-lation of sovereignty and dependence (Souveränitäts- und Abhängigkeits-verhältnis)*, in short, the *corresponding specific form of the State* . . .

So much is evident with respect to labour rent, the simplest and most primitive form of rent: Rent is here the primeval form of surplus-labour and coincides with it. But this identity of surplus-value with unpaid labour of others need not be analysed here, because it still exists in its visible, palpable form, since *the labour of the direct producer for himself is still separated in space and time from his labour for the landlord*, and the latter appears directly in the brutal form of enforced labour for a third person (*Capital*, Vol. III, pp. 771–2).

This text contains four major points (I shall take them in a different order):
– a new formulation of the principle of periodization: 'what distinguishes one historical epoch from another'. Here it is the mode of dependence of the social structure with respect to the mode of production, i.e., the mode of articulation of the social structure, which Marx gives us as equivalent to the previous determinations, from the point of view of its concept;
– the specific difference in the relation between labour and surplus-labour implied by the difference between the social relations in the feudal mode of production and in the capitalist mode of production (property/possession of the means of production): in the latter case there is a coincidence 'in space and time', simultaneously of labour and surplus-labour, but not in the former;
– the non-coincidence of the two processes, the labour process and the surplus-labour process, requires 'other than economic pressure' if surplus-labour is actually to be carried out;

– these other than economic pressures take the form of the feudal master/ slave relationship.

It seems to me that several conclusions follow.

Firstly, Marx tells us that surplus-value exists in its *visible, palpable* form (*in sichtbarer, handgreiflicher Form existiert*) in this mode of production, although surplus-value can only be recognized in its essence in the capitalist mode of production where it is hidden and therefore needs to be 'analysed'. Surplus-value is *par excellence* a category of the capitalist mode of production which takes its meaning from the analysis of the 'process of producing *value*' (*Verwertungsprozess*), i.e., of a production process whose aim is an increase in exchange value (the latter, by the same token, being generalized as a form of value).

The justification for this statement is the fact that *surplus-value is not a 'form'* in the same way that profit, rent and interest are; surplus-value is *no more nor less than surplus-labour*. The specific mode of exploitation of this surplus-labour in capitalist production, i.e., ultimately the mode of constitution of *revenues* (the mode of distribution), and therefore of the *classes*, is the constitution of profit, interest and capitalist rent, i.e., of what Marx calls the 'transformed forms' of surplus-value. In the capitalist mode of production, the forms of class struggle are first inscribed in the forms of the production process in general, they appear as a confrontation of forces within certain *limits* which are directly determined in the production process and analysable in it (limits of the working day, of wages, of profit and its subdivisions).

In other words, if we inquire about the structure of the class relations in a given society of which we have already said that it was distinguished by a certain mode of extraction of surplus-value, we are inquiring first of all about the 'transformed forms' peculiar to that society.[9]

But it is no accident that the point which this passage singles out as the characteristic difference between the feudal mode of production and the capitalist mode of production – the coincidence and non-coincidence of necessary labour and surplus-labour – is also the essential point of the whole of Marx's analysis in *Capital* of the capitalist mode of production alone: this coincidence is another way of expressing the term by term coincidence of *the labour process and the process of producing value*. The distinction between constant capital and variable capital which defines the process of producing value will always be found to correspond to the distinction between labour power and means of production peculiar to the labour process. Many examples from *Capital* could be adduced to show how the analysis demands reference to this correspondence (notably in the whole analysis of turnover). The worker's

[9] First of all, since it is always necessary at the theoretical level to *begin* with what is determinant 'in the last instance'. The reason is clear: the very *names* of the problems depend on it.

labour materially transforms raw materials into a product by setting to work the means of production; the same labour transfers to the product the value of the means of production and materials consumed, and produces a new value, part – but only part – of which is equal to the value of the labour-power. In the last analysis, therefore, the dual character of the production process, which expresses this coincidence, refers to the dual character of 'living' labour.

It is easy to see that in the case Marx is describing here, the case of a form of feudal production, the coincidence exists in neither of the two forms: not only are labour and surplus-labour distinct 'in time and space', but even given a retrospective projection of the category of value, neither of the terms can strictly speaking be called a process of producing value.

In other words:

– in the capitalist mode of production, the two processes coincide 'in time and space', *which is an intrinsic feature of the mode of production* (of the economic instance); this coincidence is itself the effect of the form of *combination* of the factors of the production process peculiar to the capitalist mode of production, i.e., of the form of the two relations of property and real appropriation. The corresponding 'transformed forms' in this social structure, i.e., the forms of the relations between classes, are then *directly economic forms* (profit, rent, wages, interest), which implies notably that *the State does not intervene in them* at this level.

– in the feudal mode of production there is a *disjunction* between the two processes 'in time and space', which is always an intrinsic feature of the mode of production (of the economic instance) and an effect of the form of combination peculiar to it (the property relation appears in it in the dual form of 'possession' and 'property'). Surplus-labour cannot then be extorted without 'other than economic pressure', i.e., without '*Herrschafts- und Knechtschafstverhältnis*'. Even before we have analysed the 'transformed forms' for themselves, we can conclude that in the feudal mode of production they will not be the transformed forms of the economic base alone, but of the '*Herrschafts- und Knechtschaftsverhältnis*'. *Not directly economic, but directly and indissolubly political and economic*;[10] which means, finally, that different modes of production do not combine *homogeneous* elements, and do not allow differential divisions and definitions like the 'economic', the 'legal' and the 'political'. Historians and ethnologists today often attest the discovery of this effect, though usually in a theoretically blind fashion.

We may also be able to understand why this politics was not conscious as such, why it did not think its relative autonomy, even in the moment when

---

[10] Pierre Vilar writes of the feudal mode of production: 'In general, growth seems to depend on a re-occupation of waste lands, on an investment in labour rather than in capital, *and the owning classes' levy on production is legal and not economic*' (*Premiere Conférence Internationale d'Histoire Économique*, Stockholm 1960, p. 36). To this point we should add the oft-repeated comment that it is difficult to find specifically *economic* crises outside capitalism.

it occupied the determinant place, either in the form of 'pure' violence, or in the forms of a law, because it emerged as one of the presuppositions of the mode of production itself. Indeed, as we know, this relative autonomy of politics was not recognized in thought until much later: it is peculiarly a 'bourgeois' thought.

I think that it is possible to draw from this, one of Marx's most detailed texts, the principle explicitly present in Marx of a definition 'of the determination in the last instance of the economy. In different structures, *the economy is determinant in that it determines which of the instances of the social structure occupies the determinant place*. Not a simple relation, but rather a relation between relations; not a transitive causality, but rather a structural causality. In the capitalist mode of production it happens that this place is occupied by the economy itself; but in each mode of production, the 'transformation' must be analysed. Here I merely suggest that we could try to re-read the first pages of *The Origins of the Family* in this perspective, the pages in which Engels expresses the following notion which he presents as a mere 'correction' of Marx's general formulations:

> According to the materialist conception, the determining factor in history is, in the last resort, the production and reproduction of material life. *But this itself is of a two-fold character*. On the one hand, the production of the means of subsistence, of food, clothing and shelter and the tools requisite therefore; *on the other, the production of human beings themselves, the propagation of the species*. The social institutions under which men of a definite historical epoch and of a definite country live are conditioned by both kinds of production: by the stage of development *of labour, on the one hand, and of the family, on the other*. The less the development of labour . . . the more preponderatingly does the social order appear to be dominated by ties of sex (Marx-Engels: *Selected Works*, pp. 455–6).

A surprising text, which not only plays impudently on the term *production*, but demands the application of the technological model of the advance of the productive forces to the forms of kinship, presented as social relations of procreation! Perhaps it would be more worthwhile, as a number of Marxist anthropologists have been attempting, to show how, in certain 'primitive' or 'self-subsistent' societies, the mode of production determines a certain articulation of the social structure in which the kinship relations determine even the forms of transformation of the economic base.[11]

---

[11] On this point, see particularly the works of Claude Meillassoux: 'Essai d'interprétation des phénomènes économiques dans les sociétés d'auto-subsistence', *Cahiers d'Études Africaines*, 1960, No. 4; *Anthropologie Économique des Gouro de Cote d'Ivoire*, Mouton, The Hague, 1964.

Chapter 2

The Elements of the Structure
and their History

The definition of every mode of production as a *combination* of (always the same) elements which are only notional elements unless they are put into relation with each other according to a determinate mode, and the possibility this affords of periodizing the modes of production according to a principle of the *variation* of these combinations, are two propositions which of themselves alone deserve our attention. In fact, they convey the radically *anti-evolutionist* character of the Marxist theory of the history of production (and therefore of society). Nothing conforms less to the dominant ideology of the nineteenth century, the century of history and evolution to which Marx belonged, if we are to believe chronology. As we shall see better later, this is because Marx's concepts are not intended to reflect, reproduce and *mimic* history, but to produce the knowledge of it: they are the concepts of the structures on which the historical effects depend.

In consequence, here there is neither a progressive *movement of differentiation* of the forms, nor even a *line of progress* with a logic akin to a destiny. Marx does tell us that all the modes of production are *historical moments*, but *he does not tell us that these moments descend one from the other*: on the contrary, the way his basic concepts are defined excludes such a facile solution. As Marx says in the *1857 Introduction* that we have already quoted, '*certain* determinations are common to the most modern and to the most ancient epochs' (e.g., co-operation and certain forms of direction, of *accountability*, which are common to 'Asiatic' modes of production and to the capitalist mode of production more than to all the others). This breaks the identity between *chronology* and a law of the internal development of forms which is at the root of evolutionism as of all historicisms of 'supersession'. Marx's aim was to show that the distinction between different modes is necessarily and *sufficiently* based on a variation of the connexions between a small number of elements which are always the same. The announcement of these connexions and of their terms constitutes the exposition of the primary theoretical concepts of historical materialism, of the few general concepts which form the rightful beginning of his exposition and which characterize the scientific method of *Capital*, conferring on its theory its axiomatic form; i.e., the announcement of a determinate form of this variation, one which directly depends on the concepts of labour-power, means of production, property, etc., is a constantly necessary presupposition of the 'economic' proofs in *Capital*.

But is this some kind of 'structuralism'? The suggestion is a tempting one, despite the risk of a confusion with thoroughly unscientific contemporary ideologies, in that it would redress the balance, for readings have traditionally leaned towards evolutionism and historicism. The 'combination' that Marx analyses is, to be sure, a system of 'synchronic' connexions obtained by variation. However, this science of combinations is not a *combinatory*, in which only the places of the factors and their relationships change, but not their nature, which is not only *subordinate* to the system in general, but also *indifferent*: it is therefore possible to abstract from it and proceed *directly* to the formalization of the systems. This suggests the possibility of an *a priori* science of the modes of production, a science of *possible* modes of production, whose realization or non-realization in real-concrete history would depend on the result of a throw of the dice or on the action of an optimum principle. Historical materialism does authorize the prediction or even the reconstruction of 'notional' modes of production (as one might describe the 'mode of simple commodity production') which, never having been dominant in history, have never existed in an undeformed state. However, it does so in a different way, as will be explained later, on the basis of modifications in an existing mode of production. Otherwise, this would presuppose that the 'factors' of the combination were the very concepts I have listed, that these concepts *directly* designated the elements of a construction, the atoms of a history. In reality, as I have already said in a very general way, these concepts designate the elements of the construction only mediately: what I have called the 'differential analysis of forms' is an essential intermediate step in the determination of the historical forms taken by labour-power, property, 'real appropriation', etc. These concepts designate only what might be called the *pertinences* of historical analysis. It is this feature of the 'combinatory', which is therefore a pseudo-combinatory, that explains why there are general concepts of the science of history although there can never be a history in general.

In order to show how this pertinence works, I shall now return in a little more detail to a few of the problems of definition involving the two 'connexions' which I have distinguished, taking the two articulations of the 'combination' separately in order to bring out their peculiar effects on the definition of the *elements* ('factors'). These specifications are indispensable if we are to see that Marx was right to speak of a *structure* of the process of production, and if the combination of the factors is to be no mere descriptive juxtaposition, but an effective explanation of a functional unity.

(1) WHAT IS 'PROPERTY'?

The first connexion that we inscribed in the 'combination' of a mode of production was designated as the 'property' connexion, or connexion of surplus-value appropriation; in fact, Marx constantly defines the 'relations of production' characteristic of a historical mode of production (and notably of capitalism) by its *kind of ownership* of the means of production, and therefore by the mode of appropriation of the social product which depends on it. The principle of this definition is well known. But a number of specifications are necessary, in order to bring out its exact structural function.

In the previous chapter, I concentrated above all on showing the difference between two concepts of *appropriation*, each of which refers to one aspect of the *dual* production process contained in every mode of production, and therefore defines one of the two connexions which constitute the combination of the 'factors' of production. But it is no less important to take up Marx's many hints and distinguish between the *relations of production* themselves, which are all that concern us here, and their 'legal expression', which does not belong to the structure of production considered in its relative autonomy. In this case, it is a question of distinguishing sharply between the connexion that we have called 'property' and the *law of property*. This analysis is of fundamental importance in characterizing the degree of relative autonomy of the economic structure with respect to the equally 'regional' structure of the 'legal and political forms', i.e., in initiating an analysis of the articulation of regional structures or instances within the social formation.

This is also a decisive point for the history of theoretical concepts: Althusser has already recalled that the Marxist concept of 'social relations' marks a break with the whole of classical philosophy and with Hegel in particular, insofar as these relations do not represent forms of *inter-subjectivity* but relations which assign a necessary function to *things* as well as to men. Let us add that the Hegelian concept of 'civil society', adopted from the classical economists and designated by Marx as the main site of his discoveries, i.e., of his theoretical transformations, includes *both* the *economic system* of the division of labour and exchange, *and the sphere of private law*. There is therefore an immediate identity of appropriation in the 'economic' sense and legal property, and, in consequence, if the second can be designated as an 'expression' of the first, it is a necessarily *adequate* expression, or a duplication.

It is particularly interesting to note that certain of the clearest texts Marx devoted to the distinction between the social relations of production and their legal expression, concern precisely the possibility of a dislocation between base and superstructure, which, without this distinction, would obviously be incomprehensible. For example, in his analysis of the 'Genesis of Capitalist Ground Rent', he writes:

> Since the direct producer [in the feudal mode of production] is not the owner, but only a possessor, and since all his surplus-labour *de jure* actually belong to the landlord, some historians have expressed astonishment that it should be at all possible for those subject to forced labour,

or serfs, to acquire any independent property, or relatively speaking, wealth, under such circumstances. However, it is evident that *tradition* must play a dominant role in the primitive and undeveloped circumstances on which these social production relations and the corresponding mode of production are based. It is furthermore clear that here as always it is in the interest of the ruling section of society *to sanction the existing order as law* and legally to establish its limits given through usage and tradition. Apart from all else, this, by the way, comes about of itself as soon as the constant reproduction of the basis of the existing order and its fundamental relations assumes a regulated and orderly form in the course of time. And such regulation and order are themselves indispensable elements of any mode of production, if it is to assume social stability and indifference from mere chance and arbitrariness. These are precisely the form of its social stability and therefore its relative freedom from mere arbitrariness and mere chance. . . . It achieves this form by mere repetition of *its own reproduction* (*Capital*, Vol. III, pp. 773–4, modified).

Such a gap or discordance between *the law* and a 'tradition' which might seem a sub-law or a debased law, is therefore in reality the expression of a gap or discordance between the law and an economic relation (the individual producer's necessary disposition of his plot of land), characteristic of periods of the formation of a mode of production, i.e., of the transition from one mode of production to another. A remarkable instance of the same effect is also featured in the analysis of the *factory legislation* that dates from the first period of the history of industrial capitalism and codifies the conditions of the 'normal' exploitation of wage labour-power (see *Capital*, T.II, pp. 159ff.; Vol. I, pp. 480ff.).

Since such gaps are possible, or more precisely, since contradictions are induced within the law itself by its *non-correspondence* with the relations of production, law must be distinct and *second* in order of analysis to the relations of production. And this is confirmed if we compare the passages where Marx reveals the specificity of 'bourgeois' property, e.g.:

> In each historical epoch, property has developed differently and under a set of entirely different social relations, thus to define bourgeois property is nothing else than to give an exposition of all the social relations of bourgeois production. To try to give a definition of property as of an independent relation, a category apart, an abstract and eternal idea, can be nothing but an illusion of metaphysics or jurisprudence (*Poverty of Philosophy*, op. cit., p. 154).

with those that recall the chronological *precedence*, the precession of the ('Roman') legal forms of the right of property with respect to the capitalist mode of production, which alone generalizes the private ownership of the means of production. On this point I could refer to the text of *Pre-Capitalist*

Economic Formations that has already been quoted (and is a very legal text, both in its object and in its terminology), or else to a letter from Engels to Kautsky:

> Roman law was the consummate law of simple, i.e., pre-capitalist commodity production, *which however included most of the legal relations of the capitalist period*. Hence precisely what our city burghers needed at the time of their rise and did not find in the local law of custom (26 June 1884).

This comparison retrospectively illuminates the text on 'The Genesis of Capitalist Ground Rent' that I quoted above. It shows that the problem of the gap between a 'tradition' and a 'law' must not be interpreted as a theory of the genesis of the law out of the economic relations: for although the transition from a custom to a law does occur in history, this transition is not a continuity, but on the contrary, a rupture, a change in the law, or better: a change *in the nature of law* which is achieved by re-activating an older law ('Roman' law) which has already been superseded once. Nor is the *repetition* that seems to play an essential part in the articulation of the law with the economic relations here an element of this genesis, which, would explain the formation of a codified superstructure by virtue of its duration: its function is necessarily quite different, and refers us to the theoretical analysis of the functions of *reproduction* found in every mode of production, which we will discuss later. What we can see from the reproduction of economic relations is the necessary function of the law with respect to the system of economic relations itself, and the structural conditions to which it is therefore subordinate; but not the generation of the *instance* of the law itself in the social formation.

It is difficult, firstly, to distinguish clearly between the relations of production and their 'legal expression'; this very concept of expression is difficult, too, once it no longer means duplication but rather the articulation of two heterogeneous instances; finally, so is the possible dislocation between the economic relations and the legal forms. All these preliminary difficulties are not accidental, they explain the method of investigation which must necessarily be followed here (and to which Marx himself shows the way, notably in his texts on pre-capitalist modes of production, which are closer to investigations than to systematic expositions). This method consists of looking for the relations of production *behind* the legal forms, or better: behind the secondary unity of production and law, which has to be disentangled. Only by this method will it eventually be possible to trace the theoretical boundary while still taking into account the ambivalent function that Marx assigns to legal forms: they are necessary and yet 'irrational', *expressing and codifying* the 'economic' reality which each mode of production defines in its own way, and yet simultaneously *masking* it. This represents a commitment to a regressive course – another attempt to determine *gaps* or differences which will be expressed negatively on the basis of the forms of the law, but this time within a completely self-contemporaneous system (a highly determinate mode of production: here the capitalist mode of production). Hence a difficult *terminological* problem as well, since the concepts in which the relations of production are expressed are precisely concepts in which the economic and the legal are indistinct, starting with the concept of *property*. What is 'property' insofar as it forms a system within the relatively autonomous structure of production, and logically precedes the law of property peculiar to the society considered? Such is the problem which must be initiated for capitalism *too*.

This commitment to an analysis of the relations between the economic structure of the capitalist mode of production and the law that corresponds to it demands a complete study of its own: that is why I must be satisfied here by giving a few hints which will serve as reference points. The steps in a proof can be outlined as follows:

(1) the whole of the economic structure of the capitalist mode of production from the immediate process of production to circulation and the distribution of the social product, presupposes the existence of a *legal system*; the basic elements of which are the *law of property* and the *law of contract*. Each of the elements of the economic structure receives a legal qualification in the context of this system, notably the various elements of the immediate production process: the owner of the means of production, the means of production ('capital'), the 'free' labourer, and the process itself, characterized legally as a contract.

(2) the peculiarity of the legal system we are discussing here (but not, of course, of every historical legal system) is its *abstract universalistic* character: by which I mean that this system simply distributes the concrete beings which can support its functions into two categories within each of which there is no pertinent distinction from the legal point of view: the category of *human persons* and the category of *things*. The property relation is established exclusively between human persons and things (or between what are *reputed* to be persons and what are *reputed* to be things); the contract relation is established exclusively between persons. Just as, in law, there is no diversity between persons, who are all or can all be owners and contractors, so there is no diversity between things, which are all or can all be property, whether they are means of labour or means of consumption, and whatever the use to which this property is put.

(3) this universality of the legal system *reflects*, in the strict sense, another universality which is part of the economic structure: *the universality of commodity exchange*, which as we know is only realized on the basis of the capitalist mode of production (although the *existence* of commodity exchange and the forms that it implies are much older); only on the basis of the capitalist mode of production is the set of elements of the economic structure distributed entirely as commodities (including labour-power) and exchangers (including the direct producer). These two categories thus correspond adequately to those which define the legal system (persons and things).

Thus the general problem of the relationship between the capitalist mode of production and the legal system which its functioning presupposes depends historically and theoretically on another problem: that of the relationship between the *economic* structure of the immediate process of production and the *economic* structure of the circulation of commodities. This necessary presence of 'commodity categories' in the analysis of the process of production explains the necessary presence of the corresponding legal categories.

(4) *the social relations of production* which are part of the structure of the capitalist mode of production can be characterized on the basis of their legal expression, by comparison, uncovering a series of *dislocations* between them.

Firstly, whereas the 'law of property' is characterized as universalistic, introducing no differences between the things possessed and their uses, the only property which is significant from the point of view of the structure of the production process is the ownership of the *means of production*, to the extent that, as Marx constantly reiterates, the latter function as means of production, i.e., are consumed productively, combined with 'living' labour and not hoarded or consumed unproductively. Whereas legal property is a right of consumption *of any kind* (in general: the right 'to use and abuse', i.e., to consume individually, to consume productively, to alienate – exchange – or to 'squander' – *Capital*, Vol. III, p. 804), the economic ownership of the means of production is not so much a legal 'right' to them as the power to consume them productively, depending on their material nature, on their adaptation to the conditions of the labour process, as a means of appropriating surplus-labour. This power does not come down to a law, but, as Althusser has already suggested, to a distribution of the means of production (notably a suitable *concentration* in quantity and quality). The economic relation is not based on the indifference of 'things' (and, correlatively, of *commodities*), but on an appreciation of their differences, which can be analysed according to two lines of opposition:

elements of individual consumption
elements of productive consumption

and:

labour-power/means of production

(the reader will realize that this system of differences recurs in the analysis of the departments of aggregate social reproduction). Thus the gap between the social relations of production and the law of property can be characterized as a movement of *extension* or protraction, as an abolition of the divisions required by the structure of production: from 'ownership of the means of production' to property 'in general'.

Secondly, the relationship established between the owner of the means of production (the capitalist) and the wage-labourer is, legally, a special form of contract: a *labour* contract. This is established on condition that labour is legally reputed to be an exchange, i.e., that labour-power is legally reputed to be a 'commodity', or a *thing*. Note that in its concept this transformation of labour-power into a commodity and the establishment of the labour contract are completely independent of the *nature of the labour* in which the labour is consumed. That is why the legal form of the *wage-earner* is, just as before, a universal form which applies both to *productive labour*, the work of transformation that produces surplus-value, and to all the other forms of labour that can generally be designated by the term 'services'. But only 'productive' labour determines a *relation of production*, and productive labour cannot generally be defined by the relationship between the employer and the wage-earner, a relationship between 'persons': it presupposes that the economic *sphere* in which it takes place is taken into account (the sphere of immediate production, the source of surplus-value), i.e., the material nature of the labour and its objects, i.e., the nature of the means of labour with which it is combined. A few moments ago the ownership of the means of production, in the form of a legal relation between a person and a thing, appeared to us as a power over 'living' labour through the disposition of the means of production (which alone confer this power); in the same way, wage labour, insofar as it is a relationship *inside the structure of production*, in the legal form of a wage-service contract, appears to us now as a power over the means of production through the disposition of productive labour (which alone confers this power, i.e., determines an adequate consumption, not just any consumption). Thus the gap between wage labour as a social relation of production and the law of labour can be characterized as a movement of *extension* or protraction formally similar to the preceding one.

Hence two conclusions of the first importance:

– whereas from the legal point of view (from the point of view of the law implied by the *capitalist* mode of production, of course) the property relation, a relation between a 'person' and a 'thing', and the contract relation, a relation between a 'person' and a 'person', are two *distinct* forms (even if they are based on a single system of categories), the same is no longer the case from the point of view of the economic structure: the ownership of the means of production and productive wage labour define *a single connexion, a single relation of production*. This follows directly from the two analyses outlined above.

– because this social relation is not legal in nature, although, for reasons that lie in the very nature of the capitalist mode of production, we are obliged (and Marx first of all) to describe it in the peculiar terminology of legal categories, it cannot be supported by the same concrete beings. The legal relations are universalistic and abstract: they are established between 'persons' and 'things' in general; it is the systematic structure of law which defines its supports as individuals (persons) confronted by things. Similarly, it is through their functions in the production process that the means of production are the supports of a connexion in the economic structure, and this connexion (as opposed to property and contract) cannot be defined for individuals, but only for *social classes* or representatives of social classes. The definition of the capitalist class or of the proletarian class therefore does not precede that of the social relations of production, but *vice versa*, the definition of the social relations of production implies a 'support' function defined as a class.

But a class cannot be the *subject* of property in the sense in which – legally – the individual is the subject of *his* property, nor a *partner*, nor 'third party', of a contract. We are not dealing here with the inherence of the object in its subject, or with the mutual recognition of subjects, but with the mechanism of the constant distribution of the means of production, hence with the entire capital and in consequence the entire social product (as Marx shows in the penultimate chapter of Volume Three of *Capital*: 'relations of production are relations of distribution'). Classes are not the subjects of this mechanism but its supports, and the concrete characteristics of these classes (their types of revenue, their internal *stratification*, their relations to the different levels of the social structure) are the *effects* of this mechanism. The economic relation of production appears therefore as a relation between three functionally defined terms: owner class/means of production/class of exploited producers. Confirmation of this may be found especially in Part 7 of Volume One ('The Accumulation of Capital'), where Marx shows how the mechanism of capitalist production, by productively consuming the means of production and the workers' labour power, produces the labourers' existence as an appendage of capital and makes the capitalist the instrument of accumulation, capital's functionary. There is nothing individual about this connexion, it is in consequence not a contract, but 'invisible threads' which bind the worker to the capitalist class, the capitalist to the working class (*Capital*, T.III, pp. 16, 20; Vol. I, pp. 573-4, 577-8). We therefore find that the social relation which determines the distribution of the means of production is instituted as a necessary relation between each individual of one class and the whole of the opposing class.

(2) PRODUCTIVE FORCES (HANDICRAFTS AND MECHANIZATION)

Among the general concepts to whose systematic articulation by Marx I referred in my analysis of the *Preface* to *A Contribution*, none, perhaps, presents such difficulties, despite all its apparent simplicity, as that of the *productive forces*, or, more exactly, of the *level* of the productive forces (or their degree of development). Indeed, the announcement of the concept alone immediately suggests two consequences which have been the source of fundamental misconstructions of Marx's theory, but of which it must be said that they are not easy to avoid: first, to speak of 'productive forces', 'forces' of production, immediately suggests the possibility of a *list* – 'the productive forces are the population, the machines, science, etc.'; at the same time, it suggests that the 'advance' of the productive forces may take the form of a cumulative progress, an addition of new productive forces or a replacement of *certain* of them by other, more 'powerful' ones (the craftsman's tool by the machine). This leads to an interpretation of the 'level' or 'degree of development' which is all the more tempting in that it seems to be implied by the words themselves: a linear and cumulative *development*, a quasi-biological continuity. But if that were so, how could we explain the historical discontinuities expressly contained in the general theory, except by a theory of 'qualitative change', of the transformation 'of quantity into quality', i.e., a descriptive theory of the *pattern* of a movement which does not suppress its general structure? How could we avoid a mechanistic theory of historical movement in which the 'dialectic' is merely another name for a periodic, and periodically compensated and adjusted, *dislocation* or *lateness* of the other instances with respect to this development against which they are measured?

However, such a distribution quickly runs into remarkable difficulties: and all of them are related to the heteronomy of the 'elements' that must be added together to make Marx's concept coincide directly with a description of the 'facts'. Marx's bourgeois critics have not failed to note that the 'productive forces' ultimately include not only technical instruments, but also the application of scientific knowledge to the perfection and replacement of those instruments, and ultimately science itself; not only a population of working strengths, but also the technical and cultural customs of this population, which history (for earlier modes of production) and industrial social psychology show to be more and more historically and sociologically 'dense' and complex; not only techniques, but also a certain organization of labour, or even a social and political organization ('planning' is an obvious example), etc. These are not arbitrary difficulties: they reflect the fact that Marx's concept cannot be made to coincide with the categories of a sociology which, for its part, does proceed by the distribution and adding together of levels – the technological, the economic, the legal, the social, the psychological, the political, etc. – and which bases its peculiar historical classifications on these distributions (traditional societies and industrial societies, liberal societies and centralized-totalitarian societies, etc.). Moreover, these difficulties provide us with an index to an essential *formal* difference between Marx's concept and categories of this kind: the fact that the concept of the productive forces has nothing to do with a distribution of this type. We must therefore start looking for its real features.

First let us stop and examine Marx's formulation itself: 'level' and 'degree', are certainly expressions which suggest the possibility of at least a notional measurement, and the measurement of a growth. These expressions are thought to characterize the essence of the productive forces, and in consequence to define them in the specificity of a historical mode of production. But it is a common-place to note that the *productivity* of any labour, i.e., the 'measure' of this development, increased more in a few decades of industrial capitalism than in centuries of previous modes of production, whereas the 'relations' of production and the legal and political forms maintained a comparable rate of change; the same is true of the transformation of the means of labour (the equipment) which Marx calls the '*Gradmesser der Entwicklung der menschlichen Arbeitskraft*'. Besides, Marx says much more correctly, and whenever this level plays a direct part in economic analysis: *the* productive power *of labour*, the productivity of *the* power of labour (*Produktivkraft*).

In other words, as we shall see, the 'productive forces' are not really *things*. If they were things, the problem of their transport, their importation, would, paradoxically enough, be easier to resolve for bourgeois sociology (with the exception of a few 'psychological' problems of cultural adaptation) than it is for Marx – since his theory claims that there is a necessary connexion or correlation between certain productive forces and a certain type of society (defined by its social relations). Bypassing the verbal illusion created by the term, we can already say that the most interesting aspect of the 'productive forces' is no longer their distribution or composition, but the *rhythm* and *pattern* of their development, for this rhythm is directly linked to the nature of the relations of production, and the structure of the mode of production. What Marx proved, notably in *Capital*, and what is alluded to in some well-known sentences in the *Manifesto*, is not the fact that capitalism has *liberated* the development of the productive forces once and for all, but the fact that capitalism has imposed on the productive forces a determinate *type of development* whose rhythm and pattern are *peculiar to it*, dictated by the form of the process of capitalist accumulation. It is this pattern which best characterizes, descriptively, a mode of production, rather than the level attained at any moment. ('The law of increased productivity of labour is not, therefore, *absolutely* valid for capital. So far as capital is concerned, productivity does not increase through a saving in living labour, but only through a saving in the *paid* portion of living labour, as compared to labour expended in the past' – *Capital*, Vol. III, p. 257).

But from the theoretical point of view, the 'productive forces', too, are a connexion of a certain type within the mode of production, in other words, they, too, are a *relation of production*: precisely the one I have tried to suggest by introducing into the constitutive connexions inside the mode of production, as well as a 'property' connexion, a connexion, B, of 'real appropriation', between the same elements: means of production, direct producers, even 'non-labourers', i.e., in the context of the capitalist mode of production, the *non-wage-earners*. I should now like to show that this really is a *connexion*, or more rigorously a relation of production, by tracing the analysis to be found in the chapters of *Capital* devoted to the methods of formation of relative surplus-value; at the same time, we shall see better what the differential analysis of forms is.

Marx's analysis takes up three chapters of *Capital* (Volume One, Chapters XIII, XIV and XV in the English translation) which are devoted to the forms of co-operation in manufacture and modern industry, and the transition from the one to the other which constitutes the 'industrial revolution'. But this development is incomprehensible unless we refer it on the one hand to the definition of the *labour process* (Volume One, Chapter VII) and on the other to Chapter XVI of Volume One ('Absolute and Relative Surplus-Value') which is its conclusion.

The transition from manufacture to modern industry inaugurates what Marx calls the 'specific mode of production' of capitalism, or again the 'real subsumption' of labour beneath capital. In other words, modern industry constitutes the form of our connexion which belongs organically to the capitalist mode of production.

> At first, capital subordinates labour on the basis of the technical conditions given by historical development. It does not change immediately the mode of production. The production of surplus-value in the form considered by us – by means of a simple extension of the working day, proved, therefore, to be independent of any change in the mode of production itself (*Capital*, T.I, p. 303; Vol. I, p. 310).
>
> The production of relative surplus-value revolutionizes out and out the technical processes of labour, and the forms of social grouping (*die gesellschaftlichen Gruppierungen*). It therefore presupposes *a specific mode, the capitalist mode of production*, a mode which, along with its methods, means and conditions, arises and develops itself spontaneously on the basis provided by the formal subsumption of labour under capital. In the case of this development, the formal subsumption is replaced by *the real subsumption of labour under capital* (*Capital*, Vol. I, p. 510, retranslated from Marx-Engels: *Werke*, Bd. XXIII, pp. 532–3).

The following considerations may be regarded merely as a commentary on these texts.

Firstly, the difference between formal subsumption and 'real' subsumption indicates the existence of a chronological *dislocation* in the formation of the different elements of the structure: capital as a 'social relation', i.e., the capitalist ownership of the means of production, exists before and independently of the 'real' subsumption, i.e., the specific form of our connexion (real appropriation) which corresponds to the capitalist mode of production. The explanation for this dislocation and for the possibility of such dislocations in general is found in a theory of the *forms of transition* from one mode of production to another, which I shall leave aside for the moment. Let me merely underline the following: the simple, purely chronological dislocation is indifferent to the theory that we are studying; the 'synchrony' in which *the concept* of a mode of production is given simply suppresses this aspect of temporality and hence excludes from the theory of history every mechanical form of thought where time is concerned (any theory which asserts that anything featured at the same level in a chart of chronological concordances belong to the same time). Not only is there a dislocation between the emergence of the capitalist ownership of the means of production and the 'industrial revolution', but the industrial revolution is *itself dislocated* from one branch of production to another. The second dislocation is also *suppressed* by the theory. Finally, within a single branch, it *proceeds* by successive replacements of manual labour by 'mechanized' labour, in a rhythm subject to structural and conjunctural economic necessities; so much so that the 'transition' which is our object here appears as a *tendency* in the strict sense Marx gave that term, i.e., as a structural property of the capitalist mode of production: the essence of the 'productive forces' in the capitalist mode of production is to be constantly *in the process of transition* from manual labour to mechanized labour.

Let us recall in what this transition from manufacture to modern industry consists.

Both are forms of co-operation between the labourers (the direct producers), and this co-operation is only possible through their subjection to capital, which employs them all simultaneously. Both therefore constitute what can be called organisms of production, instituting a 'collective labourer': the labour process which is defined by the delivery of a *finished use product* (whether this use be an individual consumption or a productive consumption) requires the intervention of several labourers in a specific form of organization. Manufacture and modern industry are thus equally opposed to the individual handicraft. *However, that is not the real break.*

All co-operation may take simple or complex forms: in simple co-operation, there is a juxtaposition of labourers and operations. 'Numerous labourers work together side by side, whether in one and the same process, or in different but connected processes.' This form of co-operation is still found, particularly in agriculture. In the workshop of the guild master, the labour of the journeymen is usually performed in simple co-operation. The same is true of the primitive forms of manufacture, which consist simply in gathering the artisans into a single place of work. Complex co-operation, on the contrary, consists of an *imbrication*, of an intertwining of the labour. The operations performed by each worker successively or simultaneously are complementary, and only together do they give birth to a finished product. This form of co-operation (which is found in quite distant times in some sectors, e.g., metallurgy) constitutes the essence of the *division of labour in manufacture: one* piece of work is divided among the workers (until the eighteenth century this was called a single *'oeuvre'* or *'ouvrage'* in France).

Obviously, this division may have different origins. It may derive from a real 'division', after the complex operations of a single handicraft have been shared out among different labourers who thus become specialists in one fraction of the labour: or it may derive from the junction of several different handicrafts, subordinated to the production of a single useful product to which they all contribute, thus transforming these handicrafts *post festum* into fractions of a single labour. Marx analyses examples of both (the manufacture of pins, the manufacture of carriages); they depend on the physical properties of the product, but in any case, this process of formation disappears in the result which is a division of labour of the same form. The basic principle, the importance of which we shall soon discover, is *the fact that the fractional operations can be performed as manual labour.*[12] All the advantages of the manufacturing division of labour are derived from the rationalization of each component operation which is made possible by its isolation and by the specialization of the labourer: the improvement of movements and tools, increased speed, etc. It is therefore essential that this specialization is in fact possible, that each simplest possible operation is individualized. Instead of a break, we therefore find a continuity between handicraft and manufacture: the manufacturing division of labour arises as the extension of the analytical movement of specialization peculiar to handicrafts, a movement which simultaneously affects both the perfection of technical operations and the psycho-physical characteristics of the workers' labour-power. These are merely two aspects, two faces of one and the same development.

Indeed, manufacture is merely the extreme radicalization of the distinctive feature of handicrafts: *the unity of labour-power and means of labour.* On the one hand, the means of labour (the tool) must be adapted to the human organism; on the other, a tool is no longer a technical instrument in the hands of someone who does not know how to use it: its effective use demands of the worker a set of physical and intellectual qualities, a sum of cultural habits (an empirical knowledge of the materials, of the tricks of the trade, up to and including the craft secret, etc.). That is why handicrafts are indissolubly linked to apprenticeship. Before the industrial revolution, a '*technique*' was *the indissociable ensemble* of a means of labour or tool, *and a worker*, moulded to its use by apprenticeship and habit. The technique is essentially individual, even if the organization of labour is collective. Manufacture retains these properties and pushes them to the limit: the inconveniences denounced from the beginning of fractional labour arise precisely from the fact that it maintains a rigorous coincidence of the *technical process*, which gives rise to more and more differentiated operations, adapted to more and more numerous and distinct materials, with the *anthropological process*, which makes individual abilities more and more specialized. The tool and the worker reflect one and the same movement.

The main consequence of this immediate unity is what Marx calls 'manual labour as a regulating principle of social production'. This means that co-

---

[12] Obviously, we are here using a general concept of 'manual labour', one not restricted to actions performed by the hands, although the hands are the dominant organs, but extended to the work of the whole psycho-physiological organism. Similarly, 'machine' should not be understood in the restricted sense of machines which are mechanical.

operation in manufacture brings workers into relationship, and only through their mediation, means of production. This fact emerges clearly if, for example, we consider the constraints to which the constitution of the 'organisms of production' must conform where the proportion of workers employed in different tasks is concerned: these are dictated by the characteristics of labour-power. The number of manual operations into which it is most advantageous to divide the labour, and the number of workers detailed to each functional task so that there is 'work' for all of them all the time, must be established empirically. This will fix the composition of a unity-group which is paralysed if even one of its members is missing, in exactly the same way as an artisan would be paralysed in the continuity of his labour-process if for some reason he could not perform any one of the operations required for the manufacture of his product (See *Capital*, T.II, p. 37; Vol. I, p. 347).

By replacing human strength in the function of *tool-bearer*, i.e., by suppressing its direct contact with the object of labour, mechanization produces a complete transformation of the connexion between the labourer and the means of production. From then on, the *information* of the object of labour no longer depends on the culturally acquired characteristics of the labour-power, but is pre-determined by the form of the production instruments and by their functioning mechanism. The basic principle of the organization of labour becomes *the necessity to replace the operations of manual labour as completely as possible by the operations of machines*. The machine-tool makes the organization of production completely independent of the characteristics of human labour-power: at the same stroke, the means of labour and the labourer are completely separated and acquire different forms of development. The previous relationship is inverted: rather than the instruments having to be adapted to the human organism, that organism must adapt itself to the instrument.

This separation makes possible the constitution of a completely different type of unity, *the unity of the means of labour and the object of labour*. The machine-tool, says Marx, makes possible the constitution of a 'material skeleton independent of the labourers themselves' (*Capital*, T.II, p. 56; Vol. I, p. 367). An organism of production is now no longer the union of a certain number of workers, it is a set of fixed machines ready to receive any workers. From now on, 'a technique' is a set of certain materials and instruments of labour, linked together by a knowledge of the physical properties of each of them, and of their properties as a system. The process of production is regarded in isolation as a *natural* labour process: within the elements of the labour process, it constitutes a relatively autonomous subset. This unity is expressed in the emergence of technology, i.e., the application of the natural sciences to the techniques of production. But this application is only possible on the existing basis provided by the objective unity of the *means of production* (means and object of labour) in the labour process.

The collective labourer acquires the determination of what Marx calls *'socialized labour'*. It is impossible to explain the totality of conditions *actually required* by a particular labour process (leading to a determinate useful product) without considering it as a component labour process, an element of social production as a whole. And notably, the *intellectual labour* which produces the knowledges which are applied in any particular labour process must appear in its analysis (in the analysis of the technical division of this labour process). There are labourers in this co-operation who are not present at the work-place. The fact that this product of intellectual labour, science, is a *free* element so far as the capitalist is concerned (which besides is not completely the case) and seems to be a gift of society, is a different problem, one which does not arise in the analysis of the labour process. Similarly, the set of workshops or factories in which the same technique is applied, independently of the distribution of property, tends to become its field of application and experiment, constituting what Marx calls 'practical experience on a wide scale':

> It is only the experience of the collective worker which discovers and reveals . . . the simplest methods of applying the discoveries, and the ways to overcome the practical frictions arising from carrying out the theory – in its application to the production process, etc. (*Capital*, Vol. III, p. 103, modified).

Thus we see that as a consequence of the relationship between the elements of the combination, the natures of those elements themselves are transformed. This 'collective worker' in a relationship with the unity of the means of production is now a completely different individual from the one who formed the characteristic unity of artisan-manufacturing labour with different means of labour; at the same time, the determination of 'productive labour' has changed it support:

> Once . . . the individual product has been transformed into a social product, produced by a collective labourer, each member of which participates to a very different extent and from near or far or not at all in the manipulation of the material, the determinations of *productive labour*, and of the *productive labourer* become extended as a necessary consequence. In order to labour productively, it is no longer necessary for you to do manual work yourself; it is enough that you are an organ of the collective labourer, and perform one of its subordinate functions. The first determination given above of productive labour, a definition deduced from the very nature of the production of material objects, still remains correct for the collective labourer, considered as a single person. But it no longer holds good for each of its members taken individually (*Capital*, T.II, pp. 183–4; Vol. I, pp. 508–9).[13]

[13] In the text of *Capital*, this determination is followed by a second one, which notes that in the capitalist mode of production the description 'productive labourer' is at the same

In our pseudo-combinatory, therefore, we do not really find *the same* *'concrete' elements* when we move from one variant to the next. Nor is their particularity defined by a mere place, *but rather as an effect of the structure, differing every time*, i.e., an effect of the combination which constitutes the mode of production. I have taken this connexion as an example because the analysis in *Capital* unravels every inch of it, but it is clear that an analysis of the same type could be conducted for the forms of *property*, not in the legal sense of the term, but in the sense of the *relations of production* presupposed and formalized by the legal forms. Marx outlines a hint towards such an analysis in the retrospective texts on *The Genesis of Capitalist Ground Rent* (*Capital*, Volume Three) and *Pre-Capitalist Economic Formations* (*Grundrisse*), making use notably of a formal distinction between 'property' and 'possession'. His hints are enough to show that we should find forms which are as complex as those he reveals with respect to real appropriation.[14]

(3) DEVELOPMENT AND DISPLACEMENT

Before announcing the further consequences we can draw from this analysis, I must first show that it depends entirely on criteria for the differentiation of forms which are contained in the definition of *the labour process*.

> The simple elements (*die einfache Momente*) into which the labour process breaks down are: (1) the personal activity of man, or labour strictly speaking (*zweckmässige Tätigkeit*); (2) the object on which that labour acts (*Gegenstand*); (3) the means with which it acts (*Mittel*) (*Capital*, T.I, p. 181; Vol. I, p. 178).

What most people remember about Marx's analysis of the industrial revolution is what distinguishes it from other explanations of the same

---

time restricted to the *wage labourer*, the labourer who corresponds to an advance of variable capital for the capitalist. These two inverse movements (extension-limitation) *are not mutually exclusive or contradictory. Each corresponds to one of the two internal connexions* of the mode of production, or more exactly to the determination of one element – the direct labourer – with respect to each of the two connexions, according to the specific form that the latter take in the capitalist mode of production. In the one that we have taken as the object of our study, the element (the labourer) which has the ability actually to set to work the social means of production is constituted not only by wage labourers and non-wage labourers (intellectual workers), but also by the capitalists themselves, insofar as they have the technical function of supervision and organization. The same double movement (extension-limitation) will recur later in this exposition, when I analyse the specific types of development of the productive forces in the capitalist mode of production and *the historical tendency of that mode of production*.

[14] The function of ownership of the means of production may be performed by individuals, collectivities, real or imaginary representatives of the collectivity, etc.; it may appear in a unique form, or, on the contrary, be duplicated – 'property' and 'possession', etc.

'phenomenon': the fact that he attributed the origin of the technical and social upheavals to the introduction of the *machine-tool*, to the replacement of man as the tool-bearer, instead of attributing it to the introduction of *new sources of energy* (the steam engine), to the replacement of man as the motor. But it is less usual to dwell on the theoretical expression of this originality, which is contained in the definition of the labour process. The industrial revolution (the transition from manufacture to modern industry) can be completely defined, with the assistance of these concepts, *as the transformation of the relationship* which followed from the replacement of the means of labour. Returning to what I said above about this transformation, summarizing Marx, it could be represented as the succession of two 'material forms of existence' of the labour process:[15]

– unity of the means of labour and of the labour power,
– unity of the means of labour and of the object of labour;

in both cases, the pattern of the relationship between the three elements is completely characterized by designating the sub-set which has a unity and relative autonomy.

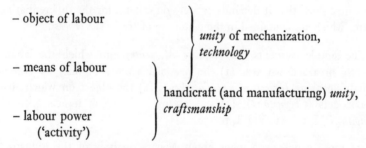

– object of labour

unity of mechanization, *technology*

– means of labour

handicraft (and manufacturing) *unity*, *craftsmanship*

– labour power ('activity')

It is obvious straightaway that the three concepts of the definition of the labour process have nothing to do with the abstraction of an empirical description (subject, object, 'mediation'), which can always be recast by distinguishing other elements. They are not derivatives of the analysis of the two successive forms of the connexion. They make that analysis possible.

Thus the movement from one form to the other can be completely analysed: *not as the mere dissolution of a structure* (the separation of the labourer from the means of labour), *but as the transformation of one structure into another*. Nor as the constitution *ex nihilo* of a structure although it is original (the unity of object and means of labour in a single system of physical interactions) (or as the accidental formation of that structure by the convergence of those two abstractions ('science' and 'technique'): *for it is the forms of the labour*

[15] 'The means of labour acquire in mechanization *a material form of existence* (*materielle Existenzweise*) which is the condition for the substitution of natural forces for human force, and the conscious application of science instead of empirical routine' (*Capital*, T.II, p. 71; Vol. I, p. 386).

process which have changed. The new system of the productive forces, of which modern capitalist mechanized industry is the first example, is neither an absolute end nor an absolute origin, but a reorganization of the entire system, of the relation of the real appropriation of nature, of the 'productive forces'.

But at the same time it is quite clear that this change in form could not have been analysed at all as the linear movement of a development, as a *lineage*. There is such a lineage between handicrafts and manufacture, since, as we have seen, manufacture can be regarded, from the point of view which concerns us, as the continuation of a movement peculiar to handicrafts, and one which conserves all its characteristics. But the machine which replaces the ensemble of tools and educated, specialized labour-power is in no way a product of the development of that ensemble. It merely occupies *the same place*. It replaces the previous system by a different system: the continuity is not that of elements or individuals, but of functions. This type of transformation can be designated by the general term *displacement*.

Here I should like to make a digression, though not an arbitrary one, and compare this kind of reasoning with the very interesting and very surprising method followed by Freud in his texts on the *history of the libido* (notably the *Three Essays on the Theory of Sexuality*). The analogy is precise enough to encourage this comparison, which will perhaps seem even more justified if we think how akin were the ideological situations in which and against which Marx and Freud had to construct their theories, and how alike sometimes even the concepts of those ideologies were. *Evolutionism* reigns as supreme in the science of history as it does in 'psychology'. The terms Freud uses in the *Three Essays* refer to a psychological evolutionism, exactly as Marx's terms 'level', 'degree of development' of the productive forces, refer to a historical evolutionism (in the Preface to *A Contribution*, Marx speaks of the replacement of the existing social relations by 'new, higher' relations). Therefore (to forestall any ambiguity) I am not interested here in the *articulation* of the objects of psycho-analysis and historical materialism, but in the possibility of revealing *epistemological analogies* between Marx's theoretical work and Freud's.

Indeed, on the one hand we find in these texts of Freud's a whole biological or quasi-biological theory of the *stages of development* of the libido (sexual instinct), a problematic of the congenital constitution and established nature of the 'germs' whose development will constitute the successive stages. We find a theory of development and of its intermediate degrees, which at the same time justifies a theory of the pathological as the fixation on one stage of development or a regression to it (but a regression is always merely the revelation of a fixation), etc.

But on the other hand, in contrast with what would be a real evolutionist theory, although in the very same terms, we find something completely different.

For example, in the following passage:

A difficult question and one which cannot be evaded: what is the general characteristic which enables us to recognize the sexual manifestations of children? *The concatenation of phenomena* into which we have been given an insight by psycho-analytic investigation justifies us, in my opinion, in regarding thumb-sucking as a sexual manifestation and in choosing it for our study of the essential features of infantile sexual activity (*Three Essays*, pp. 180–1).[16]

This is one example of a reasoning Freud generalizes in this study, which consists of making a series of organizations of the search for pleasure into the successive forms of a single sexual instinct. 'The *final outcome* of sexual development lies in what is known as the normal sexual life of the adult' (the formulation in the *Introduction to Psychoanalysis* gives a more complex chain, since Freud uses in his definition both infantile sexuality and 'abnormal' adult sexuality: hence the final outcome of the development is either 'normal' sexuality or perversion and neurosis, which have the same *place* in the 'abnormal' outcome). Paradoxically, the origins of the development are the stages which are least obviously of a 'sexual' character. In reality, they only acquire this character because analysis discovers for them *the same function*. The succession of these stages is much better analysed as a series of *displacements* than as a continuity: a displacement of the erotogenic zones, i.e., of the parts of the body invested with a sexual 'value' in a given libidinal organization (Freud tells us that there is hardly any part of the body that cannot be treated in this way); a displacement of the biological functions which 'prop up' the sexual instinct initially; a displacement of the objects of the instinct, from what Freud calls the absence of an object, but which is a particular modality of an object, to the object of genital love. Each of these displacements corresponds to one variant of the relations between what Freud calls the 'component instincts', i.e., the *components of the complex sexual instinct*.

In the second place we have found that some of the perversions which we have examined are only intelligible if we assume the *convergence* of several motive forces. If such perversions admit of analysis, that is, if they can be taken to pieces, then they must be of a composite nature. This gives us a hint that perhaps *the sexual instinct itself may be no simple thing*, but put together from components which have come apart again in the perversions. If this is so, the clinical observation of these abnormalities will have drawn our attention to amalgamations which have been lost to view (*Three Essays*, p. 162).

[16] References to the 'Three Essays on the Theory of Sexuality' are to *The Standard Edition of the Complete Works of Sigmund Freud*, translated and edited by James Strachey, Vol. VII, London 1953.

Each of these variants is a system of organization of the complex sexual instinct, implying a relation of dominance or hierarchy within the 'component instincts' (pre-genital or genital organizations – primacy of the genital erotogenic zone) (see *Three Essays*, pp. 197ff.).

Thus Freud's reasoning in these pages sets to work a series of concepts which only superficially have anything to do with a theory of the evolution of the individual, or with a biological model of the latter. This reasoning must answer *two questions at once*: what form does the development take and what is its subject, what is it that develops?[17] This reasoning seems to be inseparable from a new definition of the 'sexuality' which is the object of the analysis (Freud is constantly dealing with objections which are related to this 'extension' of the notion of sexuality and which confuse it with the protraction of 'genital' sexual activity to periods before puberty). *Finally, it emerges that sexuality is defined quite simply by the succession of forms between which such 'displacements' can be analysed.* Anything is sexual which in an element of an organization of the component instincts, the final outcome of whose variations is genital organization.

But what makes it possible to analyse these displacements is a set of theoretical concepts which plays a part analogous to that of the concepts which define the labour process in the analysis of the forms of the connexion of real appropriation ('productive forces'): activity/object/means of labour. In Freud, these concepts are used systematically in the *Three Essays* and presented systematically in the article *Instincts and their Vicissitudes* (*Standard Edition*, Vol. XIV): they are the concepts of the source (*Quelle*), pressure (*Drang*), object (*Objekt*) and aim (*Ziel*) of the instinct. Of course, there is no question of any correspondence between Freud's concepts and those of Marx: but rather one of the same type of analysis, and hence of an identity of the functions of these concepts in the method.

[17] In reality, these questions are necessarily posed to any theory of development, notably in its original domain: the biological (whether individuals or species are concerned). The Darwinian revolution can be situated in a history of theories of development as a new way of posing them, which introduces a new answer ('evolution', restricted to the species and distinct from individual development). On this point, it has been possible to write: 'Originally such a development was understood as applying to a unique and qualified individual. No doubt, around the middle of the [nineteenth] century, it became hard to tell what was the *subject* of this development (*what* developed). This invariant behind the embryological transformations could not be assimilated to surface and volume (as in an unfolding), nor to the adult structure (as in a maturation) . . . Other than [a] pseudo-unity in instantaneity (ecological, etc.), the only universe left for Darwin was a unity in a succession reduced almost to a minimum: that of a continuous lineage (*filiation*), both in the genealogical sense (all species deriving from the same stock) and in an almost mathematical sense (tiny elementary variations). This lineage explained the relative persistence of types and plans of organization: *it was not the substratum or foundation of the history: it was merely a consequence of it*' (G. Canguilhem, G. Lapassade, J. Piquemal and J. Ulman: 'Du développement à l'évolution au XIXe siècle', *Thales*, T.XI, 1962). In Freudian (and Marxist) pseudo-development, we do not even find this minimum – we are dealing with the radical absence of any pre-existing unity, i.e., any germ or origin.

Perhaps in return we shall now be able to illuminate the problems posed by Marx's text. Notably the difficulty Marx found in isolating the connexion that I have discussed, or, what amounts to the same thing, in thinking the 'level of the productive forces' as a connexion within the combination, i.e., as a *relation of production* with the same status as the forms of the ownership of the means of production.[18]

This difficulty is accompanied by the temptation to *list* the productive forces, and, for example, to divide them between nature and man. Similarly, these texts of Freud's contain formulations which attempt to situate the sexual instinct, as described by analysis, with respect to the domains of biology and psychology; Freud ends by defining instinct as a *frontier* between the biological and the psychological, and he even locates this ambiguity at the level of the 'source' of instinct (see *Instincts and their Vicissitudes*, op. cit., p. 123: 'By the source of an instinct is meant the somatic process which occurs in an organ or part of the body and whose stimulus is represented in mental life by an instinct. We do not know whether this process is invariably of a chemical nature . . . The study of the sources of instincts lies outside the scope of psychology. Although instincts are wholly determined by their origin in a somatic source, in mental life we know them only by their aims'). In the analysis of forms, the biological is therefore always absent as such. The sought after 'frontier' is thereby strictly non-existent. But we should add that in another sense the psychological, too, is absent: in its traditional conception, it, too, was defined by its opposition and relation to the biological. If the latter disappears as such, the psychological is transformed into something other than itself: into precisely what Freud called the 'psychical'. We are therefore always dealing with *a series of reorganizations and displacements of the domains* whose links Freud himself has very clearly conceived. In the *Introductory Lectures on Psychoanalysis*, Freud writes:

> Whereas for most people 'conscious' and 'psychical' are the same, we have been obliged to *extend* the concept of 'psychical' and to recognize something 'psychical' that is not 'conscious'. And in just the same way, whereas other people declare that 'sexual' and 'connected with reproduction' (or, if you prefer to put it more shortly, 'genital') are identical, we cannot avoid postulating something 'sexual' that is not 'genital' – has nothing to do with reproduction. The similarity here is only a formal one, but it is not without a deeper foundation (*Standard Edition*, Vol. XVI, p. 321).

We should add, simply, that this 'extension' is in fact a completely new definition, in content as well as in the nature of the theoretical discourse by which it is justified.

---

[18] Althusser has proposed the term 'technical relations of production', which clearly marks the distinction. But we should remember that 'relations' in itself implies their *social* character.

The same is true of 'nature' in the analysis of the productive forces. For although Marx writes that 'labour is, in the first place, an action which takes place between man and nature ... In it man has the role of a natural power with respect to nature', it would perhaps be equally correct to say that nature has the role of a social element. In this sense, too, 'nature' as such is absent.

Insofar as the Marxist analysis of the 'productive forces' is systematically inscribed in the definition of a mode of production, i.e., insofar as it is not a simple list or description of the 'technical' aspects of production or its 'resources', but rather the definition of a form of variation of the 'technical' social relations of production, it therefore achieves the same effect of displacement and rupture with respect to the traditional theoretical division of labour as that which we have found in Freud. This rupture effect is characteristic of the founding of a new science which is in the process of constituting its object and defining for it a domain which a variety of disciplines were previously occupying and for that reason ignoring completely. In the domain of historical materialism, as a scientific theoretical discipline, the analysis of the productive forces does not arise as a technical or geographical *preliminary*, formulating the *conditions* or bases on which a 'social' structure of human institutions and practices can be constructed, as an essential, but external limitation imposed on history: on the contrary, it is *inside* the definition of the social structure of a mode of production (no definition of a 'mode of production' can be regarded as satisfactory unless it includes a definition of the productive forces which are typical of that mode of production); it therefore completely transforms the meaning of 'social'.

But, as we have seen, the analogy goes further: it also extends to the *type of object* and history that Marx and Freud defined. Just as the 'sexual' that Freud discusses is not the subject of the development staked out by the organizations of the instincts, just as the organizations of the instincts do not strictly speaking descend one from another, so *in Marx's analysis we are never dealing with anything other than the combination itself and its forms.* Thus, in Marx's case, too, we can say that *the subject of development is nothing but what is defined by the succession of the forms of organization of labour* and the displacements that it achieves. Which reflects exactly the theoretical, non-empirical character of the constitution of his object.

(4) HISTORY AND HISTORIES: ON THE FORMS OF HISTORICAL INDIVIDUALITY

This analysis has very important consequences for the theory of history. Indeed, we should ask what has really been achieved by this analysis of two successive forms: we should pose the question of whether this can be called '*a history*'. This definition would be manifestly meaningless unless we could at the same time designate the object of this history. Whatever the mode of this designation, by a concept or by a mere name, we can never conceive history in general, but only *the history of something*.

We should note that most historians have, until really quite recently, avoided the necessity of giving a theoretical answer to this problem of their *object*. Take for example Marc Bloch's reflections on the 'science of history'; it is clear that all his efforts are devoted solely to the constitution of a *methodology*. The attempt to define the object of the historian's work is indeed revealed as aporetic, once it has been demonstrated that this object cannot be 'the past', nor ultimately any pure and simple definition of time: 'the very idea that the past as such could be the object of science is absurd' (Marc Bloch: *The Historian's Craft*, trans. Peter Putnam, Manchester 1954, p. 22). Nevertheless, after this negative and perfectly cogent conclusion (although its consequences have not always been drawn – by the philosophers), attempts such as Bloch's are content with an *incomplete* definition of their science which relegates the problem of the *object* to the indefiniteness of a totality: 'man, let us say rather, men', and characterizes knowledge solely as a certain set of *methods*. Here is not the place to analyse the empiricism that ultimately flows from this incomplete definition, but we should note that the problem evaded theoretically is necessarily solved practically at every moment. That is why we have political histories, histories of institutions, histories of ideas, histories of the sciences, economic histories, etc.

In this perspective we could undoubtedly define the object which was the concern of the above analysis as 'labour' and say that it was a *history of labour*, or a moment of such a history.

But at the same time, we see that Marx's analysis was presented in an essentially polemical situation with respect to what is usually called 'labour history' or 'technical history'. Such histories exist, and they receive but do not constitute objects which are claimed to persist in a certain identity of nature, through all their changes. These histories require a 'subject' to unify them, and they find one in technology, regarded as a 'fact' (even as a 'fact of civilization'), or in labour, regarded as a kind of cultural 'behaviour'. To say that they *receive* these objects is quite simply to say that the moment of their constitution lies outside the historian's theoretical practice itself, but is a part of other practices, theoretical or otherwise. From the viewpoint of theoretical practice, the constitution of the object is therefore presented as a *designation*, as a *reference* to another practice; it is therefore only possible from the point of view of the personal identities of the men who are implied in all these practices at once, in a historian's theoretical practice, and in political, economic and ideological practices. This reference is therefore only possible as an effect of the complex *historical unity* and of the historical articulation of these different practices, but as it is given, as it is reflected uncritically in a privileged site, the ideology of the period. But at the same time, because they are a paradox – a discourse (supposedly critical *par excellence*) which depends for the constitution of its object on an uncritical operation – these histories encounter, in their conceptualization and in the nature of their explanations, the insoluble problem of the mutual *frontiers* of these received objects, and finally, of the relation between this component history and other histories, and the history of the totality. As Vilar says of economic history, their description of the change, the movement of their peculiar object leads them to the insertion of this movement into a reality wider than their objects considered in their 'purity' (the 'pure' economy, 'pure' technique, etc.), which is the totality of human relations and explains this change (see *Contributions à la première Conférence Internationale d'Historie Économique,* Stockholm, 1960, p. 38). *They discover that their objects change, that their objects have a history because what they are not changes too.* It thus appears that the constitutive problem of each history is that of the relation between its object and history in general, i.e., other historical objects, and they solve it, when they are prepared to go beyond empiricism, sometimes by the announcement of a global, undifferentiated relation, which ultimately results in a theory of the 'spirit of the age', a 'historical psychology' (see for example Francastel's work on the history of the plastic arts, and I. Meyerson's theories), sometimes by the complete reduction of one structure to another, which thus emerges as the absolute reference, the original text of several translations (see for example the works of Lukács and his disciple Goldmann on literary history).

When I say that Marx presents his analysis in a polemical situation with respect to this historical practice, I do not mean that this analysis supresses the problem of the relation between component histories and general history – a problem which must necessarily be solved before it is possible to speak strictly of 'a history'. On the contrary, it shows that this problem cannot be solved unless history really *constitutes* its object, instead of *receiving* it. In this sense, the term *analysis* used by Marx has exactly the same significance as that given it by Freud when he speaks of the 'analysis of an individual history': just as Freud's analysis produces a new definition of his object (sexuality, the libido), i.e., really constitutes it by showing the variation of its *formations*, which is the reality of a history, so Marx's analysis constitutes his object (the 'productive forces') by constructing the history of its successive forms, i.e., forms which have a determinate place in the structure of the mode of production.

In his determination of the object of a component theory, Marx's method thus completely *abolishes* the problem of 'reference', of the empirical designation of the object of a theoretical knowledge, or of the ideological designation of the object of a scientific knowledge. In fact, this determination now depends entirely on the theoretical concepts which make it possible to analyse in a differential way the successive forms of a connexion, and the structure of the mode of production to which this connexion belongs. 'Labour' is presented as a connexion between the elements of the mode of production, and therefore its constitution, as an object of history, depends entirely on a recognition of the structure of the mode of production. We can generalize this comment and say that each of the elements of the combination (*Verbindung*) undoubedly has a kind of 'history', but it is *a history without any locatable subject*: the real subject of each component history is the *combination* on which depend the elements and their relations, i.e., it is *something which is not a subject*. In this sense we can say that the first problem for a history as a science, for a theoretical history, is the determination of the combination on which depend the elements which are to be analysed, i.e., it is to determine the structure of a sphere of relative autonomy, such as what Marx calls the process of production and its modes.

In fact, this preliminary determination provides a determination of the component object, and, at the same stroke, that of its articulation with the other component objects. Which is to say once again that the knowledge of one instance of the social formation through its structure includes the theoretical possibility of knowing *its articulation* with other instances. This problem then emerges as the problem of the mode of *intervention* of the other instances in the history of the instance analysed. On this point, too, the preceding analysis provides us with an excellent example: the example of the application of science to production, i.e., the articulation of (economic) production with another practice: the theoretical practice of the natural sciences. In his study of the ways of economizing on constant capital in order to raise the rate of profit, Marx writes:

> The development of the productive power of labour in any *one* line of production, e.g., the production of iron, coal, machinery, in architecture, etc., which may again be partly connected with progress in the field of intellectual production, notably natural science and its practical application, etc. (*Capital*, Vol. III, p. 81).

A text of this kind contains absolutely no implications that 'intellectual production' is a branch of production in the economic sense of the term. But it does mean that intellectual production intervenes in the history of the mode of production (in the strict sense) *through its products*, which are susceptible to importation (knowledges). And the analysis of the displacement of elements within the mode of production, which I have reproduced above, alone enables us to explain why and in what form this intervention takes place. This analysis cancels out all the questions that have been posed as to the technological 'routine' of the ancient world and the middle ages, since the application of science to production is not determined by the 'possibilities' of that science, but by the transformation of the labour process which is an organic part of the combination of a determinate mode of production. It is determined by the constitution of the system which I have called the unity of the means of labour and of the object of labour. Not only is it therefore essential to seek in the analysis of the mode of production itself for the conditions which explain its relation with other practices, but the definition of this relation depends on the same theoretical concepts as those that designate the structure of the mode of production itself, in which the specific form of the other practices is as such absent. These other practices intervene through their specific products under conditions, or more accurately, as Marx says, within *limits*, which express the current essence of the mode of production (we shall see this in more detail with respect to the articulation of the political practice of the class struggle with the economic structure). Such also is one of the senses of the concept of 'methods' which Marx uses in relation of the production of relative surplus-value (see the passage quoted above, *Capital*, Vol. I, p. 510) as well as in relation to the (political) 'methods' of primitive accumulation; perhaps one could suggest that for Marx this concept always designates the intervention of one practice in conditions determined by another – the articulation of two practices.

On this model, we can formulate the indispensability of *other histories* than those of the modes of production, histories whose objects remain to be constituted. Not all histories are possible: historical research, via controversies in economic history, the history of ideas, mentalities, etc., is beginning to sense this, although it has not explicitly posed the problem of this constitution. The determination of the objects of these histories must await that of the relatively autonomous instances of the social formation, and the production of concepts which will define each of them by the structure of a *combination*, like the mode of production. We can predict that these definitions, too, will always be *polemical* definitions, i.e., they will only be able to constitute their objects by destroying ideological classifications or divisions which benefit from the obviousness of the 'facts'. Attempts like that of Foucault give us a good example of this.[19] It might be suggested – to enter the realm of conjecture – that the history of ideologies, and notably the history of philosophy, are perhaps not histories of systems, but histories of *concepts organized into problematics*, whose synchronic combinations it is possible to reconstitute. I am referring here to Althusser's work on the anthropological problematic to which Feuerbach and the Young Marx belonged, and on the history of philosophy in general. Similarly, the history of literature may not be that of the 'works', but that of another object, a specific one, i.e., a certain relation to the ideological (itself already a social relation). In this case, too, as Pierre Macherey suggests ('Lénine, critique de Tolstoï', *La Pensée* no. 121, June 1965 or *Pour une théorie de la production littéraire*, Maspero, Paris 1966), the object under consideration would be defined by a complex combination whose forms all have to be analysed. Obviously, these are only programmatic hints.

If the theory of history implied by Marx's method of analysis is really like this, we can produce a new concept which belongs to that theory: I shall call it the concept of the *differential forms of historical individuality*. In the

[19] Particularly in *La Naissance de la Clinique*, op. cit.

example which Marx analysed, we see that the two successive forms of the 'productive forces' connexion imply two *different forms of historical individuality*. In the example which Marx analysed, we see that the two successive forms of the 'productive forces' connexion imply two *different forms of individuality* for the 'labourer', who is one of the elements of the connexion (and similarly, two different forms of the means of production): in the first case, the ability to set the means of production to work belonged to the individual (in the ordinary sense), it was an individual mastery of these means of production; in the second case, the same ability only belongs to a 'collective labourer', it is what Marx calls a 'social' mastery of the means of production. The productive forces developed by capitalism thus institute a norm which is not valid for any individual. On the other hand, this historical difference is strictly relative to the combination considered, i.e., it only concerns the practice of production. We can say that each relatively autonomous practice thus engenders forms of historical individuality which are peculiar to it. This observation results in a complete transformation in the meaning of the term 'men', which, as we have seen, the Preface to *A Contribution* made the support for the whole construction. We can now say that these 'men', in their theoretical status, are not *the concrete men*, the men of whom we are told, in famous quotations, no more than that they 'make history'. For each practice and for each transformation of that practice, they are the different forms of individuality which can be defined on the basis of its combination structure. Just as, in Althusser's words, there are different *times* in the social structure, none of which is the reflection of a common fundamental time, so for the same reason, i.e., what has been called the *complexity* of the Marxist totality, there are different forms of political, economic and ideological individuality in the social structure, too, forms which are not supported by the same individuals, and which have their own relatively autonomous histories.

Besides, Marx formulated the very concept of the dependence of the forms of individuality with respect to the structure of the process or the 'mode' of production. His terminology itself is marked by the epistemological fact that in the analysis of the 'combination' we are not dealing with concrete men, but only with men insofar as they fulfil certain determinate functions in the structure: – *bearers* of labour power (with respect to the labour process, in his exposition of the theoretical concepts which define the analysis, Marx does not, as we have seen, say 'man' or 'subject', but *'zweckmässige Tätigkeit'*, activity which conforms to the norms of the mode of production); – *representatives* of capital.

To designate these individuals, he systematically used the term *Träger*, which is most often translated into English as *support*. Men do not appear in the theory except in the form of supports for the connexions implied by the structure, and the forms of their individuality as determinate effects of the structure.

We might perhaps import the term *pertinence* to designate this character-istic of Marxist theory, and say that each relatively autonomous practice in the social structure must be analysed according to its own pertinence, on which depends the identification of the elements which it combines. There is no reason why the elements, which are thus determined in different ways, should *coincide* in the unity of concrete individuals, who would then appear as the local, miniature reproduction of the whole social articulation. The supposition of such a common support is, on the contrary, the product of a psychological ideology, in exactly the same way as linear time is the product of a historical ideology. It is this ideology which supports the whole prob-lematic of *mediations*, i.e., the attempt to rediscover concrete individuals, the *subjects* of psychological ideology, as the centres or 'intersections' of various progressively more external systems of determination, culminating in the structure of economic relations, systems which constitute a series of hierarchized levels. This is a modern form of what Leibniz expressed per-fectly when he said that each substance with a degree of singularity, and in particular each mind, expresses the whole universe in a specific way:

> Minds . . . *in a manner* . . . express and concentrate the whole into them-selves, so that it may be said that minds are total parts ('De rerum orig-inatione radicali', in *The Monadology and other Philosophical Writings*, trans. Robert Latta, Oxford 1898, p. 349).

Similarly, if men were the common supports of determinate functions in the structure of each social practice, they would 'in a manner express and concentrate' the entire social structure into themselves, i.e., they would be the *centres* from which it would be possible to know the articulation of these practices in the structure of the whole. At the same time, each of these practices would be effectively *centred* on the men-subjects of ideology, i.e., on consciousnesses. Thus the 'social relations', instead of expressing the structure of these practices, of which individuals are merely the effects, would be generated from the multiplicity of these centres, i.e., they would have the structure of a practical inter-subjectivity.

As we have seen, Marx's whole analysis excludes this possibility. It forces us to think, not the multiplicity of centres, but the radical absence of a centre. The specific practices which are articulated in the social structure are defined by the relations of their combination before they themselves determine the forms of historical individuality which are strictly relative to them.

Chapter 3
On Reproduction

In everything that I have said so far, I have only been *defining* a single concept: 'mode of production', on the basis of the use that Marx made of it in his analysis of the capitalist mode of production. I have outlined what might be called the first theoretical effects peculiar to this concept: all the terms the function of which in Marx's exposition I have attempted to pin-point have only acquired their meaning by reference to this first definition; their intervention in a proof thus appears as an extension of the effectivity of the 'presuppositions' implied by the definition of a mode of production; the transformations in the way history is thought contained in these terms, transformations which at the same time have the meaning of a transition from ideology to science, are merely the *effects of a single theoretical event*: the introduction of the concept of a *mode of production* into the traditional problematic of periodization.

But to stop there would leave us facing a difficulty which I have already referred to in my discussion of 'component histories' in the normal practice of historians: I have pointed out the stumbling-block of these histories, which do not constitute their object on the basis of a historical definition but receive it ready constituted, the problem of the *location* of that object in a totality of historical objects. This location is always something already established for theoretical discourse (for the discourse that aims to be theoretical), established by a *non-theoretical* operation which refers to the more or less immediate obviousness in which this object proposes its existence and consistency; thus, in the last analysis, it presents itself as a recourse to *gesture*, to the gesture which *shows* the objects of a world, whose conceptual representatives one *only then* proposes to deal with in a theoretical discourse. But we also know that this gesture is only apparently an innocent one, that in reality it is inhabited by an ideology which governs the division of the world into objects, and, in the same movement, the 'perception' of these objects, what has elsewhere been designated as the *allusive* nature of ideology. We know this from the moment a science breaks, constituting other objects in polemical rupture with the previous ones.

The difficulty we are now about to meet is of an analogous kind, and we shall not lack examples to persuade us that this difficulty is no fabrication. We now have the theoretical concept of a mode of production, or more precisely, we have it in the form of the knowledge of one particular mode of production, since, as we have seen, the concept only exists if it is specified. However, it seems that we still need to know something else, i.e., *when and where the concept is 'applicable'*, what societies, at what moments in their histories, have a capitalist mode of production. Indeed, the whole problem of periodization seems to be concentrated in this point: it is not enough to have at one's disposal a theoretical analysis of the effects which depend on the structure of each mode of production, once one has formulated its 'presuppositions' – it is also necessary to build an actual history with them, quite simply, *real history, our history*, which presents these different modes of production here or there, one after the other. A true knowledge tells us, i.e., we know theoretically, what the capitalist mode of production is, but we also want to know if this knowledge is really the knowledge of England in 1840 or of France in 1965, etc. This is a problem of *identification* or *judgement*: it seems that we need *rules* to determine which objects in experience fall within the concept of the capitalist mode of production. It is this apparent necessity which gives rise to the empiricist interpretation of theoretical practice as a practice which constitutes 'models': in this view, the entire theory of *Capital* is a study of the properties of a model, properties which are valid for every production that is an 'example' or 'case' of the structure. The identification of the cases, the actual subsumption, is, in this ideology of models, in every respect a pragmatic process, a gesture, however complicated the forms in which it is achieved (by which I mean, even if this identification is not made at one stroke, but through a series of partial identifications in which the elements of the structure and its particular effects are discovered). As such, it is a non-theoretical process which depends, not on concepts, but on properties of the identifier, properties which might well be called psychological even where a scientific consciousness is concerned. Kant already said that good judgement is a gift which cannot be learnt, and that the basis of judgement is a profound mystery (for theory).

Nevertheless, this route whose mere exercise subordinates theoretical practice to a non-theoretical faculty seems to be implied, at least negatively, like the space within a mould, in certain terms which Marx applies to his own object in *Capital*. I shall only recall a few of these texts here, for I have commented on them several times already. Marx tells us that he only studied the mode of production 'in its ideal average' (*Capital*, Vol. III, p. 810). Which does not only mean that one abstracts from the 'particular' effects, from the 'accidental' circumstances or 'superficial' traits, in order to study the general structure itself, but also that one studies a structure which is not peculiar to any particular time or place. This is also the meaning of the famous reference to England:

> In this work I have to examine the *capitalist mode of production*, and *the relations of production and exchange* corresponding to that mode. Their classical ground is England. That is the reason why I have taken the chief

facts and examples which illustrate the development of my theories from England. If, however, the German reader shrugs his shoulders . . . I must plainly tell him, '*De te fabula narratur!*' (*Capital*, preface to the first German edition, T.I, p. 18; Vol. I, p. 8).

We must take this text strictly literally, and say that the object of the theory is itself a theoretical object at a determinate level of abstraction. The mode of production, the relations of production and exchange, these things are what is known in *Capital*, not England or Germany (besides, a whole book could be written on the history of the theoretical destiny of the English *example* in Marxism, from its function here as a paradigm to the function as an *exception* which Lenin gave it, basing himself on certain of Marx's own political texts – see Lenin: ' "Left-Wing" Childishness and Petty-bourgeois Mentality', *Selected Works in Three Volumes*, Vol. II, pp. 753–5). Certain of Marx's texts allow us to go further and say that the analysis is not only in principle independent of the national historical examples it deals with, but also of the extension of the connexions that it analyses; it is a study of the properties of every possible economic system which constitutes a market subject to a structure of capitalist production:

> We here take no account of export trade, by means of which a nation can change articles of luxury either into means of production or means of subsistence, and vice versa. In order to free the general analysis of all irrelevant subsidiary circumstances, we must treat the commercial world as one nation, and assume that capitalist production is everywhere established and has possessed itself of every branch of industry (*Capital*, T.III, p. 22n; Vol. I, p. 581n).

The same is true of every mode of production.

In the chapter on the 'Genesis of Capitalist Ground Rent' (Vol. III), where he analyses the successive forms of land ownership in different modes of production, Marx could therefore generalize these epistemological suggestions, and write:

> This does not prevent the same economic basis – the same form from the standpoint of its main conditions – due to innumerable different empirical circumstances, natural environment, racial relations, external historical influences, etc., from showing infinite variations and gradations in appearance, which can be ascertained *only by analysis of the empirically given circumstances* (*Capital*, Vol. III, p. 772).

Like many others, this passage expresses perfectly the theoretical pragmatism which I have been discussing. Reading it literally, one would be perfectly justified in reserving theoretical status for the study of the 'main conditions', which coincide with the structure of the mode of production, and saying that the analysis of the empirically given circumstances is itself an empirical analysis.

But what Marx is reflecting here is quite simply the operation I was trying to explain at the beginning, when I said that the first movement of a science of history was to reduce the *continuity* of history, on which is based the impossibility of sharp 'breaks', and to constitute history as a science of discontinuous modes of production, as the science of a variation. He is reflecting this movement by re-establishing continuity as a real reference, a reference to the reality of history, and by making discontinuity a property of the concept in general. Thus the problem of the *location* of the object whose science is the science of the mode of production is not posed inside the theory itself, which is merely the production of models; this problem is posed on the frontiers of theory, or, more accurately, it makes it obligatory to presuppose that theory has a frontier, which is occupied by a subject of knowledge. 'Hic Rhodus, hic salta': theoretical analysis must be abandoned and complemented by 'empirical' analysis, i.e., by the designation of the real objects which actually obey the laws expounded. It is then really one and the same problem to collect together the examples which are realizations of the model, despite 'infinite gradations', and to designate the transitions from one mode of production to another: to say where the concept of one mode of production is applicable and where it is necessary to apply the concepts of two modes of production in succession. In either case, a residue remains which is given as the irreducibly empirical (in the last analysis, the obviousness of something observed: where its theoretical definition is concerned, on the one hand, the capitalist mode of production is a certain system of relations between labour, means of production, etc., and where its location is concerned, on the other, it is 'our' mode of production). But if we refuse to budge, and insist on staying in theoretical discourse, then this residue can be seen as really a *lacuna*, as something which *must be thought* and yet *cannot be thought* with the help of the theoretical concept of the 'mode of production' *alone*.

I have deliberately gone to this extreme conclusion and to the texts which can be used to support it, leaving aside everything in *Capital* itself which might look like an analysis of the transition from one mode of production to another, i.e., like a solution to the problem of location, namely, an analysis of the *formation* of the capitalist mode of production and an analysis of its *dissolution*. I have done so in order to underline straight away that we really do need a *second concept* at the same theoretical level as that of the mode of production, just as 'abstract', if you like, in order to constitute a theory of history as a succession of modes of production. We need it because the concept as we have developed it up to now has precisely left *succession* in parenthesis. We have only been able to define what a mode of production is by revealing the singularity of its forms, the specific *combination* that binds together these elements of every combination: labourer, means of production, non-labourers, etc. In order not to pre-judge the issue, let us say that if historical materialism were reduced to this concept alone, it would be unable to think the *transition* from one combination to another at the same theoretical level.

It follows that we must read all of Marx's analyses which deal with the formation and dissolution of a mode of production, and look in them for *this second attempt*, whether it is there explicitly or has to be disengaged. But we cannot take these analyses for descriptions pure and simple. However, the fact that Marx let ambiguities survive which allow certain of his terms to have a theory of 'models' read into them, is a warning that we shall find more difficulties in this task.

If we return to *Capital* and try to read in it a theory of the transition from one mode of production to another, we find first of all a concept which seems to be the very concept of historical *continuity*: the concept of *reproduction*. The theory of reproduction in fact seems to ensure a triple link or a triple continuity:

– a link between the different economic subjects, in the event, between the different individual capitals, which really constitute a single 'inter-twining' or a single movement. A study of the reproduction of capital is a study of this interlacing and intertwining:

> However, the circuits of the individual capitals intertwine, presuppose and necessitate one another, and form, precisely in this interlacing (*Verschlingung*), the movement of the total social capital (*Capital*, Vol. II, p. 353).

Therefore, what made it possible to imagine the movement of an individual capital was only an abstraction, and a deforming abstraction, since the movement as a whole is more complex than a mere addition.

– a link between the different levels of the social structure, since reproduction implies the permanence of the non-economic conditions of the production process, notably the legal conditions: in the chapter of *Capital* on the 'Genesis of Capitalist Ground Rent', Marx shows that the institution of a law corresponding to the real relations of production is merely the effect of the *repetition* of the process of production, of reproduction: see the passage quoted above, *Capital*, Vol. III, pp. 773–4:

> It is in the interest of the ruling section of society to sanction the existing order as law and to legally establish its limits given through usage and tradition. Apart from all else, this, by the way, comes about of itself as soon as the constant reproduction of the basis of the existing order and its fundamental relations assumes a regulated and orderly form *in the course of time*. And such regulation and order are themselves indispensable elements of any mode of production, if it is to assume social stability and indifference from mere chance and arbitrariness. These are precisely the form of its social stability and therefore its relative freedom from arbitrariness and mere chance. Under stagnant conditions of the production

process as well as the corresponding social relations, it achieves this form by mere repetition of its own reproduction. If this has continued on for some time, it entrenches itself as custom and tradition and is finally sanctioned as an explicit law.

– lastly, reproduction ensures the successive continuity of production itself, and this is the basis for all the rest. Production cannot be stopped, and its necessary continuity is inscribed in the identity of the elements as they emerge from one production process and enter another: means of production which have themselves been products, labourers and non-labourers between whom the products and means of production are shared in a certain way. It is the materiality of the elements which supports the continuity, but it is the concept of reproduction which expresses its specific form, because it envelops the different (differential) determinations of the material. Through each of the aspects that I have evoked, the concept expresses merely one and the same pregnancy of the structure which presents a 'well-bound' history. At the beginning of her book, *The Accumulation of Capital*, Rosa Luxemburg writes:

> The regular repetition of reproduction is the general *sine qua non* of regular consumption which in its turn has been the pre-condition of human civilization in every one of its historical forms. The concept of reproduction, viewed in this way, reflects an aspect of the history of civilization (*ein kultur-geschichtliches Moment*) (trans. Agnes Schwarz-schild, London 1951, p. 31).

Thus, the analysis of reproduction seems genuinely to set in motion what has hitherto been seen only in a static form, and to articulate together levels which have hitherto been isolated; reproduction appears to be the general form of permanence of the general conditions of production, which in the last analysis englobe the whole social structure, and therefore it is indeed essential that *it should be the form of their change and restructuration, too*. That is why I shall dwell on it, for this concept implies more than the previous ones.

(1) THE FUNCTION OF 'SIMPLE' REPRODUCTION

In the series of expositions that have the title 'reproduction', Marx always prefaced the exposition of the reproduction peculiar to the capitalist mode of production, which is capitalist *accumulation* (the capitalization of surplus-value) and its peculiar conditions, with a prior exposition of 'simple repro-duction'. Marx calls this simple reproduction an 'abstraction', or better, 'a strange assumption' (*Capital*, Vol. II, p. 395). Several explanations of this might be advanced.

It might be thought that this was a matter of an *exposition procedure*, that 'simple' reproduction is only a *simplification*. At the level of Volume Two (the reproduction schemes), i.e., of the conditions of reproduction which affect the exchanges between the different departments of production, it seems obvious enough why such a simplification should be attempted. It allows the presentation of the general form of these connexions in the form of equations, before presenting them in the form of *inequalities*. The disequilibrium, or disproportion which constitutes the motor of accumulation of the social capital is made intelligible with respect to a simple equilibrium pattern.

It might also be thought that the study of simple reproduction is the study of a *particular case*, which is partly the same thing, insofar as this particular case is simpler than the general case. But this would not just be an exposition procedure: it would give the knowledge of the movement of reproduction of certain capitals, those which are content to maintain production in certain periods when accumulation temporarily ceases.

Finally, it might be thought that the study of simple reproduction is the study of a *part*, an always necessary part, of extended reproduction. However much of the surplus-value is capitalized, it is added on over and above an automatic capitalization, which is merely the conservation of the existing capital. The quantity of capitalized surplus-value varies, and it depends on the initiative of the capitalists, in appearance at any rate; simple reproduction cannot be altered, once a capital of a given size is considered, without the capitalist ceasing to be a capitalist to the precise extent of the decrease. That is why it is important to study simple reproduction in itself (Marx writes: 'As far as accumulation does take place, simple reproduction is always a part of it, and can therefore be studied by itself, and is an actual factor of accumulation', *Capital*, Vol. II, p. 395), and only afterwards accumulation or extended reproduction, as a *supplement* added on to simple reproduction. To be precise, this supplement cannot be added on at will: it has to conform to quantitative conditions which depend on the technical composition of capital; hence it may be intermittent in its actual application. Simple reproduction, on the other hand, is autonomous, continuous and automatic.

None of these explanations are false, nor are they incompatible. But they leave room for a different explanation, one which is more important for us. In *Capital*, Marx does first present us with the concept of reproduction in the forms of the accumulation of capital, or more accurately, since we want to indicate both 'simple' and 'extended' reproduction, in the forms of the *capitalization of the product*, and he first installs us in a quantitative problematic. It is a question of analysing the conditions under which the capitalist or ensemble of capitalists can realize this practical objective: to increase the scale of production, i.e., the scale of exploitation, i.e., the quantity of surplus-value appropriated; which presupposes, in principle at least, the possibility of a practical *choice* between a simple reproduction and an expansion. But as we know, or are about to discover, this choice is really illusory, a fake, and if we look at the whole of capital, it is a fictive choice. There is no alternative, there are only the real conditions of extended reproduction. Marx tells us that *the premiss of simple reproduction is incompatible with capitalist production,* 'although this does not exclude the possibility that in an industrial cycle of ten to eleven years some year may show a smaller total production than the preceding year, so that not even simple reproduction takes place compared to the preceding year' (*Capital*, Vol. II, p. 520). Which amounts to saying quite clearly this: the conceptual distinction between simple reproduction and accumulation does not cover the quantitative variations in accumulation, which depend on various circumstances (Marx analyses them) and are the effects of the general law of capitalist accumulation.

Simple reproduction, reproduction on the same scale, appears as an abstraction, inasmuch as on the one hand the absence of all accumulation or reproduction on an extended scale is a strange assumption in capitalist conditions, and on the other hand conditions of production do not remain exactly the same in different years (*and this is assumed*) . . . The value of the annual product may decrease, although the quantity of use-values may remain the same; or the value may remain the same although the quantity of use-values may decrease; or the quantity of value and of the reproduced use-values may decrease simultaneously. All this amounts to reproduction taking place either under more favourable conditions than before or under more difficult ones, which may result in imperfect – defective – reproduction. *All this can refer only to the quantitative aspect of the various elements of reproduction, not to the role which they play as reproducing capital or as reproduced revenue in the entire process* (*Capital*, Vol II, pp. 394–5).

When 'simple' reproduction such that $I_{v+s} = II_c$ (which, from the *economic* point of view, is not the expression of a state of equilibrium anyway, but that of a crisis) occurs during accumulation, this occurrence has precisely only the sense of an occurrence, of a coincidence, i.e., it has *no particular theoretical significance.* The same is true if we consider the reproduction of an individual capital, which may be extended, simple, or less than simple, and may have a rhythm higher than, equal to or lower than that of the social capital as a whole, etc. These variations make no conceptual difference, in exactly the same way and for the same reason, that variations in the prices of commodities *never make them anything but prices*: it may be that a commodity is actually sold 'at its value' without this being any more than a coincidence. Moreover, it is a coincidence that cannot be registered in a general rule, i.e., cannot be measured: only prices are assessed in the exchange of commodities, not values. In both cases, Marx presents an important conceptual distinction between two levels of the structure, or, better, between the structure and its effects, in the mild form of a 'provisional assumption', to be lifted later ('the prices of commodities coincided

with their values', 'the conditions of reproduction remain the same').
*The assumption of 'invariant conditions' is not an analysis of the effects, but of
the conditions themselves.*

We are thus led to look for another explanation for this duplication of the
analysis of reproduction, and we find it in a series of indications of Marx's
such as the following:

> This illustration of fixed capital, on the basis of an unchanged scale of
> reproduction, is striking. A disproportion of the production of fixed and
> circulating capital is one of the favourite arguments of the economists in
> explaining crises. That such a disproportion can and must arise even
> when the fixed capital is merely *preserved*, that it can and must do so *on
> the assumption of ideal normal production on the basis of simple reproduction
> of the already functioning social capital* is something new to them (*bei
> Voraussetzung einer idealen Normalproduktion*) (*Capital*, Vol. II, p. 469).

This ideal 'normal' production is obviously production *in its concept*,
production as Marx studies it in *Capital*, telling us to make it as the 'norm'
or the 'ideal average'. Before it is a simplification of the exposition or the
study of one particular case, one which we have just seen to be without
theoretical significance, even before it makes possible a quantitative analysis
of capitalized value and of the origin of its different parts, 'simple reproduction' is therefore the analysis of the *general formal conditions of all reproduction*.
And even before it is an exposition of the general forms of the connexions
between the different departments of production, in the mathematical sense
of the term, it is an exposition of the 'form' of the reproduction process in
the sense in which we have already analysed the 'capitalist form' of a mode
of production.

This is indeed the sense of the first exposition of 'simple reproduction'
(*Capital*, Vol. I, Chapter XXIII). Marx starts from the definition of reproduction as a simple *repetition* of the immediate production process in the
way we have just analysed it, and he writes:

> The production process periodically begins again and always passes
> through the same phases in a given time, but is always repeated on the old
> scale. Nevertheless, this repetition, or continuity, gives certain new
> characteristics to the process, *or, rather* (*oder vielmehr,*) *causes the disap-
> pearance of some apparent characteristics which it possessed as an isolated
> act* (*die Scheincharaktere seines nur vereinzelten Vorgangs*) (*Capital*, T.III,
> p. 10; Vol. I, p. 567).

The essential aspect of simple reproduction is not therefore that all
surplus-value is unproductively consumed instead of being partially capitalized; it is this uncovering of the essence by the removal of illusions, this
virtue of repetition which retrospectively illuminates the nature of the
'first' production process (in the manuscript *Pre-Capitalist Economic Forma-*

tions, Marx also writes: 'the true nature of capital does not appear *until the end of the second cycle*').

However, the point of view of repetition itself implies the possibility of an illusion which might conceal the orientation of Marx's reflection on this point. This would be to wish to follow capital in its successive '*acts*', to wish to understand what happens when, after a 'first' production cycle, capital undertakes to pursue a 'second' cycle. In this way, instead of arising as the knowledge of the determinations of the production process itself, reproduction appears as a *continuation* of production, as a supplement to the analysis of production. Thus the analysis of capital seems to follow in the tracks of the destiny of an object which is capital: at the moment of reproduction, this capital meets others on the market, its freedom of movement is suppressed (it cannot grow in arbitrary proportions because it is in competition with other capitals), and it seems that the movement of social capital is not the sum of the movements of the individual capitals, but a complex movement of its own which has been called an 'intertwining'. For example, this is the path urged on us at the beginning of Rosa Luxemburg's *Accumulation of Capital*, which starts from a literal reading of Marx ('The literal meaning of the word "reproduction" is repetition . . .') and asks what *new conditions* reproduction implies with respect to production. The passage of Marx's which I have quoted shows us that, on the contrary, it is a matter of *the same conditions*, initially implicit (transposed and deformed in the eyes of the agents of production into 'apparent characteristics'; and presented in Marx's exposition of the 'immediate' production process in the forms of admitted 'assumptions' or 'presuppositions').

In reality, it is a matter of a more complex operation than a mere repetition. In Marx's text, simple reproduction is from the beginning identified with the consideration of *the ensemble of social production*. The movement that destroys this appearance which arises from the study of the immediate production process and is also what the capitalist and the worker 'imagine' (*Capital*, T.III, p. 13; Vol. I, p. 569: '*die Vorstellung des Kapitalisten*') is at once a 'repetition' and the transition to capital as a totality:

> *The matter takes a quite different aspect*, when we contemplate, not the single capitalist, and the single labourer, but the capitalist class and the labouring class, *not isolated acts of production*, but capitalist production in its full continuous renewal, and on its social scale (*Capital*, T. III, pp. 14–15; Vol. I, p. 572).

The analysis of Volume Two will show clearly in detail how the analysis of the repetition (of the succession of cycles of production) and that of capital as a form of the ensemble of production are inter-dependent. But this unity is already present here. The 'isolated act of production' is twice characterized negatively: as something which is not repeated and as something which is done by an individual. Or rather, 'isolated act' is a way of saying the same thing twice. Once the isolation has been suppressed, we are no longer dealing with an *act*, i.e., with a subject, an intentional structure of means and ends, if it is true, as Marx says in the *1857 Introduction*, that 'to treat society as a single subject is to treat it from a false position – speculatively' (*Grundrisse*, p. 15). There can therefore be no question in this analysis of *following* the reproduction process, of attempting effectively – and fictively – to 're-new' the production process.

This analytical operation is in principle the one which the *1857 Introduction* to *A Contribution to the Critique of Political Economy* installed in parallel to the comparative analysis of the modes of production. It is now no longer a question of identifying the variants of the 'combination' of the 'relations of production' and the 'productive forces' on the basis of historical material, but of examining what Marx calls 'the general determination of production at a given social stage', i.e., the relation between the *totality* of social production and its particular forms (branches) in a *given synchrony* (as this term has been illuminated for us from now on, since the analysis of the 'repetition' of production, of the continuity of production in a series of cycles, depends on the analysis of production as a whole, of production as a totality – *Totalität*). For there is totalization only in the actuality of the social division of labour at a given moment, not in the individual adventures of capitals. This is expressed by Marx when he says that the analysis of reproduction envisages social production exclusively in its *result* ('If we study the annual function of social capital . . . in its results', *Capital*, Vol. II, p. 392 – modified). As we know, this result is production as a whole and its division into different departments: the operation that reveals it is not therefore a section through the movement of the different branches of production, of the different capitals, at a moment chosen with reference to a common external time, and hence dependent both in principle and in actual realization on this movement; it is an operation in which the peculiar movement of the capitals, the movement of production in each of its divisions, is completely set aside, suppressed, without any kind of conservation. Marx bases his whole analysis of reproduction from the first very general exposition of simple reproduction (Volume One) to the system of reproduction schemes (Volume Two) on this transformation of succession into synchrony, into 'simultaneity' (in his own term: *Gleichzeitigkeit*). Paradoxically, the continuity of the movement of production finds its concept in the analysis of a system of synchronic dependencies: the succession of the cycles of individual capitals and their intertwining depend on it. In this 'result', *the movement which has produced it is necessarily forgotten, the origin is 'obliterated'* (*die Herkunft ist aufgelöscht*) (*Capital*, Vol. II, p. 110).

To move from the isolated act, from the immediate production process, to the *repetition*, to the *ensemble* of social capital, to the *result* of the production process, is to install oneself in a fictive contemporaneity of all the movements, or, to put it more accurately, applying one of Marx's theoretical metaphors, in a fictive *planar space*, in which all the movements have been suppressed, in which all the moments of the production process appear in projection side by side with their connexions of dependence. It is the movement of this transition that Marx describes for the first time in the chapter of Volume One on 'Simple Reproduction'.

(2) THE REPRODUCTION OF THE SOCIAL RELATIONS

We can list the 'appearances' (*Scheincharaktere*) which are dissipated in this operation as follows:

First the appearance of the separation and the relative independence of the different 'moments' of production in general: the separation of production in the strict sense from circulation, of production from individual consumption, of the production and distribution of the means of production from that of the means of consumption. If we consider an 'isolated act' of production or even a plurality of such 'acts', all these moments seem to belong to a different *sphere* from that of production ('sphere' is a word which Marx very often uses). Circulation belongs to the *market* on which commodities are presented after 'leaving' production, without any certainty that they will actually be sold; individual consumption is a private act which takes place outside the sphere of circulation itself:

> The labourer's productive consumption, and his individual consumption, are therefore totally distinct. In the former, he acts as the motive power of capital, and belongs to the capitalist. In the latter, he belongs to himself, and performs his vital functions outside the process of production. The result of the one is, that capital lives; of the other, that the labourer himself lives (*Capital*, T.III, p. 14; Vol. I, p. 571).

The distribution of the means of production and consumption appears either as the contingent origin of production, or as revenue (and then it passes into the sphere of consumption).

> *The introductory act* (*der einleitende Akt*), which constitutes an act of circulation – the purchase and sale of labour-power – itself rests on a distribution of the *elements* of production which preceded and presupposed the distribution of the social *products*, namely on the separation of labour-power as a commodity of the labourer from the means of production as the property of non-labourers (*Capital*, Vol. II, p. 385).

The analysis of reproduction shows that these moments have no relative autonomy or laws of their own, but are determined by those of production. If we consider the ensemble of social capital in its *result*, the sphere of circulation disappears as a 'sphere', since all exchanges are predetermined in the division of the departments of production and in the material nature of their production. The individual consumption of the worker and capitalist, too, is predetermined in the nature and quantity of the means of consumption produced by the total social capital: while one portion of the annual product is 'destined for productive consumption from the very first' (T.III, p. 9; Vol. I, p. 566), another is destined from the very first (*von Haus aus*) for individual consumption. The *limits* within which individual consumption can oscillate depend on the internal composition of capital and are fixed at each moment.

The individual consumption of the labourer, whether it proceeds within the workshop or outside it, forms therefore an element (*Moment*) of the reproduction of capital; just as cleaning machinery does, whether it be done during the labour process or at moments when it is interrupted (*Capital*, T.III, p. 15; Vol. I, p. 572).

Lastly, the distribution of the means of production and consumption, or the division of the different elements, ceases to appear as a contingent factual state: once he has consumed the equivalent of his wages, the worker leaves the production process as he entered it, stripped of property, and the capitalist as he entered it, owner of the products of labour, which include new means of production. Production continually determines the same distribution.

Thus is appears that the capitalist mode of production determines the modes of circulation, consumption and distribution. More generally, the analysis of reproduction shows that *every mode of production determines modes of circulation, distribution and consumption as so many moments of its unity*.

Further, the analysis of reproduction destroys the appearance involved in the 'beginning' of the production process, the appearance of a 'free' contract between the worker and the capitalist, which is renewed on each occasion, the appearance which makes variable capital an 'advance' from the capitalist to the labourer (on account of the product, i.e., of the 'end' of the production process). In a word, all the appearances which seem to reduce to *chance* the face to face meeting of the capitalist and the worker as buyer and seller of labour power. Reproduction reveals the 'invisible threads' which chain the wage-earner to the capitalist class.

The capitalist production process reproduces . . . the conditions which force the labourer to sell himself in order to live, and enable the capitalist to purchase him in order that he may enrich himself. It is no longer a mere accident, that capitalist and labourer confront each other in the market as buyer and seller. It is the dilemma (*Zwickmühle* – 'double mill') of the process itself that incessantly hurls back the labourer onto the market as a vendor of his labour-power, and that incessantly converts his product into a means by which another man can purchase him. In reality, the labourer belongs to the capitalist class before he has sold himself to an individual capitalist (*Capital*, T.III, pp. 19–20; Vol. I, p. 577).

Simultaneously, reproduction destroys the appearance according to which capitalist production merely applies the laws of commodity production, i.e., of the *exchange of equivalents*. Each sale-purchase of labour-power is a transaction of that form, but the general movement of capitalist production appears as the movement by which the capitalist class continually appropriates a portion of the product created by the working class without giving any equivalent for it. This movement no longer has any beginning or termination (a division duplicated and designated by the legal structure of the contract, precisely a terminal contract or '*contrat à terme*'), i.e., there is no longer any isolated structure in which the elements of production meet. In the concept of the elements of production provided by the analysis of reproduction, they no longer need to meet because they are *always already* together.

Thus simple reproduction destroys in the production process even the appearance of an *isolated act*: an act whose agents were individuals, transforming things under determinate conditions which eventually obliged them to make these things into commodities and surplus-value for the capitalist. In this appearance the individuals retained their identity, just as capital seemed to be a sum of value which was conserved throughout the succession of acts of production.[20]

And, conversely, these material elements, in the specificity of their material nature, and in the differential distribution of these natural properties through all the branches of production and all the capitals of which they are composed, now express the conditions of the process of social reproduction. Thus reproduction reveals that things are transformed in the hands of the agents of production without their being aware of it, without it being possible for them to be aware of it if the production process is taken for the acts of individuals. Similarly, these individuals change and they really are only *class representatives*. But these classes are obviously not sums of individuals, which would not change anything: it is impossible to make a class by adding individuals together on whatever scale. Classes are *functions of the process of production as a whole*. They are not its subjects, on the contrary, they are determined by its form.

Precisely in these chapters of Volume One on reproduction, we find all the images which Marx uses to help us grasp the mode of existence of the agents of the production process as the *supports* (*Träger*) of the structure.

---

[20] 'The capitalist imagines that he is consuming the surplus-value, and is keeping intact the capital-value; but what he thinks cannot change the fact that after a certain period, the capital-value he then possesses is equal to the sum total of the surplus-value that he has acquired for nothing during this period, and the value he has consumed is equal to that which he advanced. Of the old capital which he advanced out of his own pocket, not an atom remains. It is true, he has in hand a capital whose amount has not changed, and of which a part, viz., the buildings, machinery, etc., were already there when the work of his business began. But what we have to do with here, is not the material elements, but the value, of that capital' (*Capital*, T.III, pp. 12–13; Vol. I, pp. 569–70).

On the stage of reproduction, where things 'come to light' (*Capital*, T.III, p. 26; Vol. I, p. 586) and look quite different (*ganz anders aussehen*), the individuals quite literally *come forward masked* ('it is only because his money constantly functions as capital that the economic guise of a capitalist – *die ökonomische Charaktermaske des Kapitalisten* – attaches to a man', *Capital*, T.III, p. 9; Vol. I, p. 566): *they are nothing more than masks.*

These are therefore the analyses in which Marx shows us the movement of transition (*but this transition is a rupture*, a radical innovation) from a concept of production as an act, the objectivation of one or more subjects, to a concept of production without a subject, which in return determines certain classes as its peculiar functions. This movement, in which Marx pays retrospective homage to Quesnay (for whom 'the innumerable individual acts of circulation are at once brought together in their characteristic social mass movement – the circulation between great functionally determined economic classes of society', *Capital*, Vol. II, p. 359), is carried out in exemplary fashion with respect to the capitalist mode of production, but in principle it is valid for every mode of production. As opposed to the movement of reduction and then constitution which characterizes the transcendental tradition of classical philosophy, it directly achieves an extension which excludes any possibility of production being the acts of any subjects, their practical *cogito*. It embraces the possibility, which I can only suggest here, of formulating a new philosophical concept of production in general.

All the preceding can be summarized by saying that, in a single movement, reproduction replaces and transforms the things, but retains the *relations* indefinitely. These relations are obviously what Marx calls 'social relations'; the relations which are drawn, 'projected', in the fictive space which I have mentioned.[21] the term itself is Marx's own:

> This natural faculty of labour (to conserve old value, while it creates new) takes the appearance of the self-sustaining faculty of the capital,

[21] In Volume One, Marx defines them in their *concept* (but not in all their effects) by the analysis of the *abstract* object which he calls a 'fraction of the total social capital promoted into autonomy' (*Capital*, Vol. II, p. 353). By which we are obviously to understand, as Establet notes (*Lire le Capital*, first edition, Vol. II, p. 343), not a *real* firm or enterprise which is capitalist in form, but a *fictive* capital which is necessarily a *productive* capital and yet carries out all the functions historically assumed by different types of 'capital' (merchant's capital, interest-bearing capital, etc.). The division of social capital is an essential property: it is therefore possible to represent capital *in general* by *one* capital.

For their part, only the analyses of reproduction in Volume Two, Part 3 ('Reproduction and Circulation of the Aggregate Social Capital'), which make way for the establishment of *schemes* of reproduction, and thus allow the mathematical formalization of economic analysis, explain by what mechanism the reproduction of the social relations is assured, by subjecting the qualitative and quantitative composition of the total social product to invariable conditions. But these structural conditions are not *specific* to the capitalist mode of production: in their theoretical form they imply no reference to the social form of the production process, to the form of the product ('value'), to the type of circulation of the social product which it in which it is incorporated, just as the social productive forces take the appearance of a property of capital, and as the constant appropriation of surplus-labour by the capitalist takes that of a constant self-expansion of capital. All faculties of labour are projected (*projektieren sich*) as faculties of capital, just as all forms of commodity value are projected as forms of money (*Capital*, T.III, p. 47; Vol. I, pp. 606–7).

The relations thus revealed mutually imply one another: notably the relations of property and the relations of real appropriation ('productive forces') in their complex unity. They comprehend the hitherto disjointed 'moments' (production, circulation, distribution, consumption) in a necessary and complete unity. And at the same time, they comprehend everything which appeared during the analysis of the immediate production process as its 'presuppositions', as the necessary 'conditions' for the process to be able to proceed in the form described: e.g., in capitalist production, the autonomy of the economic instance or of the legal forms corresponding to the forms of commodity exchange, i.e., a certain form of *correspondence* between the various instances of the social structure. This is what might be called the 'consistency' of the structure as it appears in the analysis of reproduction. It might also be said that for Marx the conceptual pair production/ reproduction contains the definition of the *structure* involved in the analysis of a mode of production.

On the plane instituted by the analysis of reproduction, production is not the production of things, it is the production and conservation of social relations. At the end of the chapter on simple reproduction, Marx writes:

> The capitalist production process, therefore, considered in its interconnexion (*Zusammenhang*) or as reproduction, produces not only commodities, not only surplus-value, but *it also produces and eternalizes the social relation between the capitalist and the wage-earner* (*Capital*, T.III, p. 20; Vol. I, p. 578).

This formulation is repeated at the end of the whole work, just as Marx is locating the relationship of the classes to the different forms of revenue:

> On the other hand, if the capitalist mode of production presupposes this definite social form of the conditions of production, so does it reproduce it continually. It produces not merely the material products, but reproduces continually the production relations in which the former are

---

implies ('exchange'), or to the concrete space which supports this circulation ('market'). On this point, I refer the reader in particular to the various recent works of Charles Bettelheim, and to his critical comments in *Problèmes de la Planification*, No. 9 (École Pratique des Hautes Études) – *Note of 1967.*

produced, and thereby also the corresponding distribution relations (*Capital*, Vol. III, p. 857).

The same goes for any mode of production. Each mode of production continually reproduces the social relations of production presupposed by its functioning. In the manuscript *Pre-Capitalist Economic Formations*, Marx had already expressed this by assigning the production and reproduction of the social relations to the corresponding production as its unique result (instead of a 'not merely . . .'):

> Property – and this applies to its Asiatic, Slavonic, Antique and Germanic forms – therefore originally signifies a relation of the working (producing) subject (or self-reproducing subject) to the conditions of his production or reproduction as his own. Hence, according to the conditions of production, property will take different forms. The aim of production itself is to reproduce the producer in and together with these objective conditions of his existence (*Grundrisse*, p. 395; *PCEF*, p. 95).

What is the meaning of this double 'production'?

Let us note first of all that it provides us with a key to a number of formulations of Marx's which have been regarded, precipitately perhaps, as fundamental theses of historical materialism. For the lack of a complete definition of the terms which they contain, they have lent authority to a number of rather divergent readings. For example, the formulations in the Preface to *A Contribution* which I discussed at the outset: '*In the social production of their life, men enter into definite relations that are indispensable and independent of their will . . . therefore mankind always sets itself only such tasks as it can solve*'; or the formulations in Engels's letter to Bloch: '*We make our history ourselves, but, in the first place, under very definite assumptions and conditions*'. The whole philosophical interpretation of historical materialism is indeed at stake here: if we take this double 'production' literally, i.e., if we think that the objects transformed and the social relations which they support are modified or conserved by the production process in the same way, if, for example, we group them *within a single concept of 'practice'*, we are giving a rigorous foundation to the idea that 'men make history'. Only on the basis of such a unique, unified concept of practice-production can this formulation have any theoretical meaning, can it be an immediately theoretical thesis (and not simply a moment in the ideological struggle against a mechanistic-materialist determinism). But this concept really belongs to an anthropological conception of production and practice, centred precisely on those 'men', who are the 'concrete individuals' (notably in the form of the masses) who produce, reproduce and transform the conditions of their former production. In respect to this activity, the constraining *necessity* of the relations of production only appears as a form which the object of their practice already possesses and which restricts the possibilities of creating a new form. The necessity of the social relations is simply the work of the former production activity, which necessarily leaves to the succeeding one determinate conditions of production.

But our analysis of reproduction has shown us that this double 'production' must be taken *in two different senses*: to take the unity of the expression literally is precisely to reproduce the *appearance* which makes the production process an isolated act enclosed in the determinations of the *preceding* and the *succeeding*. An isolated act, insofar as its only connexions with the other acts of production are supported by the structure of linear temporal continuity in which there *can be no* interruption (whereas in the conceptual analysis of reproduction, these connexions are, as we have seen, supported by the structure of a *space*). Only the 'production of things' can be thought as an activity of this kind – it already almost contains the concept of it in its determination of the 'raw' material and the 'finished' product; but the 'production of the social relations' is far rather a production of things and individuals *by the social relations*, a production in which the individuals are determined so as to produce and the things so as to be produced in a specific form by the social relations. That is, it is a determination of the functions of the social process of production, a process without a subject. These functions are no more men than, on the plane of reproduction, the products are things. Therefore (re)production, i.e., social production in its concept, does not strictly speaking produce the social relations, since it is only possible on condition that these social relations exist; but on the other hand, neither does it produce commodities in the sense of producing things which *subsequently* receive a certain social qualification from the system of economic relations which invests them, objects which subsequently 'enter into relations' with other things and men; production only produces (*ever already*) *qualified things, indices of relations*.

Marx's formulation ('the process of production does not only produce material objects but also social relations') *is not therefore a conjunction but a disjunction*: either it is a matter of the production of things, or else it is a matter of the (re)production of the social relations of production. There are *two* concepts, the concept of the 'appearance' and the concept of the effectivity of the structure of the mode of production. As opposed to the production of things, the production of social relations is not subject to the determinations of the preceding and the succeeding, of the 'first' and the 'second'. Marx writes that 'every process of social production is at the same time a process of reproduction. The conditions of production are also those of reproduction'; and at the same time they are the conditions which reproduction reproduces: in this sense the 'first' process of production (in a determinate form) is *always-already* a process of reproduction. There is no 'first' process of production for production in its concept. All the definitions concerning the production of things must therefore be transformed: in the production of the social relations, what appeared as the conditions of the first production really *determines identically all the other productions*.

> This transaction, which pertains to circulation – the sale and purchase of labour power – not only *inaugurates* the process of production, but also *determines implicitly* its specific character (*Capital*, Vol. II, p. 385).

The concept of reproduction is thus not only the concept of the 'consistency' of the structure, but also the concept of the necessary determination of the movement of production by the permanence of that structure; it is the concept of the permanence of the initial elements in the very functioning of the system, hence the concept of the necessary conditions of production, conditions which are precisely *not created by it*. This is what Marx calls the *eternity* of the mode of production:

> This incessant *reproduction or eternalization* (*Verewigung*) of the labourer, is the *sine qua non* of capitalist production (*Capital*, Vol. I, p. 571; retranslated from the German text).

Chapter 4
Elements for a Theory
of Transition

Let us return to the question posed above: the question of the transition from one mode of production to another. The analysis of reproduction seems merely to have erected a number of obstacles to its theoretical solution. Really, it enables us to pose the problem in its true terms, for it subjects the theory of transition to two conditions.

First, all social production is a re-production, i.e., a production of social relations in the sense suggested. All social production is subject to structural social relations. The 'transition' from one mode of production to another can therefore never appear in our understanding as an irrational hiatus between two 'periods' which are subject to the functioning of a structure, i.e., which have their specified concept. The transition cannot be a moment of destructuration, however brief. It is itself a movement subject to a structure which has to be discovered. We can give a strong sense to these comments of Marx's (reproduction expresses the continuity of production because it can never stop) which he often presented as 'obvious', as things 'every child knows' (that the labourer can never have lived on 'the air of time', that 'a nation which ceased to work, I will not say for a year, but even for a few weeks, would perish' – Letter to Kugelmann, 11 July 1868). They mean that the invariant structure of production can never disappear, although it may take a particular form in each mode of production (the existence of a fund for the maintenance of labour, i.e., the distinction between necessary labour and surplus-labour; the division of the product into means of production and means of consumption, a distinction that Marx calls *original*, or again the expression of a natural law, etc.). They therefore mean that the forms of transition themselves are particular 'forms of manifestation' (*Erscheinungsformen*) of this general structure: they are therefore themselves *modes of production*. They therefore imply the same conditions as every mode of production, and notably a certain form of complexity of the relations of production, of correspondence between the different levels of social practice (I shall try to suggest what form). The analysis of reproduction shows that if we can formulate the concept of the modes of production which belong to periods of transition between two modes of production, at the same stroke the modes of production are no longer suspended in an indeterminate time (or site): the problem of their location has been resolved once we can explain theoretically how they follow one another, i.e., once we know the moments of their succession in their concepts.

But on the other hand (second consequence), the transition from one mode of production to another, e.g., from capitalism to socialism, cannot consist of the transformation of the structure by its functioning itself, i.e., of any transition of quantity into quality. This conclusion follows from what I have said about the double sense in which the term 'production' has to be understood in the analysis of reproduction (the production of things, and the 'production' of social relations). To say that the structure can be transformed in its functioning itself is to identify two movements which manifestly cannot be analysed in the same way with respect to it: on the one hand, the very functioning of the structure which, in the capitalist mode of production, takes the particular form of the law of accumulation; this movement is subject to the structure, *it is only possible on condition that the latter is permanent*; in the capitalist mode of production it coincides with the 'eternal' reproduction of capitalist social relations. On the contrary, the movement of dissolution is not subject in its concept to the same 'presuppositions', it is apparently a movement of a completely different kind, since *it takes the structure as the object of transformation*. This conceptual difference shows us that where a 'dialectical logic' would quickly solve the problem, Marx holds firmly to non-dialectical logical principles (obviously, non-Hegelian-dialectical principles): what we have recognized as distinct in essence shall not become a single process. And more generally, *the concept of the transition* (from one mode of production to another) *can never be the transition of the concept* (to one other-than-itself by internal differentiation).

And yet we do have a text where Marx presents the transformation of the relations of production as a dialectical process of the negation of the negation. This is the passage on the 'Historical Tendency of Capitalist Accumulation' (*Capital*, Vol. I, Chapter XXXII). It groups into a single schema those of Marx's analyses which deal with the origin of the capitalist mode of production ('primitive accumulation'), those which deal with its peculiar movement of accumulation, and those which deal with its end, which Marx here calls its 'tendency', using this term in the way he does in Volume Three. I shall be obliged to take each of these three moments separately, according to the aggregate of the analyses that Marx devotes to them in *Capital*. But first of all, I should like to demonstrate the remarkable form of this passage, which already determines certain conclusions.

In principle, Marx's reasoning in this text implies that the *the two transitions are of the same nature*. First transition: from the individual private ownership of the means of production, based on personal labour ('the pygmy property of the many') to capitalist private ownership of the means of production, based on the exploitation of the labour of others ('the huge property of the few'). First transition, first expropriation. Second transition: from capitalist ownership to individual ownership, based on the acquisitions of the capitalist era, on co-operation and the common possession of all the means of production, including the land. Second transition, second expropriation.

These two successive negations are of the same form, which implies that all the analyses Marx devoted to primitive accumulation on the one hand (origin), to the tendency of the capitalist mode of production on the other, i.e., to its historical future, are similar in principle. But as we shall see, in *Capital* these analyses *in fact* present a remarkable disparity: the analysis of primitive accumulation seems to be relatively independent of the analysis of the mode of production strictly speaking, or even to be an enclave of 'descriptive' history in a work of economic theory (on this opposition I refer the reader to the preceding paper by Louis Althusser); on the contrary, the analysis of the historical tendency of the capitalist mode of production seems to be one moment of the analysis of the capitalist mode of production, a development of the intrinsic effects of the structure. It is this last analysis which suggests that the (capitalist) mode of production is transformed 'by itself', through the play of its own peculiar 'contradiction', i.e., through its structure.

In the passage on the 'Historical Tendency of the Capitalist Mode of Production', the two transformations are reduced to the second type, which is all the more surprising in that the text constitutes the conclusion to the analysis of the forms of primitive accumulation. The capitalist mode of production, too, appears in these formulations to be the result of the spontaneous evolution of the structure:

> This industrial regime of small independent producers . . . engenders *by itself* the material agents for its dissolution which are contained in its peculiar contradiction (it prevents the advance of production) (*Capital*, T.III, pp. 203–4; Vol. I, pp. 761–2).

> The second movement, 'This expropriation is accomplished by the action of the immanent laws of capitalist production itself, which lead to the concentration of capitals . . . The socialization of labour and the concentration of the means of production at last reach a point where they become incompatible with their capitalist integument (*Hülle*) . . . Capitalist production begets its own negation with the fatality that presides over the metamorphoses of nature' (T.III, pp. 204–5; Vol. I, p. 763).

Thus, while summing up the analyses that Marx devoted to the formation and dissolution of the capitalist mode of production, these formulations claim to give the very concept of the transition that we are looking for. They must therefore be compared with these analyses themselves. But the apparent disparity between these analyses must not be allowed to prevail over the unity postulated by the text on the 'Historical Tendency' via the forms of the 'negation of the negation': on the contrary, it must be reduced if it is to be possible to formulate the concept of the transition. (Obviously, there can be no question of maintaining that all transitions from one mode of production to another have the same concept: the concept is specified each time, like that of the mode of production itself. But just as all historical modes of production have appeared as forms of a combination of the same nature, historical transitions must have concepts *of the same theoretical nature*. This is what is strictly implied by the preceding quotations, even if they do go on to suggest that this nature is that of an external dialectical supersession.) Let us look at these 'transitions' again, one by one.

(1) PRIMITIVE ACCUMULATION: A PRE-HISTORY

The chapters which Marx devotes to 'so-called primitive accumulation' (*die sogennante ursprüngliche Akkumulation*) are presented as the solution to a problem which arose in the study of reproduction (capitalist accumulation) and which was provisionally left on one side. The movement of accumulation of capital is only possible because a surplus-value susceptible to capitalization exists. This surplus-value itself can only be the result of a previous production process, and so on, apparently indefinitely. But in given technical conditions the minimum sum of value capable of functioning as capital and its division into constant and variable capital are also given, and condition every extraction of surplus-value. The production of this original capital therefore constitutes a threshold and crossing this threshold cannot be explained by the action of the law of capitalist accumulation alone.

But it is not really just a question of measuring a sum of value. The movement of reproduction is not only continually the origin of a capitalizable surplus-value, it implies the permanence of capitalist social relations, and it is only possible on condition that they exist. The question of primitive accumulation therefore simultaneously involves the formation of capitalist social relations.

What characterizes the myth of primitive accumulation in classical economics is the *retrospective projection* of the forms of capitalist production, and of the forms of exchange and law which correspond to it: by pretending that the original minimum capital was saved by the future capitalist out of the product of his labour before being advanced in the form of wages and means of production, classical economics gave some retroactive validity to the laws of exhange between equivalents and of the ownership of the product based on the legitimate disposal of the set of factors of production. This retrospective projection does not lie in the distinction between a necessary labour and a surplus-labour, and hence between a wage and a profit, with respect to a hypothetical individual production (for these distinctions can serve conventionally to distinguish between various portions of the product even in non-capitalist modes of production, even in modes of production without exploitation where these portions do not constitute the revenues of different classes: Marx himself uses this convention, for example, in the chapter on the 'Genesis of Capitalist Ground Rent' in Volume

Three); the retrospective projection lies precisely in the idea that the formation of capital and its development are part of a single movement subject to common general laws. The basis for the bourgeois myth of primitive accumulation is therefore, in a reading of absolute reversibility, the formation of capital by the movement of an already potentially capitalist private production, and the self-generation of capital. But it would be even more accurate to say that the entire movement of capital (the movement of accumulation) thus appears as a *memory*: the memory of an initial period in which, by his personal labour and saving, the capitalist acquired the possibility of indefinitely appropriating the product of others' surplus-labour. This memory is inscribed in the form of the bourgeois *rights of property* which base the appropriation of the product of labour indefinitely on the previous ownership of the means of production:

> At first the rights of property seemed to us to be based on a man's own labour. At least, some such assumption was necessary since only commodity-owners with equal rights confronted each other, and the sole means by which a man could become possessed of the commodities of others, was by alienating his own commodities; and these could be re-placed by labour alone. Now, however, property turns out to be the right, on the part of the capitalist, to appropriate the unpaid labour of others or its product, and to be the impossibility, on the part of the labourer, of appropriating his own product. The separation of property from labour has become the necessary consequence of a law that apparently originated in their identity (*Capital*, Vol. I, pp. 583–4).

If we adopt the view-point of classical economics we must retain both faces of this 'law of appropriation' at once, the universally equal commodity right (and the hypothetical personal labour which it presupposes and induces through its own consistency) on the one hand, and on the other the exchange without equivalence which is an expression of the essence of the process of capitalist accumulation. It is in the constantly present space of these two forms that the memory of the mode of production is inscribed, the continuing present of an origin homogeneous with the current process.

As we know, this is a myth. Marx sets himself the task of proving that, historically, things did not happen like that. At the same stroke, what he calls the 'apologetic' function of the myth is exposed, expressed in the perenneal nature of the economic categories of capitalism. I shall presume that the reader has this study in mind and draw attention to its very remarkable form.

Both *a history and a pre-history* are involved in the study of 'primitive accumulation' (the name has been retained, but it now designates a quite different process). *A history*: we have discovered that the bourgeois theory of primitive capital is no more than a myth, a restrospective construction, very precisely the projection of a current structure which is expressed in the 'law of appropriation' and depends on the capitalist structure of production. It has therefore become clear that the 'memory' inscribed in this law of appropriation is a purely fictive one: it expresses a current situation in the form of a past whereas this situation's real past had another form, a completely different one, demanding an analysis. The study of primitive accumulation is this replacement of memory by history. *A pre-history*: this study reveals to us a different world at the origin of capital. Knowledge of the laws of the development of capitalism is useless to us here because this is a completely different process, not subject to the same conditions. Thus a complete rupture appears, a rupture reflected in theory, between the history of the formation of capital (of capitalist social relations) and the history of capital itself. Thus the real history of the origins of capitalism is not just different from the *myth* of origins; by the same token it is different in its conditions and principles of explanation from what has appeared to us to be the *history* of capital; it is a pre-history, i.e., a history of a different age.

But in their turn, these determinations are in no sense vague or mysterious to us, for we know that a different age is precisely *a different mode of production*. Let us call it the feudal mode of production, following Marx's historical analysis, but without asserting any law of necessary and unique succession of these modes of production, an assertion which nothing in the concept of a 'mode of production' allows us to make immediately, if the nature of the latter really is that of a varied combination. We see that to recognize the history of the origins of capital as a real pre-history is at the same time to pose the problem of the relationship between this pre-history and the history of the feudal mode of production, which, just like the history of the capitalist mode of production, can be known by the concept of its structure. In other words, we must ask ourselves whether this pre-history is identical with the history of the feudal mode of production, simply dependent on it or distinct from it. The set of conditions for this problem is summed up by Marx as follows:

> The capitalist system is based on the radical separation of the producer from the means of production. As soon as capitalist production is once established, it reproduces this separation on a continually extending scale; but as the latter is the basis of the former, it could not have been established without it. In order that the capitalist system should come into existence it is therefore necessary that the means of production have already, at least in part, been seized absolutely from the producers who had been using them to realize their own labour, and that they are already held by commodity producers who use them to speculate on the labour of others. 'primitive' accumulation, therefore, is nothing else than the *historical movement* which divorces labour from its external conditions, and it is called 'primitive' because it forms the prehistoric stage of the bourgeois world.

The capitalist economic order emerged from the entrails of the feudal economic order. The dissolution of the latter set free the constitutive elements of the former (*Capital*, T.III, pp. 154–5; Vol. I, pp. 714–15).

Marx returned to this problem several times, using the same method on each occasion, and the texts in which he did so should be assembled for an analysis of their content: in *Capital*, besides Part 8 of Volume One ('The So-called Primitive Accumulation'), the chapters in Volume Three devoted to the 'Historical Facts about Merchant's Capital', to 'Pre-Capitalist Relationships', and to the 'Genesis of Capitalist Ground Rent'. We shall find that this dispersion is not accidental. Marx himself calls Part 8, on so-called primitive accumulation, a 'sketch' (T. III, p. 156; Vol. I, p. 716, but we have various preparatory manuscripts on the same subject to which to refer, above all the already cited text on *Pre-Capitalist Economic Formations*.

All these studies have a common *retrospective* form, but in a sense which we have to specify, since we have just been criticizing the form of retrospective projection of the bourgeois myth of primitive accumulation. It is very clear from the preceding text that the study of primitive accumulation takes as its guiding thread precisely the elements which were distinguished by the analysis of the capitalist structure: these elements are grouped together here under the heading of the 'radical separation of the labourer from the means of production'. The analysis is therefore retrospective, not insofar as it projects backwards the capitalist structure itself, presupposing precisely what had to be explained, but insofar as it· depends on knowledge of the *result* of the movement. On this condition it escapes empiricism, the listing of the events which merely precede the development of capitalism: it escapes vulgar description by starting from the connexions essential to a structure, but this structure is the 'current' structure (I mean that of the capitalist system insofar as it has currently come into its own). The analysis of primitive accumulation is therefore, strictly speaking, merely *the genealogy of the elements which constitute the structure of the capitalist mode of production*. This movement is particularly clear in the construction of the text on *Pre-Capitalist Economic Formations*, which depends on the action of two concepts: that of the *presuppositions (Voraussetzungen)* of the capitalist mode of production, thought on the basis of its structure, and that of the *historical conditions (historische Bedingungen)* in which these presuppositions happen to be fulfilled. The outline history of the different modes of production in this text, rather than being a true history of their succession and transformation, is a historical *survey (sondage)* of the routes by which the separation of the labourer from his means of production and the constitution of capital as a sum of disposable value were achieved.

For this reason, the analysis of primitive accumulation is a fragmentary analysis: the genealogy is not traced on the basis of a global result, but distributively, element by element. And notably, it envisages separately the formation of the *two* main elements which enter into the capitalist structure: the 'free' labourer (the history of the separation of the producer from the means of production) and capital (the history of usury, of merchant capital, etc.). In these conditions, the analysis of primitive accumulation does not and never can coincide with the history of the previous mode or modes of production as known from their structures. The indissoluble unity possessed by the two elements in the capitalist structure is suppressed in the analysis, and it is not replaced by a comparable unity in the previous mode of production. That is why Marx writes: 'The capitalist economic order emerged from the entrails of the feudal economic order. *The dissolution of the latter set free the constitutive elements of the former.*' The dissolution of the latter, i.e., the necessary evolution of its structure, is not identical to the constitution of the former in its concept: instead of being thought at the level of the structures, the transition is thought at the level of the elements. This form explains why we are not dealing with a true history in the theoretical sense (since, as we know, such a history can only be produced by thinking the dependence of the elements with respect to a structure), but it is also the condition on which we can discover a very important fact: the relative independence of the formation of the different elements of the capitalist structure, and the *diversity of the historical roads* to this formation.

The two elements necessary for the constitution of the structure of capitalist production each have their relatively independent history. In the text of *Pre-Capitalist Economic Formations*, after running through the history of the separation of the labourer from the means of production, Marx writes:

> These, then, *on the one hand*, are the historical presuppositions for the labourer to be found as a free labourer, as objectiveless, purely subjective labour-power, confronting the objective conditions of production as his *non-property*, as someone else's property, as value existing for itself, as capital. *On the other hand*, we must now ask what conditions are necessary for him to find *a capital confronting him* (*Grundrisse*, pp. 397–8; *PCEF*, p. 99).

We ought to be even more precise, and say: for him to find a capital confronting him in the form of *money*-capital. Marx then goes on to the history of the constitution of the second element: capital in the form of money-capital, and he returns to this second genealogy in *Capital* after the chapters devoted respectively to merchant's capital and interest-bearing capital, i.e., once the elements necessary to the constitution of the capitalist structure have been analysed within that structure. The history of the separation of the labourer from the means of production does not give us money-capital ('the question remains: whence came the capitalists originally? For it is clear that the expropriation of the agricultural population creates, directly, none but great landed proprietors', *Capital*, T.III, p. 184; Vol. I, p. 742); for its part, the history of money-capital does not give the 'free' labourer (Marx notes this twice in *Capital, vis-à-vis* merchant's capital – Vol. III, pp. 321–3 – and *vis-à-vis* finance capital – Vol. III, p. 582 – and in *Pre-Capitalist Economic Formations* he writes:

> The mere existence of monetary wealth, even its conquest of a sort of supremacy, is not sufficient for this dissolution to result in capital. If it were, then ancient Rome, Byzantium, etc., would have concluded their history with free labour and capital, or rather, they would have begun a new history. There the dissolution of the old relations of property was also tied to the development of monetary wealth – of commerce, etc. However, in fact the result of this dissolution was not industry, but the domination of the countryside over the city . . . Its [capital's] original formation occurs simply because the historical process of the dissolution of an old mode of production allows value existing in the form of monetary wealth to buy the objective conditions of labour on the one hand, and to exchange the living labour of the now free workers for money on the other. *All these moments are already in existence. What separates them out is a historical process, a process of dissolution, and it is this which enables money to turn into capital – Grundrisse* pp. 405–6; *PCEF*, pp. 109–10).

In other words, the elements combined by the capitalist structure have different and independent origins. It is not one and the same movement which makes free labourers and transferable wealth. On the contrary, in the examples analysed by Marx, the formation of free labourers appears mainly in the form of transformations of agrarian structures, while the constitution of wealth is the result of merchant's capital and finance capital, whose movements take place outside those structures, 'marginally', or 'in the pores of society'.

Thus the unity possessed by the capitalist structure once it has been constituted is not found in its rear. Even when the study of the pre-history of the mode of production takes the form of a genealogy, i.e., when it aims to be explicitly and strictly dependent, *in the question that it poses*, on the elements of the constituted structure, and on their identification, which requires that the structure is known as such in its complex unity – even then the pre-history can never be the mere retrospective projection of the structure. All it requires is that the meeting should have been produced and rigorously thought, between those elements, which are identified on the basis of the result of their conjunction, and the historical field within which their peculiar histories are to be thought. *In their concepts*, the latter have nothing to do with that result, since they are defined by the structure of a *different* mode of production. In this historical field (constituted by the previous mode of production), the elements whose genealogy is being traced have precisely only a 'marginal' situation, i.e., a *non-determinant* one. To say that the modes of production are constituted as combination variants is also to say that they transpose the order of dependence, that they make certain elements move in the structure (which is the object of the theory) from a place of historical domination to a place of historical subjection. I am not saying that the problematic is complete in this form, that it leads us to the threshold of a solution: but at any rate, this is how we can disengage it from the way in which Marx practices the analysis of primitive accumulation, explicitly closing all the roads ideology might take.

But already at this point, we can introduce a different consequence: it is the fact that the analysis of primitive accumulation, in its genealogical form, is adequate for one basic characteristic of the process of formation of the structure: the *diversity of the historical roads* by which the elements of the structure are constituted, by which they lead to the point at which they can join together and constitute that structure (the structure of a mode of production) by coming under its jurisdiction, *becoming its effects* (thus the forms of merchant's capital and finance capital only become forms of capital in the strict sense on the 'new bases' of the capitalist mode of production – see *Capital*, Vol. III, pp. 322-3 and 583-4). Or again, to return to the terms mentioned above: the same set of *presuppositions* corresponds to several series of *historical conditions*. Here we are touching on a point which is all the more important in that Marx's analyses in Volume One of *Capital* have led to misunderstandings, despite all his precautions: these analyses are explicitly the analyses of *certain* forms, certain 'methods' among others, of primitive accumulation, found in the history of Western Europe and mainly in that of England. Marx explained his position on this very point very clearly in his letter to Vera Zasulich of 8 March 1881 (the different drafts of which need to be read). There are therefore a plurality of processes of constitution of the structure which *all reach the same result*: their particularity depends on each occasion on the structure of the historical field in which they are situated, i.e., on the structure of the existing mode of production. The 'methods' of primitive accumulation which Marx describes in the English example must be related to the specific characteristics of the mode of production which is dominant in that particular case (the feudal mode of production), and notably to the systematic utilization of extra-economic (legal, political and military) power, which, as I recalled briefly above, was founded in the specific nature of the feudal mode of production. More generally, the result of the transformation process depends on the nature of the historical environment, of the existing mode of production: Marx shows this for merchant's capital (*Capital*, Vol. III, pp. 326-7). In a text such as *Pre-Capitalist Economic Formations*, Marx describes *three distinct forms* of constitution of the free labourer (of the separation of the producer from his means of production), which constitute different historical processes, correspond to specific earlier forms of property, and are designated as so many different forms of 'negation' (*Grundrisse*, pp. 398-9, *PCEF*, pp. 99-101). Further on, and this list is referred to again in *Capital*, he similarly describes three distinct forms of the constitution of money-capital (which obviously have no one-to-one correspondence with the three forms of constitution of the free labourer):

> There is, consequently, a three-fold transition: *First*, the merchant becomes directly an industrial capitalist. This is true in crafts based on trade, especially crafts producing luxuries and imported by merchants, together with raw materials and labourers from foreign lands, as in Italy from Constantinople in the fifteenth century. *Second*, the merchant turns the small masters into his middlemen, or buys directly from the independent producer, leaving him nominally independent and his mode of production unchanged. *Third*, the industrialist becomes a merchant and produces directly for the wholesale market (*Capital*, Vol. III, p. 330).

(We should also add the forms of usury which constitute the pre-history of interest-bearing capital and one of the processes of constitution of capital.)

The relative independence and historical variety of the constitution processes of capital are gathered together by Marx into a single word: the constitution of the structure is a 'find' (*trouvaille*); the capitalist mode of production is constituted by 'finding already there' (*vorfinden*) the elements which its structure combines (*Grundrisse*, p. 407; *PCEF*, p. 111). This find obviously does not imply chance: it means that the formation of the capitalist mode of production is completely indifferent to the origin and genesis of the elements which it needs, 'finds' and 'combines'. Thus it is impossible for the reasoning whose movement I have retraced to be looped into a circle: the genealogy is not the other side of a genesis. Instead of re-uniting the structure and the history of its formation, the genealogy *separates* the result from its pre-history. It is not the old structure which itself has transformed itself, on the contrary, it has really 'died out' as such ('All in all, the entire guild system – both master and journeyman – dies out, where the capitalist and the labourer emerge', *Grundrisse*, p. 405; *PCEF*, p. 109). The analysis of primitive accumulation thus brings us into the presence of the radical *absence of memory* which characterizes history (memory being only the reflection of history in certain pre-determined sites – ideology or even law – and as such, anything but a faithful reflection).

(2) TENDENCY AND CONTRADICTION OF THE MODE OF PRODUCTION

Here I shall set aside this analysis of primitive accumulation, although I have not drawn every consequence from it, and turn to the study of the second movement, that of the dissolution of the capitalist mode of production (which I am using here as a paradigm). This second analysis deals with everything Marx tells us about the historical *tendency* of the capitalist mode of production, the peculiar movement of its *contradiction*, the development of the *antagonisms* implied by the necessity of its structure, and all that can be revealed in that structure of the exigency of a new organization of social production. If, as I have said, it is true that these two analyses have, *by right*, an object of the same nature (the transition from one mode of production to another) – which identity of object is perfectly clear in the text on the 'Historical Tendency of Capitalist Accumulation' (*Capital*, T.III, pp. 203–5; Vol. I, pp. 761–5) – it is no less clear that Marx treats them differently. The difference lies not just in the literary realization (on the one hand – for primitive accumulation – a historical analysis which is fairly extensive and detailed, but dissociated from the body of the exposition and apparently less systematic; on the other – the dissolution of capitalism – insights only, but formulated in general terms and organically linked to the analysis of the capitalist mode of production), it is the expression of two complementary theoretical situations: on the one hand, we have identified the elements whose genealogy has to be retraced, but we do not have in concept the knowledge of the historical field which is the theatre of this genealogy (the structure of the previous mode of production); on the other, we do have the knowledge of this historical field (the capitalist mode of production itself) and nothing else. Before formulating a complete problematic, we must therefore carry out a second preliminary reading.

In the first place, we can establish the strict theoretical equivalence of a number of 'movements' analysed by Marx at the level of the aggregate social capital: the concentration of capital (of the ownership of the means of production), the socialization of the productive forces (by the application of science and the development of co-operation), the extension of capitalist social relations to all branches of production and the formation of one world market, the constitution of an industrial reserve army (relative over-population), and the progressive decline in the average rate of profit. The 'historical tendency' of capitalist accumulation is identical in principle with the 'tendential law' analysed in Volume Three, which Marx calls the 'real tendency of capitalist production', and of which he writes:

> The progressive tendency of the general rate of profit to fall is, therefore, *just an expression peculiar to the capitalist mode of production of the progressive development of the social productivity of labour . . . It is thereby proved a logical necessity proceeding from the nature of the capitalist mode of production*, that in its development the general average rate of surplus-value must express itself in a falling general rate of profit (*Capital*, Vol. III, p. 209 – modified).

In fact, the tendency for the average rate of profit to fall is merely the immediate effect of the rise in the average organic composition of capital, of the constant capital expended as means of production compared with the variable capital expended as labour-power, which is the expression of the peculiar movement of accumulation. To say that all these movements are theoretically equivalent is therefore to say that they are different expressions in a single tendency, dissociated and expounded separately merely in the interests of the *order of exposition* (proof) of *Capital*. But their separation expresses no succession: from the view-point of the *system* of concepts, we are dealing with the same movement of analysis of the structure.

This movement is none other than the movement that Marx calls *the development of the contradiction* peculiar to the capitalist mode of production. Defined first in a very general way as the 'contradiction' between the social-ization of the productive forces (which defines their development in the capitalist mode of production) and the character of the relations of production (private ownership of the means of production), it is then specified *in the forms peculiar to the capitalist mode of production* as the contradiction between an increase in the *mass* of value produced, and hence of profit, and a decrease in the *rate* of profit. But the search for profit is the sole motor of the develop-ment of production in the capitalist mode of production.

But what kind of movement is this? It seems that we could define it as a *dynamics* of the system, whereas the analysis of the complex combination which constitutes the structure of the mode of production fulfils the function of a *statics*, This pair of concepts does enable us to account for the movement insofar as it depends solely on the internal connexions of the structure, insofar as it is the *effect* of that structure, i.e., *its existence in time*. Knowledge of this movement implies no other concepts than those of production and reproduction, in the form peculiar to the historical mode of production considered. Thus the 'contradiction' is not something different from the structure itself, it is indeed 'immanent' to it, as Marx says: but inversely, the contradiction by itself includes a dynamics: it is only given as a contradiction, i.e., it only produces contradictory effects in the temporal existence of the structure. It is therefore perfectly accurate to say, as Marx also does, that the contradiction 'develops' in the historical movement of capitalism.

The question we must examine can then be formulated as follows: is the dynamics of the structure at the same time – in the same 'time' – *its history*? In other words, is this movement at the same time a movement *towards the historical future* of capitalism? (and more generally towards the future of the mode of production considered, since each mode has its own specific 'contradiction', i.e., 'an expression peculiar to' it 'of the progressive develop-ment of the social productivity of labour'). And since the relationship be-tween the statics and the dynamics allows us to make the development of the contradiction the very movement which produces the effects of the structure, can we also say that it constitutes the 'motor' of its supersession? The identity – or difference – which we are looking for between this dynamics and this history is obviously *the unity of the concepts*, and cannot be satisfied by the coincidence provided *ipso facto* by a merely empirical temporality: if the development of the contradiction is inscribed in the chronology of a succession, it is quite simply that history. Since, on the contrary, we want to construct the relationship between these two concepts, Marx's text forces us here to start from the most explicit concept (the dynamics of the development of the structure) in order to go on to, or attempt to go on to, the other (its historical future).

If we try to define more accurately what Marx meant by the 'contradictory' nature and 'tendency' of the mode of production, his repeated formulations confront us with the problem of the relationship between the structure and its effects. The 'tendency' is defined by a restriction, a diminution, a postponement or a travesty of effectivity. Tendency is a law 'whose absolute action is checked, retarded and weakened, by counteracting causes (*entgegenwirkende Ursachen*)' (*Capital*, Vol. III, p. 229 – modified), or even one whose effects (*Wirkung, Verwirklichung, Durchführung*) are annulled (*aufheben*) (p. 227) by these opposed causes. The tendency character thus appears first of all as a failure of the law, but an extrinsic failure, caused by the obstacle of external circumstances which do not depend on it, and whose origins are not explained (for the time being). The exteriority of the opposed causes is enough to justify the fact that their effectivity is purely negative: the result of their intervention is not to *alter* the result of the law itself, the nature of its effects, but merely the chronology of their production; we are thus led to define a tendency as something which is only realized *in the long run*, and the retarding causes as a set of empirical circumstances which merely *mask* the essence of the process of development. 'Thus', writes Marx, 'the law acts only as a tendency. And it is only under certain circumstances and only after long periods that its effects become strikingly prounced' (*Capital*, Vol. III, p. 233).

But this definition is unsatisfactory, because, in its empiricist and mechanistic character, it is a return precisely to what Marx criticized in the economists, particularly Ricardo: the study of 'factors' called 'independent' because of an inability to find their common origin in the unity of a structure, a study which belongs to the 'exoteric' or 'vulgar' side of political economy. It also ignores Marx's systematic use of the term tendency to designate *the laws of production themselves*, or else the laws of the movement of production insofar as this movement depends on its structure. In the Preface to the first German edition of *Capital*, Marx wrote:

> It is not a question of the more or less complete development of the social antagonisms that result from the natural laws of capitalist production, but *of these laws themselves, of these tendencies* manifesting and realizing themselves with iron necessity (*Capital*, T.I, p. 18; Vol. I, p. 8).

And also in Volume One, to formulate the law of the production of relative surplus-value:

> The general result is treated, here, as if it were the immediate result directly aimed at. When a capitalist cheapens shirts by increasing the productivity of labour, he does not necessarily aim thereby to reduce

the value of labour-power and shorten the portion of the day in which the worker works for himself. But it is only insofar as he ultimately contributes to this result, that he contributes to raising the general rate of surplus-value. *The general and necessary tendencies (Tendenzen) of capital must be distinguished from the forms in which they appear (Erscheinungsformen).*

It is not our intention to consider here the way in which *the immanent* laws of capitalist production (*immanente Gesetze*) appear in the external movements of capitals, assert themselves as coercive laws of competition, and thereby impose themselves on the capitalist as the motives of their operations (*Capital*, T.II, p. 10; Vol. I, p. 316).

Here it seems that Marx's term 'tendency' designates not a restriction on the law due to external circumstances, which necessarily belong to the sphere of 'appearances', of 'surface' phenomena, *but the law itself*, independently of any extrinsic circumstance. If Marx's vocabulary is rigorous here, we may think that it is only as a first appearance that the law of the development of production (expressed in the fall in the rate of profit, etc.) is externally limited.

But if we examine the 'causes' hindering the realization of the tendency one by one, we find that they are all *either the immediate effects* of the structure *or determined* by the structure which sets limits (*Grenzen*) on the variation of their effects. Under the first heading we can list the increasing intensity of exploitation, the depreciation of existing capital, relative over-population and its restriction to less developed branches of production, the increase in the scale of production (and the creation of an external market); under the second, the depression of wages below the value of labour-power. Now, it is peculiar to all causes which are immediate effects of the structure that they are *ambivalent*: so much so that all the causes that counteract the action of the law are at the same time the causes which produce its effects:

> But since the same causes which raise the rate of surplus-value (even a lengthening of the working-time is a result of large-scale industry) tend to decrease the labour-power employed by a certain capital, it follows that they also tend to reduce the rate of profit and to retard this reduction (*Capital*, Vol. III, p. 229 – modified).

Similarly, the depreciation of the existing capital is linked to the increase in the productivity of labour, which cheapens the elements of constant capital, and thus prevents the value of constant capital from increasing in the same proportion as its material volume, etc. In a general way, if the aggregate social capital is considered, 'the same causes which produce a tendency in the general rate of profit to fall, also call forth counter-effects' (*Capital*, Vol. III, p. 233 – modified). This is a crucial point, for it enables us to establish the fact that the reduction of the law of development to the status of a *tendency* is not a determination external to that law, influencing only the chronology of its effects, but *an intrinsic determination of the production of its effects*. The effect of the opposed causes, i.e., of the law itself, is not to delay the historical effects of capitalist production, but to determine a specific rhythm for the production of those effects, a determination which only appears *negatively* (as a 'restriction', etc.) with reference to the ahistorical absolute of a 'free', 'unlimited' growth of the productivity of labour (leading to an increase in the organic composition of capital and a fall in the rate of profit). Moreover, the definition of the mode of action peculiar to the structure, which includes the reduction of the apparent exteriority of the opposing causes, is once again linked to the consideration of the social capital (or what comes to the same thing, of the 'individual capital as an aliquot part of the total capital' – Vol. III, p. 216), which is the theoretical support for Volume One and the first half of Volume Two, i.e., the consideration of a capital in the theoretical 'synchrony' which I discussed with respect to *reproduction*. All the reasoning that enables Marx to establish the existence and level of a general average rate of profit depends on such a synchrony (Marx calls it a simultaneity) in which the addition together of the capitals portion by portion is possible by definition; if we were obliged to ask to what extent does the cheapening of the means of production one by one hinder the value of constant capital from increasing with respect to that of the corresponding variable capital, it would become impossible to establish such a law. The impure theoretical status of the 'causes' which 'counteract' the fall in the general rate of profit merely reveals, in a number of formulations (which I have cited), Marx's difficulty in thinking this 'synchrony' explicitly, insofar as it was a matter of a *law of development* of the structure. But in fact he closes the circle nevertheless, since *it is the tendential fall in the rate of profit which arouses the competition of capitals, i.e., the mechanism by which the equalization of profits* and the formation of the general rate of profit *are actually achieved* (*Capital*, Vol. III, p. 250). (At the same stroke, this clarifies and limits the place of competition, for Marx excludes the analysis of its mechanism from the analysis of capital in general, since it merely ensures this equalization without determining the *level* at which it is established, just as it did for the market price of a particular commodity.) The development of the structure according to a tendency, i.e., a law which does not only (mechanically) include the production of effects, but also the production of effects according to a specific rhythm, therefore means that *the definition of the specific internal temporality* of the structure is part of the analysis of that structure itself.

It is now clear what is 'contradictory' about tendency, which enables us to illuminate the true status of contradiction in Marx. Marx defines the terms between which there is a contradiction as *the contradictory effects of a single cause*:

> Thus, the same development of the social productiveness of labour
> expresses itself with the progress of capitalist production on the one

hand in a tendency of the rate of profit to fall progressively and, on the other, in a progressive growth of the absolute mass of the appropriated surplus-value, or profit; so that on the whole a relative decrease of variable capital and profit is accompanied by an absolute increase of both. *This two-fold effect* (*doppelseitige Wirkung*), as we have seen, can express itself only in a growth of the total capital at a pace more rapid than that at which the rate of profit falls . . . To say that the mass of profit is determined by two factors – first, the rate of profit, and, secondly, the mass of capital invested at this rate, is *mere tautology*. It is therefore but a corollary of this tautology to say that there is a *possibility* for the mass of profit to grow even though the rate of profit may fall at the same time. It does not help us one step further . . . But if *the same causes* which make the rate of profit fall, entail the accumulation, i.e., the formation of additional capital, and if each additional capital employs additional labour and produces additional surplus-value; if, on the other hand, the mere fall in the rate of profit implies that the constant capital and with it the total old capital, have increased, then this process ceases to be mysterious (*Capital*, Vol. III, pp. 219–21).

(Obviously, it is one and the same thing to say that the fall in the rate of profit is slowed down by the growth in the scale of production, as above, or to say, as here, that the mass of accumulation is relatively diminished by the fall in the rate of profit.) This very important definition includes both the refutation of an empirical notion of contradiction (which Marx links to Ricardo's name – *Capital*, Vol. III, p. 243), and the limitation of its role. The empiricism of classical economics could only reveal contradictory terms as in 'peaceful coexistence', i.e., in the relative autonomy of distinct phenomena, e.g., successive 'phases' of development dominated inversely by one or other of the contradictory tendencies. . . . Marx, on the contrary, produced the theoretical concept of the *unity* of the two contradictory terms (which he calls a 'combination' here too: 'the tendency of the rate of profit to fall is combined with – *ist verbunden mit* – a tendency of the rate of surplus-value to rise, hence with a tendency for the rate of labour exploitation to rise' – *Capital*, Vol. III, p. 234 – modified), i.e., he produces the knowledge of the contradiction's foundation in the nature of the structure (of capitalist production). Classical economics reasons from independent 'factors' whose interaction 'may' induce such and such a result: the whole problem is therefore to measure these variations and relate them empirically to other variations (the same is true of prices, and of the values of commodities, which are supposed to depend on the variation of certain factors: wages, average profit, etc.). Marx does not regard the law (or tendency) as a *law of variation* in the size of the effects, but as a *law of production* of the effects themselves: it determines these effects on the basis of the *limits* within which they can vary, and which do not depend on this variation (the same is true of wages, the working day, prices, and the different fractions into which surplus-value is divided); *it is these limits alone which are determined as effects of the structure, and in consequence they precede the variation instead of being its average resultant.* It is by the law of its production from a single cause that contradiction is given us here, and not in the variation of its result (the level of accumulation).

But this definition also includes the limitation of the role of contradiction, i.e., its situation of *dependence* with respect to the cause (the structure): there is only a contradiction between the effects, the cause is not divided in itself, it cannot be analysed in antagonistic terms. Contradiction is therefore not original, but derivative. The effects are organized in a series of particular contradictions, but the process of production of these effects is in no way contradictory: the increase in the *mass* of profit (and hence the scale of accumulation) and the decrease in its *rate* (hence the peculiar speed of accumulation) are the expression of one and the same increasing movement of the quantity of means of production set to work by capital. That is why only an *appearance of contradiction* is found in the knowledge of the cause: 'this law', says Marx, 'this inner and necessary connexion between two *seeming* contradictions' (Vol. III, p. 220); the inner and necessary connexion which defines the law of production of the effects of the structure excludes logical contradiction. From this point of view, the 'two-fold effect' is thus merely the 'double-edged' (*zwieschlächtig* – Vol. III, p. 215) nature of the law. It is particularly noteworthy that here, in order to express the derivative and dependent character of the contradiction between certain effects of the structure, we find Marx returning to the same term that he used at the beginning of *Capital* to designate the false contradiction '*in adjecto*' of the commodity (on this point see Pierre Macherey's paper).[22] For their part, the effects present a *simple* contradiction (a term-by-term contradiction: relative over-population and relative over-production, etc.) and one *distributed* into several contradictory aspects or component contradictions which, for all that, do not constitute an overdetermination, but simply have inverse effects on the scale of accumulation.

Just as the cause which produces the contradiction is not itself contradictory, so the result of the contradiction is always a certain *equilibrium*, even when this equilibrium is attained by way of a *crisis*. Thus it seems that contradiction has a status analogous to that of competition in the movement of the structure: it determines neither its tendency nor its limits, rather it is a local, derivative phenomenon, whose effects are pre-determined in the structure itself:

> These different influences may at one time operate predominantly side by side in space, and at another succeed one another in time. From time to time the conflict of antagonistic agencies finds vent in crisis. The crises

[22] *Lire le Capital*, first edition, Vol. I.

are always but momentary and forcible solutions of the existing contradictions. They are violent eruptions which for a time restore the disturbed equilibrium. . . . The periodical depreciation of existing capital – *one of the means immanent in the capitalist mode of production* to check the fall of the rate of profit and hasten accumulations of capital-value through formation of new capital – disturbs the given conditions, within which the process of circulation and reproduction of capital takes place, and is therefore accompanied by sudden stoppages and crises in the production process. . .

The ensuring stagnation of production would have prepared – within capitalistic limits – a subsequent expansion of production. *And thus the cycle would run its course anew* (*Capital*, Vol. III, pp. 244 and 250 – modified).

Thus the only intrinsic result of the contradiction, which is completely immanent to the economic structure, does not tend towards the supersession of the contradiction, but to the perpetuation of its conditions. The only result is the *cycle* of the capitalist mode of production (the crisis is cyclical because the reproduction of the aggregate capital depends on the turnover of fixed capital – see *Capital*, Vol. II, p. 186 – but it is possible to say metaphorically that the crisis manifests the circle in which the whole mode of production moves with an immobile movement).

Marx also says that the crisis reveals the *barriers* (*Schranken*) of the mode of production:[23]

Capitalist production seeks continually to overcome these immanent barriers (*immanenten Schranken*), but overcomes them only by means which again place these barriers in its way and on a more formidable scale.

The *real barrier* (*die wahre Schranke*) of capitalist production *is capital itself* (*Capital*, Vol. III, p. 245).

The 'limits' towards which the movement of the mode of production tends (its dynamics) are not therefore a question of a ladder, of a *threshold* to attain. If the tendency cannot pass these limits, it is because they are inside it, and as such *never reached*: in its movement it carries them with it, they coincide with the causes which make it a 'mere' tendency, i.e., they are simultaneously its actual conditions of possibility. To say that the capitalist mode of production has internal limits is quite simply to say that the mode of production is not a 'mode of production in general', but a *delimited, determinate* mode of production:

The capitalist mode of production meets in the development of its productive forces a barrier which has nothing to do with the production

---

[23] These *limits* must not be confused with the *limits of variation* (*Grenzen*) which we discussed above.

of wealth as such: and this peculiar barrier testifies to (*bezeugt*) the limitations (*Beschränktheit*) and to the merely historical, transitory character of the capitalist mode of production; testifies that for the pro-production of wealth, it is not an absolute mode, moreover, that at a certain stage (*auf gewisser Stufe*) it rather conflicts with its further development (*Capital*, Vol. III, p. 237).

(The term wealth should always be regarded as strictly synonymous with use-value.)

These limits are therefore the same as those whose effects we have already met in the determination of the tendency: a mode of production of wealth in itself does not exist, i.e., there only exists a determinate type of development of the productive forces, depending on the nature of the mode of production. The rise in the productivity of labour is limited by the nature of the relations of production which make it into a means of formation of relative surplus-value. For its part, the extorsion of surplus-value is limited by the productivity of labour (within the limits of variation of the working day, the relationship between necessary labour and surplus-labour is given by this productivity at each moment). What we see here therefore is not the contradiction, but the *complexity* of the mode of production, which was defined at the beginning of this exposition as a double articulation of the mode of production ('productive forces', relations of ownership of the means of production): the internal limits of the mode of production are none other than the *limitation of each of these two connexions by the other*, i.e., the form of their 'correspondence' or of the 'real subsumption' of the productive forces beneath the relations of production.

But if the limits of the mode of production are internal ones, they only determine what they affirm and not what they *deny* (i.e., via the idea of an 'absolute mode of production', a mode of production 'of wealth in itself', the possibility of all the other modes of production which have their own peculiar internal limitations). Only in this sense do they imply the transition to a different mode of production (the historical, transitional character of the existing mode of production): they designate the necessity for a way out and a different mode of production whose delimitation is absolutely absent from them; and since the limits consist of the 'correspondence' which articulates the two connexions within the complex structure of the mode of production, the movement suppressing these limits implies the supression of the correspondence.

But it is also clear that the transformation of these limits does not simply belong to the time of the dynamics. Indeed, if the effects within the structure of production do not by themselves constitute any challenge to the limits (e.g., the crisis, which is 'the mechanism [with which] capitalist production spontaneously gets rid of the obstacles that it happens on occasion to create' – *Capital*) there may be *one of the conditions* (the 'material basis') of a *different result,* outside the structure of production: it is this other result which Marx suggests marginally in his exposition when he shows that the movement of production produces, by the concentration of production and the growth of the proletariat, one of the conditions of the particular form which the class struggle takes in capitalist society. But the analysis of this struggle and of the political social relations which it implies is not part of the study of the structure of production. The analysis of the transformation of the limits therefore requires a theory of the different times of the economic structure and of the class struggle, and of their articulation in the social structure. To understand how they can join together in the unity of a *conjuncture* (e.g., how, if other conditions are fulfilled, the crisis can be the occasion for a – revolutionary – transformation of the structure of production) depends on this, as Althusser has shown in an earlier study ('Contradiction and Over-determination', in *For Marx*).

(3) DYNAMICS AND HISTORY

The preceding analyses constitute a number of still disjointed moments of the problematic within which it is possible to think theoretically the transition from one mode of production to another. It will not be possible to *articulate* this problematic effectively, i.e., to produce the *unity* of the questions which have to be answered, until we succeed in situating with respect to one another the concepts that we have proposed up to this point (history, gene-alogy, synchrony – diachrony, dynamics, tendency) and in defining differ-entially their peculiar objects.

All these concepts, which are still largely descriptive and will remain so precisely so long as they are not articulated, seem to be so many conceptual-izations of *historical time.* In an earlier paper, Althusser showed that, in any theory of history (whether scientific or ideological), there was a rigorous and necessary correlation between the structure of the *concept of history* peculiar to that theory (a structure itself dependent on the structure of the concept of the social *totality* peculiar to that theory), on the one hand, and the *concept of temporality* in which that theory of history thinks the 'changes', 'movements', 'events', or, more generally, the phenomena which appertain to its object, on the other. The fact that this *theory* is usually absent as such, that it is reflected in the form of a non-theory, i.e., of empiricism, does not contradict such a demonstration. The structure of temporality is then quite simply that provided by the ruling ideology, and it is never reflected in its function as a presupposition. We have even found that in Hegel the structure of historical temporality, being dependent, from the point of view of the articulation of the system, on the structure of the simple Hegelian totality, i.e. of the expressive totality, merely took up on its own accord the very form of the empiricist ideological conception of time, providing it with its concept and theoretical foundation.

At the same time, we have found that the form of this time was not only the continuous linearity, but also, by way of consequence, the *uniqueness* of time. Because time is unique, its present has the structure of contemporaneity, and all the moments whose chronological simultaneity can be established must also necessarily be determined as the moments of one and the same current whole, they must necessarily belong to the same history. Here we should note that, in this ideological conception, the peculiar form of time precedes the determination of historical objects in relation to it: the order and duration of this time always precede any determination of a phenomenon as 'unfolding over time' and thereby as a historical phenomenon. Of course, the effective estimation of order or duration always presupposes a connexion with or reference to the temporality of certain objects, but the form of their possibility is always already given. In reality, this is to move in a circle, since it is to admit the structure of a time which is merely the effect, either of a perception, or of an ideological conception of the social totality. But this movement of real dependence, before the location of 'historical' phenomena in time, is not thought as such in the representation of time which serves as its premiss, and it is possible to take the short cut of *discovering* (in reality, rediscovering) in the determinations of history the presupposed structure of this time. From this movement we get the determination of the historical object as an *event*, present even when it is doubted, i.e., in the idea that there are *not only* events, i.e., not only 'short'-term phenomena, but also non-events, i.e., *long events, long-term permanences* (which are wrongly christened 'structures').

If we then remember the problematic within which Marx originally thought his theoretical undertaking, but which was not peculiarly his problematic, the problematic of *periodization*, we can draw several conclusions. If we pose the problem of the transition from one mode of production to another solely in the framework of this problematic, it is impossible for us to escape the form of unique linear time: we must think the effects of the structure of each mode of production on an equal footing with the phenomena of transition, situating them in the unique time which serves as a *framework* or *common support* for every possible historical determination. We have no right to establish differences in principle or method between analyses of the effects of a mode of production and analyses of the transition between two modes of production which succeed one another or coincide with one another in the framework of this time, and we can only distinguish the movements by determinations of the 'structure' of this time: long-term, short-term, continuity, intermittency, etc. The time of periodization is therefore a time for which any true diversity is impossible: the supplementary determinations which are *inserted* in the course of a historical sequence, e.g., during transitions from one mode of production to another, are part of the same time as them, *and have the movement of their production in common with them.*

Moreover, a superficial reading of Marx is more than likely not to dissipate the forms of this illusion, if it is content to take the different 'times' implied by the analysis in *Capital* as *so many descriptive aspects or subordinate determinations of time in general*. It would then be possible to try practising the fundamental operation implied by the ideological theory of time: *the insertion of the different times one within another*. It would be possible to inscribe the segmented times (labour times, production times, circulation times) in *cycles* (the cyclical process of capital); these cycles themselves would necessarily be complex cycles, cycles of cycles, because of the different turnover speeds of the different elements of capital, but as a whole they in their turn could be inserted in the general movement of capitalist reproduction (accumulation), which Marx, following Sismondi, describes as a *spiral*; and finally this 'spiral' would manifest a general *tendency*, an orientation – precisely that of the transition from one mode of production to another, of the succession of the modes of production and of periodization. In such a reading the *harmonization* of the different 'times' and the imbrication of their forms would obviously raise no difficulties in principle, for their *possibility* would already be inscribed in the uniqueness of time in general which serves as a support for all these movements. The only difficulties would be difficulties of *application*, difficulties in identifying the phases and in forecasting the transitions.

What is most noteworthy in such a reading – which is, as we shall see, not just a purely polemical expository device on my part – is that it necessarily implies that each 'moment' of time is thought simultaneously as a *determination* of all the intermediate times which have been inserted into one another in this way – whether this determination is immediate, or, on the contrary, merely mediated. And to draw the most extreme consequence straightaway, it is absolutely consistent with this conception to determine a given time during which the worker expends his labour-power as a certain *quantity of social labour, as a moment of the cycle* of the production process (in which capital exists in the form of productive capital), as a *moment of the reproduction* of social capital (of capitalist accumulation) and finally as a *moment of the history* of the capitalist mode of production (which tends towards its transformation, however distant the latter may be).

Such an ideological reading provides the base from which it is possible to characterize the whole Marxist theory of the economic structure as a *dynamics*. The concept has been re-introduced in this way in order to oppose Marx to classical and modern political economy, while situating both on the same terrain, and assigning them the same 'economic' object: Marx thus becomes one of the innovators, perhaps the main one, who have introduced 'dynamic' theory into political economy (see for example Granger's *Méthodologie économique*). This has made it possible to present classical and neoclassical economics as theories of *economic equilibrium*, i.e., of a 'statics' of the connexions of the economic structure; while Marx, on the contrary, is supposed never to have seen the study of equilibrium as anything more than a provisional moment, operational in scope, an expository simplification; the essential object of Marx's analysis is *the time of the evolution of the economic structure*, analysed in its successive components, the different 'times' of *Capital*:

> As for the particular object of Marx's study, capitalist production, it is necessarily presented as a dynamic process. Capitalist *accumulation* is the object of Volume One of *Capital*. The notion of a static equilibrium is obviously *a priori* incorrect as a description of this phenomenon. The 'simple reproduction' of capital is *already a temporal process*; but it is little more than a first abstraction. The system is characterized precisely by 'reproduction on an extended scale', the growth and continuous qualitative metamorphosis of capital through the accumulation of surplus-value. The various forms of crisis appear as a chronic disorder of the system, not as accidents. *The general picture of economic reality is thus made totally dynamic* (G. G. Granger: *Méthodologie économique*, p. 98).

Such an interpretation, in which the dynamics of the capitalist system is itself a moment, a local aspect of the 'claim that the laws of the economy are relative and evolutionary in character', is really an example of the structure of *temporal insertion* that I outlined above. The concepts of history and dynamics then become twins, one popular (history), the other learned (dynamics), since the second expresses very accurately the determination of the historical movement on the basis of a structure. This makes it possible to add a third term to these two: *diachrony*, which does not produce any new knowledge here, since it simply expresses the form of unique linear temporality which is implied by the identification of the first two concepts.

But in reality, such a reading of Marx completely ignores the mode of constitution of the concepts of temporality and history in the theory of *Capital*. It may have been possible to adopt (or interpret) these concepts in their normal sense, i.e., in their ideological use, in a text such as the Preface to *A Contribution*, from which we started: there they merely have the function of *registering* and *designating a theoretical field which has not yet been thought in its structure*. But in the analysis of *Capital*, as our studies of *primitive accumulation* and of the *tendency* of the mode of production have shown, they are produced separately and differentially: their unity, instead of being presupposed in an always already given conception of time in general, must be constructed out of an initial diversity which reflects the complexity of the whole which is analysed. On this point it is possible to generalize from the way Marx posed the problem of the unity of the different cycles of the individual capitals in a complex cycle of the social capital: this unity must be constructed as an 'intertwining' whose nature is initially problematic. On this, Marx writes:

Therefore, the manner in which the various component parts of the aggregate social capital, of which the individual capitals are but constituents functioning independently, mutually replace one another in the process of circulation – in regard to capital as well as surplus-value – is *not ascertained from the simple intertwinings of the metamorphoses in the circulation of commodities* – intertwinings which the acts of capital circulation have in common with all other circulation of commodities. *That requires a different method of investigation.* Hitherto one has been satisfied with uttering phrases which upon closer analysis are found to contain nothing but indefinite ideas borrowed from the intertwining of metamorphoses common to all commodity circulation (*Capital*, Vol. II, p. 115).

We know that this '*different method of investigation*' which peculiarly constitutes the analysis of the reproduction of the total social capital, leads to a paradoxical result: a synchronic structure of the relation between the different sectors of social production, in which the peculiar form of a *cycle* has completely disappeared. But this method alone allows us to think the intertwining of the different individual production cycles. In the same way, the complex unity of the different 'times' of historical analysis, those which depend on the permanence of the social relations and those in which is inscribed the transformation of the social relations, is initially problematic: it must be constructed by a '*different method of investigation*'.

The relationship of theoretical dependence between the concepts of *time* and *history* is thus *inverted* with respect to the preceding form, which belongs to empiricist or Hegelian history, or to a reading of *Capital* which implicitly reintroduces empiricism or Hegelianism. Instead of the structures of history depending on those of time, it is the structures of temporality which depend on those of history. The structures of temporality and their specific differences are *produced in the process of constitution of the concept of history*, as so many necessary determinations of its object. Thus the definition of temporality and its various forms becomes *explicitly* necessary; similarly, the necessity of thinking the relationship (the harmony) between the different movements and the different times becomes a basic necessity for theory.

In Marx's theory, therefore, a synthetic concept of time can never be a pre-given, but only a *result*. The preceding analysis in this paper allows us to anticipate this result to a certain extent, and to propose a differential definition of concepts which have been confused until now. We have seen that the analysis of the relations which appertain to a determinate mode of production and constitute its structure must be thought as the constitution of a theoretical 'synchrony': this is reflected with respect to the mode of production by Marx in the concept of *reproduction*. The analysis of all the peculiar effects of the structure of the mode of production is necessarily part of this synchrony. The concept of *diachrony* will therefore be reserved for the time of the *transition* from one mode of production to another, i.e., for the time determined by the replacement and transformation of the relations of production which constitute the double articulation of the structure. Thus it appears that the 'genealogies' contained in the analyses of primitive accumulation are *elements of diachronic analysis*: and thus the *difference* in problematic and methods between the chapters of *Capital* devoted to primitive accumulation and all the others, irrespectively of their degree of theoretical perfection, has been established as more than a mere difference in style or literary form. This difference is a consequence of the strict distinction between 'synchrony' and 'diachrony', and we have met another example of this in what goes before, an example to which I shall return: when I analysed the forms of the two connexions (property, 'real appropriation') peculiar to the capitalist mode of production and the relationship between them, we observed a 'chronological dislocation' in the constitution of these two forms, the capitalist form of property ('capitalist relations of production') chronologically preceding the capitalist form of real appropriation ('capitalism's productive forces'); this dislocation was reflected by Marx in his distinction between the 'formal subsumption' of labour to capital and its 'real subsumption'. At the time, I remarked that this chronological dislocation was *suppressed as such* in the synchronic analysis of the structure of the mode of production, that it was then indifferent to the theory. In fact, this dislocation, which then purely and simply disappears, can only be thought in a theory of the diachrony; it constitutes a *relevant problem for diachronic analysis.* (Here we should note that the expressions 'diachronic analysis' and 'diachronic theory' are not absolutely rigorous; it would be better to say 'analysis – or theory – *of the diachrony*'. For if the terms 'synchrony' and 'diachrony' are taken in the sense which I have proposed here, the expression 'diachronic theory' has no meaning, strictly speaking: all theory is synchronic insofar as it expounds a systematic set of conceptual determinations. In an earlier essay, Althusser has criticized the synchrony-diachrony distinction insofar as it implies a *correlation* between objects or aspects of a single object, showing how it was, in fact, a version of the empiricist – and Hegelian – structure of time, in which the diachronic is merely the development (*devenir*) of the present – the 'synchronic'. It is clear straightaway that this cannot be the case in the usage which I have proposed here, since the synchrony is not *a real self-contemporaneous present*, but the present of the theoretical analysis in which all its determinations are given. This definition *therefore excludes any correlation* between the two concepts, one of which designates the structure of the thought process, while the other designates a particular relatively autonomous object of analysis, and only by extension the knowledge of it.)

For its part, the synchronic analysis of the mode of production implies that we stress several concepts of 'time' which differ in function. All these times are not *directly, immediately historical*: they are not in fact constructed out of the general historical movement, but quite independently of it, and independently of one another. Thus, the *time of social labour* (which measures the value produced) is constructed on the basis of the distinction between socially necessary labour and socially unnecessary labour, which depends at each moment on the productivity of labour and the proportions in which social labour is divided among the different branches of production (see *Capital*, T.I, pp. 59ff.; Vol. I, pp. 44ff.: *Theories of Surplus Value*, Vol. I, pp. 225–6). Thus it does not coincide at all with the empirically observable time during which a labourer works. In the same way, the cyclical time of the *turnover* of capital, with its different moments (production time, circulation time) and its peculiar effects (regular disengagement of money-capital, change in the rate of profit), is constructed on the basis of the metamorphoses of capital and the distinction between fixed and circulating capital.

In the same way, finally, the analysis of the *tendency* of the capitalist mode of production produces the concept of the dependence of the advance of the productive forces in relation to the accumulation of capital, and therefore the concept of the peculiar temporality of the productive forces in the capitalist mode of production. Only this movement can be called a *dynamics* as I have proposed, i.e., a movement of development *inside* the structure and sufficiently determined by it (the movement of accumulation), proceeding according to a peculiar *rhythm* and *speed* determined by the structure, with a necessary and irreversible *orientation*, and indefinitely retaining (*reproducing*) the properties of the structure on a different scale. The peculiar rhythm of capitalist accumulation is inscribed in the cycle of crises, while its peculiar speed expresses the 'limitation' of the development of the productive forces, as Marx says, simultaneously accelerated and decelerated, i.e., the reciprocal limitation of the two connexions articulated in the structure (capitalist 'productive forces', relations of production). The necessary orientation of the movement consists of the increase in constant capital with respect to variable capital (in the production of means of production with respect to the production of means of consumption). The retention of the properties of the structure is particularly clear in the expansion of the market: one of the means employed by the capitalist or by an ensemble of capitalists to counteract the fall in the rate of profit being to expand the field of his or their market (by 'external' trade):

> This internal contradiction [between production and consumption] seeks to resolve itself through expansion of the *out-lying fields* of production. But the more productiveness develops, the more it finds itself at variance with the narrow basis on which the conditions of its consumption rest (*Capital*, Vol. III, p. 240).

In this '*out-lying*' adventure, therefore, capitalist production always meets its own peculiar *internal* limitation, i.e., it never escapes being determined by its own peculiar structure.

Only in the 'time' of this dynamics can the 'age' of capitalist production, of one of its branches, or of a set of branches of production, be determined: this age is measured precisely by the level of the relation between constant capital and variable capital, i.e., by the *internal organic composition* of capital:

It goes without saying that the more advanced *the age of capitalist production*, the more money is accumulated in all hands, and therefore the smaller the quantity annually added to this hoard by the production of new gold, etc. (*Capital*, Vol. II, p. 473 – modified).

This is a very important point, for it shows that only in the 'time' of the dynamics – which, as I have said, is not immediately the time of history[24] – is it possible to determine and assess *the forwardnesses or backwardnesses of development*; indeed, only in this internal orientated time can historical unevennesses of development be thought simply as temporal dislocations:

What is true of different *successive stages of development* in one country, is also true of *different coexisting stages of development* in different countries. In an *undeveloped* (*unentwickelt*) *country*, in which the former composition of capital is the average, the general rate of profit would $= 66\frac{2}{3}$ per cent, while in a country with the latter composition and a much higher stage of development it would $=$ 20 per cent. The difference between the two national rates of profit might disappear, or even be reversed, if labour were less productive in the *less developed country* . . . The labourer would then spend more of his time in reproducing his own means of subsistence, or their value, and less time in producing surplus-value (*Capital*, Vol. III, p. 210).

The consequences of this differential determination of time, and of the distinction between the time of the dynamics and the time of history in

---

[24] Not even the time of *economic history*, of course, if by that is meant the relatively autonomous history of the economic base of the mode of production. This is for two main reasons: firstly, such a history, dealing as it does with concrete-real social formations, always studies economic structures dominated by *several* modes of production. It therefore has nothing to do with the 'tendencies' determined by the theoretical analysis of isolated modes of production, but with the compounded effects of several tendencies. This considerable problem lies outside the field of the present analysis, and it is only touched on incompletely in the next section (on the 'phases of transition'). Secondly, the 'age' of production which we are discussing here is not, clearly, a *chronological* feature, it does not indicate *how old* capitalist production is: for it is an age compared between several economic zones (or 'markets') subject to the capitalist mode of production, which is important because of the effects which lead to an unevenness in the organic composition of capital from one region to another or from one department to another. According to the closeness of the analysis, it will be a matter of an average organic composition or of a differentiated analysis of the organic composition of capital from branch of production to branch of production: this is the beginning of a study of the effects of domination and uneven development implied by the unevenness of the organic composition between competing capitals. Obviously, this is not our object here. I am only suggesting it as a possibility.

general for the contemporary problem of 'under-development' (which is a favourite haunt for every theoretical confusion) cannot be expounded here; at least what we have said gives us a foretaste of its critical importance.

Like the preceding ones, this 'time' of the dynamics (of the tendency) is determined in the *synchronic* analysis of the mode of production. The distinction between *dynamics* and *diachrony* is therefore a strict one, and the former cannot appear as one determination in the field of the latter, in which it is not relevant in the form in which Marx analyses it. It is easy to cast light on this distinction by borrowing a paradox from the analysis of the societies 'without a history' (strictly speaking a meaningless expression, for it designates social structures in which the dynamics appears in the peculiar guise of a *non-development*, as in the Indian communities which Marx discusses in *Capital*, T.II, pp. 46–8; Vol. I, pp. 356–9): the *event* constituted by the meeting between these societies and 'Western' societies in transition to capitalism (in conquest, colonization, or the various forms of commercial connexion) is obviously part of the *diachrony* of those societies, since it determines – more or less brutally – a transformation of their modes of production: but it is no part of these societies' *dynamics*. This event in their history is produced *in the time of their diachrony without being produced in the time of their dynamics*: a limit-case which brings out the conceptual difference between the two times, and the necessity of thinking their articulation.

We must therefore finally situate the concept of *history* with respect to these different concepts: should we for example assimilate it to the concept of diachrony, remembering the old problematic of periodization? Can we say that 'history' is this diachrony, the basic theoretical problem of which is the analysis of the *modes of transition* from one structure of production to another? No, obviously, for this old problematic has now been transformed. It is no longer defined by the necessity of 'cutting up' linear time, which would presuppose this reference time as an *a priori*. The question now is to think theoretically the *essence of the transition periods* in their specific forms and the variations of these forms. The problem of periodization in the strict sense has therefore been suppressed, or rather it has ceased to be part of the moment of scientific proof, of what Marx called the *order of exposition* (only exposition *is* science): periodization as such is at most a moment of the *investigation*, i.e., a moment of the preliminary critique of the theoretical materials and their interpretations. Here the concept of history is therefore not identical with any of the particular moments produced in theory in order to think the differential forms of time. *The concept of history in general, unspecified, is simply the designation of a constitutive problem* of the 'theory of history' (of historical materialism): it designates that theory as a whole as *the site* of the problem of the articulation of the different historical times and the variants of this articulation. This articulation no longer has anything to do with the simple model of the *insertion* of one time into another; it accepts *coincidences* not as obviousnesses, but as problems: for instance, the transition from one mode of production to another may seem to be the moment of a collision, or collusion, between the times of the economic structure, of the political class struggle, of ideology, etc. The question is to discover how each of these times, e.g., the time of the 'tendency' of the mode of production, *becomes* a historical time.

But if the general concept of history has the peculiar function of designating a constitutive problem of the theory of history, then, as opposed to the preceding concepts, it does not belong to that theory of history. *And indeed, the concept of history is no more a concept of the theory of history than the concept of 'life' is a concept of biology.* These concepts belong to the epistemologies of these two sciences, and, as 'practical' concepts, to the practice of the scientists, locating and staking out the field of that practice.

(4) CHARACTERISTICS OF THE PHASES OF TRANSITION

Here I can only outline a number of the concepts that belong to the theory of the 'diachrony' and enable us to think the nature of periods of transition from one mode of production to another. Indeed, as we have seen, Marx devoted far less theoretical effort to this second moment of the theory of history than he did to the first. On this point, I have no other aim here than to draw up a balance-sheet of results.

The analysis of Primitive Accumulation is part of the field of diachronic study, but not *in itself* part of the definition of the periods of transition (to capitalism). In fact, the analysis of primitive accumulation, of the *origin* of the capitalist mode of production, gives an element by element genealogy which passes through the transition period, but which in the same movement ascends to the heart of the previous mode of production. The outline definitions which can be borrowed from it must therefore be related to a different analysis which is not an analysis of the *origins* but one of the *beginnings* of the capitalist mode of production, and which in consequence does not proceed element by element, but from the point of view of the whole structure. In the study of *manufacture* we have a notable example of this analysis of the beginnings. The forms of transition are in fact necessarily modes of production in themselves.

In the first part of this paper, when I examined manufacture as a certain form of the connexion of real appropriation, a certain form of the 'productive forces', I set aside the problem posed by the chronological *dislocation* in the constitution of the structure of capitalist production between the formation of its specific property relations and that of its specific 'productive forces'. As I showed, this was not part of the examination of the structure of the mode of production. In contrast, *this dislocation constitutes the essence of manufacture as a form of transition*. The concepts which Marx uses to designate this dislocation are those of 'real subsumption' and 'formal subsumption' (of labour to capital). The 'formal subsumption' which begins with the form of outwork on behalf of a merchant capitalist and ends with the industrial revolution includes the whole history of what Marx calls 'manufacture'.

In the 'real subsumption' of modern industry, the labourer's belonging to capital is doubly determined: on the one hand he does not possess the material means to work on his own behalf (the ownership of the means of production); on the other, the form of the 'productive forces' takes away his ability to set the social means of production to work on his own, outside an organized and inspected process of co-operative labour. This double determination reveals a *homology* in the form of the two connexions constituting the complex structure of the mode of production: they can both be characterized as the 'separation' of the labourer from his means of production. Which amounts to saying that they divide up their 'supports' in the same way, that they determine coincident forms of individuality for the labourer, the means of production and the non-labourer. The labourers who are in a relationship of absolute non-ownership with the means of production, constitute a collective in the production process which coincides with the 'collective labourer' who can set to work the 'socialized' means of production of modern industry, and thereby really appropriate nature (the objects of labour). What is here called 'real subsumption' is what Marx introduced in the Preface to *A Contribution* as a *'correspondence'* between the relations of production and the level of the productive forces. We can therefore specify the sense in which the term 'correspondence' is to be understood. Since the two connexions between which there is a homology both belong to the same level, constituting the complexity of the structure of production, this *'correspondence'* cannot be a relation of translation or reproduction of one by the other (of the form of the productive forces by that of the relations of production): it is not one of the two which is 'subsumed' beneath the other, it is labour which is 'subsumed' beneath capital, and this subsumption is 'real' when it is thus doubly determined. The correspondence therefore lies completely in the unique division of the 'supports' of the structure of production and in what I called above the *reciprocal limitation* of one connexion by the other. At the same time, it is clear that this correspondence is in its essence completely different from any 'correspondence' between *different levels of the social structure*: it is established in the structure of one particular level (production) and depends completely on it.

In 'formal subsumption', on the other hand, the labourer's belonging to capital is only determined by his absolute non-ownership of the means of production, but not at all by the form of the productive forces, which are still organized according to craft principles. It seems not impossible that each labourer might return to handicrafts. That is why Marx says that the labourers' belonging to capital is still 'accidental' here:

> In the early stages of capital, its command over labour has a purely formal and almost accidental character. The worker at this time only

works under capital's orders because he has sold it his labour-power: he only works for it because he does not have the material means to work on his behalf (*Capital*, T.II, p. 23; Vol. I, p. 330).

However, this absence of ownership of the means of production for the direct labourer is by no means 'accidental': it is the result of the historical process of primitive accumulation. In these conditions, there is not strictly speaking any homology between the forms of the two connexions: in manufacture the means of production continue to be set to work by individuals in the strict sense, even if their component products have to be assembled to constitute a useful object on the market. We can therefore say that the form of 'complexity' of the mode of production may be *either the correspondence or the non-correspondence* of the two connexions, of the productive forces and the relations of production. In the form of non-correspondence, which is that of the phases of transition such as manufacture, the relationship between the two connexions no longer takes the form of a reciprocal limitation, but becomes *the transformation of the one by the effect of the other*: this is shown by the whole analysis of manufacture and the industrial revolution, in which the capitalist nature of the relations of production (the necessity of creating surplus-value in the form of relative surplus-value) determines and governs the transition of the productive forces to their specifically capitalist form (the industrial revolution arises as a method of formation of relative surplus-value beyond any predetermined quantitative limit). The 'reproduction' of this specific complexity is the reproduction of this effect of the one connexion on the other.

It thus seems that, neither in the case of correspondence, nor in that of non-correspondence, can the relationship between the two connexions ever be analysed in terms of a transposition or translation (even a distorted one) of one into the other, *but only in terms of an effectivity and a mode of effectivity*. In one case we are dealing with the reciprocal limitation of the effectivities of the two connexions, in the other with the transformation of one by the effectivity of the other:

> We now see that a certain minimum amount of capital in the hands of individuals is the concentration of wealth necessitated for the transformation of individual labour into combined, social labour; it becomes the material base for the changes which the mode of production will undergo' [here 'mode of production' should be understood in the restricted sense of 'form of the productive forces'] (*Capital*, T.II, p. 23; Vol. I, p. 330).

What has occasionally been called the 'law of correspondence' between the productive forces and the relations of production should therefore rather be named, as Charles Bettelheim has proposed, 'the law of necessary correspondence or non-correspondence between the relations of production and the character of the productive forces' ('Les cadres socio-économiques et l'organization de la planification sociale', *Problèmes de Planification*, V, École Pratique des Hautes Études, Paris 1965). This would express the fact that the 'law of correspondence' has as its peculiar object the determination of effects within the structure of production and the varying mode of this determination, and not a connexion of *expression* which would merely be the inverse of a mechanical causality.

The mode of 'correspondence' *between the different levels of the social structure*, which has more strictly been called the mode of articulation of these levels, depends in turn on the form of the internal correspondence of the structure of production. We have already encountered this articulation above in two forms: on the one hand, in the determination of the determinant 'last instance' in the social structure, which depends on the combination peculiar to the mode of production considered; on the other, with respect to the form of the productive forces peculiar to capital and to the mode of intervention of *science* in their history, as the determination of the *limits* within which the effect of one practice can modify another practice from which it is relatively autonomous. Thus the mode of intervention of science in the practice of economic production is determined by the peculiar new form of the 'productive forces' (unity of means and object of labour). The particular form of correspondence depends on the structure of the two practices (practice of production, theoretical practice): here it takes the form of the *application* of the science, in conditions determined by the economic structure.

We can generalize this kind of relationship between two relatively autonomous instances; it recurs, for example, in the relationship between *economic practice* and *political practice*, in the forms of class struggle, law and the State. Marx's indications here are much more precise, although *Capital* does not contain any theory of the class struggle as such, or of law or the State. Here, too, the correspondence is analysed as the mode of intervention of one practice within limits determined by another. This is the case with the intervention of the *class struggle* within limits determined by the economic structure: in the chapters on the *working day* and on *wages*, Marx shows us that the sizes of these are subject to a variation which is not determined in the structure and depends purely and simply on the balance of forces. But the variation only takes place between certain limits (*Grenzen*) which are set by the structure: it thus possesses only a relative autonomy. The same is true of the intervention of law and of the State in economic practice, which Marx analyses in the example of *factory legislation*: the State intervention is doubly determined, by its generalized form, which depends on the particular structure of the law, and by its effects, which are dictated by the necessities of economic practice itself (family and education laws govern child labour, etc.).

In this case, too, there is therefore no relationship of simple transposition, translation or expression between the various instances of the social structure.

Their 'correspondence' can only be thought on the basis of their relative autonomy, of their peculiar structure, as *the system of interventions* of this type, of one practice in another (here, obviously, I am only locating a theoretical problem, not producing a knowledge). These interventions are of the same type as those we have just recalled, and in consequence, they are in principle *non-reversible*: the forms of intervention of law in economic practice are not the same as the forms of intervention of economic practice in legal practice, i.e., as the *effects* which a transformation dictated by economic practice may have on the legal system, precisely by virtue of its systemacity (which also constitutes a system of internal 'limits'). And in the same way, it is clear that the class struggle cannot be reduced to the struggle for wages and a shorter working day, which only constitute one moment of it (the autonomization and exclusive consideration of this moment, within the political practice of the working class is peculiar to 'economism', which claims precisely to reduce all the non-economic instances of the social structure purely and simply to reflections, transpositions of phenomena of the economic base). The 'correspondence' of the levels is thus not a simple connexion, but a complex set of interventions.

We can now return to the problems of the transition from one mode of production to another, on the basis of the *differential analysis* of the interventions of the State, law and political power in the constituted mode of production, and in the phase of transition. Marx's analysis of *factory legislation* (*Capital*, T.II, pp. 159–78; Vol. I, pp. 480–503) and of the '*bloody legislation*' which is a part of primitive accumulation (*Capital*, T.III, pp. 175–83; Vol. I, pp. 734–41) contains this differential analysis implicitly. Instead of an intervention governed by the limits of the mode of production, primitive accumulation shows us an intervention of political practice, in its different forms, whose result is to *transform* and *fix* the limits of the mode of production:

> The bourgeoisie, at its rise, cannot do without the constant intervention of the State; it uses it to 'regulate' wages, i.e., to depress them to the suitable level, to lengthen the working day and to keep the labourer himself in the desired degree of dependence. This is an essential moment of primitive accumulation (*Capital*, T.III, p. 179; Vol. I, p. 737).

> Some of the methods [of primitive accumulation, introduced by the capitalist epoch] depend on the use of brute force, but without exception they all exploit the power of the State, the concentrated and organized force of society, to hasten violently the transition from the feudal economic order to the capitalist economic order, and to shorten the transition phase. Indeed, force is the midwife of every old society pregnant with a new one. Force is an economic agent' (T.III, p. 193; Vol. I, p. 751).

In the transition period, the forms of law and of State policy are not, as hitherto, adapted to the economic structure (articulated with the peculiar limits of the structure of production) but *dislocated* with respect to it: as well as showing force as an economic agent, the analyses of primitive accumulation also reveal the *precession of law* and of the forms of the State with respect to the forms of the capitalist economic structure. This dislocation can be translated by saying that the correspondence appears here, too, in the form of a *non-correspondence* between the different levels. In a transition period, there is a 'non-correspondence' because the mode of intervention of political practice, instead of conserving the limits and producing its effects within their determination, displaces them and transforms them. There is therefore no general form of correspondence between the levels, but a variation of the forms, which depend on the degree of autonomy of one instance with respect to another (and to the economic instance) and on the mode of their mutual intervention.

I shall close these very schematic suggestions with the comment that the theory of *dislocations* (within the economic structure, between the instances) and of the forms of non-correspondence is only ever possible by a *double reference* to the structure of two modes of production, in the sense which I defined at the beginning of this paper. In the case of manufacture, for example, the definition of non-correspondence depends on definitions of the forms of individuality as determined in handicrafts on the one hand, and in the capitalist ownership of the means of production on the other. Similarly, an understanding of the precession of law requires a knowledge of the structures of political practice in the previous mode of production as well as of the elements of the capitalist structure. The use of violence and its accommodated forms (accommodated by the intervention of State and law) depends on the form and function of the political instance in feudal society.

Periods of transition are therefore characterized by the *coexistence* of several modes of production, as well as by these forms of non-correspondence. Thus manufacture is not only a continuation of handicrafts from the point of view of the nature of its productive forces, it also presupposes the persistence of handicrafts in certain branches of production (T.II, p. 56; Vol. I, p. 367) and even causes handicrafts to develop alongside itself (T.II, pp. 43, 56; Vol. I, pp. 353, 368). Manufacture is therefore never *one* mode of production, its unity is the coexistence and hierarchy of two modes of production. Modern industry, on the contrary, is rapidly propagated from one branch of production to all the others (T.II, p. 69; Vol. I, p. 383). Thus it seems that the *dislocation* between the connexions and instances in transition periods merely reflects *the coexistence of two* (or more) *modes of production in a single 'simultaneity', and the dominance of one of them over the other.* This confirms the fact that the problems of diachrony, too, must be thought within the problematic of a theoretical 'synchrony': the problems of the transition and of the forms of the transition from one mode of production to another are problems of a more general synchrony than that of the mode of production itself, englobing several systems and their relations (according to Lenin, at the beginning of the period of the transition to socialism in Russia, there were up to five coexisting modes of production, unevenly developed and organized in a hierarchy in dominance). The analysis of these *relations of domination* is only outlined by Marx, and it constitutes one of the main fields open for investigation by his successors.

*

As can be seen, this paper closes with a number of *open* problems, and it cannot claim more than that it has indicated or produced open problems, for which it is impossible to propose solutions without further and deeper investigation. It cannot be otherwise, so long as we realize that *Capital*, the object of our reflections, founds a new discipline: i.e., *opens up a new field* for scientific investigation. As opposed to the closure which constitutes the structure of an ideological domain, this *openness* is typical of a scientific field. If we can claim anything for our exposition, it is only that it has defined, as far as possible, the theoretical problematic which installed and opened this field, it has recognized, identified and formulated the problems already posed and resolved by Marx, and finally discovered in these acquisitions, in Marx's concepts and forms of analysis, all that may enable us to identify and pose the new problems which are inscribed in the analysis of the problems already solved, or which are outlined on the horizons of the field already explored by Marx. The openness of this field is the existence of these problems *to be solved*.

I add that it is no accident that even today some of these problems, which I have posed solely on the basis of a reading of *Capital*, a book which is a hundred years old, concern directly certain questions of contemporary economic and political practice. In the problems of theoretical practice, all that is ever at issue, beneath their peculiar form as theoretical problems, i.e., beneath the form of the production of concepts which can give their knowledge are the tasks and problems of the other practices.

Glossary

The present form of this Glossary requires some explanation. Many of the entries are the same as those in the Glossary which I prepared for the English translation of *For Marx*. Included here as well, however, are concepts from *Reading Capital*, making it, in effect, a completely new Glossary.

Althusser's *Letter to the Translator*, written originally to accompany the Glossary in *For Marx*, explains the nature of his own corrections – marked 'L.A.' in the text.

Technical Marxist terms are only included in this Glossary when they have a special meaning for Althusser and Balibar. The same is true for the terms from the Freudian theory of instincts used by Balibar in Chapter 2 of his paper.

Ben Brewster

ABSTRACT (*abstrait*). For Althusser, the theoretical opposition between the abstract and the concrete lies wholly in the realm of *theory*. The abstract is the starting-point for theoretical practice, its Generality I (q.v.), while the concrete is its end-point (Generality III). The common theoretical view that regards theory as abstract and reality as concrete is characteristic of the works of Feuerbach and of Marx's own youth.

ALIENATION (*aliénation, Entäusserung*). An ideological concept used by Marx in his Early Works (q.v.) and regarded by the partisans of these works as the key concept of Marxism. Marx derived the term from Feuerbach's anthropology where it denoted the state of man and society where the essence of man is only present to him in the distorted form of a god, which, although man created it in the image of his essence (the species-being), appears to him as an external, pre-existing creator. Marx used the concept to criticize the State and the economy as confiscating the real self-determining labour of men in the same way. In his later works, however, the term appears very rarely, and where it does it is either used ironically, or with a different conceptual content (in *Capital*, for instance).

BREAK, EPISTEMOLOGICAL (*coupure épistémologique*). A concept introduced by Gaston Bachelard in his *La Formation de l'esprit scientifique*, and related to uses of the term in studies in the history of ideas by Canguilhem and Foucault (see Althusser's *Letter to the Translator*, which follows this glossary). It describes the leap from the pre-scientific world of ideas to the scientific world; this leap involves a radical break with the whole pattern and frame of reference of the pre-scientific (ideological) notions, and the construction of a new pattern (problematic q.v.). Althusser applies it to Marx's rejection of the Hegelian and Feuerbachian ideology of his youth and the construction of the basic concepts of dialectical and historical materialism (q.v.) in his later works.

CAUSALITY, LINEAR, EXPRESSIVE AND STRUCTURAL (*causalité linéaire, expressive et structurale*). Whereas classical theories of causality have only two models, linear (transitive, mechanical) causality, which only describes the effects of one element on another, and expressive (teleological) causality, which can describe the effect of the whole on the parts, but only by making the latter an 'expression' of the former, a phenomenon of its essence, Marxist theory introduces a new concept of the effect of the whole on the parts, structural, complex causality, where the complex totality (q.v.) of the structure in dominance (q.v.) is a structure of effects with *present-absent causes*. The cause of the effects is the complex organization of the whole, *present-absent* in its economic, political, ideological and knowledge effects. Marx himself often used the theatrical analogy of the *Darstellung* (representation, *mise en scéne*). Empiricist ideologies, seeing the action on the stage, the effects, believe that they are seeing a faithful copy of reality, recognizing themselves and their preconceptions in the mirror held up to them by the play (see DENEGATION). The Hegelian detects the hand of God or the Spirit writing the script and directing the play. For the Marxist, on the contrary, this is a theatre, but one which reflects neither simple reality nor any transcendental truth, a theatre without an author; the object of his science is the mechanism which produces the stage effects.

COMBINATION/COMBINATORY (*combination, Verbindung/combinatoire*). The only theory of the totality (q.v.) available to classical philosophy is the Leibnizian conception of an expressive totality (*totalité expressive*) in which each part 'conspires' in the essence of the totality, so that the whole can be read in each of the parts, which are total parts (*partes totales*) homologous with it. Modern structuralism (q.v.) reproduces this ideology in its concept of a *combinatory*, a formal pattern of relations and (arbitrarily occupied) places which recur as homologous patterns with a different content throughout the social formation and its history. Theoretically, the combinatory will produce all the possible structures of the social formation, past, present and future, which are or will be realized or not according to chance or to some kind of principle of natural selection. Marxism has an apparently similar concept, that of *combination* or *Verbindung* (Marx). The *Verbindung*, however, has nothing in common with the formalism of the combinatory: it is a complex structure, doubly articulated (in the mode of production, by the productive forces connexion and the relations of production connexion – q.v.), and one that specifies its content (its 'supports' – q.v.), which changes with a change in the formation or mode of production analysed.

CONCRETE-IN-THOUGHT/REAL-CONCRETE (*concret-de-pensée/concret-réel*). In Feuerbach's ideology, the speculative abstract (q.v.), theory, is opposed to the concrete, reality. For the mature Marx, however, the theoretical abstract and concrete both exist in thought as Generalities I and III (q.v.). The concrete-in-thought is produced wholly in thought, whereas the real-concrete 'survives independently outside thought before and after' (Marx).

CONJUNCTURE (*conjoncture*). The central concept of the Marxist science of politics (cf. Lenin's 'current moment'); it denotes the exact balance of forces, state of overdetermination (q.v.) of the contradictions at any given moment to which political tactics must be applied.

CONSCIOUSNESS (*conscience*). A term designating the region where ideology is located ('false consciousness') and superseded ('true consciousness'), contaminated by the pre-Marxist ideology of the Young Marx. In fact, Althusser argues, ideology is profoundly *unconscious* – it is a structure imposed involuntarily on the majority of men.

CONTRADICTION (*contradiction*). A term for the articulation of a practice (q.v.) into the complex whole of the social formation (q.v.). Contradictions may be antagonistic or non-antagonistic according to whether their state of overdetermination (q.v.) is one of fusion or condensation, or one of displacement (q.v.). Balibar also uses contradiction in a more limited sense in relation to the theory of 'tendency' (q.v.). The 'causes' which counter-act the tendency of the rate of profit to fall are identical with the 'causes' of the original tendency – these causes (non-contradictory) have reciprocally limiting (contradictory) effects: they define the possible *limits of variation* (*Grenzen*) within which an element or relation within the mode of production or social formation moves. They also define other limits (*Schranken*): the barriers beyond which the mode of production or social formation itself cannot go.

CONTRADICTIONS, CONDENSATION, DISPLACEMENT AND FUSION OF (*condensation, déplacement et fusion des contradictions*). Condensation and displacement were used by Freud to indicate the two ways dream-thoughts are represented in the dream-work – by the compression of a number of dream-thoughts into one image, or by transferring psychical intensity from one image to another. Althusser uses the analogy of these processes of psychical overdetermination to denote the different forms of the overdetermination (q.v.) of contradictions in the Marxist theory of history. In periods of stability the essential contradictions of the social formation are neutralized by displacement; in a revolutionary situation, however, they may condense or fuse into a revolutionary rupture.

DENEGATION (*dénégation, Verneinung*). Freud used the term *Verneinung* (normally translated into English as *negation*, but *denegation* has been used in this text because of the Hegelian ambiguity of *negation*) to designate an unconscious denial masked by a conscious acceptance, or *vice versa* (in fetishisms, for example, there is a denegation of the female's absence of a penis). Translated into French as *dénégation*, it is one of a set of concepts for the place of the conscious system in the total psychic mechanism (the unconscious) which Althusser applies by analogy to the place of ideology in the social formation. The role of historical materialism is to analyse (in the strict sense) the mechanisms producing the ideological recognition of the obvious, given facts, just as psycho-analysis explains the mechanism producing the mirror-recognition of Narcissistic identification with the other. This mythical recognition structure, typical of ideology, explains the latter's closed circular nature, its homology with wish-fulfilment (*plein-du-désir*) in analysis, as ideology fulfilment (*plein-de-idéologie*). Science and analysis, on the other hand, are open systems of concepts, because they cannot be defined by any spatial metaphor.

DEVELOPMENT, UNEVEN (*développement inégal*). A concept of Lenin and Mao Tse-tung: the overdetermination (q.v.) of all the contradictions in a social formation (q.v.) means that none can develop simply; the different overdeterminations in different times and places result in quite different patterns of social development.

DIALECTIC OF CONSCIOUSNESS (*dialectique de la conscience*). The Hegelian dialectic, or any dialectic where the various elements or moments are externalizations of a single, simple, internal principle, as Rome in Hegel's *Philosophy of History* is an expression of the abstract legal personality, etc.

DISLOCATION (*décalage*). Empiricist and historicist problematics assume a one-to-one correspondence (*correspondence biunivoque*) between the concepts of a science and its real object, and a relation of expressive homology between these objects themselves (although these correspondences may be direct or inverted – i.e., the order of emergence of the concepts in the science may follow the historical sequence, or, on the contrary, follow a reverse order). Althusser argues, on the contrary, that the relations between ideology and the other practices, between the different practices in general, between the elements in each practice, and between ideology and science, are, in principle, relations of *dislocation*, staggered with respect to one another: each has its own time and rhythm of development. The totality is the theory of their articulation together, so it cannot be discovered by making an 'essential section' (q.v.) through the current of historical movement at any time one. This dislocation plays an important part in the theory of transition (q.v.).

EFFECTIVITY, SPECIFIC (*efficacité spécifique*). The characteristic of Marx's later theory: the different aspects of the social formation are not related as in Hegel's dialectic of consciousness (q.v.) as phenomena and essence; each has its precise influence on the complex totality, the structure in dominance (q.v.). Thus base and superstructure (q.v.) must not be conceived as vulgar Marxism conceives them, as essence and phenomenon, the State and ideology are not mere expressions of the economy, they are autonomous within a structured whole where one aspect is dominant, this dominance being determined in the last instance by the economy.

EMPIRICISM (*empirisme*). Althusser uses the concept of empiricism in a very wide sense to include all 'epistemologies' that oppose a given subject to a given object and call knowledge the abstraction by the subject of the essence of the object. Hence the knowledge of the object is part of the object itself. This remains true whatever the nature of the subject (psychological, historical, etc.) or of the object (continuous, discontinuous, mobile, immobile, etc.) in question. So as well as covering those epistemologies traditionally called 'empiricist', this definition includes classical idealism, and the epistemology of Feuerbach and the Young Marx.

FETISHISM (*fétichisme*). Fetishism is the mechanism which conceals the real functioning (the real movement – *wirkliche Bewegung*) of the dominant structure in the social formation, i.e., it is the constitutive dislocation (q.v.) between the ideological practice and the other practices (q.v.). This is not a subjective mystification, but the mode of appearance of reality (Marx calls it a reality – *Wirklichkeit*). In the capitalist mode of production it takes the form of *the fetishism of commodities*, i.e., the personification of certain things (money-capital) and the 'reification' of a certain relationship (labour). It does not consist of a *general* 'reification' of *all* relationships, as some humanist interpretations of Marx argue, but only of this particular relationship. Fetishism is not absent from other modes of production, it is merely displaced onto whichever level is dominant in the social formation characterized by that mode of production.

FORMATION, SOCIAL (*formation sociale*). [A concept denoting 'society' so-called. L.A.]. The concrete complex whole comprising economic practice, political practice and ideological practice (q.v.) at a certain place and stage of development. Historical materialism is the science of social formations.

GENERALITIES I, II AND III (*Généralités I, II et III*). In theoretical practice (q.v.), the process of the production of knowledge, Generalities I are the abstract, part-ideological, part-scientific generalities that are the raw material of the science, Generalities III are the concrete, scientific generalities that are produced, while Generalities II are the theory of the science at a given moment, the means of production of knowledge (q.v.).

HISTORICISM (*historicisme*). A currently widespread interpretation of Marxism which originated around the time of the October Revolution, and which dominates the ideas of authors as diverse as Lukács, Korsch, Gramsci, Della Volpe, Colletti and Sartre. It is characterized by a linear view of time (q.v.) susceptible to an essential section (q.v.) into a present at any moment. The knowledge of history is then the self-consciousness of each present. This self-consciousness of the present may take a number of forms (different 'mediations' may intercede between the historian and the totality): the class consciousness of the revolutionary proletariat (Lukács), the organic ideology of the ruling (hegemonic) class (Gramsci), or the practice of human inter-subjectivity as a whole, human 'praxis' (Sartre). Historicisms may or may not be humanist (Sartre and Colletti respectively).

HUMANISM (*humanisme*). Humanism is the characteristic feature of the ideological problematic (q.v.) from which Marx emerged, and more generally, of most modern ideology; a particularly conscious form of humanism is Feuerbach's anthropology, which dominates Marx's Early Works (q.v.). As a science, however, historical materialism, as exposed in Marx's later works, implies a theoretical anti-humanism. 'Real-humanism' characterizes the works of the break (q.v.): the humanist form is retained, but usages such as 'the ensemble of the social relations' point forward to the concepts of historical materialism. However, the *ideology* (q.v.) of a socialist society may be a humanism, a proletarian 'class humanism' [an expression I obviously use in a provisional, half-critical sense. L.A.].

IDEOLOGY (*idéologie*). Ideology is the 'lived' relation between men and their world, or a reflected form of this unconscious relation, for instance a 'philosophy' (q.v.), etc. It is distinguished from a science not by its falsity, for it can be coherent and logical (for instance, theology), but by the fact that the practico-social predominates in it over the theoretical, over knowledge. Historically, it precedes the science that is produced by making an epistemological break (q.v.) with it, but it survives alongside science as an essential element of every social formation (q.v.), including a socialist and even a communist society.

KNOWLEDGE (*connaissance*). Knowledge is the product of theoretical practice (q.v.); it is Generalities III (q.v.). As such it is clearly distinct from the practical recognition (*reconnaissance*) of a theoretical problem.

KNOWLEDGE, THE PROBLEM OF (*le problème de la connaissance*). Ideological conceptions of knowledge are dominated by the 'problem' of the criteria by which a knowledge can be judged, the guarantee of its truth. These criteria may be pragmatic (practical or experimental verification) or *a priori*. Marxist theory replaces the problem of guarantees by the problem of the mechanisms producing a knowledge effect (see CAUSALITY) the 'criteria' are defined within the science by its scientificity, its axiomatics. Knowledge effects are of two kinds (with two mechanisms): ideological and scientific.

MATERIALISM, DIALECTICAL AND HISTORICAL (*matérialisme dialectique et historique*). Historicists, even those who claim to be Marxists, reject the classical Marxist distinction between historical and dialectical materialism since they see philosophy as the self-knowledge of the historical process, and hence identify philosophy and the science of history; at best, dialectical materialism is reduced to the historical method, while the science of history is its content. Althusser, rejecting historicism, rejects this identification. For him, historical materialism is the science of history, while dialectical materialism, Marxist philosophy, is the theory of scientific practice (see THEORY).

MODEL (*modèle*). The theory of models is a variant of empiricism (q.v.). According to this theory, *Capital*, for example, analyses not the real capitalist world, but the properties of an ideal, simplified *model* of it, which is then *applied* to empirical reality, which, of course, it only fits approximately. For Althusser, the theory in *Capital* is only 'ideal' in the sense that it only involves the object of knowledge, like all theory, not the real object, and the knowledge it produces is perfectly adequate to its object, not an approximation to it. Related to the general theory of models are both the view that Volume Three of *Capital* is a concretization, removing the simplifications of the ideal model of Volume One, and the theory of the 'English example' in *Capital* as a model for capitalist development everywhere else. For Althusser, Volume Three is as much concerned with the object of knowledge as Volume One, and England is only a source of illustrations in *Capital*, not a theoretical norm.

NEGATION OF THE NEGATION (*négation de la négation*). A Hegelian conception that Marx 'flirts' with even in his mature works. It denotes the process of destruction and resumption (supersession/*Aufhebung*, q.v.) whereby the Spirit moves from one stage of its development to another. For Marx, it describes the fact that capitalism, having come into being by the destruction of feudalism, is itself destined to be destroyed by the rise of socialism and communism [this description makes a *metaphorical* use of the notion. L.A.].

OVERDETERMINATION (*surdétermination*, *Überdeterminierung*). Freud used this term to describe (among other things) the representation of the dream-thoughts in images privileged by their condensation of a number of thoughts in a single image (condensation/*Verdichtung*), or by the transference of psychic energy from a particularly potent thought to apparently trivial images (displacement/*Verschiebung-Verstellung*). Althusser uses the same term to describe the effects of the contradictions in each practice, q.v.) constituting the social formation (q.v.) on the social formation as a whole, and hence back on each practice and each contradiction, defining the pattern of dominance and subordination, antagonism and non-antagonism of the contradictions in the structure in dominance (q.v.) at any given historical moment. More precisely, the overdetermination of a contradiction is the reflection in it of its conditions of existence within the complex whole, that is, of the other contradictions in the complex whole, in other words its uneven development (q.v.).

'PHILOSOPHY'/PHILOSOPHY (*'philosophie'/philosophie*). 'Philosophy' (in inverted commas) is used to denote the reflected forms of ideology (q.v.) as opposed to Theory (q.v.). See Althusser's own 'Remarks on the Terminology Adopted': *For Marx*, p. 162. Philosophy (without inverted commas) is used in the later written essays to denote Marxist philosophy, i.e., dialectical materialism.

PRACTICE, ECONOMIC, POLITICAL, IDEOLOGICAL AND THEORETICAL (*pratique économique, politique, idéologique et théorique*). Althusser takes up the theory introduced by Engels and much elaborated by Mao Tsetung that economic, political and ideological practice are the three practices (processes of production or transformation) that constitute the social formation (q.v.). Economic practice is the transformation of nature by human labour into social products, political practice the transformation of social relations by revolution, ideological practice the transformation of one relation to the lived world into a new relation by ideological struggle. In his concern to stress the distinction between science and ideology (q.v.), Althusser insists that theory constitutes a fourth practice, theoretical practice, that transforms ideology into knowledge with theory. The determinant moment in each practice is the work of production which brings together raw materials, men and means of production – *not* the men who perform the work, who cannot therefore claim to be the subjects of the historical process. Subsidiary practices are also discussed by Althusser, e.g. technical practice (*pratique technique*).

PROBLEMATIC (*problématique*). A word or concept cannot be considered in isolation; it only exists in the theoretical or ideological framework in which it is used: its problematic. A related concept can clearly be seen at work in Foucault's *Madness and Civilization* (but see Althusser's *Letter to the Translator*). It should be stressed that the problematic is *not* a world-view. It is not the essence of the thought of an individual or epoch which can be deduced from a body of texts by an empirical, generalizing reading; it is centred on the *absence* of problems and concepts within the problematic as much as their presence; it can therefore only be reached by a symptomatic reading (*lecture symptomale*) on the model of the Freudian analyst's reading of his patient's utterances.

PRODUCTION/DISCOVERY OF A KNOWLEDGE (*production/découverte d'une connaissance*). Engels noted the difference between Priestley's *production* of oxygen without realizing the theoretical significance of the new substance, and Lavoisier's *discovery* of (the concept of) oxygen, with its revolutionary consequences for the science of chemistry. He compared this with the difference between the *production* of the reality of surplus-value in classical economic theory and Marx's *discovery* of the concept of surplus-value. The slightly pejorative use of *production* here should not be confused with Althusser's insistence that knowledge is a specific mode of production (q.v.).

PRODUCTION, MODE OF (*mode de production, Produktionsweise*). The mode of material production is the central concept of the theory of the economic practice of the social formation. It is itself a complex structure, doubly articulated by the productive forces connexion and the relations of production connexion (q.v.), and containing three elements: the labourer, the means of production (sub-divided into object of labour and instrument of labour), and the non-labourer. The term can also be applied by analogy to any other practice or level, for they are all also doubly articulated, contain a similar set of elements, and produce a specific product.

PRODUCTIVE FORCES/RELATIONS OF PRODUCTION (*forces productives/rapports de production*). These concepts are generally taken (even by some Marxists) to mean the machines or their productivity on the one hand, and the human relations between the members of a society on the other. For Althusser and Balibar, on the contrary, they are the two different articulations of the combination (q.v.) of the mode of production: they are both 'relations' (connexions – *relations*) combining together labourers, means of production and non-labourers within the mode of production. The productive forces constitute the connexion of real appropriation (*wirkliche Aneignung*) of nature, or the 'possession' connexion, while the relations of production are the relations of expropriation of the product or the 'property-ownership' connexion (not the corresponding 'law of property' which is not even an 'expression' of the relations of production, but a structure dislocated from them, a superstructure). This double articulation appears in every aspect of the mode of production, in the difference between use-value and exchange value, and in the difference between the technical and the social division of labour, etc. While the productive forces cannot be reduced to machines or quantifiable techniques, the relations of production can not be reduced to relations between men alone, to human relations or inter-subjectivity, as they are in the historicist ideology (q.v.).

READING (*lecture*). The problems of Marxist theory (or of any other theory) can only be solved by learning to read the texts correctly (hence the title of this book, *Lire le Capital*, 'Reading Capital'); neither a superficial reading, collating literal references, nor a Hegelian reading, deducing the essence of a corpus by extracting the 'true kernel from the mystified shell', will do. Only a symptomatic reading (*lecture symptomale* – see PROBLEMATIC), constructing the problematic, the unconsciousness of the text, is a reading of Marx's work that will allow us to establish the epistemological break that makes possible historical materialism as a science (q.v.). Both Hegelian and empiricist readings are attempts to return to the myth of direct communication, to the Logos, and they therefore have a religious inspiration. Marx's own reading of the classics provides an example of symptomatic reading. While apparently merely recording the discoveries of the classics, their sightings (*vues*) and at the same time noting their omissions (*manques*) and oversights (*bévues*), Marx in fact shows that the classical texts contain something in their omissions that the classics did not know they contained. The symptomatic reading analyses the textual mechanism which produces the sightings and oversights rather than merely recording it.

REPRODUCTION (*reproduction*). Simple reproduction is often regarded as a simplified 'model' (q.v.) of extended reproduction, and the analysis of reproduction as the realization of production in history, the introduction of temporality into the analysis of production, in the form of the conditions of its continuation. Balibar shows, however, that simple reproduction is the *concept* of social production. Social production is only apparently the production of things; in reality it is the production of a social relation, i.e., the reproduction of the relations of production. Hence simple and extended reproduction are synchronic (q.v.) concepts of the mode of production.

SCIENCE (*science*). See IDEOLOGY and PRACTICE.

SECTION, ESSENTIAL (*coupe d'essence*). Ideological theories (empiricism, idealism, historicism) see the historical totality as analysable in a present, a contemporaneity, in which the relations between the parts can be seen and recorded. To see this present implies the possibility of cutting a section through the historical current, a section in which the essence of that current is visible. This essential section is impossible for Althusser and Balibar because there is no present for all the elements and structures at once in their conceptual system (see TIME). The possibility of an essential section is one of the positive tests for an empiricist ideology of history.

SPONTANEITY (*spontanéité*) A term employed by Lenin to criticize an ideological and political tendency in the Russian Social Democratic movement that held that the revolutionary movement should base itself on the 'spontaneous' action of the working class rather than trying to lead it by imposing on this action, by means of a party, policies produced by the party's theoretical work. [For Lenin, the *real* spontaneity, capacity for action, inventiveness and so on, of the 'masses', was to be respected as *the most precious* aspect of the workers' movement: but at the same time Lenin condemned the 'ideology of spontaneity' (a dangerous ideology) shared by his opponents (populists and 'Social Revolutionaries'), and recognized that the *real* spontaneity of the masses was to be sustained and criticized in the mean time in order to 'liberate' it from the influence of bourgeois ideology. L.A.]. In this sense, Lenin argued that to make *concessions* to 'spontaneity' was to hand the revolutionary movement over to the power of bourgeois ideology, and hence to the counter-revolution.

Althusser generalizes this by arguing that each practice (q.v.) and its corresponding science must not be left to develop on their own, however successful they may temporarily be, since to do so leaves the field open for an ideology (characteristically pragmatism) to seize hold of the science, and for the counter-revolution to seize the practice. The 'unity of theory and practice' cannot be the simple unity of a reflection, it is the complex one of an epistemological break (q.v.) [in theory. In *political* practice this unity takes another form (not examined in this book). L.A.].

STRUCTURALISM (*structuralisme*). A fashionable ideology according to which only the relations between the elements (i.e., their places) in the totality are significant, and the occupants of these places are arbitrary. The set of places and relations is the structuralist combinatory (q.v.). Structuralism also conceives of the combinatory as the synchronic structure and its temporal or historical realization, its development, as the diachrony (see SYNCHRONY/DIACHRONY).

STRUCTURE, DECENTRED (*structure décentrée*). The Hegelian totality (q.v.) presupposes an original, primary essence that lies behind the complex appearance that it has produced by externalization in history; hence it is a structure with a centre. The Marxist totality, however, is never separable in this way from the elements that constitute it, as each is the condition of existence of all the others (see OVERDETERMINATION); hence it has no centre, only a dominant element, and a determination in the last instance (see STRUCTURE IN DOMINANCE): it is a decentred structure.

STRUCTURE IN DOMINANCE (*structure à dominante*). The Marxist totality (q.v.) is neither a whole each of whose elements is equivalent as the phenomenon of an essence (Hegelianism), nor are some of its elements epiphenomena of any one of them (economism or mechanism); the elements are asymmetrically related but autonomous (contradictory); one of them is *dominant*. [The economic base '*determines*' ('in the last instance') *which* element is to be *dominant* in a social formation. L.A.]. Hence it is a structure in dominance. But the dominant element is not fixed for all time, it varies according to the overdetermination (q.v.) of the contradictions and their uneven development (q.v.). In the social formation this overdetermination is, in the last instance, determined by the economy (*determiné en dernière instance de l'économie*). This is Althusser's clarification of the classical Marxist assertion that the superstructure (q.v.) is relatively autonomous but the economy is determinant in the last instance. The phrase 'in the last instance' does not indicate that there will be some ultimate time or ever was some starting-point when the economy will be or was solely determinant, the other instances preceding it or following it: 'the last instance never comes', the structure is always the co-presence of all its elements and their relations of dominance and subordination – it is an 'ever-pre-given structure' (*structure toujours-déjà-donnée*).

STRUCTURE, EVER-PRE-GIVEN (*structure toujours-déjà-donnée*). See STRUC-
TURE IN DOMINANCE

SUPERSESSION (*dépassement, Aufhebung*). A Hegelian concept popular
among Marxist-humanists, it denotes the process of historical development by the destruction and retention at a higher level of an old historically
determined situation in a new historically determined situation – e.g.
socialism is the supersession of capitalism, Marxism a supersession of
Hegelianism. Althusser asserts that it is an ideological concept, and he
substitutes for it that of the historical transition, or, in the development
of a science, by the epistemological break (q.v.).

SUPERSTRUCTURE/STRUCTURE (*superstructure/structure*). In classical Marxism the social formation (q.v.) is analysed into the components economic
structure – determinant in the last instance – and relatively autonomous
superstructures: (1) the State and law; (2) ideology. Althusser clarifies
this by dividing it into the structure (the economic practice) and the
superstructure (political and ideological practice). The relation between
these three is that of a structure in dominance (q.v.), determined in the
last instance by the structure.

SUPPORT (*support, porteur, Träger*). Humanist ideologies see the social totality
as the totality of inter-subjective relations between men, as civil society, the
society of human needs. In other words, they are anthropologies strictly
homologous with the classical economic theory of the *homo oeconomicus*. In
Marxist theory, on the contrary, the real protagonists of history are the social
relations of production, political struggle and ideology, which are constituted by the place assigned to these protagonists in the complex structure of
the social formation (e.g., the labourer and the capitalist in the capitalist
mode of production, defined by their different relations to the means of production). The biological men are only the *supports* or bearers of the guises
(*Charaktermasken*) assigned to them by the structure of relations in the social
formation. Hence each articulation of the mode of production and each level
of the social formation defines for itself a potentially different form of historical individuality. The correspondence or non-correspondence of these
forms of historical individuality plays an important part in transition (q.v.).

SYNCHRONY/DIACHRONY (*synchronie/diachronie*). Althusser and Balibar
oppose the structuralist (q.v.) ideological use of these terms, and insist
that the synchrony of an object is merely the concept of that object,
existing as one of a set of concepts in the theory of that object (e.g., the
synchrony of *production* is its concept: *reproduction* – q.v.). However, they
make slightly different uses of the concept of diachrony. Althusser only
uses it to indicate the 'time' of the proof, the fact that the concepts emerge
in a certain order in the proof, an order which has nothing to do with the
historical emergence of the real objects of those concepts (see DISLOCA-
TION). Balibar, on the other hand, uses it to designate the theory of the
transition from one mode of production to another.

TENDENCY (*tendance*, *Tendenz*). Marx describes a number of aspects of the capitalist mode of production as tendencies (notably the tendency of the rate of profit to fall). These tendencies have often been seen as the patterns of historical development from one mode of production to another, as the symptoms of the 'negation of the negation' (q.v.) which leads to a higher historical phase. Balibar shows that they are in fact merely the concept of the pattern of development peculiar to a mode of production, the concept of the limits of variation (see CONTRADICTION) of its movement and of the eventual barriers to its development, i.e., they are features of the synchronic analysis (q.v.) of the mode of production, not of the diachronic analysis of the transition from one mode of production to another (see TIME).

THEORY, 'THEORY', THEORY (*théorie*, '*théorie*', *Théorie*). For Althusser theory is a specific, scientific theoretical practice (q.v.). In *For Marx*, Chapter 6, 'On the Materialist Dialectic', a distinction is also made between 'theory' (in inverted commas), the determinate theoretical system of a given science, and Theory (with a capital T), the theory of practice in general, i.e., dialectical materialism (q.v.). [In a few words in the preface to the Italian translation of *Lire le Capital*, reproduced in this English translation, I have pointed out that I *now* regard my definition of philosophy (Theory as 'the Theory of Theoretical practice') as a unilateral and, in consequence, *false* conception of dialectical materialism. Positive indications of the new definition I propose can be found: (1) in an interview published in *L'Unità* in February 1968 and reproduced in the Italian translation of *Lire le Capital* (Feltrinelli) (not included here), and in *La Pensée* (April 1968); (2) in *Lénine et la philosophie*, the text of a lecture I gave to the Société Française de Philosophie in February 1968, and published under the same title by François Maspero in January 1969. The new definition of philosophy can be resumed in three points: (1) philosophy 'represents' the class struggle in the realm of *theory*, hence philosophy is neither a science, nor a pure theory (Theory), but a *political practice of intervention* in the realm of theory; (2) philosophy 'represents' scientificity in the realm of political practice, hence philosophy is not *the* political practice, but a theoretical practice of intervention in the realm of politics; (3) philosophy is an original 'instance' (differing from the instances of *science* and *politics*) that represents the one instance alongside (*auprès de*) the other, in the form of a specific *intervention* (political-theoretical). L.A.].

TIME (*temps*). Hegelian theories of history see time as the mode of existence (*Dasein*) of the concept (*Begriff*). There is therefore a unique linear time in which the totality of historical possibilities unfolds. Empiricist theories of history as a chronology of 'events' accept the same conception of time by default. This simple unilinear time can then be divided into 'events' (short-term phenomena) and 'structures' (long-term phenomena), or periodized in evolutionist fashion into self-contemporaneous 'modes of production', the static or 'synchronic' analysis of which has a dynamic or 'diachronic' development in time into another mode of production. This dynamics or diachrony is then history. For Althusser and Balibar, on the contrary, there is no simple unilinear time in which the development of the social formation unfolds: each level of the social formation and each element in each level has a different temporality, and the totality is constituted by the articulation together of the dislocations (q.v.) between these temporalities. It is thus never possible to construct a self-contemporaneity of the structure, or essential section (q.v.). Historical time is always complex and multi-linear. The synchrony of the social formation, or of one of its levels or elements, is the concept of its structure, i.e., of its dislocation and articulation into the totality. It therefore includes both 'static' and 'dynamic' elements (tendencies – q.v.). The term diachrony (q.v. synchrony) can only be applied to the concept of the phase of transition (q.v.). History itself is not a temporality, but an epistemological category designating the object of a certain science, historical materialism.

TOTALITY (*totalité, Totalität*). An originally Hegelian concept that has become confused by its use by all theorists who wish to stress the whole rather than the various parts in any system. However, the Hegelian and the Marxist totalities are quite. different. The Hegelian totality is the essence behind the multitude of its phenomena, but the Marxist totality is a decentred structure in dominance (q.v.).

TRANSITION (*passage*). Marx's analysis of the transition from one mode of production to another has two sides. First there is the analysis of the pre-history of the mode of production, the *genealogy* of its constitutive elements, as they emerge in the interstices of the previous mode of production. Second there is the analysis of the phase of transition itself, which is not a destructuration-restructuration, but a mode of production in its own right, although one in which there is a dislocation (q.v.) of a special type rather than a homology between the two articulations of the structure (see PRODUCTIVE FORCES) and therefore between the modes of historical individuality (see SUPPORT) defined by the structure, a dislocation within the mode of production and between the mode of production and the other levels of the social formation. This dislocation is such that, rather than defining reciprocal limitations which maintain the structure within a certain pattern of development, one of the dislocating connexions transforms the other. Thus, the phase of manufacture is a transitional phase in the development of the capitalist mode of production. The labourer is separated from the means of labour in the property connexion; but he is still linked to them in the connexion of real appropriation, through his traditional craft skill. Labourer and instrument of labour are opposed to object of labour. Hence the labour process still has its feudal form, whereas the property relation is capitalist. The introduction of machines breaks down this feudal connexion between the labourer and his means of labour, replacing it by one homologous with the property connexion, in which the means and the object of labour are connected and opposed to the labourer.

WORKS OF MARX, EARLY, TRANSITIONAL AND MATURE (*Oeuvres de jeunesse, de maturation et de la maturité de Marx*). Althusser rejects the view that Marx's works form a theoretical unity. He divides them as follows: Early Works (up to 1842); Works of the Break (*Oeuvres de la Coupure* – 1845); Transitional Works (1845–7); Mature Works (1857–83). It should be remembered, however, that the epistemological break (q.v.) can neither be *punctual*, nor made once and for all: it is to be thought as a 'continuous break', and its criticism applies even to the latest of Marx's works, which 'flirt' with Hegelian expressions and contain pre-Marxist 'survivals'.

A Letter to the Translator

Thank you for your glossary; what you have done in it is *extremely* important from a political, educational and theoretical point of view. I offer you my warmest thanks.

I return your text with a whole series of corrections and interpolations (some of which are fairly long and important, you will see why).

A minor point: you refer twice to Foucault and once to Canguilhem *vis-à-vis* my use of 'break' and, I think, of 'problematic'. I should like to point out that Canguilhem has lived and thought in close contact with the work of Bachelard for many years, so it is not surprising if he refers somewhere to the term 'epistemological break', although this term is rarely to be found as such in Bachelard's texts (on the other hand, if the term is uncommon, the *thing* is there all the time from a certain point on in Bachelard's work). But Canguilhem has not used this concept *systematically*, as I have tried to do. As for Foucault, the uses he explicitly or implicitly makes of the concepts 'break' and 'problematic' are echoes either of Bachelard, or of my own systematic 'use' of Bachelard (as far as 'break' is concerned) and of what I owe to my unfortunate friend Martin (for 'problematic'). I am not telling you this out of 'author's pride' (it means nothing to me), but out of respect both for the authors referred to and for the readers.

As for these authors: *Canguilhem*'s use of the concept 'break' differs from mine, although his interpretation does tend in the same direction. In fact, this should be put the other way round: *my debt to Canguilhem is incalculable*, and it is my interpretation that tends in the direction of his, as it is a *continuation* of his, going beyond the point where his has (for the time being) stopped. *Foucault*: his case is quite different. He was a pupil of mine, and 'something' from my writings has passed into his, including certain of my formulations. But (and it must be said, concerning as it does his own philo-sophical personality) under his pen and in his thought even the meanings he gives to formulations he has borrowed from me are transformed into another, quite different meaning than my own. Please take these corrections into account; I entrust them to you insofar as they may enlighten the English reader (who has access in particular to that *great* work, *Madness and Civili-zation*), and guide him in his references.

Much more important are the corrections I have suggested for some of your rubrics. In most cases they are merely *corrections* (*précisions*) which do not affect the state of the theoretical concepts that figure in the book (*For Marx*). They cast a little more light on what you yourself have very judi-ciously clarified. But in other cases they are corrections of a different kind: bearing on a certain point in Lenin's thought, for example (my interpolation on the question of spontaneity). And finally, in other cases (see my last interpolation), I have tried to give some hints to guide the English reader in the road I have travelled since the (now quite distant) publication of the articles that make up *For Marx*. You will understand why I am so *insistent* on all these corrections and interpolations. I urge you to give them a place in your glossary, and add that (1) I have myself gone over the text of the glossary line by line, and (2) I have made changes in matters of detail (which need not be indicated) and a few *important interpolations*.

As a result, everything should be perfectly clear. And we shall have removed the otherwise inevitable snare into which readers of 1969 would certainly have 'fallen', if they were allowed to believe that the author of texts that appeared one by one between 1960 and 1965 has *remained in the position* of these old articles whereas time has not ceased to pass. . . . You can easily imagine the theoretical, ideological and political misunderstandings that could not but have arisen from this 'fiction', and how much time and effort would have had to be deployed to 'remove' these misunderstandings. The procedure I suggest has the advantage that it removes any misunderstanding of this kind *in advance*, since, *on the one hand*, I leave the system of concepts of 1960 to 1965 as it was, while *on the other*, I indicate the *essential point* in which I have developed in the intervening years – since, *finally*, I give *references* to the new writings that contain the new definition of philosophy that I now hold, and I summarize the *new conception* which I have arrived at (provisionally – but what is not provisional?).

Louis Althusser, 19 January 1970

Index

Index